RESEARCH IN ECONOMIC HISTORY

Supplement 1 · 1977

RECENT DEVELOPMENTS
IN THE STUDY OF BUSINESS
AND ECONOMIC HISTORY:
ESSAYS IN MEMORY OF
HERMAN E. KROOSS

"RESEARCH IN ECONOMIC HISTORY"

Supplement 1 · 1977

RECENT DEVELOPMENTS IN THE STUDY OF BUSINESS AND ECONOMIC HISTORY: ESSAYS IN MEMORY OF HERMAN E. KROOSS

Editor: Robert E. Gallman
University of North Carolina

JAI PRESS
Greenwich, Connecticut

Copyright © 1977 by JAI Press
321 Greenwich Avenue
Greenwich, Connecticut 06830
All rights reserved. No part of this publication may be reproduced, stored on a retrieval system, or
transmitted, in any form or by any means, electronic, mechanical, photocopying, recording or
otherwise, without prior permission in writing from the publisher.
ISBN: 0-89232-035-4
Library of Congress Catalog Card Number: 76-13956
Manufactured in the United States of America

HC
1
.R471
J.1
1977

CONTENTS

Preface

At his death in the spring of 1975, Herman Krooss was at work on two series of books in economic and business history, which he had agreed to edit for Johnson Associates. One set was to consist of monographs, the other of volumes of essays, and he had already commissioned several papers for the latter. After Herman's death, Jeffrey Williamson agreed to take on the task of editing the monograph series and Paul Uselding the essay series. But it was decided that the essays Herman had commissioned should be brought together in a separate volume to honor Herman's memory. I was asked to assemble and edit these papers, together with a few others that I was to commission, and to bring the volume to publication. While there are those who knew Herman longer and better than I and there are those better equipped by training and research to appraise his intellectual contribution, nonetheless, it seemed to me that it would not be presumptuous of me to accept the assignment. We had worked together off and on for over a dozen years in the practical business of the Economic History Association, a kind of activity in which one learns a good deal about the character and personality of his associates. If he enjoyed our association half as much as I did and if he reciprocated my feelings of affection and respect—which I hope he did—then there was a bond between us that makes it fitting that I serve in this capacity.

My first meeting with Herman Krooss came at a joint conference of the Economic History Association and the Conference on Research in Income and Wealth. The two groups had received an invitation from William Parker and

Milton Heath to meet at Chapel Hill, but by the time the invitation had been accepted, Parker had taken a new position at Yale and Heath had made plans for an extended visit to England. When I arrived in Chapel Hill in September of 1962 to fill the position vacated by Parker, Heath's first duty toward his new colleague was to break the news that I had fallen heir to the job of chairing the local arrangements committee for the meeting, then one year off, a piece of news not altogether welcome. But Heath communicated it to me over a leisurely luncheon in so graceful and indirect a way that I barely felt the shock.

In the course of the next several months I heard from every officer of the Economic History Association, except for the Treasurer, Krooss. Each officer reminded me of some facet of the local arrangements that I must not forget, a meeting room that must be provided for this, a dining room for that, a list that must be made up, an event for which special staff would be required, etc. But no word came from Krooss, the officer who kept the Association moving along from year to year, who signed contracts and paid bills and generally ran things. In May I wrote him to report on the state of affairs and to enquire as to what we had forgotten to arrange. His answer, which has somehow survived the years, begins: "The local arrangements committee does better with each passing year." It goes on to give a concise and clear answer to each question I had raised and ends: ". . . I am sure we shall have an excellent meeting.

This is pure Krooss, reassuring and encouraging the panicky colleague, with the light touch. He must have written a good many letters of this type, as a practical man running an association composed of academics. Certainly I have several more around that are like it, some gathered when I was editing the *Journal of Economic History* and Herman was serving as Business Manager and chief shield against the slings and arrows of outraged contributors and printers. He was a good defender and a man who could raise your spirits.

The morning of the day the conference was to begin, I walked over to the Carolina Inn, which was providing accommodations. Standing at the main desk, elbow on the desk, chin in hand, one foot cocked over the other, was a lean, sandy haired man, with a jaunty air. He had on a bow tie and, it may be, black and white shoes and he was talking out of the side of his mouth to the desk staff, all of whom were gathered around him. I never found out what he was saying, but it seemed to please the staff, since they were patently in good humor, even cheery. Certainly they exhibited an animation I had never drawn from them. As I came up to the group, the sandy haired man's eyes swiveled around and caught me and his right hand shot out in my direction, although he made no other movement. "Krooss," he said. "You're Gallman." I liked him on sight.

I also decided he had everything under control, which was true. The meeting went well, including the Treasurer's report, the first of those witty annual performances that I had the pleasure to witness. At that time the books of the Association were audited each year by a committee of the Association and the chairman of the

committee that year was Raymond De Roover. De Roover said that the Association had chosen wisely in selecting him to chair the audit committee, since only an expert in Medieval bookkeeping could make any sense of the books of the Association. Herman chuckled delightedly. But from De Roover's report it was evident that the books were in excellent condition and that if any Medieval businessmen had been at work on them, it must have been one of the cleverer of the Medici, so flourishing was the financial state of the Association.

My memories of Herman are all of this type: of a friendly, witty, good-humored, jaunty, supportive, decent man. Also of a man of wisdom and scholarly gifts. But I am just the gatekeeper to this volume and will leave the treatment of these subjects to Thomas Cochran and J. R. T. Hughes, whose essays follow. I want to convey only the picture and the personality of the man, as they came to me that first day and remain in my mind's eye today.

With the exception of the pieces by Cochran and Hughes, the volume is much as Herman had planned it. He had in mind to bring together a group of essays that would treat recent work in various functional and geographic divisions of the fields of economic and business history, summarizing, criticizing and pointing the way toward future work. Not all of the topics he hoped to encompass are represented in this book and, in that sense, it is an unfinished work. But much has been completed and the range of subjects suggests the scope of his initial undertaking, as the emphasis on lines of new and promising work indicates the forward-looking quality of his mind.

Finally, I must thank Jane N. Gallman, who shared with me the task of editing these essays, and Helen Krooss, who has been most cooperative and helpful in every way.

Robert E. Gallman
Chapel Hill

RESEARCH IN ECONOMIC HISTORY

Supplement 1 · 1977

RECENT DEVELOPMENTS
IN THE STUDY OF BUSINESS
AND ECONOMIC HISTORY:
ESSAYS IN MEMORY OF
HERMAN E. KROOSS

RECOLLECTIONS OF HERMAN KROOSS

Thomas C. Cochran, UNIVERSITY OF PENNSYLVANIA

At its start the *Journal of Economic History* had a small office on the top floor of a building otherwise given over to the School of Education of New York University. There one morning early in January, 1945, a slender, sandy haired young man in his early thirties introduced himself as Herman Krooss, a fellow alumnus of the University of Pennsylvania. After taking an MA in economics in 1935, at the age of twenty-three, he had entered business, but he had spent the last three years recovering from an attack of tuberculosis. Now he wanted to teach, which, of course, meant writing a thesis and securing a doctor's degree. Since the Economics Department indulgently regarded me as an affiliated member, I could supervise the thesis.

In the course of many conversations I learned that Herman and I also had in common birth in New York City, a rarity among the itinerant academic community of those days whose fathers appeared usually to have been professors in country colleges or small-town clergymen. But Herman's attendance for four years at Muhlenberg (PhB., 1933) and his German family background always made him seem more a Pennsylvanian than a New Yorker. Perhaps the family heritage and a Manhattan upbringing were jointly responsible for his quick wit and incisiveness, coupled with skepticism and a strong will, particularly in money matters affecting the Economic History Association.

His half a dozen years' experience in business, which should probably be a requirement for all scholars in business or economic history, served him well

3

throughout his career. After a brief period with a well-known Wall Street broker-age firm he had gone with Penn Mutual, where he became, in 1937, a Certified Life Underwriter. Forecasting his later aptitudes he then taught the training course for CLUs. In 1939 he married Helen Bausher of Reading, whom he had met while at Muhlenberg, and everything seemed in order for Herman to become a suburban New York insurance broker. It was at this juncture that tuberculosis intervened and gave Herman many months to look at hospital ceilings and think about his future career. His ultimate decision to teach was warmly supported by Helen.

Returning to January, 1945, in the office on top of the School of Education, I can't recall who made the suggestion that he write on the thinking of businessmen between the two wars; at least, I was then doing the same type of study of nineteenth-century railroad leaders. Since Herman was only ten years younger than I, our academic relationship quickly developed into a personal friendship, made more intimate by his becoming the Treasurer of the Economic History Association in 1948, while I was still an editor of the *Journal*. As a lazy man, who didn't want to proofread a lot of copy (we all copyedited in those days), I got on well with Herman by keeping the *Journal* small.

From the start Herman's Treasurer's reports were gems of wit and brevity. They insured large attendance at the business meetings, and should be collected and published as a guide or admonition to officers making annual reports. Since he always showed a surplus in the treasury and knew more about finance than his amateur auditors, we were happy to assume that everything was in good order and in strong hands. When Ralph Hidy retired from the Secretaryship of the Associa-tion to become its president in 1970, Herman, with the help of Helen, now called Suzy, carried on both offices from their home in Allentown during the ensuing five years. At any time during this period I believe the nominating committees of the Association would have been delighted to select Herman as president, but he steadily refused.

With his new PhD, in 1947, Herman joined the Economics Department of the New York University School of Commerce and Finance and, in 1950, also that of the Graduate School of Business Administration. In the old open office of the Economics Department, where no one but the Chairman had privacy, Herman soon formed a friendship with a brilliant Russian twenty-five years his senior, Paul Studenski, an association that was strongly to influence Herman's early academic career.

Studenski, a former student of both the University of St. Petersburg in law and the University of Paris in natural science, came to the United States in 1911 as a licensed French airplane pilot. With aviation all but moribund in America, Studenski embarked on a long career in teaching, interspersed with service on an incredible number of boards and bureaus, both state and national. During this period he acquired a doctorate from Columbia and wrote books on government administration, taxation and fiscal policy. Finding in Herman a young man who could write well and knew United States economic history, Studenski suggested

that they collaborate on a much needed financial history of the United States.[1] The excellent result was published in 1952, one year before Studenski retired from the NYU department at age sixty-six.

During this first decade of his teaching career Herman was an economic historian with a primary interest in finance. Three years after the *Financial History of the United States* he published a book on *American Economic Development* which ultimately went through three editions, the last only a year before his death.[2] This predominantly financial and economic phase of his career is also illustrated in the publication of *The Origins and Development of the American Economy*, coauthored with E.A.J. Johnson; *Security Credit: Its Role and Regulation* with Jules Bogen; and *A Short History of Financial Intermediaries*.[3]

The departure of Ralph Hidy from NYU in 1957, to take the Strauss Professorship in the Harvard Business School, undoubtedly helped to turn Herman's attention back toward his original interest in business history. The course he inherited at the Graduate School of Business, separated from Wall Street only by the cemetery of Trinity Church, has always had among its students some of the men and women destined to reach high executive levels, and for nearly twenty years Herman exchanged ideas and witticisms with these sophisticated students. In addition he had active business contacts as a director of MONY Mortgage Investors and on the Board of Arbitrators of the American Stock Exchange.

Transfer from the Economics Department at Washington Square to the GBA as well as experience with business executives may have heightened Herman's initial unwillingness to become caught up in the changing fads of theory. Although he was well versed in both theoretical and applied economics, his writing was illuminated by a skeptical but understanding humanism, the mark of a true historian.

One product of the business history course was *American Business History*, written jointly with his former student Charles Gilbert of Hofstra University.[4] No preceding historians of business had attempted a synthesis of what should be included in a course from colonial days to 1970, and consequently Krooss and Gilbert became a major influence in defining the field.

But the book that gave Herman the greatest chance to display his mature wit and ability at interpretation was *Executive Opinion: What Business Leaders Said and Thought 1920's–1960's* published in 1970.[5] This study should insure him a lasting place in the history of American business long after transitory theoretical approaches have been superceded. In spite of the fact that he had made a practical beginning in this field some thirty-five years earlier and had written on it a decade after that, *Executive Opinion* represented chiefly the results of mature consideration and systematic sampling. His conclusion to the Preface illustrates the mordant wit so frequent in all of his writing: ''Businessmen were not as much out of step with the truth as I had once thought they were. Neither they nor their opinions seemed in retrospect to be more ridiculous than those of other groups in our society. Indeed, they sometimes were superior to the opinions offered by those

who should have known better . . . or who thought they did." I will not attempt a review of the book, which has already been done in a memorial session reported in the *Journal of Economic History*.[6] It is a study that compresses the results of a lifetime of attention to what was literally going on around him. The concluding chapter is a masterful summary of this half a century of formal pronouncements by business leaders. "The much publicized revolution in business opinion that is supposed to have taken place in the last twenty years," writes Herman, "is, like the equally publicized revolution in sex, greatly exaggerated." But he does conclude that "The spectrum from the most 'conservative' to the most 'liberal' is much narrower than it was then. There are successors to Swope and Sloan, but there are no counterparts to Filene and Girdler".[7]

Herman was only sixty-two at his death, the age at which many productive scholars begin the most important period of their work. Just a year earlier he had won the Great Teacher award at N.Y.U. Yet in scarcely more than thirty years of writing he had produced books that will be indispensable to the next generation of business and economic historians. He also was the central figure in the growth and effective operation of the Economic History Association. He alone knew the background of every problem from publishing the *Journal* to monitoring the membership and arranging the annual meetings. In the learned associations with which I have had experience none has been as indebted to a single man as was the Economic History Association to Herman Krooss.

FOOTNOTES

1. Krooss and Studenski (1952).
2. Krooss (1955).
3. Krooss and Johnson (1953), Krooss and Bogan (1961), Krooss (1971).
4. Krooss and Gilbert (1972).
5. Krooss (1970).
6. Hughes (March 1976), pp. 166–172.
7. Krooss (1970), pp. 374, 380.

REFERENCES

Hughes, J.R.T., (March 1976), "Krooss on Executive Opinion," *The Journal of Economic History*, 36, pp. 166–172.
Krooss, Herman E., (1955), *American Economic Development*, Englewood Cliffs, N.J.: Prentice-Hall.
———. (1970), *Executive Opinion: What Business Leaders Said and Thought 1920's–1960's*, Garden City, N.Y.: Doubleday and Company.
———. (1971), *A Short History of Financial Intermediaries*, New York: Random House.
Krooss, Herman E. and Bogan, Jules (1961), *Security Credit: Its Role and Regulation*, Englewood Cliffs, N.J.: Prentice-Hall.

Krooss, Herman E. and Gilbert Charles (1972), *American Business History*, Englewood Cliffs, N.J.: Prentice-Hall.

Krooss, Herman E. and Johnson, E.A.J. (1973), *The Origins and Development of the American Economy*, Englewood Cliffs, N.J.: Prentice-Hall.

Krooss, Herman E. and Studenski, Paul (1952), *Financial History of the United States*, New York: McGraw-Hill.

KROOSS ON EXECUTIVE OPINION*

J.R.T. Hughes, NORTHWESTERN UNIVERSITY

Those who knew Herman Krooss will not object if I refer to him in the familiar in this paper on this occasion. He would laugh at me if I added "Professor" in my references; and if I followed academic custom and called him by his surname only, those who knew him would be offended too. The reason for this special session is that in Herman Krooss there was a man with whom familiarity did not breed contempt.

In years to come, when this association has either recovered from the loss of Herman's management of its affairs, or has succumbed from its failure to do so, I think his fame as a student of this country's financial development will have been augmented considerably by his book, *Executive Opinion*.[1] It is that book I want to talk about today. Others knew Herman better than I did, and are more qualified than I am to discuss his work on finance. I have two qualifications to discuss *Executive Opinion*, however.

I

First, when I was writing my book on American business leaders some years ago, I had the experience of reading through a mountain of printed whitewash and blanket condemnation, together with some of the most boring and platitudinous material—speeches by business leaders—I had ever seen. It seemed to me at the

9

time quite incredible that men who, in their lives, had played such dramatic roles in this country's development could have had such puerile, childish opinions of what they had accomplished, and of the world in which those accomplishments were achieved. But I considered my subjects to be eccentric, and indeed I had partly chosen them for their eccentricity. In any case, I considered that I had more than a slight acquaintance with the written legacy of the country's past business leadership.

Now, were it not for Herman, that would have been about the extent of my interest and feelings concerning the opinions of business executives of the past. Their ideas about public affairs were not my conception of interesting reading.

This brings me to my second qualification. During the 1964 Presidential campaign I got my first glimpse of a larger pattern from Herman in a Madison, Wisconsin, beer parlor. He explained, in all seriousness, and for hours, the origins, nature and implications of the Republican Presidential candidate's ideas about economic and social matters. The evening was an exquisite pleasure. Herman had a way of saying things. Placed in a context of the modern history of American business opinion by Herman, one could see Senator Goldwater as an American Macmillan, or perhaps at least, a Lord Home. It turned out, upon careful examination and by Herman's explanation, that the vapid platitudes of the 1964 campaign were part of a body of very traditional and systematic thought, that we had a sort of Tory tradition. And why not? Surely our business community has become the American version of the British landed class. It is in business over here that the great fortunes were made, and defended by argument, against those who would threaten wealth and its privileges. Our Tory tradition has not had its Disraelis and Churchills to give it wings. But elegance apart, there is consistency, content and relevance. Indeed, executive opinion, as much as any other publicly expressed opinion, makes the headlines and competes for broad public attention. In the economic realm executive opinion must have carried special weight. Goldwater's views represented part of this tradition.

II

Executive Opinion is a very extended essay on the tradition of business thought in this century. Herman's procedure was to use the great events of the half century after World War I as his sounding board. He sought executive opinion on those great issues, and then divided up his data in a taxonomy compounded of institutional and ideological categories. Anyone who has attempted to organize and weigh such material can well appreciate the problems he faced. It is not a public opinion poll, because the questions have already been asked by "history," and the "responses" (who Herman listened to) were determined by a complex social structure, by "spokesmen," some representing merely themselves, some speaking for industry, or trade associations, firms; there were business publications,

annual reports of firms, responses to congressional enquiries etc. Herman sent out questionnaires, combed the printed sources and thus systematically gathered information for this historical argosy.

The resulting compilation is unique. It could never be repeated. Systematic Herman was, and a system can be repeated. But the essential element involved in selection, analysis and commentary in *Executive Opinion* was judgment, not a system, not a formula, but a brain, not a selection process, but a connoisseur's taste. Herman admitted that he was a sympathetic listener,[2] so he pursued this material to remote sources. Like the happy connoisseur who *likes* the taste of the wine he judges, Herman clearly enjoyed dipping into this ocean of verbiage. He also clearly understood that, viewed in the rough, this material is mainly absurd. But as he says, by way of warning to the reader, after nearly 400 pages: "Nonsense and naiveté are not the monopoly of any one group."[3]

III

Executive Opinion is in the end a disquieting and dispiriting book, and I don't think Herman wanted it to be that way. But he reported what he found. What he shows by careful and judicious sifting is that on all the great issues of the mid-twentieth century, the country's business and labor leaders, statesmen, journalists, and yes, economists, simply did not, in a very profound sense, know what they were talking about. Where there was wisdom Herman was grateful enough to find it and note it. But he was careful always to give the reader a full and fair sample of his sources; and surveying them is a dismaying experience, expecially if one supposes that the words, arguments and explanations we are getting on today's great questions are of no higher quality than those in *Executive Opinion*.

Partly this long and almost ubiquitous catalog of error is due to the off-the-cuff nature of public utterances business leaders make. Men who managed their own and their companies' affairs successfully on the basis of solid technical expertise would, again and again, make public comments on great national and international problems with a kind of headlong recklessness. This might be excused were it not for the volume of such commentary and the thought that it may have been to some extent influential in its time. But also the tendency for men to believe on the basis of unquestioned axioms produced structured responses, decade after decade, to novel questions which required real mental ingenuity—as we can see with hindsight—to produce even a minimally adequate understanding. This is a routine enough experience in this country in public discussion. It is, after all, embarrassing, even humiliating, to read the election speeches, ten years later, of our leaders. What Herman shows is that the quality of executive opinion is no better than the words of our politicians. It also is no worse. The impression one gets is a grasping after straws mixed with angry denunciation and witless mumbo-jumbo. When real understanding does come through, it stands like a monolith in the surrounding

desert of nonsense and platitudes. For example, Alfred Sloan in the 1930's said of the impending unionization of industry what even our university presidents have since learned.

> It is axiomatic in employer-employee relationships that organized labor, as such, can never be satisfied. It cannot afford to be satisfied, for being dissatisfied is the very foundation of its continued existence.[4]

Labor problems would not be removed, but merely changed, by unionization established by government. Presumably our leaders did not believe that when the Wagner Act was passed. Herman wove this into his tapestry with the comment merely that some of the business conservatives like Sloan had a clearer understanding of what was at stake than did the "sentimental liberals." Solutions to problems created new problems.

Another general and, to me at least, demoralizing impact of the book is the extent to which apparently almost everything has been said before in given circumstances. One gets the impression that a page from Krooss could be taken at random and inserted in tomorrow's *Wall Street Journal* and it would be taken as serious commentary on whatever is going to be in tomorrow's *Wall Street Journal*.

IV

There are general results in Herman's conclusions of great interest. He found that, although there has always been considerable diversity of executive opinion, in our own time, the diversity has narrowed, This is due, he says, to the decline of the entrepreneurial leader. Professional business managers who now run the top companies are less eccentric than the Carnegies and Fords. They have to be. A lifetime spent satisfying conflicting demands of owners, labor, government and public opinion alike, wears off the corners of thought. So paradoxically, although the modern executive is more educated, more sophisticated, the range of his ideas has narrowed. This conclusion is of course in accord with Galbraith's assertion in *The New Industrial State* that the great corporations, at the commanding heights of the economy, are committee affairs, rendering committee decisions. These constantly tend toward the center of discussion. No university professor needs to be told about this social phenomenon.

Herman found that whereas the American executive has come to accept the *fact* of established national labor unions, the paternalistic and sympathetic view of labor that characterized the 1920's has vanished. The unions are viewed as "an adult form of juvenile delinquency." They are accepted as such. Government is an accepted part of the business world too. Its expanding role, once the object of executive opposition, is now no longer seriously questioned.

If such changes might be seen as a weakening of sturdy old ideological positions

in American society, Herman emphasized that this results from a fatal ambiguity in the corporate business community's view of itself.

> Labor leaders wanted, in the words of Samuel Gompers, "more and more, now and now." Farmers wanted their "fair share of the national income." Politicians wanted to get elected. Academic economists were ostensibly interested in finding out how man used his scarce resources for maximum want satisfaction. But businessmen were not sure whether their objective was to maximize profits, or to act as stewards, or to be socially responsible, or to hold the organization together.[5]

Herman noted, in conjunction with a statement of Schumpeter's, that the decline of the old-time business faith in its own role went with the general decline of conservative American values during and after the depression of the 1930's. That those who held a philosophy which could no longer attract the allegiance of the young finally lost faith in themselves. When doubts about government as the solution to all problems began to reappear in the 1960's, and economists looked again to their favorite abstraction, "the market," to solve problems, there was no swing back to business opinion for support. Few cared what business executives thought. Especially the entrepreneur had gone into decline as a source of wisdom, he was viewed as "nothing more than a robot." That part of our tradition has finally been left to moulder in history books.

V

What Herman produced in *Executive Opinion* was both a cautionary tale and a fable for our time. It is not surprising. Business executives, of whatever persuasion, must change as their social environment changes. Few want to see their careers end as did Sewell Avery, out of touch with his times. American capitalism in this century has been rocked by a series of cataclysmic events, and the Federal Goverment has risen as the focal point of national power, thought, policymaking, wisdom. Those whose views of themselves, their roles, their claims to be heard, were once warranted by their observable and known contributions to the creation of modern American society, have had their voices muted.

If I taught in a graduate business school I would require *Executive Opinion* to be read by all the students. I would do so in order that they should understand how the fallacy of composition works out as wisdom over time. I would do so also as an exercise in the intellectual history of American business. Whereas few indeed of these individual opinions are of any lasting value, Herman has put them together in a verbal collage which is extremely valuable, which shows from the actors' mouths how the great and disastrous events of our era changed them and their world. It is, after all, the decline of a force that once was real, for good or ill, in this country's economic development. Herman has catalogued its demise in *Executive Opinion*; and on the internal evidence, we are perhaps fortunate that so few listened.

Also I would use *Executive Opinion* as an example of style of thought, the wit, the care and the economy of words that characterized Herman Krooss. It would have been tempting to lay out this long array of folly with broad strokes. But not as effective. Herman did it with finesse. He understood and relished the nonsense of it, as he did Senator Goldwater's campaign addresses. But he also saw the tragedy of *Executive Opinion* in our century: that on those great issues, it was the best we could muster from this crucially important part of our leadership, and it really was not good enough. Events ruled, and we coped with the consequences. Herman asked the opinions of American economic leaders on the great issues of four decades, and faithfully and sympathetically recorded for posterity their pitiable replies. No doubt a similar study of economists' opinions, or any other group on these issues would resemble *Executive Opinion*. The fact that our economy still soldiers on, despite such leadership, is evidence of Adam Smith's wisdom when he observed that "every country has a great deal of ruin in it."

Executive Opinion is a book which will last a long time as a starkly honest witness to the Twentieth Century. And it also is for those of us who knew, loved and respected Herman Krooss, one small monument to a man with a remarkably clear head about important things, who is, and will be, sorely missed by the members of this association.

FOOTNOTES

* This paper was delivered at the 1975 meetings of the Economic History Association, as part of a session honoring the memory of Herman Krooss. It was published in the *Journal of Economic History* of March 1976 (pp. 166–172) and is reprinted here with the kind permission of the author and the *Journal of Economic History*. ED.

1. The complete title of Krooss' *Executive Opinion* is *Executive Opinion: What Business Leaders Said and Thought, 1920's–1960's*. It was published by Doubleday in 1970.

2. *Executive Opinion*, p. XIV.

3. *Ibid.*, p. 383.

4. *Ibid.*, p. 356.

5. *Ibid.*, p. 384.

BUSINESS HISTORY: A BIBLIOGRAPHICAL ESSAY

Ralph W. Hidy, HARVARD UNIVERSITY

Since the publication of an article on the status of business history six years ago,[1] writers have continued to produce a flow of books and a substantial number of articles in a variety of periodicals. Given the volume of literature to be considered, this essay wil be confined to analysis of *books* on the history of business in the United States. It will categorize types of studies by content and characterize a few in more detail.

Among a host of books valuable for understanding the setting in which businessmen have operated, three were quite intriguing. Gilbert's analysis of the intellectual pursuit of collectivism since 1880 will not be the last work on the subject, but it advances ideas worthy of thought. More definitive was the collection of essays edited by Israel on associational activities in modern America and the book on the bureaucratization of the world by Jacoby;[2] these two books provide invaluable perspectives on the history of business institutions in the United States.

As usual in business history, biographers ranged over a wide spectrum. Two studies centered on outstanding merchants: Chyet on Aaron Lopez of Newport (Rhode Island), Seaburg and Patterson on T.H. Perkins of Boston.[3] Alberts presented a limited view of the policies and practices of H.J. Heinz. In contrast, Bruce produced a comprehensive book on Alexander Graham Bell, indicating his limitations as a businessman. (Brooks' history of the telephone did less than justice to the business aspects of that development.) Bryant dealt with a promoter, Arthur

E. Stillwell; and Ferguson began editing the papers of Robert Morris. Pusey's book on Eugene Meyer, publisher and public figure, and Ward's on engineer-businessman Herman Haupt, though useful, were less than definitive. More satisfying, though probably to a more limited readership, was Tinkle's biography of E.L. DeGolyer, oil expert and businessman.[4] Two scholars, Klein and Spence, decided that second-rank railroaders in the South merited study.[5] Two books on agents of the Hudson's Bay Company added small bits to the written history of that great firm in the American West.[6] Also illustrative of the range of interest were Colonel Sanders' slight autobiographical memoir and Hessen's detailed appraisal of Charles M. Schwab.[7]

Several prominent businessmen continued to be topics of scholarly investigation. Gustin produced the best study to date of Billy Durant, though it cannot be called definitive. Goulder subjected John D. Rockefeller's years in Cleveland to detailed examination. While Wik assessed the relationship of rural America to Henry Ford's business career, Anne Jardim attempted to explain his behavior by psycho-historical analysis. Kakar utilized similar techniques in seeking to understand Frederick Taylor. Neither user of the new tool won unqualified praise. Of course, the same statement is true for Tutorow's conventional study of Leland Stanford.[8] Canfield evaluated J.P. Morgan as a remarkable art collector, but Wheeler attributed much of Morgan's reputation as a financier to his friends, especially some of his partners.[9]

Among the biographies of leading businessmen, three deserve special recognition. Coauthors Chandler and Salsbury concentrated on the decision-making and administrative actions of Pierre S. Dupont in the growth of two large firms—Dupont and General Motors; this resulted in a prime example of business history, one to which even general historians of the United States might well refer. Similarly, those interested in Andrew Carnegie were provided with two definitive works: in a massive study, Wall provided chapter and verse supporting his statements and conclusions about the steel magnate and his achievements; using Wall's study as a base, Livesay wrote a lively, brief book, giving general readers and beginning students all they will need (or want?) to know about Carnegie and the emergence of large-scale enterprise in the United States.[10]

Business historians seeking to analyze the performance of businessmen in the political arena and of politicians reflecting business points of view were provided data by several authors. Included were biographies of William Gibbs McAdoo by Broesamle (little on business), Richard Olney by Eggert, the senior Stettinius by Forbes, Louis McLane by Munroe (an outstanding book) and John Barrett (publicist and diplomat) by Prisco. Truman's third Secretary of Commerce, businessman Charles Sawyer, contributed an autobiographical memoir.[11] Five authors examined varied aspects of Herbert Hoover's career and left readers with mixed views of the man.[12]

The crusading and philanthropic concerns of some businessmen were the subjects chosen by other researchers. Wyatt-Brown studied Lewis Tappan's war

against slavery; Swain analyzed Horace M. Albright's concern for conservation; and Sibley surveyed the record of George W. Brackenridge, a West Texan "maverick" philanthropist.[13]

Recent literature on the history of the colonial period tended to touch upon business rather than deal directly with it. Among general studies in this category, five might be cited: those by Davies, Kammen, Nash, Platt and Skaggs, and Rainbolt. Shepherd and Walton provided a more rigorous framework within which to study and evaluate business institutions and performance in colonial North America.[14] Five other books throw light on the history of business somewhat more directly: Coleman on debtors and creditors, Clowse on economic beginnings in South Carolina to 1730, Edgar on a merchant in the rice trade, Smith on religion and trade in New Netherland, and Price on the French tobacco monopoly.[15] Of these, the last named was by far the most detailed and informative. Papenfuse traced the efforts of merchants of Annapolis to seize a prominent place in the Maryland sun.[16] Two analyses dealt with forest products, one quite general (Carroll on the timber economy of Puritan New England), the other more narrowly focused (Smith's comprehensive survey of papermaking to 1969).[17]

Operations in foreign trade and shipping engaged at least five historians. Hao presented comprehensive detail on the role of the comprador in the China trade of the nineteenth century. Kirker again reviewed the activities of Americans in the southern oceans to 1812. While Lockwood gave a glimpse of the operations of Augustine Heard & Company in a monograph covering only six years, Baughman recorded the ventures of six generations of the Mallory family in maritime enterprise. On a little studied topic, the legitimate trade of the United States with West Africa in the nineteenth century, Brooks produced an objective analysis which left room for others to contribute additional information on the businessmen involved.[18]

As might be expected, some historians explored aspects of agribusiness. Brunson and Chazanof investigated land-development companies and Holden revised and added to *The Spur Ranch* published in 1934. A livestock association aroused the interest of Savage, cattle-trailing contractors that of Skaggs, and beef-cattle feeding that of Whitaker.[19]

Mining as a business received relatively little historical examination. Chaput "dug into" the history of America's first great copper mine while Gibson was assessing zinc mining in the Missouri-Kansas-Oklahoma area. Neither of these answered as many questions as readers could easily ask. Nor could historians find much on the relationship of business to western mining in the compendium by Otis E. Young, Jr.[20]

As the same time, the petroleum business sustained its interest for historians. Biographies of Joseph S. Cullinan by King and of Walter Teagle by Wall and Gibb added to knowledge about the personalities and roles of leaders of the Texas Company and Exxon, respectively.[21] Darrah reiterated the story of Pithole, while Schruben told that of oil in Kansas for the first time.[22] Anderson and Stocking

threw new light on the relation of petroleum to United States policy in East Asia and the Middle East, respectively.[23] Writers on histories of firms were represented by Ironside on Skelly and Jones on Richfield.[24]

Most importantly, the long awaited third volume of the history of Standard Oil Company (New Jersey) was produced by Larson, Knowlton and Popple.[25] This terminated the most comprehensive analysis of the historical performance of a giant, multinational American corporation. The multivolume study has already stimulated other research on the history of the petroleum industry and promises to long remain the standard work on the background of Exxon.

In addition to the Carroll and Smith studies on the history of forest products, several books provided new information on lumbering. Smith approached the post-1861 years on lumbering in Maine through the records of business firms.[26] Kohlmeyer and Twining utilized the histories of two firms in the Upper Mississippi Valley to elaborate, extend and, in some instances, correct points made by Hidy, Hill and Nevins in *Timber and Men: The Weyerhaeuser Story* (1963). Paul Neils performed a familial task by recording the history of the J. Neils Lumber Company of Montana and associated areas.[27] More comprehensively, Thomas R. Cox related, in a first-class study, the history of Pacific Coast lumbering not only to the producing region but to the trade of the Pacific Ocean. The impact of business (sawmill operations in particular) on the town of Everett, Washington, especially on workers, was the topic tackled by Norman H. Clark.[28]

Historians of manufacturing enterprises studied topics from colonial times to the present. Hood examined the first American porcelain factory.[29] Manufacturing in underdeveloped areas was the preoccupation of four researchers: Crockett—woolen mills in the Midwest; Lomax—woolen mills in Oregon; Jackson—"mills of yesteryear"; and Walsh—pioneer industry in Wisconsin, 1830–1860.[30] Both Cromwell's study of the Virginia state armory and Cudd's of the Chicopee Manufacturing Company answered a disappointingly limited number of questions on those nineteenth-century institutions. Siegenthaler exposed the monopolistic element in the American textile industry to 1880.[31] Six authors narrated the histories of firms active primarily in the twentieth century: Foy on IBM, Damman on Buick, Gray on Stellite, Mahan on McNally of Pittsburgh and Wright on the American Ship Building Company. A comprehensive view of patterns in American manufacturing was offered by Niemi.[32]

Manufacturing of aircraft began to receive a modicum of particularized attention. Ingells told the "story" of the Boeing 747, and Kuter thoroughly studied the negotiations concerned with its construction. At the same time, Francis provided in *Mr. Piper and His Cubs* an example of the history of a firm assembling small planes.[33]

No academic historian delved deeply into the record of the electric-energy suppliers. Two books that can be mentioned were either amateurish or journalistic or both. A retired executive demonstrated *How Edison's Lamp Helped Light the*

West and Bush brought the history of the Consumers Power Company into the light of day. Even the history of Detroit Edison by Raymond C. Miller, an academician, did not measure up to his earlier *Kilowatts at Work*.[34] Electric-power producers and marketers deserve more and better analysis.

One most significant function in American business, marketing, continues to attract historians less than it should, even though there have been some recent noteworthy additions to the literature. Semipopular books dealt with a chain store and a supermarket: Hoyt on the first, Marnell on the second.[35] Sturdivant completed Smalley's careful study of Spiegel, a mail-order enterprise, and also produced a history of a wholesale hospital-supply firm.[36] Advertising and promotion intrigued several writers: Emmons (boomer literature of the Central Great Plains), Fahey (Charles Sweeny, a mining promoter), and Preston (puffery in advertising and selling).[37]

Though relatively short, the most significant book in the marketing area was written by Porter and Livesay.[38] It dealt with the changing structure of marketing in the nineteenth century, particularly the rise and decline of the wholesaler. Geographical expansion of the economy, the emergence of large-scale manufacturing enterprises and other factors entered the analysis. The study not only added to the information and interpretations available to business historians but also promised to influence the research of other scholars.

In two other books, marketing was only one of the functions considered. As Atherton portrayed him, the frontier merchant was not only a merchant but often also a manufacturer, a farmer, a civic leader and a banker. Similarly, American cooperative enterprise, as viewed by Knapp, involved not only selling but buying.[39]

In the recent history of transportation, railroads practically preempted the field. Yoder investigated the Delaware Canal,[40] while numerous books on railroading were being published. In the Macmillan series, three histories of companies appeared: the Santa Fe by Bryant, the Louisville & Nashville by Klein and the Illinois Central by Stover.[41] In addition, Alexander assessed the Pennsylvania Railroad in the nineteenth century, Klein analyzed the Richmond Terminal as an agency in the combination of southeastern railway systems, and Weller recorded the rise and fall of the New Haven railway.[42] For the Trans-Mississippi West, Ames reappraised the builders (including members of his family) of the Union Pacific while Athearn analyzed the territory served by the company. Fair published a semipopular history of the Missouri & North Arkansas Railroad, and Miner studied seriously the project to build a transcontinental from St. Louis to San Francisco along the thirty-fifth parallel.[43] Other authors catered to the demand for picture books on companies.[44]

Although centered on other topics, several studies involved railroads and their influence. Adler's analysis of British investment in American railways in the nineteenth century added considerable depth to the historian's knowledge of

suppliers and transmitters of funds. Olson's history of railroad use of lumber demonstrated that the early depletion of timber in the United States was exaggerated. Henderson fleshed out information available on Harvey's restaurants. The relation between the "Communication Revolution" and American foreign policy was significant, according to Schonberger. Similarly, railroads were not unimportant, in the view of Scott, in the rise of the agricultural extension services to 1914. Probably surprising to opponents of monopoly, Taylor found railroad control of New England coastal steamship lines, 1870–1916, satisfactorily "productive" in a broad sense.[45] Comstock presented railroad buffs and historians alike with pictures of the steam locomotives used by railroads for more than a century.[46]

Several studies focused on railroading in individual states, with varying degrees of attention to regulation. Least impressive was Dunbar's narrative on railroads in Michigan. Parks' examination of public enterprise in Jacksonian Michigan was probably best on the reasons for failure of the railroad and canal projects in the state.[47] According to Caine, regulation of railroads in Wisconsin, 1903–1910, fell short of its goals. Carson decided that poor administration was primarily responsible for the decline of New York railroads in the twentieth century. The role of railroads in the history of California, 1850–1911, was the subject of McAfee's relatively brief analysis.[48]

Two other books illustrate strikingly different approaches to analyses of broad general topics. Railroading in the western part of the United States was, to O'Connor, the history of robber barons and the plundering of the region. The portrayal is onesided and replete with loaded words and phrases. In contrast, using coolly dispassionate terminology and tone, Stover presented the construction, technology, operation and decline of the railroads of the nation.[49] While Stover may have underplayed the misdemeanors and mistakes of railroad leaders, O'Conner practically disregarded their constructive achievements in the West.

Two special analyses of railroad regulation promise to have greater impact on the writing of American business history than most similar projects of recent years. In 1971, Miller synthesized recent studies and the results of his own investigations to bring up to date the relation between growth of railroads and the Granger laws; neither specialists nor general historians can ignore his book. In a well-written, challenging analysis (almost a brief), Martin asserted that government policy, including that of the Interstate Commerce Commission's response to requests for increases in rates, must bear heavy responsibility for the beginning of the decline of American railroads before 1917. The quality of the exposition and the implications of Martin's findings will almost certainly stimulate additional research.[50]

As might be expected, given the preeminence of the motorcar in American life, the automobile continued to receive scholarly attention. Two books by Flink and one by Rae together presented an evaluation of the impact of the mode of transportation on the way Americans live and on the structure of life and institutions in the United States since the 1890's. Both constructive and destructive

influences of the automobile on American culture were evaluated. Meanwhile, White analyzed the state of the industry about 1970, with summaries of background materials since 1945.[51]

Semipopular books have dominated the recently published histories of air transport. Mills dramatized the role of Northeast Airlines, Serling emphasized the contributions of Robert Six to the growth of Continental Airlines, and Williams produced a popular history of National Airlines. Whitehouse gave rather superficial treatment to the history of airlines generally in the United States. In contrast, Jordan and Redford made successful attempts to assess in scholarly fashion the effects and imperfections of airline regulation in the nation.[52]

In banking and finance, writers of business history were largely academicians. Two authors illuminated the role of firms in American foreign trade and finance: Perkins detailed the performance of the house of Brown, antecedent of Brown Brothers Harriman, and Buist that of Hope & Company, the Amsterdam firm that has had strong connections with American business for two centuries.[53] Four scholars took four different views of investment banking: Cohen studied the interaction of business and politics in the life of W.W. Corcoran; McFerrin traced the rise and fall of a southern firm, Caldwell & Company (a reissue of a 1939 book); Willis recorded the changes over time in investment banking in New England; and Carosso presented an overview of investment banking in the history of the United States, the standard work on the subject to date.[54]

Substantial additions were made to the literature on the history of commercial banking. Examples of treatment of individual banks were the People's Bank of Bloomington, Indiana, by Crissey, the Bank of South Carolina by Lesesne, the National Bank of Commerce of Seattle by Marple and Olson, and the Bank of Virginia by Wessells.[55] Two scholars analyzed banking in individual states: Erickson in Iowa to 1865, Green in Louisiana to 1861, the latter combining economic theory and historical narrative more effectively than any similar study to my knowledge.[56] Hammond demonstrated the interaction of banking and politics on the national level in the Civil War; Sharp, the politics of banking in the states after 1837; and Shade, the same in Western areas, 1832–1865.[57] Kennedy provided a detailed analysis of the banking crisis of 1933, while Klebaner took a comprehensive overview of the history of commercial banking structure, practice, operation and regulation in the United States. For deeper analysis, Krooss offered a comprehensive collection of documents on the history of banking and currency in the nation.[58]

Good books on stock markets were few. Axon's narrative on the crash of 1929, a rehash of ideas on that subject, was of limited utility. Scholars could find use for only small segments of Wyckoff's publication on Wall Street and the stock market. Meanwhile, Sobel wrote two interesting surveys, one on speculative orgies in the United States and another on the origins of the American Stock Exchange.[59]

Two types of histories illustrate the range of recent publications in the financial

area. Three books dealt with consumer finance: Crews with the Michigan Credit Union League, Moody and Fite with the growth of credit unions since 1850, and Michelman with the history of consumer finance in general.[60] At the other end of the spectrum, Krooss and Blyn published the first synthesis of the history of all financial intermediaries in the United States.[61] This was at once an impressive performance and a most useful book.

Most encouraging has been the publication of books on multinational corporations. Within a few short years after the impact of such enterprises became evident, scholars began to analyze their growth and significance. In two studies—*The Emergence of Multinational Enterprise* and *The Maturing of Multinational Enterprise*—Wilkins[62] produced a historical survey of outstanding quality. Containing considerable detail, it covered the pertinent activities of almost every American firm of significance. Destructive criticism of the books has been minimal. At the same time, Vernon summarized in two books part of the findings of the multiyear study at the Harvard Business School of multinational American firms—their spread, the impact on the concept of sovereignty in host nations, and the changing relationships that emerged in western Europe prior to the recent recession.[63] Gilpin added an evaluation of American power in relation to the multinational corporation.[64] These products of research, when coupled with an initial estimate of the evolution of international management structures,[65] have given economic and business historians an amazingly good perspective and body of data for analyzing the process of change in an area pregnant with potential power for alteration of the world economy. At present, most needed is a study of European multinational firms to match and parallel those put out on American enterprise.

Other analyses of the multinational corporate spread dealt with limited topics. Teichova provided an interesting tidbit—the United States supplied only 3.5 percent of the foreign investment in Czechoslovakia prior to World War II. Levitt offered what amounted to a political tract against domination of the Canadian economy by U.S. corporations. In contrast, Moran published a well-balanced analysis of government-business relations over copper in Chile; particularly impressive was the inclusion of the reasoning back of the various moves by the protagonists.[66]

Recent histories of cities reflect an increasing recognition of business as a factor in the process of urban change. Among the cities examined were Boston, by Bunting; New Orleans, by Clark; Wilmington (Delaware), by Hoffecker; and San Francisco, by Barth as well as by Lotchin.[67] Relations between actions of private transport companies and the growth of Milwaukee intrigued McShane, while Hilton examined the cablecar and its role.[68] For background information, the historian of business can now turn to Teaford's search for origins of modern American municipal government. A significant addition to the literature helpful to the business historian was Pred's investigation of the relationship between urban

growth and the circulation of information, one offering new insights as well as a model of methodology.[69]

A number of publications reflected interest in the interaction between business and government. The general setting was provided by Armitage, on the politics of decontrol of industry; and by Glyn and Sutcliffe, on the prevailing "crisis" in capitalism.[70] Armentano attacked the "myths" about antitrust regulation, Cuff produced a thorough analysis of the performance of the War Industries Board and Ratner offered a brief survey of the tariff in American history.[71] In a remarkable undergraduate thesis, Godfrey assessed government operation of railroads in World War I.[72] Studies on the inter-war period demonstrated the connection of bankers with monetary stabilization in the 1920's (Meyer, 1970) and with New Deal banking reforms (Burns, 1974). Funigiello investigated the attempt of New Dealers to establish a national power policy, and McGraw made a thorough study of the pulling and hauling in the early life of the TVA.[73] Other authors examined the politics involved in various enterprises: launching the Trans-Canada pipeline, particularly its financing (Kilbourn, 1976), slum housing (Friedman, 1968), life insurance (Orren, 1974), and Montana's liquor control system (Quinn, 1970).[74] Stimulated in part by Williams, some authors sought to evaluate the relation of business to foreign policy; Wilson took a comprehensive look at the period 1920–1933.[75] Meanwhile, Hurst examined the changing status of economic instruments in the law.[76]

Most authors dealing with technological change gave little space to the business implications of their subjects. Biographies of inventors accounted for two excellent books: Harry Ferguson by Fraser (Fraser, 1973) and Elmer Sperry by Hughes (Hughes, 1971).[77] Four other studies provide background for evaluating the relation of the growth in technology to business decisions: Pursell's analysis of the migration of steam-engine technology, Sinclair's history of the Franklin Institute to 1865, Rosenberg's investigation of technology and economic growth, and David's examination of technical choice, innovation and economic growth.[78]

A selection of titles from a substantial body of literature must suffice to show the interest in management-labor interaction. On slavery in the United States, the books by Blassingame, Curtin, Davis, Fogel and Engerman, McManus, Smith and Thompson were probably the most pertinent to the concerns of business historians; noteworthy was Blassingame's conclusion that management was important in explaining the difference between successful and unsuccessful planters.[79] The implications of the work by Fogel and Engerman are so well known as to need no explication. Analyses of labor-management confrontation, peaceful and militant, characterized most of the research in labor history that had direct pertinence to business historians. Among these were studies by Carpenter on the needle trades, by Galarza on fieldworkers in California, by Garnel on teamsters in the West, by Gitelman on workers in Waltham, by Graham on unions in the pulp and paper industry, by McLaurin on activities of southern cotton-textile workers and by

Suggs on struggles of militant unions in Colorado.[80]

Five authors concerned themselves with relatively recent business responses to varied stimuli. Two tested and refined the Chandler hypothesis on the relation of structure to strategy: Channon in British enterprise and Rumelt on the role of profits in encouraging diversification (showing that the relationship was positive).[81] That businessmen are representative Americans was indicated by Michelman in a semipopular but useful book demonstrating that executives tended to wait for social issues to reach the crisis stage before taking effective action. Whisenhunt's look at the ecological crisis provided a specific but brief and limited documentation of Michelman's point.[82] Examples of public reactions by business leaders to economic issues since World War I were presented by Krooss in *Executive Opinion*.[83]

In the early 1970's, scholarly studies of business response to its social responsibility, broadly defined, were still few. Gelber recorded the growing acceptance of the necessity to accord equal employment opportunity to blacks.[84] Corporate policies on contributions to education in the United States were analyzed by K.G. Patrick and Richard Eells.[85] Although not as comprehensive in coverage as might be desired, Heald produced the best-to-date analysis of the increasingly complex business-community relationships from 1900 to 1960.[86]

Blacks in the history of American business received a measure of attention. A book edited by Bailey provided some historical perspectives on black business enterprise; Weare gave a specific example in a social history of the North Carolina Mutual Life Insurance Company; and Light did a comparative analysis of business and welfare among Chinese, Japanese and blacks.[87]

Some researchers ventured into topics concerned with the internal working of firms. Partly stimulated by the Academy of Accounting Historians, projected and/or published writing on the history of accounting showed signs of increasing. Chatfield synthesized the growing body of literature in a historical survey of accounting thought. Carey centered his investigation of the accounting profession on the period since 1937, while Zeff adopted a comparison of national developments in his analysis of trends in the history of accounting. In addition, Arno Press announced plans for a number of publications, none of which I have seen.[88]

A few writers attempted to discuss changes in professional managerial thought. Wolf published an introduction to Barnard's theories of organization and management, and Wren ventured a historical survey of management thought.[89] The latter is probably the best available book on the topic but can remain of only limited value for analyzing an intellectual area of marked complexity. Christian dared to look at ethics in business conduct generally, and Milton assessed ethics in personnel management.[90] Meanwhile, Burch challenged the assumption that almost all large-scale enterprises are administered by professional managers; his data suggested that approximately 50 percent of the 500 largest manufacturing and mining firms in the United States were dominated in the mid-1960's by various family or entrepreneurial interests.[91]

In three books of essays on a range of topics, business historians may find numerous stimulating ideas. Some theories helpful to historians appeared in the book on the corporate economy edited by Marris and Wood. The essays published in honor of Harold F. Williamson present considerable data and some theories on the history of business. In the work on social structure and cultural values edited by Jaher, the chapter on the Boston Brahmins is the most pertinent to business historians and one of the best in the collection.[92] That essay may be read in conjunction with Udy's study of the changing attitude toward the work ethic and Greene's examination of American heroes over time.[93]

As a manifestation of increasing interest in the synthesis of available knowledge about business, historians of industries recorded more activity than in earlier years. In *The Image Empire,* Barnouw brought his 3-volume history of broadcasting in the United States up to 1970. It promises to long remain the standard work in the field. More popular and less comprehensive was Schicke's historical "biography" of the recording industry; but Tebbel's study of book publishing set a high standard—comprehensive, scholarly and definitive, it was an outstanding performance and will be the best available on the subject for some time to come.[94] Several other such books have been mentioned in other connections.[95]

Parenthetically, although they are focused on families or technology, three special studies illuminated the histories of industries. Durden's major concern was the three business leaders of the Duke family, but of necessity his book contained much information relevant to the history of the tobacco industry. Similarly, Whiteman's portrayal of the Hendricks family's activities contributed considerable data on the history of the copper industry. In the first serious history of photography in the United States, Jenkins centered his attention on the industry and its technology to 1925, but he showed that major changes emanated from decisions of businessmen. Understandably, George Eastman's activities were presented in some detail. This book combines most effectively the history of decision-making and changes in the application of technological knowledge.[96]

Other recent histories of industries were less impressive than those on broadcasting and book publishing. Some covered limited areas or time periods, others were not as scholarly or definitive. Among those with a national view were Cobrin on the history of the men's clothing industry, Haber on the chemical industry, 1900–1932, Hess on the moving and storage industry, and Landing on the peppermint and spearmint industry (sketchy on business side).[97] Three other authors concentrated on industries within individual states: Grindle on Maine's lime industry, Blakey on Florida's phosphate industry and Campbell on pharmacy in Mississippi.[98] Kochiss investigated oystering from New York to Boston. Still more limited geographically were Decker on the whaling industry of New London (little on business aspects) and Downward on the brewing industry in Cincinnati.[99]

In books on the general history of American business, accentuation of the negative continued to appeal to some critics and publishers. According to Debouzy, leaders of big business in the twentieth century consolidated the economic

and political power seized by the robber barons in the late nineteenth, leaving the defense of the status quo since 1920 to business historians and sociologists! Demaris gleefully recorded all the sins of both corporations and individuals that he could crowd into 442 pages. To the pro-Marxist eyes of Dowd, American capitalist development was but a "twisted dream." Although not as extreme as Dowd, Seligman was extremely critical of the exercise of power by leaders of big business.[100] Family use and abuse of power to the present day occupied one popular, inaccurate book on the Duponts and two semipopular, more acceptable ones on the Rockefellers.[101]

In the 1970's, several historians of American business synthesized available knowledge on specific areas in objective fashion. Douglas tried to establish the relationship of three centuries of business activity to economic growth; although the linkage is not clearly or consistently maintained, the massive opus is useful as a summary. Porter's essay on the rise of big business, 1860–1910, incorporated the latest findings, and Sobel's narrative on the "age of giant corporations" brought the "story" down to 1970. Material covered by both Porter and Sobel was given a different interpretation by Cochran in his survey (an update of a 1957 book) of American business in the twentieth century. Business as a major transfer agent loomed large in Woodruff's assessment of America's impact on the world from 1750 to 1970. Davis and North sought, with some success, to work out theories of institutional change and link them to economic growth.[102]

Four general histories of American business were directed at different reader-ships. Alex Groner et al published one for the general reader; it is valuable for its photographs but the text contains some inaccuracies and does not reflect recent research.[103] The book by Cochran assesses the interaction of business with major categories of social organization in American life, including education and philan-thropy, and serves best as a reference work summarizing what is known in each area.[104] An introduction to a "business and society" course seemed to be one aim of Walton's small book. Far more significantly, Krooss and Gilbert, *American Business History*, answered quite effectively the long felt need for a textbook on the subject.[105] Although no historian of American business would agree with everything in the book, the caliber of selectivity and writing is most impressive.

Among several features of the writing on the history of American business since the 1960's one stands out. Most of the books published followed the traditional descriptive, qualitative pattern. No new concept comparable to that of Chandler's *Strategy and Structure* appeared in print. The use of economic tools was reflected in a number of studies, particularly those dealing with the corporate economy and business-government relations. The large number of books on business history produced, a high percentage by university presses, emphasized the need for, and stimulated greater interest in, synthesis of information in several areas. The most remarkable feature, however, was the output of Herman Krooss during the last five years of his life. He published a volume of documents on opinions of business

executives about economic issues in the twentieth century, four volumes of documents on banking and currency in the history of the country, a synthesis of data on the history of financial intermediaries and the first good textbook on business history in the United States (the latter two with coauthors). Those publications constitute an impressive memorial and are certain to leave a lasting imprint on his chosen field.

FOOTNOTES

1. Hidy (Winter 1970), pp. 483–497.
2. Gilbert (1972), Israel (1972), and Jacoby (1973).
3. Chyet (1970) Seaburg and Patterson (1971).
4. Alberts (1973), Bruce (1973), Brooks (1976), Bryant (1971), Ferguson (1973), Pusey (1974), Tinkle (1970), and Ward (1973).
5. Klein (1971), and Spence (1971).
6. Sampson (1973), and Cline (1974).
7. Sanders (1974), and Hessen (1975).
8. Gustin (1973), Goulder (1972), Wik (1972), Jardim (1970), Kakar (1970), and Tutorow (1971).
9. Canfield (1974), and Wheeler (1973).
10. Chandler and Salsbury (1971), Livesay (1975), and Wall (1970).
11. Broesamle (1973), Eggert (1974), Forbes (1974), Munroe (1973), Prisco (1973), and Sawyer (1968).
12. Huthmacher and Susman (1973), Lloyd (1972), Schwarz (1970), and Wilson (1975).
13. Wyatt-Brown (1969), Swain (1970), and Sibley (1973).
14. Davies (1974), Kammen (1970), Nash (1970), Platt and Skaggs (1971), Rainbolt (1974), and Shepherd and Walton (1972).
15. Coleman (1974), Clowse (1971), Edgar (1972), Smith (1973), and Price (1973).
16. Papenfuse (1975).
17. Carroll (1973), and Smith (1970).
18. Hao (1970), Kirker (1970), Lockwood (1971), Baughman (1972), and Brooks (1970). For a small item on trade in ice, see Everson (1970).
19. Brunson (1970), Chazanof (1970), Holden (1970), Savage (1973), Skaggs (1973), and Whitaker (1975).
20. Chaput (1971), Gibson (1972), and Young (1970).
21. King (1970), and Wall and Gibb (1974).
22. Darrah (1972), and Schruben (1972).
23. Anderson (1975), and Stocking (1970).
24. Ironside (1970), and Jones (1972).
25. Larson, Knowlton and Popple (1971).
26. Smith (1972).
27. Kohlmeyer (1972), Twining (1975), and Neils (1971).
28. Cox (1974), and Clark (1970).
29. Hood (1972).
30. Crockett (1970), Lomax (1974), Jackson (1971), and Walsh (1972).
31. Cromwell (1975), Cudd (1974), and Siegenthaler (1972).
32. Foy (1975), Damman (1973), Gray (1974), Mahan (1972), Wright (1969), and Niemi (1974).

33. Ingells (1970), Kuter (1973), and Francis (1973).
34. Dierdorff (1971), Bush (1973), and Mill (1971).
35. Hoyt (1969), and Marnell (1971).
36. Smalley (1973), and Sturdivant (1970).
37. Emmons (1971), Fahey (1971), and Preston (1975).
38. Porter and Livesay (1971).
39. Atherton (1971), and Knapp (1969).
40. Yoder (1972).
41. Bryant (1974), Klein (1972), and Stover (1975).
42. Alexander (1971), Klein (1970), and Weller (1969).
43. Ames (1969), Athearn (1971), Fair (1969), and Miner (1972).
44. Wood and Wood (1974, 1972).
45. Adler (1970), Olson (1971), Henderson (1969), Schonberger (1971), Scott (1970), and Taylor (1970).
46. Comstock (1971).
47. Dunbar (1969), and Parks (1972).
48. Caine (1970), Carson (1971), and McAfee (1973).
49. O'Connor (1973), and Stover (1970).
50. Miller (1971), and Martin (1971).
51. Flink (1970), Flink (1975), Rae (1971), and White (1971).
52. Mills (1972), Serling (1974), Williams (1970), Whitehouse (1971), Jordan (1970), and Redford (1969).
53. Perkins (1975), and Buist (1974).
54. Cohen (1971), McFerrin (1969), Willis (1973), and Carosso (1970).
55. Crissey (1969), Lesesne (1970), Marple and Olson (1972), and Wessells (1973).
56. Erickson (1971), and Green (1972).
57. Hammond (1970), Shade (1972), and Sharp (1970).
58. Kennedy (1973), Klebaner (1974), and Krooss (1969).
59. Axon (1974), Wyckoff (1972), and Sobel (1973, 1970).
60. Crews (1971), Moody and Fite (1971), and Michelman (1970).
61. Krooss and Blyn (1971).
62. Wilkins (1970, 1974).
63. Vernon (1971, 1974).
64. Gilpin (1975).
65. Williamson (1975).
66. Teichova (1974), Levitt (1971), Moran (1974), and Preston (1972). Except indirectly through trade unions, Preston's book was of little value to the historian of business.
67. Bunting (1971), Clark (1970), Hoffecker (1974), Barth (1975), and Lotchin (1974).
68. McShane (1974), and Hilton (1971).
69. Teaford (1975), and Pred (1973).
70. Armitage (1969), and Glyn and Sutcliffe (1972).
71. Armentano (1972), Cuff (1973), and Ratner (1972).
72. Godfrey (1974).
73. Meyer (1970), Burns (1974), Funigiello (1973), and McCraw (1971).
74. Kilbourn (1970), Friedman (1968), Orren (1974), and Quinn (1970).
75. Williams (1970), and Wilson (1971).
76. Hurst (1970, 1973).
77. Fraser (1973), and Hughes (1971).
78. Pursell (1969), Sinclair (1974), Rosenberg (1972), and David (1975).
79. Blassingame (1972), Curtin (1969), Davis (1975), Fogel and Engerman (1974), McManus (1973), Smith (1973), and Thompson (1975).

80. Carpenter (1972), Galarza (1970), Garnel (1972), Gitelman (1974), Graham (1970), McLaurin (1971), and Suggs (1972).
81. Channon (1973), and Rumelt (1974).
82. Michelman (1973), and Whisenhunt (1974).
83. Krooss (1970).
84. Gelber (1974).
85. Patrick and Eells (1969).
86. Heald (1970).
87. Bailey (1971), Weare (1973), and Light (1972).
88. Chatfield (1974), Carey (1970), and Zeff (1972). Among publications announced by Arno Press in 1975 were several specialized studies: Brief, Richard P., *Nineteenth Century Capital Accounting and Business Investment*; Bruchey, Stuart W., *Robert Oliver and Mercantile Accounting in the Early Nineteenth Century*; Sprouse, Robert T., *The Effect of the Concept of the Corporation on Accounting*; and Zeff, Stephen A., ed., *Asset Appreciation, Business Income and Price-Level Accounting, 1918–1935*.
89. Wolf (1974), and Wren (1972).
90. Christian (1971), and Milton (1970).
91. Burch (1972).
92. Marris and Wood (1971), Cain and Uselding (1973), and Jaher (1968).
93. Udy (1970), and Greene (1970). In *Steeped in Two Cultures: A Selection of Essays Written by Fritz Redlich* (Redlich, 1971), the segment on entrepreneurship is short and not to be compared with that in *Der Unternehmer* by the same author.
94. Barnouw (1970), Schicke (1974), and Tebbel (1972, 1975).
95. See Carroll (1973), Smith (1970), Cox (1974), Crockett (1970), Dunbar (1969), Parks (1972), Stover (1970), Flink (1970, 1975), Rae (1971), White (1971), Whitehouse (1971), Willis (1973), Carosso (1970), Klebaner (1974), and Krooss and Blyn (1971).
96. Durden (1975), Whiteman (1971), and Jenkins (1975).
97. Cobrin (1970), Haber (1971), Hess (1973), and Landing (1969).
98. Grindle (1971), Blakey (1973). and Campbell (1974).
99. Decker (1973), Downward (1973), and Kochiss (1974).
100. Debouzy (1972), Demaris (1974), Dowd (1974), and Seligman (1970).
101. Zilg (1974), Kutz (1974), and Collier and Horowitz (1976).
102. Douglass (1971), Porter (1973), Sobel (1972), Cochran (1972, 1975), and Davis and North (1971).
103. Groner and the Editors of *American Heritage* and *Business Week* (1972).
104. Cochran (1972).
105. Walton (1971), and Krooss and Gilbert (1972).

REFERENCES

Adler, Dorothy R. (1970), *British Investment in American Railways, 1834–1898*, (edited by Hidy, Muriel E.) Charlottesville: University of Virginia for the Eleutherian Mills–Hagley Foundation.

Alberts, Robert C. (1973), *The Good Provider: H. J. Heinz and His 57 Varieties,* Boston: Houghton Mifflin Company.

Alexander, Edwin P. (1971), *On the Main Line: The Pennsylvania Railroad in the 19th Century,* New York: Clarkson N. Potter, Inc.

Ames, Charles E. (1969), *Pioneering the Union Pacific: A Reappraisal of the Builders of the Railroad,* New York: Appleton–Century–Crofts.

Anderson, Irvine H., Jr. (1975), *The Standard–Vacuum Oil Company and United States East Asian Policy, 1933–1941*, Princeton: Princeton University Press.

Armentano, D. T. (1972), *The Myths of Antitrust: Economic Theory and Legal Cases*, New Rochelle, N.Y.: Arlington House.

Armitage, S.M.H. *The Politics of Decontrol of Industry: Britain and the United States*, London: Weidenfield and Nicolson.

Athearn, Robert G. (1971), *Union Pacific Country*, New York: Rand, McNally and Company.

Atherton, Lewis E. (1971), *The Frontier Merchant in Mid-America*, Columbia: University of Missouri Press.

Axon, Gordon V. (1974), *The Stock Market Crash of 1929*, New York: Mason and Lipscomb.

Bailey, Ronald W., ed. (1971), *Black Business Enterprise: Historical and Contemporary Perspectives*, New York: Basic Books.

Barnouw, Erik (1970), *The Image Empire: A History of Broadcasting in the United States from 1953*, New York: Oxford University Press.

Barth, Gunther (1975), *Instant Cities: Urbanization and the Rise of San Francisco and Denver*, New York: Oxford University Press.

Baughman, James P. (1972), *The Mallorys of Mystic: Six Generations in American Maritime Enterprise*. Middletown, Conn.: Wesleyan University Press.

Blakey, Arch F. (1973), *The Florida Phosphate Industry: A History of the Development and Use of a Vital Mineral*, Cambridge, Mass.: Harvard University Press.

Blassingame, John W. (1972), *The Slave Community: Plantation Life in the AnteBellum South*, New York: Oxford University Press.

Broesamle, John J. (1973), *William Gibbs McAdoo: A Passion for Change, 1863–1917*, Port Washington, New York: Kennikat Press, Inc.

Brooks, John (1976), *Telephone: The First 100 Years*, New York: Harper and Row.

Brooks, George E., Jr. (1970), *Yankee Traders, Old Coasters and African Middlemen: A History of American Legitimate Trade with West Africa in the Nineteenth Century*, Boston: Boston University Press.

Bruce, Robert V. (1973), *Bell: Alexander Graham Bell and the Conquest of Solitude*, Boston: Little, Brown and Company.

Brunson, B. R. (1970), *The Texas Land Development Company*, Austin: University of Texas Press.

Bryant, Keith L., Jr. (1971), *Arthur E. Stillwell: Promoter with a Hunch*, Nashville, Tenn.: Vanderbilt University Press.

———. (1974), *History of the Atchison, Topeka and Sante Fe*, New York: Macmillan Company.

Buist, Marten G. (1974), *At Spes Non Fracta: Hope and Co., 1770–1815*, The Hague: Martinus Nijhoff.

Bunting, W. H. (1971), *Portrait of a Port: Boston, 1852–1914*, Cambridge: Belknap Press of Harvard University Press.

Burch, Philip H., Jr. (1972), *The Managerial Revolution Reassessed: Family Control in America's Large Corporations*, Lexington, Mass.: D. C. Heath and Company.

Burns, Helen M. (1974), *The American Banking Community and New Deal Banking Reforms, 1933–1935*, Westport, Conn.: Greenwood Press.

Bush, George (1973), *Future Builders*, New York: McGraw-Hill Book Company.

Cain, Louis P. and Uselding, Paul J. eds. (1973), *Business Enterprise and Economic Change: Essays in Honor of Harold F. Williamson*, Kent, Ohio: Kent State University Press.

Caine, Stanley P. (1970), *The Myth of Progressive Reform: Railroad Regulation in Wisconsin, 1903–1910,* Madison: The State Historical Society of Wisconsin.

Campbell, Leslie C. (1974), *Two Hundred Years of Pharmacy in Mississippi,* Jackson, Miss.: University Press of Mississippi.

Canfield, Cass (1974), *The Incredible Pierpont Morgan: Financier and Art Collector,* New York: Harper and Row.

Carey, John L. (1970), *The Rise of the Accounting Profession to Responsibility and Authority, 1937–1969,* New York: American Institute of Certified Public Accountants.

Carosso, Vincent P. (1970), *Investment Banking in America,* Cambridge: Harvard University Press.

Carpenter, Jesse J. (1972), *Competition and Collective Bargaining in the Needle Trades, 1910–1967,* New York: State School of Industrial and Labor Relations.

Carroll, Charles F. (1973), *The Timber Economy of Puritan New England,* Providence: Brown University Press.

Carson, Robert B. (1971), *Main Line to Oblivion: The Disintegration of the New York Railroads in the Twentieth Century,* Port Washington, N.Y.: Kennikat Press, Inc.

Chandler, Alfred D., Jr. and Salsbury, Stephen (1971), *Pierre S. Dupont and the Making of the Modern Corporation,* New York: Harper and Row.

Channon, Derek F. (1973), *The Strategy and Structure of British Enterprise,* Boston: Division of Research, Graduate School of Business Administration, Harvard University.

Chaput, Donald (1971), *The Cliff: America's First Great Copper Mine,* Kalamazoo, Mich.: Sequoia Press Publishers.

Chatfield, Michael (1974), *A History of Accounting Thought,* Hinsdale, Ill.: Dryden Press.

Chazanof, William (1970), *Joesph Ellicott and the Holland Land Company: The Opening of Western New York,* Syracuse: Syracusè University Press.

Christian, Portia (1971), *Ethics in Business Conduct,* Detroit: Gale Research Company.

Chyet, Stanley F. (1970), *Lopez of Newport: Colonial American Merchant Prince,* Detroit: Wayne State University Press.

Clark, John G. (1970), *New Orleans, 1718–1812: An Economic History,* Baton Rouge: Louisiana State University Press.

Clark, Norman H. (1970), *Mill Town: A Social History of Everett, Washington from Its Earliest Beginnings on the Shores of Puget Sound to the Tragic and Infamous Event Known as the Everett Massacre,* Seattle: University of Washington Press.

Cline, Gloria Griffen (1974), *Peter Skene Ogden and the Hudson's Bay Company,* Norman: University of Oklahoma Press.

Clowse, Converse D. (1971), *Economic Beginnings in Colonial South Carolina, 1670–1730,* Columbia: University of South Carolina Press.

Cobrin, Harry A. (1970), *The Men's Clothing Industry: Colonial through Modern Times,* New York: Fairchild Publications.

Cochran, Thomas Co. (1972), *Business in American Life: A History,* New York: McGraw-Hill Book Company.

———. (1972), *American Business in the Twentieth Century,* Cambridge: Harvard University Press.

Cohen, Henry (1971), *Business and Politics in America from the Age of Jackson to the Civil War: The Career Biography of W. W. Corcoran,* Westport, Conn.: Greenwood Publishing Corporation.

Coleman, Peter J. (1974), *Debtors and Creditors in America: Insolvency, Imprisonment for Debt, and Bankruptcy, 1607–1900,* Madison: The State Historical Society of Wisconsin.

Collier, Peter and Horowitz, David (1976), *The Rockefellers: An American Dynasty*, New York: Holt, Rinehart and Winston.

Comstock, Henry B. (1971), *The Iron Horse: America's Steam Locomotives, A Pictorial History*, New York: Thomas Y. Crowell.

Cox, Thomas R. (1974), *Mills and Markets: A History of the Pacific Coast Lumber Industry to 1900*. Seattle: University of Washington Press.

Crews, Cecil R. (1971), *The History of the Michigan Credit Union League*, Detroit: Wayne State University Press.

Crissey, Elwell (1969), *People's Bank of Bloomington: First 100 Years, 1869–1969*, Bloomington, Ind.: People's Bank of Bloomington.

Crockett, Norman L. (1970), *The Woolen Industry of the Midwest*, Lexington: University Press of Kentucky.

Cromwell, Giles (1975), *The Virginia Manufactory of Arms*, Charlottesville: University Press of Virginia.

Cudd, John Michael (1974), *The Chicopee Manufacturing Company, 1823–1915*, Wilmington, Del.: Scholarly Resources, Inc.

Cuff, Robert D. (1973), *The War Industries Board: Business-Government Relations during World War I*, Baltimore: Johns Hopkins Press.

Curtin, Philip D. (1969), *The Atlantic Slave Trade: A Census*, Madison: University of Wisconsin Press.

Damman, George H. (1973), *Seventy Years of Buick*, Glen Ellyn, Ill.: Crestline Publishing.

Darrah, William C. (1972), *Pithole, The Vanished City: A Story of the Early Days of the Petroleum Industry*, Gettysburg, Pa.: Privately printed.

David, Paul A. (1975), *Technical Choice, Innovation and Economic Growth: Essays on American and British Experience in the Nineteenth Century*, London: Cambridge University Press.

Davies, K. G. (1974), *The North Atlantic World in the Seventeenth Century*, Minneapolis: University of Minnesota Press.

Davis, David B. (1975), *The Problem of Slavery in the Age of Revolution, 1770–1823*, Ithaca, N.Y.: Cornell University Press.

Davis, Lance E. and North, Douglass (1971), *Institutional Change and American Economic Growth*, London: Cambridge University Press.

Debouzy, Marianne (1972), *Le Capitalisme "Sauvage" aux Etats-Unis (1860–1900)*, Paris: Editions du Seuil.

Decker, Robert O. (1973), *Whaling Industry of New London*, York, Pa.: Liberty Cap Books.

Demaris, Ovid (1974), *Dirty Business: The Corporate-Political-Money-Power Game*, New York: Harper's Magazine Press.

Dierdorff, John (1971), *How Edison's Lamp Helped Light the West*, Portland, Ore.: Pacific Power and Light Company.

Douglass, Elisha P. (1971), *The Coming of Age of American Business: Three Centuries of Enterprise, 1600–1900*, Chapel Hill: University of North Carolina Press.

Dowd, Douglas F. (1974), *The Twisted Dream: Capitalist Development in the United States since 1776*, Cambridge, Mass.: Winthrop Publishers, Inc.

Downward, William L. (1973), *The Cincinnati Brewing Industry: A Social and Economic History*, Athens, O.: Ohio University Press.

Dunbar, Willis F. (1969), *All Aboard! A History of Railroads in Michigan*, Grand Rapids, Mich.: Erdmans Publishing Company.

Durden, Robert F. (1975), *The Dukes of Durham, 1865–1929*, Durham: Duke University Press.

Edgar, Walter B., ed. (1972), *The Letterbook of Robert Pringle, Vol. I., April 2, 1737-September 25, 1742; Vol. II, October 9, 1742-April 29, 1745,* Columbia: University of South Carolina Press.

Eggert, Gerald G. (1974), *Richard Olney: Evolution of a Statesman,* University Park: Pennsylvania State University Press.

Emmons, David M. (1971), *Garden in the Grasslands: Boomer Literature of the Central Great Plains,* Lincoln: University of Nebraska Press.

Erickson, Erling A. (1971), *Banking in Frontier Iowa, 1836-1865,* Ames: Iowa State University Press.

Everson, Jennie G. (1970), *Tidewater Ice of the Kennebec River,* Freeport, Me.: Bond Wheelwright Company for the Maine State Museum.

Fahey, John (1971), *The Ballyhoo Bonanza,* Seattle: University of Washington Press.

Fair, James R., Jr. (1969), *The North Arkansas Line: The Story of the Missouri and North Arkansas Railroad.* Berkeley: Howell-North Books, 1969.

Ferguson, E. James, ed. (1973), *The Papers of Robert Morris, 1781-1784, Vol. I: February 7-July 31, 1781,* Pittsburgh: University of Pittsburgh Press.

Flink, James J. (1970), *America Adopts the Automobile, 1895-1910,* Cambridge, Mass.: M.I.T. Press.

———. (1975), *The Car Culture,* Cambridge Mass.: M.I.T. Press.

Fogel, Robert W. and Engerman, Stanley (1974), *Time on the Cross,* Boston: Little, Brown and Company.

Forbes, John D. (1974), *Stettinius, Sr.: Portrait of a Morgan Partner,* Charlottesville: University Press of Virginia.

Foy, Nancy (1975), *The Sun Never Sets on IBM,* New York: William Morrow and Company.

Francis, Devon (1973), *Mr. Piper and His Cubs,* Ames: Iowa State University Press.

Fraser, Colin (1973), *Tractor Pioneer: The Life of Harry Ferguson,* Athens: Ohio University Press.

Friedman, Lawrence M. (1968), *Government and Slum Housing: A Century of Frustration,* Chicago: Rand McNally.

Funigiello, Philip J. (1973), *Toward a National Power Policy: The New Deal and the Electric Utility Industry, 1933-1941,* Pittsburgh: University of Pittsburgh Press.

Galarza, Ernesto (1970), *Spiders in the House and Workers in the Field,* Notre Dame, Ind.: University of Notre Dame Press.

Garnel, Donald (1972), *The Rise of Teamster Power in the West,* Berkeley: University of California Press.

Gelber, Steven M. (1974), *Black Men and Businessmen: The Growing Awareness of a Social Responsibility,* Port Washington, N.Y.: Kennikat Press, Inc.

Gibson, Arrell M. (1972), *Wilderness Bonanza: The Tri-State District of Missouri, Kansas, and Oklahoma,* Norman: University of Oklahoma Press.

Gilbert, James (1972), *Designing the Industrial State: The Intellectual Pursuit of Collectivism in America, 1880-1960,* Chicago: Quadrangle Books.

Gilpin, Robert (1975), *U.S. Power and the Multinational Corporation,* New York: Basic Books, Inc.

Gitelman, Howard M. (1974), *Workingmen of Waltham: Mobility in American Urban Industrial Development, 1850-1890,* Baltimore: The Johns Hopkins University Press.

Glyn, Andrew and Sutcliffe, Bob (1972), *Capitalism in Crisis,* New York: Pantheon Books.

Godfrey, Aaron A. (1974), *Government Operation of the Railroads: Its Necessity, Suc-*

cess, and Consequences, 1918–1920, Austin, Texas: The San Felipe Press.

Goulder, Grace (1972), *John D. Rockefeller: The Cleveland Years*, Cleveland: The Western Reserve Historical Society.

Graham, Harry E. (1970), *The Paper Rebellion: Development and Upheaval in Pulp and Paper Unionism*, Iowa City: University of Iowa Press.

Gray, Ralph D. (1974), *Stellite: A History of the Haynes Stellite Company, 1912–1972*, Kokomo, Ind.: Stellite Divison, Cabot Corporation.

Green, George D. (1972), *Finance and Economic Development in the Old South: Louisiana Banking, 1804–1861*, Stanford: Stanford University Press.

Greene, Theodore P. (1970), *America's Heroes: The Changing Models of Success in American Magazines*, New York: Oxford University Press.

Grindle, Roger L. (1971), *Quarry and Kiln: The Story of Maine's Lime Industry*, Rockland, Me.: The Courier-Gazette, Inc.

Groner, Alex and the Editors of *American Heritage* and *Business Week* (1972), *The History of American Business and Industry*, New York: American Heritage Publishing Company.

Gustin, Lawrence R. (1973), *Billy Durant, Creator of General Motors*, Grand Rapids, Mich.: W. B. Erdmans Publishing Company.

Haber, L. F. (1971), *The Chemical Industry, 1900–1930: International Growth and Technological Change*, Oxford: Oxford University Press.

Hammond, Bray (1970), *Sovereignty and an Empty Purse: Banks and Politics in the Civil War*, Princeton: Princeton University Press.

Hammond, Bray (1970), *Sovereignty and an Empty Purse: Banks and Politics in the Civil War*, Princeton: Princeton University Press.

Hao, Yen-p'ing (1970), *The Comparador in Nineteenth Century China: Bridge between East and West*, Cambridge: Harvard University Press.

Heald, Morrell (1970), *The Social Responsibilities of a Business: Company and Community, 1900–1960*, Cleveland, O.: Press of Case Western Reserve University.

Henderson, James D. (1969), *"Meals by Fred Harvey": A Phenomenon of the American West*, Fort Worth: Texas Christian University Press.

Hess, John (1973), *The Mobile Society: A History of the Moving and Storage Industry*, New York: McGraw-Hill Book Co.

Hessen, Robert (1975), *Steel Titan: The Life of Charles N. Schwab*, New York: Oxford University Press.

Hidy, Ralph W. (Winter 1970), "Business History: Present Status and Future Needs," *The Business History Review*, 44.

Hilton, George W. (1971), *The Cable Car in America*, Berkeley, Cal.: Howell-North Books.

Hoffecker, Carol E. (1974), *Wilmington, Delaware: Portrait of an Industrial City*, Charlottesville: University Press of Virginia.

Holden, W. C. (1970), *The Espuela Land and Cattle Company*, Austin: Texas State Historical Association.

Hood, Graham (1972), *Bonnin and Morris of Philadelphia: The First American Porcelain Factory, 1770–1772*, Chapel Hill: University of North Carolina Press.

Hoyt, Edwin P. (1969), *That Wonderful A&P!*, New York: Hawthorn Books.

Hughes, Thomas P. (1971), *Elmer Sperry: Inventor and Engineer*, Baltimore: Johns Hopkins University Press.

Hurst, James W. (1970), *The Legitimacy of the Business Corporation in the Law of the United States*, Charlottesville: University Press of Virginia.

———. (1973), *A Legal History of Money in the United States, 1774–1970*, Lincoln: University of Nebraska Press.

Huthmacher, J. Joseph and Susman, Warren I., eds. (1973), *Herbert Hoover and the Crisis of American Capitalism*, Cambridge, Mass.: Schenkman Publishing Company.

Ingells, Douglas J. (1970), *747: Story of the Boeing Superjet*, Fallbrook, Cal.: Aero Publications.

Ironside, Roberta (1970), *An Adventure Called Skelly: A History of Skelly Oil Company through Fifty Years*, New York: Appleton-Century-Crofts.

Israel, Jerry, ed. (1972), *Building the Organizational Society; Essays on Associational Activities in Modern America*, New York: Free Press.

Jackson, A. T. (1971), *Mills of Yesterday*, El Paso, Tex.: Texas Western Press.

Jacoby, Henry (1973), *The Bureaucratization of the World*, Berkeley: University of California Press.

Jaher, Frederic C., ed. (1968), *The Age of Industrialism: Essays in Social Structure and Cultural Values*. New York: Free Press.

Jardim, Anne (1970), *The First Henry Ford: A Study in Personality and Business Leadership*, Cambridge, Mass.: M.I.T. Press.

Jenkins, Reese V. (1975), *Images and Enterprise: Technology and the American Photographic Industry, 1839 to 1925*, Baltimore: Johns Hopkins University Press.

Jones, Charles S. (1972), *From the Rio Grande to the Arctic: The Story of the Richfield Oil Corporation*, Norman: University of Oklahoma Press.

Jordan, William A. (1970), *Air Line Regulation in America: Effects and Imperfections*, Baltimore: Johns Hopkins University Press.

Kakar, Sudhir (1970), *Frederick Taylor: A Study in Personality and Innovation*, Cambridge, Mass.: M.I.T. Press.

Kammen, Michael (1970), *Empire and Interest: The American Colonies and the Politics of Mercantilism*, Philadelphia: J. B. Lippincott Company.

Kennedy, Susan E. (1973), *The Banking Crisis of 1933*, Lexington: University Press of Kentucky.

Kilbourn, William (1970), *Pipeline: Trans-Canada and the Great Debate—A History of Business and Politics*, Toronto: Clark, Irwin and Company, Ltd.

King, John O. (1970), *Joseph Stephen Cullinan: A Study of Leadership in the Texas Petroleum Industry, 1897–1937*, Nashville, Tenn.: Vanderbilt University Press for the Texas Gulf Coast Historical Association.

Kirker, James (1970), *Adventures to China: Americans in the Southern Oceans, 1792–1812*, New York: Oxford University Press.

Klebaner, Benjamin J. (1974), *Commercial Banking in the United States: A History*, Hinsdale, Ill.: Dryden Press.

Klein, Maury (1970), *The Great Richmond Terminal: A Study in Businessmen and Business Strategy*, Charlottesville: University Press of Virginia for the Eleutherian Mills-Hagley Foundation.

———. (1971), *Edward Porter Alexander*, Athens: University of Georgia Press.

———. (1971, *History of the Louisville and Nashville Railroad*, New York: Macmillan Company.

Knapp, Joseph G. (1969), *The Rise of American Cooperative Enterprise, 1620–1920*, Danville, Ill.: Interstate Printers and Publishers.

Kochiss, John M. (1974), *Oystering from New York to Boston*, Middletown, Conn.: Wesleyan University Press.

Kohlmeyer, Fred W. (1972), *Timber Roots: The Laird, Norton Story, 1855–1905*, Winona, Minn.: County Historical Society.

Kroos, Herman E. and Blyn, Martin R. (1971), *A History of Financial Intermediaries*, New York: Random House.

Kroos, Herman E., ed. (1969), *Documentary History of Banking and Currency in the*

United States, 4 vols., New York: Chelsea House Publishers.

————. (1970), *Executive Opinion: What Business Leaders Said and Thought on Economic Issues, 1920's–1960's,* Garden City, N.Y.: Doubleday and Company.

Kroos, Herman E. and Blyn, Martin R. (1971), *A History of Financial Intermediaries,* New York: Random House.

Kroos, Herman E. and Gilbert, Charles (1972), *American Business History,* Englewood Cliffs, N.J.: Prentice-Hall, Inc.

Kuter, Laurence S. (1973), *The Great Gamble: The Boeing 747,* University, Ala.: University of Alabama Press.

Kutz, Myer (1974), *Rockefeller Power,* New York: Simon and Schuster.

Landing, James E. (1969), *American Essence: A History of the Peppermint and Spearmint Industry in the United States,* Kalamazoo, Mich.: Kalamazoo Public Museum.

Larson, Henrietta M., Knowlton, Evelyn H. and Popple, Charles S. (1971), *New Horizons, 1927–1950: History of Standard Oil Company (New Jersey),* III, New York: Harper and Row.

Lesesne, J. Mauldin (1970), *The Bank of the State of South Carolina: A General and Political History,* Columbia: University of South Carolina Press.

Levitt, Kari (1971), *Silent Surrender: The American Economic Empire in Canada,* New York: Liveright.

Light, Ivan H. (1972), *Ethnic Enterprise in America: Business and Welfare among Chinese, Japanese, and Blacks,* Berkeley: University of California Press.

Livesay, Harold C. (1975), *Andrew Carnegie and the Rise of Big Business,* Boston: Little, Brown and Company.

Lloyd, Craig (1972), *Aggressive Introvert: A Study of Herbert Hoover and Public Relations Management, 1912–1932,* Columbus: Ohio State University Press.

Lockwood, Stephen C. (1971), *Augustine Heard and Company, 1858–1862: American Merchants in China,* Cambridge: Harvard University Press.

Lomax, Alfred L. (1974), *Later Woolen Mills in Oregon: A History of the Woolen Mills which Followed the Pioneer Mills,* Portland, Ore.: Binsford and Mort, Publishers.

Lotchin, Roger W. (1974), *San Francisco, 1846–1856: From Hamlet to City,* New York: Oxford University Press.

McAfee, Ward (1973), *California's Railroad Era, 1850–1911,* San Marino, Cal.: Golden West Books.

McCraw, Thomas K. (1971), *TVA and the Power Fight, 1933–1939,* Philadelphia: J. B. Lippincott Company.

McFerrin, John B. (1969), *Caldwell and Company: A Southern Financial Empire,* Nashville, Tenn.: Vanderbilt University Press.

McLaurin, Melton A. (1971), *Paternalism and Protest: Southern Cotton Mill Workers and Organized Labor, 1875–1905,* Westport, Conn.: Greenwood Publishing Corporation.

McManus, Edgar J. (1973), *Black Bondage in the North,* Syracuse: Syracuse University Press.

McShane, Clay (1974), *Technology and Reform: Street Railways and the Growth of Milwaukee, 1887–1900,* Madison: State Historical Society of Wisconsin.

Mahan, Ernest (1972), *The History of McNally, Pittsburgh,* Wichita, Kan.: McCormick-Armstrong Company.

Marnell, William H. (1971), *Once Upon A Store: Biography of the World's First Supermarket,* New York: Herder and Herder.

Marple, Elliot and Olson, Bruce H. (1972), *The National Bank of Commerce of Seattle,* Palto Alto, Cal.: Pacific Books.

Marris, Robin and Wood, Adrian, eds. (1971), *The Corporate Economy: Growth, Competition and Innovative Potential,* Cambridge: Harvard University Press.

Martin, Albro (1971), *Enterprise Denied: Origins of the Decline of American Railroads, 1897–1917,* New York: Columbia University Press.

Meyer, Richard H. (1970), *Bankers' Diplomacy: Monetary Stabilization in the Twenties,* New York: Columbia University Press.

Michelman, Irving S. (1970), *Consumer Finance: A Case History in American Business,* New York: Augustus M. Kelley.

———. (1973), *The Crisis Meeters: Business Response to Social Crisis,* Clifton, N.J.: Augustus M. Kelley.

Miller, Raymond C. (1971), *The Force of Energy: A Business History of the Detroit Edison Company,* East Lansing: Michigan State University Press.

Miller, George H. (1971), *Railroads and the Granger Laws,* Madison: University of Wisconsin Press.

Mills, Stephen E. (1972), *More than Meets the Sky,* Seattle: Superior Publishing Company.

Milton, Charles R. (1970), *Ethics and Expediency in Personnel Management: A Critical History of Personnel Philosophy,* Columbia: University of South Carolina Press.

Miner, H. Craig (1972), *The St. Louis-San Francisco Transcontinental Railroad: The Thirty-fifth Parallel Project, 1853–1890,* Lawrence: University Press of Kansas.

Moody, J. Carroll and Fite, Gilbert C. (1971), *The Credit Union Movement: Origins and Development, 1850–1970,* Lincoln: University of Nebraska Press.

Moran, Theodore H. (1974), *Multinational Corporations and the Politics of Dependence: Copper in Chile,* Princeton: Princeton University Press.

Morison, E. E. (1974), *From Know-how to Nowhere: The Development of American Technology,* New York: Basic Books, Inc.

Munroe, John A. (1973), *Louis McLane: Federalist and Jacksonian,* New Brunswick, N.J.: Rutgers University Press.

Nash, Gary B. (1970), *Class and Society in Early America,* Englewood Cliffs, N.J.: Prentice-Hall.

Neils, Paul (1971), *Julius Neils and the J. Neils Lumber Company,* Seattle: Frank McCaffrey.

Niemi, Albert J., Jr. (1974), *State and Regional Patterns in American Manufacturing,* Westport, Conn.: Greenwood Press.

O'Connor, Richard (1973), *Iron Wheels and Broken Men: The Railroad Barons and the Plunder of the West,* New York: G. P. Putnam's Sons.

Olson, Sherry H. (1971), *The Depletion Myth: A History of Railroad Use of Timber,* Cambridge: Harvard University Press.

Orren, Karen (1974), *Corporate Power and Social Change: The Politics of the Life Insurance Industry,* Baltimore: Johns Hopkins University Press.

Papenfuse, Edward C. (1975), *In Pursuit of Profit: The Annapolis Merchants in the Era of the American Revolution,* Baltimore: Johns Hopkins University Press.

Parks, Robert J. (1972), *Democracy's Railroads: Public Enterprise in Jacksonian Michigan,* Port Washington, N.Y.: Kennikat Press, Inc.

Patrick, Kenneth G. and Eells, Richard (1969), *Education and the Business Dollar: A Study of Corporate Contributions Policy and American Education,* New York: Macmillan Company.

Perkins, Edwin J. (1975), *Financing Anglo-American Trade: The House of Brown, 1800–1880,* Cambridge: Harvard University Press.

Platt, Virginia B. and Skaggs, David C., eds. (1971), *Of Mother Country and Plantations: Proceedings of the Twenty-seventh Conference in Early American History,* Bowling Green, Ohio: Bowling Green University Press.

Porter, Glenn and Livesay, Harold C. (1971), *Merchants and Manufacturers: Studies in*

the Changing Structure of Nineteenth-Century Marketing, Baltimore: Johns Hopkins University Press.

——. (1973), The Rise of Big Business, 1860–1910, New York: Thomas Y. Crowell Company.

Pred, Allan R. (1973), Urban Growth and the Circulation of Information: The United States System of Cities, 1790–1840, Cambridge: Harvard University Press.

Preston, Ivan L. (1973), The Great American Blowup Puffery in Advertising and Selling, Madison: University of Wisconsin Press.

Preston, Richard A., ed. (1972), The Influence of the United States on Canadian Development: Eleven Case Studies, Durham, N.C.: Duke University Press.

Price, Jacob M. (1973), France and the Chesapeake: A History of the French Tobacco Monopoly, 1674–1791, and of Its Relationship to the British and American Tobacco Trades, 2 vols., Ann Arbor: University of Michigan Press.

Prisco, Salvatore, III (1973), John Barrett, Progressive Era Diplomat: A Study of a Commercial Expansionist, 1887–1920, University: University of Alabama Press.

Pursell, Carroll W., Jr. (1969), Early Stationary Steam Engines in America: A Study in the Migration of a Technology, Washington, D.C.: Smithsonian Institution Press.

Pusey, Merlo J. (1974), Eugene Meyer, New York: Alfred A. Knopf.

Quinn, Larry D. (1970), Politicians in Business: A History of the Liquor Control System in Montana, Missoula: University of Montana Press.

Rae, John B. (1971), The Road and the Car in American Life, Cambridge, Mass.: M.I.T. Press.

Rainbolt, John C. (1974), From Prescription to Persuasion: Manipulation of Seventeenth Century Virginia Economy, Port Washington, N.Y.: Kennikat Press.

Ratner, Sidney, (1972), The Tariff in American History, New York: D. Van Nostrand Company.

Redford, Emmette S. (1969), The Regulatory Process, with Illustrations from Commercial Aviation, Austin: University of Texas Press.

Redlich, Fritz (1971), Steeped in Two Cultures: A Selection of Essays written by Fritz Redlich, New York: Harper and Row.

Rosenberg, Nathan (1972), Technology and American Economic Growth, New York: Harper and Row.

Rumelt, Richard P. (1974), Strategy, Structure, and Economic Performance, Boston: Division of Research, Graduate School of Business Administration, Harvard University.

Sampson, William R., ed. (1973), John McLoughlin's Business Correspondence, 1847–1848, Seattle: University of Washington Press.

Sanders, Col. Harland (1974), Finger Lickin' Good, Carol Stream, Ill.: Creation House.

Savage, William W., Jr. (1973), The Cherokee Strip Live Stock Association: Federal Regulation and the Cattleman's Last Frontier, Columbia: Unviersity of Missouri Press.

Sawyer, Charles (1968), Concerns of a Conservative Democrat, Carbondale: Southern Illinois University Press.

Schicke, C. A. (1974), Revolution in Sound: A Biography of the Recording Industry, Boston: Little Brown and Company.

Schmookler, Jacob (1972), Patents, Inventions, and Economic Change: Data and Selected Essays, (edited by Griliches, Zvi and Hurwicz, Leonid, Cambridge: Harvard University Press.

Schonberger, Howard B. (1971), Transportation to the Seaboard: The "Communication Revolution" and American Foreign Policy, 1860–1900, Westport, Conn.: Greenwood Publishing Corporation.

Schruben, Francis W. (1972), *WEA Creek to Eldorado: Oil in Kansas,* Columbia: University of Missouri Press.

Schwarz, Jordan A. (1970), *The Interregnum of Despair: Hoover, Congress, and the Depression,* Urbana: University of Illinois Press.

Scott, Roy V. (1970), *The Reluctant Farmer: The Rise of Agricultural Extension to 1914,* Urbana: University of Illinois Press.

Seaburg, Carl and Patterson, Stanley (1971), *Merchant Prince of Boston: Colonel T. H. Perkins, 1764–1854,* Cambridge: Harvard University Press.

Seligman, Ben B. (1970), *The Potentates: Business and Businessmen in American History,* New York: Dial Press.

Serling, Robert J. (1974), *Maverick: The Story of Robert Six and Continental Airlines,* New York: Doubleday.

Shade, William G. (1972), *Banks or no Banks: The Money Issue in Western Politics, 1832–1865,* Detroit: Wayne State University Press.

Sharp, James R. (1970), *The Jacksonians versus the Banks: Politics in the State after the Panic of 1837,* New York: Columbia University Press.

Shepherd, James F. and Walton, Gary M. (1972), *Shipping, Maritime Trade, and the Economic Development of Colonial North America,* New York and London: Cambridge University Press.

Sibley, Marilyn M. (1973), *George W. Brackenridge: Maverick Philanthropist,* Austin: University of Texas Press.

Siegenthaler, Hansjorg (1972), *Das Gewicht Monopolistischer Elemente in Der Amerikanischen Textilindustrie, 1840–1880,* Berlin: Duncker and Hambolt.

Sinclair, Bruce (1974), *Philadelphia's Philosopher Mechanics: A History of the Franklin Institute, 1824–1865,* Baltimore: John Hopkins University Press.

Skaggs, Jimmy M. (1973), *The Cattle Trailing Industry: Between Supply and Demand, 1866–1890,* Lawrence: University Press of Kansas.

Smalley, Orange A. and Sturdivant, Frederick D. (1973), *The Credit Merchants: A History of Spiegel, Inc.,* Carbondale: Southern Illinois University Press.

Smith, David C. (1970), *History of Papermaking in the United States (1691–1969),* New York: Lockwood Publishing Company.

———. (1972), *A History of Lumbering in Maine, 1861–1960,* Orono: University of Maine Press.

Smith, George, L. (1973), *Religion and Trade in New Netherland: Dutch Origins and American Development,* Ithaca: Cornell University Press.

Smith, Julia F. (1973), *Slavery and Plantation Growth in Antebellum Florida, 1821–1860,* Gainesville: University of Florida Press.

Sobel, Robert (1970), *The Curbstone Brokers: The Origins of the American Exchange,* New York: Macmillan Company.

———. (1972), *The Age of Giant Corporations: A Microeconomic History of American Business,* Westport, Conn.: Greenwood Press.

———. (1973), *The Money Manias: The Eras of Great Speculation in America, 1770–1970,* New York: Weybright and Talley.

Spence, Vernon G. (1971), *Colonel Morgan Jones: Grand Old Man of Texas Railroading,* Norman: University of Oklahoma Press.

Stocking, George W. (1970), *Middle East Oil: A Study in Political and Economic Controversy,* Nashville, Tenn.: Vanderbilt University Press.

Stover, John F. (1970), *The Life and Decline of the American Railroad,* New York: Oxford University Press.

———. (1975), *History of the Illinois Central Railroad,* New York: Macmillan Company.

Sturdivant, Frederick D. (1970), *Growth through Service: The Story of American Hospital*

Supply Corporation, Evanston: Northwestern University Press.

Suggs, George G., Jr. (1972), *Colorado's War on Militant Unionism: James H. Peabody and the Western Federation of Miners,* Detroit: Wayne State University Press.

Swain, Donald C. (1970), *Wilderness Defender: Horace M. Albright and Conservation,* Chicago: University of Chicago Press.

Taylor, William L. (1970), *A Productive Monopoly: The Effect of Railroad Control on New England Coastal Steamship Lines, 1870–1916,* Providence, R.I.: Brown University Press.

Teaford, John C. (1975), *The Municipal Revolution in America: Origins of Modern Urban Government, 1650–1825,* Chicago: University of Chicago Press.

Tebbel, John (1972, 1975), *A History of Book Publishing in the United States,* 2 vols., New York: R. R. Bowker.

Teichova, Alice (1974), *An Economic Background to Munich: International Business and Czechoslovakia, 1918–1938,* London and New York: Cambridge University Press.

Thompson, Edgar T. (1975), *Plantation Societies, Race Relations, and the South: The Regimentation of Populations,* Durham, N.C.: Duke University Press.

Tinkle, Lon (1970), *Mr. De: A Biography of Everette Lee DeGolyer,* Boston: Little, Brown and Company.

Tutorow, Norman E. (1971), *Leland Stanford: Man of Many Careers,* Menlo Park, Cal.: Pacific Coast Publishers.

Twining, Charles E. (1975), *Downriver: Orrin H. Ingram and the Empire Lumber Company,* Madison: State Historical Society of Wisconsin.

Udy, Stanley H., Jr. (1970), *Work in Traditional and Modern Society,* Englewood Cliffs, N.J.: Prentice-Hall, Inc.

Vernon, Raymond (1971), *Sovereignty at Bay: The Multinational Spread of U.S. Enterprise,* New York: Basic Books.

———. (1974), *Big Business and the State: Changing Relationships in Western Europe,* Cambridge, Mass.: Harvard University Press.

Wall, Bennett and Gibb, George S. (1974), *Teagle of Jersey Standard,* New Orleans: Tulane University.

Wall, Joseph F. (1970), *Andrew Carnegie,* New York: Oxford University Press.

Walsh, Margaret (1972), *The Manufacturing Frontier: Pioneer Industry in Wisconsin, 1830–1860,* Madison: State Historical Society of Wisconsin.

Walton, Scott D. (1971), *Business in American History,* Columbus, O.: Grid, Inc.

Ward, James A. (1973), *That Man Haupt: A Biography of Herman Haupt,* Baton Rouge: Louisiana State University Press.

Weare, Walter B. (1973), *Black Business in the New South: A Social History of the North Carolina Mutual Life Insurance Company,* Urbana, Ill.: University of Illinois Press.

Weller, John L. (1969), *The New Haven Railroad: Its Rise and Fall,* New York: Hastings House.

Wessells, John H., Jr. (1973), *The Bank of Virginia: A History,* Charlottesville: University Press of Virginia.

Wheeler, George (1973), *Pierpont Morgan and Friends: The Anatomy of a Myth,* Englewood Cliffs, N.J.: Prentice-Hall.

Whisenhunt, Donald W. (1974), *The Environment and the American Experience: A Historian Looks at the Ecological Crisis,* Port Washington, N.Y.: Kennikat Press.

Whitaker, James W. (1975), *Feedlot Empire: Beef Cattle Feeding in Illinois and Iowa, 1840–1900,* Ames: Iowa State University Press.

White, Lawrence J. (1971), *The Automobile Industry since 1945,* Cambridge, Mass.: Harvard University Press.

Whitehouse, Arch (1971), *The Sky's the Limit: A History of the U.S. Airlines,* New York: Macmillan Company.

Whiteman, Maxwell (1971), *Copper for America: The Hendricks Family and a National Industry, 1755–1939,* New Brunswick, N.J.: Rutgers University Press.

Wik, Reynold M. (1972), *Henry Ford and Grass-roots America,* Ann Arbor: University of Michigan Press.

Wilkins, Mira (1970), *The Emergence of Multinational Enterprise: American Business Abroad from the Colonial Era to 1914,* Cambridge, Mass.: Harvard University Press.

———. (1974), *The Maturing of Multinational Enterprise: American Business Abroad from 1914 to 1970,* Cambridge, Mass.: Harvard University Press.

Williams, Brad (1970), *The Anatomy of an Airline,* New York: Doubleday.

Williams, W. A. (1970), *The Roots of the Modern American Empire: A Study of the Growth and Shaping of Social Consciousness in a Marketplace Society,* Rolling Hills Estates, Cal.: Vintage Radio Company.

Williamson, H. F., ed. (1975), *Evolution of International Management Structures,* Newark, Del.: University of Delaware Press.

Willis, Parker B. (1973), *A History of Investment Banking in New England,* Boston: Federal Reserve Bank of Boston.

Wilson, Joan Hoff (1971), *American Business and Foreign Policy, 1920–1933,* Lexington: University Press of Kentucky.

———. (1975), *Herbert Hoover: Forgotten Progressive,* Boston: Little, Brown and Company.

Wolf, William B. (1974), *The Basic Barnard: An Introduction to Chester I. Barnard and His Theories of Organization and Management,* Ithaca: New York State School of Industrial and Labor Relations.

Wood, Charles R. and Dorothy M. (1972), *Milwaukee Road—West,* Seattle: Superior Publishing Company.

———. (1974), *Spokane, Portland and Seattle Railway,* Seattle: Superior Publishing Company.

Woodruff, William (1975), *America's Impact on the World: A Study of the Role of the United States in the World Economy, 1750–1970.* New York and Toronto: John Wiley and Sons.

Wren, Daniel A. (1972), *The Evolution of Management Thought,* New York: The Ronald Press Company.

Wright, Richard J. (1969), *Freshwater Whales: A History of the American Ship Building Company and Its Predecessors,* Kent: Kent State University Press.

Wyatt-Brown, Bertram (1969), *Lewis Tappan and the Evangelical War against Slavery,* Cleveland: Press of Case Western Reserve University.

Wyckoff, Peter (1972), *Wall Street and the Stock Market,* New York: Chilton Book Company.

Yoder, C. P. (1972), *Delaware Canal Journal: A Definitive History of the Canal and the River Valley through Which It Flows,* Bethelem, Pennsylvania: Canal Press, Inc.

Young, Otis E., Jr., with the technical assistance of Lenon, Robert (1970), *Western Mining: An Informal Account of Precious-Metals Prospecting, Placering, Lode Mining, and Milling on the American Frontier from Spanish Times to 1893,* Norman: University of Oklahoma Press.

Zeff, Stephen A. (1972), *Forging Accounting Principles in Five Countries: A History and an Analysis of Trends,* Champaign, Ill.: Stipes Publishing Company.

Zilg, Gerard C. (1974), *DuPont: Behind the Nylon Curtain, Englewood Cliffs, N.J.:* Prentice-Hall, Inc.

TWENTIETH CENTURY RAILROAD MANAGERIAL PRACTICES: THE CASE OF THE PENNSYLVANIA RAILROAD

Stephen M. Salsbury, UNIVERSITY OF DELAWARE

The Penn Central's financial collapse in 1970 and the subsequent failure of the court-appointed trustee to restore the railroad's fiscal health have focused much attention on railroad problems. A considerable body of opinion has blamed goverment policy for the difficulties. Certainly unfair Interstate Commerce Regulation, and the creation of highly subsidized air, water and highway transport contributed significantly to the Penn Central's downfall, and pose grave problems for the remaining solvent systems.

Other observers, particularly the congressional committees which investigated the Penn Central's demise, blamed bad management. While it is true that the Pennsy had poor leadership, the investigations have focused on the sensational and have made no detailed study as to why the railway's management was worse than that of other private businesses.

Railroads are of particular interest to the business historian because they are the nation's oldest continuously operating large enterprises. The Pennsylvania had been a major corporation for more than a decade before the discovery of the world's first producing oil well at Titusville, Pennsylvania, in 1859. And the Pennsy was well into its second half-century when such giants as United States Steel, Ford Motor Company and General Motors came into being. With railroads we have a rare opportunity to examine the impact of age on managerial structures. It is my contention that age and the problems associated with it was one of the major factors in the Pennsy's collapse.

The career of David Bevan[1] gives a clear insight into the Pennsylvania's managerial problems. Bevan started his business life in 1931 as a banker with Philadelphia's Provident Trust and in 1946 he went to New York Life as Assistant Treasurer. In 1951, Bevan became the Pennsylvania Railroad's Vice President in Charge of Finance and continued in this position until the line was merged with the New York Central to form the Penn Central in 1968. On the Penn Central, Bevan was the Chief Financial Officer and was, with Stuart Saunders, the Chairman of the Board, and Alfred Perlman, the President, one of the top three executive officers.

When Bevan started with the railroad, his job was quite limited. It included corporate finance and debt management as well as the supervision of the system's treasury and banking functions. It did not include power over the railroad's comptroller, accounting, real estate or taxes. Bevan's first major problem was the management of the firm's large debt, which amounted to slightly more than one billion dollars. Bevan's efforts to restructure and reduce the system's debt brought him face to face with archaic managerial practices. The line's retiring chief executive, Martin Clement, who ran the railroad from 1935 until 1951, in practice served as his own chief financial officer. Clement, an operating man, distrusted statisticians. Under his management the railroad had no forward planning for debt reduction because he felt the railroad needed none. Furthermore, debt maturities were so uneven that in some years only about ten million dollars in bonds came due, whereas in others $125 million of bonds matured. Bevan quickly set about to reduce and restructure the railroad's debt and found that the system's top management was primitive by standards of American industry in the mid-20th century. The administrative structure Bevan found can only be understood against the background of American railway history.

Managerial backwardness on the Pennsylvania was an irony. In the 19th century, the railroad pioneered modern concepts of business administration in the United States. Prior to the 1840's, the merchant dominated American business. He made most of his decisions personally, trusted his distant interests to agents who were either his kin or close personal friends. It was the merchants who took the lead in the industrialization of America between 1812 and the Civil War. In most cases, the merchants provided the finance for infant industries and supervised them without changing their traditional business methods.

The emergence of railroads in the 1840's had been revolutionary. By standards of the 19th century, they were extremely large and complex enterprises. For example, Massachusetts' Western Railroad, which in 1842 had only 160 miles of single track, cost more than $7 million. Twelve years later, the Western's capital amounted to more than $10 million, even though its mileage had not increased. By contrast, the Erie Canal, which was more than 360 miles long, cost only $7 million. The Pennsylvania Railroad, when it completed its expansion program in 1873, had a total investment of more than $400 million. Railroads dwarfed textile factories, which in the 19th century were the nation's largest industrial firms. At

mid-century, only a few "cost as much as $500,000. In fact, in 1850, only 41 American plants had a capitalization of $250,000 or more."[2] As Alfred D. Chandler, Jr., observed, "Size was only one dimension of the unique challenges facing the managers of the new large railroads in the 1850's." Chandler noted that day-to-day decisions on the railways were more complicated and numerous than those required at a mill or canal. For example, a manager could view a textile factory or even a group of mills in less than half an hour, whereas, by the 1850's, several railroads already extended over hundreds of miles. Furthermore, unlike the canal which covered a large geographic area, a railroad "ran, maintained and repaired the equipment it used" in the transportation of passengers and freight.[3]

Starting with the Western Railroad of Massachusetts in the 1840's and continuing with the great trunk lines which linked the Atlantic seaboard with the Ohio and Mississippi valley in the 1850's (The Baltimore and Ohio, The Pennsylvania, The Erie and The New York Central), the railroads evolved a new type of bureaucratic administrative structure. The new methods of railway administration reached their peak of perfection on the Pennsylvania Railroad during J. Edgar Thomson's presidency. Thomson's railroad was divided into divisions about 50 miles long, each headed by a superintendent. Under the superintendent were deputies who had specific responsibilities for separate functions, such as operations, maintenance of way and maintenance of equipment. The railroad's many divisions reported directly to the system's top management. On the Pennsylvania, the president, who was the chief executive, had staff officers responsible for various functions corresponding to those at the division level—that is, operations, maintenance of way and maintenance of equipment. It was the duty of the general office and the president's staff to set the policies for running the railroad. The central office did this by the issuance of written directives. The general office enforced its will in two ways. First, it required a series of written reports which flowed upward from division level to the general office. The president and his staff analyzed these reports and, on the basis of the information contained in them, made policy decisions. The second manner in which the general office enforced its will was through actual physical inspections, which enabled the president and his staff to match the data in the written reports with actual visual perusal of a division.

One of the primary responsibilities of top management was to set rates and fares. It was important that these by set low enough to capture business from competing forms of transportation and other railroads, yet high enough to earn a profit. Yet, in J. Edgar Thomson's day, this was easier said than done since there was no readily available cost data. In order to solve this problem, top management devised a series of reports to be made at division level which carefully recorded such facts as the number of train miles run, the number of man hours worked, the amount of fuel consumed by locomotives, the amount of repairs on rolling stock and the costs of the maintenance of way. Other reports were required which detailed the nature and amount of traffic in each direction. Top management also had at its disposal data on

the nature of capital employed by the railroad, the amount of real-estate taxes and the cost of general administration. Management used the data generated by the individual divisions and the data on capital, taxes, and administrative costs to make crucial decisions in setting freight rates and passenger fares.

Because railroads pioneered in the use of statistical data in making business decisions, they became a training ground for American industrial leaders. A. D. Chandler, Jr., has noted that managerial techniques developed on J. Edgar Thomson's Pennsylvania Railroad were transferred to the steel industry by Andrew Carnegie. Later, men who received their initial administrative experience in steel helped bring modern managerial techniques to such industrial fields as electricity, explosives and chemicals, and finally automobiles. By the beginning of the 20th century, industrial managers started to refine the use of statistical data in making important policy decisions. These improvements went far beyond managerial practices developed by Thomson's Pennsylvania. The DuPont Company of Wilmington, Delaware, was one of the most important innovators in the field of statistical control.

Between 1902 and 1910, Pierre S. duPont, treasurer of the DuPont Company, used his office, which also controlled accounting to develop a highly sophisticated, statistical approach to management. It is important to review these developments because they indicate the wide divergence which developed at the beginning of the 20th century between industrial and railway managerial practices.

In 1902, when Pierre duPont became treasurer of his company, he found a situation in many respects similar to that of the Pennsylvania of David Bevan's day. The DuPont Company was a consolidation of many individual explosive firms, most of which operated independently of one another. Beginning in 1902, the DuPont Company adopted a new centralized bureaucratic administrative structure. It created three functional production departments—black powder, high explosives and smokeless powder—as well as several other centrally administered departments, such as sales, purchasing and finance, which served the entire corporation. As did J. Edgar Thomson, Pierre duPont recognized that top management could not make intelligent decisions without adequate data, and he assumed the responsibility for providing such information.

Using his position as treasurer, which included the firm's accounting function, Pierre duPont devised uniform reports which were to be submitted at the lowest level, starting with individual plants. From these, the data traveled upward, being consolidated at division level (i.e., smokeless powder, high explosives, etc.). The divisions in turn sent the data forward to the general headquarters at Wilmington, Delaware. Their reports were compiled, and summarized activity at each level on a weekly, monthly, semi-annual and yearly basis. Top management, therefore, could examine the data as it flowed forth each week and discern trends by comparing it to performance in other months and years. The data included such information as a plant's input of raw materials, cost of these materials, labor costs

and production. The standardized format allowed management to compare the costs and efficiency of each plant within a product line and also to measure the relative profitability of the various product divisions against one another. From the information management could project sales, costs and margin of profit for as much as one year in advance. This enabled DuPont's executive officers to develop an operating budget, have a solid knowledge of the firm's cash position and determine the size of proposed capital budgets. Under Pierre duPont's leadership, each factory had the responsibility of developing its own capital proposals annually. These were in turn forwarded to division level where they were consolidated and forwarded to the central mangement. At the top, management could compare competing capital requests and select those capable of generating the most profits.

Statistical flow in the DuPont Company enabled the firm to develop a rational method for decision-making. By 1910, the DuPont Company could make up a capital budget which would allocate funds to the most profitable areas of the business. Furthermore, top executives could use data to measure the relative efficiency of the management of each division and factory. Because the data were collected over a long period of time and were updated weekly, top management could quickly see whether or not their predictions of sales and profit were being fulfilled. This enabled centralized management to control the purchases of raw material (part of working capital) to coincide with actual market demands. Furthermore, it enabled top management to cancel or curtail certain capital expenditures which allowed the firm to avoid borrowing cash at times of slack business and high interest rates.[4] While the DuPont Company led American industry in adopting complex statistical methods for decision-making, such practices soon spread to such diverse ventures as automobiles, mass merchandising and the oil industry. On the eve of the Second World War, complex statistical control became the rule, rather than the exception, in large businesses.

Railroads, and particularly the Pennsylvania, failed to share in these managerial advances. Instead, their practices became frozen at the beginning of the 20th century. Nothing better illustrates this than the situation Bevan found when he began to investigate the way funds were handled and accounted for on the Pennsy in 1951. The Vice-President in Charge of Finance did not have control over real estate or taxes, nor did he supervise the comptroller or accounting. Furthermore, the railroad had no capital or income budgets. The rudimentary budgets that did exist were "made up by the staff of the operating vice-president for his use, and were changed from time to time as he saw fit. They were not generally available to top management." Consequently, there was no forward planning as to how to meet maturing obligations or to forecast the need for capital improvements in future years. When it came to the accounting deparment, Bevan was surprised. After careful examination, he concluded that he could not determine how many people were actually in accounting, but he did find the function overstaffed. He remembers that "the heads of the operating department in times past had been

much stronger than the accounting chiefs, had greater authority, and had gradually taken over many important accounting functions and absorbed them into the operating department. Therefore, no one actually knew how many people were really involved in accounting, and, as far as we could ascertain, there was not a single person in the accounting department who was a qualified certified public accountant, not even the comptroller!'' Bevan did discover that there were nearly 2,700 people in accounting alone and ''nobody knew how many more in the operating department doing accounting work.''

More significant than the confusion and overstaffing was the concept of accounting employed. The department merely followed Interstate Commerce Commission regulations. This meant that the ICC policy determined the various accounts and dictated which figures should be placed in what account. Bevan recollects that it did not take him ''long to learn that ICC accounting was not only obsolete, but actually impossible to utilize effectively in controlling costs.''

In order to comprehend what had happened, it is necessary to retrace briefly the development of railway management after the creative years of the Pennsylvania's J. Edgar Thomson and Thomas Scott. By the 1890's, the railroads had achieved a dominance in American land transportation. Managerial and accounting problems which had been unique to American business in the 1850's and 1860's had been effectively solved by the managerial innovations of Thomson and Scott. Thus, railroad management became routine and fixed in patterns that had appeared to work well for decades. Furthermore, after the end of the Civil War, there had been constant public criticism of railroad freight-rate and passenger-fare policies. The result of this criticism had been the creation of state regulatory commissions; and then, in 1887, the United States Congress passed an act establishing the Interstate Commerce Commission to provide for national railway regulation. Although the ICC has been traditionally criticized by historians for failing to achieve railroad regulation in the 1880's and the decade of the 1890's, the commission did begin to set standards of accounting which became generally accepted in the railroad industry. Almost at the same time, railroad management gravitated from the creative entrepreneurs like Thomas and Scott to men who were primarily interested in operations. The vice-presidency in charge of operations became the traditional road to the presidency on the Pennsylvania from 1900 onward. Because the railroads appeared to have a dominant position in land transportation, traditional administrative techniques seemed adequate; and because the Interstate Commerce Commission accounting practices appeared satisfactory, the operating departments came to accept them. Thus, they became fixed on the railway industry, almost by default.

As Bevan saw the ICC accounting system in use on the Pennsylvania, it had many defects. The main problem was that it could not be used as an effective management tool. The accounting system was passive—that is, it merely recorded facts. It had no built-in requirements for forward planning and, therefore, the very concepts of capital budgets, income budgets, or cash-flow statements were foreign

to the ICC system. Indeed, the ICC accountants looked backward at what had happened, rather than forward to what should happen. But the ICC formula had another grave defect as a management tool. Peat, Marwick, Mitchell, & Company, in a special analysis undertaken at Bevan's request, pinpointed the problem. The ICC format allocated costs against a division or a function regardless of whether the supervisor of that function was responsible for the costs. "For example, the Regional Superintendent of Transportation normally received charges from other departments which may approximate 35 percent of his total budget. While it is true that such charges are for services rendered on behalf of the transportation activity, the amount of the charges or effectiveness of the work performed is not within the control of the Superintendent of Transportation."[5] Under the ICC system, it was impossible to analyze the real effectiveness of a manager, since he reported statistical data over which he exercised no control. Under this system, top management could not separate out the cost over which a Regional Superintendent of Transportation had control, and, therefore, effectively compare his performance against that of others or against past data.[6]

David Bevan's attempt to restructure the Pennsylvania Railroad's debt brought him face to face with the railroad's backward managerial structure. He soon became determined to reform the system. Bevan's experience with the Provident Trust before World War II and New York Life after the war enabled him to develop a constructive program for change. Bevan talked over his ideas with presidents Walter Franklin and James Symes. Both encouraged Bevan to proceed, and gradually a number of new functions were placed under his supervision. The responsibility for taxes had been split among four departments. Those were consolidated under Bevan. In 1957, Symes placed accounting and insurance under his jurisdiction. All of this was preparatory for building a new system for recording and reporting statistical data to serve as the basis for developing new managerial tools for the railroad's top administrators. Bevan recognized that the Pennsylvania Railroad lacked employees who had experience in creating such a system. Therefore, he determined with the full support of president James Symes to select an outside consultant. Because Symes was already thinking in terms of a merger between the New York Central and the Pennsylvania Railroads, Bevan decided to retain the world's largest accounting and auditing firm, Peat, Marwick, Mitchell, & Company. Bevan selected this firm because it already audited the New York Central Railroad's accounts, and Bevan realized that if merger were a possibility it would serve the interest of both firms if they had common outside accountants. It should be noted here that prior to Bevan's selection of Peat, Marwick, Mitchell, & Company, no independent firm of certified public accountants had ever routinely audited the Pennsylvania Railroad's books. In May of 1959, Peat, Marwick undertook to advise the railroad on the adoption of two separate systems. First was a management control devices program, and the second was a centralized data processing installation.

As it started its assignment, Peat, Marwick recognized that it was breaking new

ground. It commented in a progress report to the Penn Central's top executives that "of all members of the American business community, railroads constitute perhaps the only industry which does not use a conventional industrial management control structure, consisting of budgetary control, work measurement, and responsibility accounting and reporting." The accounting firm added that while many railroads employed "certain aspects of these tools . . . only the roads owned by the United States Steel Corporation employ all of them on an integrated basis."[7] Because of the novelty of the new managerial control system, it was necessary to experiment and phase the program in over a period of several years. Peat, Marwick started its investigation in May of 1959 and introduced the first aspects of the new system by the middle of 1961. It was not, however, until the end of the following year that the program took effect over the entire railroad, and the full impact of the innovations did not become apparent until 1963.

Peat, Marwick's new control devices program utilized the regional structure which the Pennsylvania Railroad had adopted in November, 1955. Under this, the railroad had been divided into nine regions, each of which was headed by a regional manager who controlled what amounted to a separate railroad. Peat, Marwick added a comptroller to the staff of each region. The accounting firm's system had three major aspects. The first was responsibility reporting. This concept abandoned the ICC practice of allocating expenses according to a set formula which did not take into account who actually supervised the work done. Instead, responsibility reporting held each function accountable only for what is acutally expended and dispersed. This relieved a supervisor of responsibility for the effectiveness of work performed which was not under his control. Responsibility reporting attributed expenses to "the supervisor who actually controlled the money spent for labor, materials, and so forth."[8] Overhead such as taxes and insurance were not allocated to an operating department which did not control them.

Work measurement constituted the second aspect of the control devices program. The idea behind work measurement was to compare the dollars spent with the work actually produced. As the accounting firm put it, "It is not sufficient for management to assure itself that a supervisor does not exceed his dollar budget. Management must be certain that the money spent within the budget produces a reasonable amount of work." Work measurement set time standards for each operation or groups of operations on the railroad. These standards were fixed by determining the "time a normal man (or men), working at a normal rate of speed, needs to complete a unit of work."[9] Along with labor standards went material standards. Peat, Marwick worked with industrial engineers to develop these standards, which became the basis for measuring the effectiveness of the management of any single division of the Pennsylvania Railroad. As the standards were installed, management was able to compare the work actually performed with the standard (the work that should have been performed in the same time interval).

These data were reported together with payroll documents. Armed with information on the dollars spent, the work output and the material consumed, and the responsibility reports, Pennsylvania's top management was able for the first time to have detailed and accurate information on performance in each division.

Budgetary control formed the third aspect of the control devices program. Under budgetary control, each supervisor had the responsibility for building a budget for his own division. Again, included in this budget were the only expenses over which he would have direct control. These budgets were forwarded to the Pennsy's general office in Philadelphia where they could be analyzed and funds allocated for the most important projects. This was an essential step in the development of a rational and effective capital budget, a step which was largely impossible prior to the institution of the control devices program. Thus, in four years, through David Bevan's efforts, the Pennsylvania Railroad moved from a backward managerial system based on outmoded interstate commerce accounting concepts to one of the most sophisticated cost-and-control systems in American industry.

Simultaneously with the control devices program, Peat, Marwick began work on a second major undertaking: the development and installation of an integrated data processing program. The purpose of this was to install a centralized computer facility at the railroad's headquarters in Philadelphia that would comprehend "the reporting and clerical aspects of the transportation function, operating statistics, sales analysis, car utilization and distribution, and car accounting."[10] Although each of these categories utilized the same basic information, they were handled separately on the Pennsylvania in 1959. As Peat, Marwick pointed out, working up each category separately resulted in costly duplication of clerical effort. However, the old way's worst fault was the difficulty for top management to utilize the information gathered in such a cumbersome manner. Although many of the nation's largest railroads had recognized the importance and desirability of centralizing the computer capability and integrating the information on the various functions, no railroad had as late as 1961 succeeded in installing a complete program. Typically, reported Peat, Marwick, "a railroad will start by developing a data processing system to deal with . . .car tracing. The company would plan to concentrate on this new procedure until it became routinized. Then it would plan to expand the system to include, let us say, sales statistics. Thereafter each of the various functions would be absorbed sequentially until the entire program was complete. "While several railroads," concluded Peat, Marwick, "have started on such a program and have even completed the first phase of it, no appreciable progress has been made in developing and installing a comprehensive system."[11]

In 1960, Peat, Marwick developed specifications for the Pennsylvania's new centralized computer system. The effort was so striking that the *Wall Street Journal* reported that the Pennsylvania's data processing program was one of the two largest such proposals then under consideration. Experimentation with various computer prototype equipment began in 1961. In 1962, under Peat, Marwick's

supervision, the railroad began to install the final system, which by 1963 began to make an important impact on the railroad. The new centralized computer worked surprisingly well. It provided the Pennsylvania with a "comprehensive, well-disciplined data origination system [that collected] both way bill and movement information with error rates below four-tenths of one percent for movement and below seven-tenths of one percent for way bills."[12] Not only did the new system provide more reliable and accessible information to top management, it also saved money. Between 1963 and 1967, it enabled the railroad as a whole to save over "$14 million in clerical expenses."[13]

David Bevan's first twelve years with the Pennsylvania produced important results. His accomplishments included initiation of a systematic debt management program as well as a strong start in the direction of reducing the railroad's massive debt. The same twelve years saw a number of important functions, such as taxes, real estate and accounting, come under his supervision. This was essential in David Bevan's campaign to modernize the Pennsylvania's obsolete administrative procedures. Acting with the enthusiastic support of president James Symes, Bevan achieved in a short period of time the establishment of a new accounting system that, together with an administrative structure, gave management new and more effective tools in its struggle to make the railroad an economically successful venture. At the same time, Bevan's leadership resulted in the establishment of a centralized computer center which integrated the data flowing from various important railway activities. This reinforced the railroad's new control devices program.

The Pennsylvania's new managerial system worked reasonably well for a short time, but it was destroyed by forces set into motion with the formation of the Penn Central. The merger of the New York Central with the Pennsylvania faced many obstacles. Among them were the hostility of prominent politicians such as Milton Shapp who later became Governor of Pennsylvania. Other railroads feared the competition of the merged lines. Organized labor worried about lost jobs. Finally, there was mistrust from within railroad management itself, particularly that on the New York Central, which felt it would come out second best.

Stuart Saunders, who guided the merger through to completion, made a number of fatal compromises, one of the most significant of which was the selection of Alfred Perlman, chief executive of the New York Central, to be the president and chief operating officer of the merged road. Unfortunately, Perlman was an operating man of the old school. He, like Martin Clement before him, distrusted statistics and believed that a railroad could be managed on a "seat of the pants" basis from the back of the president's private railway car.

Perlman, under whose control fell accounting, did not appreciate the importance of such things as capital budgets, income budgets, or the Pennsylvania's new accounting system or its centralized computer operation. While president of the New York Central, Perlman refused to cooperate in coordinating his railroad's accounting, computer and budgeting with the Pennsylvania. When Perlman took

over as President of the Penn Central, he scrapped the system which Peat, Marwick and David Bevan had worked so hard to implement. This proved to be one of the major factors of the Penn Central's management's loss of control, which became evident as early as the second half of 1968. A merger of two giant corporations is always complex. Without careful advance planning and excellent statistical data and control of the type which Peat, Marwick provided, it was almost bound to fail.

FOOTNOTES

1. All quotations from David Bevan which are not footnoted are taken from correspondence from Mr. Bevan to the author or from papers made available to the author by Mr. Bevan.
2. Chandler and Salsbury (1965), p. 130.
3. Chandler (1965), pp. 97, 98.
4. The data on the DuPont Company is from Chandler and Salsbury (1971), Chapter 8.
5. Progress Report to the Pennsylvania Railroad Company by Peat, Marwick, Mitchell & Co. (Spring, 1961), in the Bevan Papers, p. 3.
6. *Ibid.*
7. *Ibid.*, p. 1.
8. *Ibid.*, p. 3.
9. *Ibid.*, p. 4.
10. *Ibid.*, p. 6.
11. *Ibid.*, p. 7.
12. C. G. Sempier's memorandum to W. S. Cook, "New York Central Data Processing Appraisal," dated Dec. 5, 1967, Bevan Papers.
13. *Ibid.*

REFERENCES

Burgess, George H. and Kennedy, Miles C. (1949), *Centennial History of the Pennsylvania Railroad Company 1846–1946*, Philadelphia: Pennsylvania Railroad Co.
Chandler, Alfred D. (1959), "The Beginnings of 'Big Business' in American Industry," *The Business History Review*, XXXIII, pp. 1–31.
———.(1965), *The Railroads: The Nation's First Big Business*, New York: Harcourt, Brace & World.
———. (1962), *Strategy and Structure: Chapters in the History of the Industrial Enterprise*, Cambridge: The M.I.T Press.
Chandler, Alfred D. and Salsbury, Stephen (1965), "The Railroads: Innovators in Modern Business Administrations," *The Railroad and the Space Program* (edited by Mazlish, Bruce), pp. 127–162, Cambridge: The M.I.T. Press.
———. (1971), *Pierre S. duPont and the Making of the Modern Corporation*, New York: Harper & Row.
Cochran, Thomas C. (1953), *Railroad Leaders 1845–1940: The Business Mind in Action*, Cambridge: Harvard University Press.

Livesay, Harold C. (1975), *Andrew Carnegie and the Rise of Big Business*, Boston: Little, Brown & Company.

Schotter, N. W. (1927), *The Growth and Development of the Pennsylvania Railroad Company*, Philadelphia: Allen, Lane & Scott.

Sloan, Alfred P. (1963), *My Years with General Motors*, New York: Doubleday & Company.

U.S. Congress (1972), *The Financial Collapse of the Penn Central Company: Staff Report of the Securities and Exchange Commission to the Special Subcommittee on Investigations* (With comments on H. R. 12128 by SEC and ICC), August 1972 (Subcommittee Print), Washington: U.S. Government Printing Office.

U.S. Congress (1972), *The Penn Central Failure and the Role of Financial Institutions: Staff Report of the Committee on Banking and Currency*, House of Representatives 92nd Congress, First Session (Committee Print), Washington: U.S. Government Printing Office.

FINANCIAL INTERMEDIARIES IN ECONOMIC HISTORY: QUANTITATIVE RESEARCH ON THE SEMINAL HYPOTHESES OF LANCE DAVIS AND ALEXANDER GERSCHENKRON*

Richard Sylla, NORTH CAROLINA STATE UNIVERSITY

The role of financial intermediaries in economic growth is a problem of long-standing interest to students of modern economic history. The interest is motivated by the importance of intermediaries in performing two functions of general theoretical and empirical significance in modern economies. These functions are the providing of financial instruments, which serve as a large part of the means of payment, and the providing of specialized financial services that bridge the gap between savings behavior and investment activity, a gap that increases in the process of economic modernization.[1]

Given the longevity of economic historians' interest in financial intermediaries, it is perhaps not surprising that much of the recent work on the subject is not especially original in terms of the questions asked. Instead, many of the more stimulating works of recent years are notable because of the attention they give to extracting and employing quantitative evidence bearing on older questions. These works are notable also for their explicit use of economic theory and techniques of quantitative empirical research.

In the following pages I illustrate this situation by examining the responses of recent students of the history of financial intermediaries to earlier studies by Lance Davis and Alexander Gerschenkron. Davis's work on intermediaries and the problem of regional interest rate differentials in late nineteenth-century America

was essentially empirical in nature.[2] In contrast to the work of Davis, Gerschenkron's work relating to the role of banks in financing the initial spurts of industrialization in nineteenth-century European nations was essentially interpretative in nature, and but one element of a broader canvas on which he organized the diversity of European industrialization patterns according to the concept of the relative backwardness of the several countries at the time of their industrialization.[3] Although very different, the contributions of Davis and Gerschenkron were seminal because each of them inspired a host of subsequent studies along the lines they had set out. These studies attempt to test, to refine, to amend and even to overturn their conclusions. Here, then, is a critical review of how successful the more recent authors have been in these endeavors.

I. DAVIS ON REGIONAL INTEREST RATE DIFFERENTIALS IN THE UNITED STATES, 1870–1914.

Lance Davis's work on American interest rates appeared in the *Journal of Economic History* in 1965.[4] The heart of his contribution was a collection of tables and charts based upon national bank earnings and asset data from the *Annual Reports* of the U.S. Comptroller of the Currency for the period 1870–1914. Davis interpreted various ratios of bank earnings to bank assets as proxy measures for interest rates on bank loans in different regions of the United States, and he demonstrated that while these interest rates diverged markedly across regions in the early years of the period, they tended to converge over time, particularly in the early years of this century.

Combining his empirical evidence with the truism of economic theory that there can be only one price for identical goods in a perfect market, Davis argued that the market for bank loans and also other money and capital markets were decidedly imperfect in the post Civil War American economy, but that the imperfections were gradually reduced over time. Why did the wide differentials in regional interest rates exist? And why did they narrow during the period 1870–1914? Davis answered the first question by noting that the major sources of savings in the U.S. were concentrated in the older and more developed areas of the Northeast while the demand for loanable funds was growing most rapidly in the newer and developing regions of the West and South, and by arguing that there were definite barriers to capital mobility between regions. These barriers were reflected in widely varying regional interest rates, which indicated a basic disequilibrium in the American money and capital markets. Davis's answer to the second question, that of why the regional bank interest rate differentials narrowed over time, was that nonbank financial intermediaries—in particular, commercial paper dealers—grew up in the late nineteenth century to mobilize capital in response to the profit possibilities inherent in the regional rate differentials. By competing with banks in local and regional loan markets, these intermediaries brought about a narrowing of the interregional loan-price structure.

The force of Davis's quantitative evidence together with his rather more impressionistic interpretation of what it showed and his relative inattention to the question of the wider implications of his results for the development of the American economy led a number of other students of intermediaries in the ensuing years to follow in his footsteps. Most of these later efforts have been directed toward amending and improving the explanation or interpretation of the data and toward exploring wider implications. But the data themselves have not gone without challenge.

The Bank Entry-Barrier Alternative

In one of the earlier studies motivated by Davis's work, I examined the question of whether it was necessary to look, as Davis in effect did, outside of the American banking system in order to explain the existence and narrowing of regional bank interest rate differentials between 1870 and 1914.[5] My conclusion was that it was not necessary to do so, although there was no reason in my own findings to rule out Davis's explanation—the growth of a national commercial paper market—as also being an operative factor in bringing about regional interest rate convergence.

In my study of the problem, I attempted to relate Davis's empirical findings on bank loan rates to an older historical tradition that emphasized monopolistic characteristics of late nineteenth-century American banking markets. That older tradition often emphasized the restrictions, not always intended as such, placed on American banking development by federal banking legislation of the Civil War era. For the new national banks created by that legislation, the federal laws prescribed restrictions on minimum required bank capitals, maximum allowable note issues, and permissible types of bank loans. Related legislation in the form of a prohibitive tax on nonnational bank note issues sought to obtain a uniform national paper currency by forcing the old note-issuing banks chartered by the states either to join the national system or to cease operations. The overall impact of these restrictions, I argued, was to create entry barriers which restrained the growth and geographical spread of both national and nonnational banking in the ensuing decades. Moreover, from the very nature of the legal restrictions (e.g., minimum bank capital requirements) as well as from the way in which the national banking system was first administered (e.g., the allocation of most of the total note issue allowed to banks in the developed states), the hindrances to banking development were not uniform throughout the land, but were felt to a more severe degree in the agriculturally-oriented, small-town areas of the West and South as compared to the more developed Northeast and the larger cities of all regions.

I therefore proposed that a characterization of the late nineteenth-century banking scene as being divided between fairly competitive banking in cities and older developed regions where legal entry barriers were rather ineffective, and more monopolistic banking in newer and rural areas where the entry barriers were more inhibiting, would explain both the regional and the city-country interest rate differentials found by Davis for the post Civil War era. I reasoned further that the

relaxation of legal entry barriers on a national scale, which took place, for example, through liberalization of the federal banking laws in the Gold Standard Act of 1900, would explain why regional and city-country interest rates converged after the turn of the century.

Confirmation of the validity of these characterizations involved demonstrating a number of points. One was that the observed interest rate differentials could not be adequately explained by cost differences, because banks in rural areas and newer regions where interest rates were relatively high earned on the average higher rates of profit on bank equity than did their more competitive urban and northeastern brethren. Another was that the transfer of large amounts of banking resources from places where prevailing interest rates were high to places where rates were much lower—a factor of some importance in understanding industrial growth and concentration in the late nineteenth century—followed from the existence of differential degrees of monopoly in banking across regions. Finally, I showed that when some regulatory causes of the differential degrees of bank monopoly were relaxed at the turn of the century, bank entry responded in predictable fashion, and both interest and profit differentials were attenuated. Thus, one could find in the banking system itself an explanation of regional and city-country interest differentials as well as some reasons why the differentials narrowed toward the end of the 1870–1914 period.

As I have said earlier, nothing in my own analysis of the problem suggested that Davis's explanation was incorrect. Rather, either of the two explanations could be regarded as incomplete and the question becomes one of their relative importance in accounting for observed results. That could have been, and to some degree has been, the subject of subsequent studies. The overall tone of several of these studies, however, has been to argue that both the Davis and Sylla analyses are seriously flawed and therefore to be doubted. Since such contentions naturally stimulate a critical attitude on the part of one whose analysis is so characterized, let me proceed to examine the works to which I refer.

Wisconsin Banking as a Counter Example

On the basis of an intensive study of the banking history of Wisconsin from 1863 to 1914, Richard Keehn argued in 1974 that both the Davis and Sylla analyses are doubtful.[6] The findings of Davis on the existence of interest rate differentials and their decline over the period are in general supported by Keehn's Wisconsin data; but Davis's explanation of the decline, which Keehn characterizes as "improvements in the capital market," is said by him to be "so vague as to be of little help in explaining the relationship of rates over the period."[7] Improvements in the capital market could be thought of, as Davis and I did, as *institutional changes* such as increasing bank competition and the appearance of active commercial-paper dealers. Keehn instead proposes an alternative explanation: namely, the *decline of capital transfer costs* resulting from "improvements in communications, transportation and paper handling"; and he holds that his alternative constitutes a better

explanation of regional interest rate movements. Keehn admits, however, that it would be difficult to separate changes in transfer costs from institutional changes.[8]

The brunt of Keehn's attack is directed at my analysis of bank entry barriers which, he says, "is not supported by Wisconsin data" and "should be modified."[9] The essence of Keehn's argument is that nonnational banks were "increasingly good substitutes for national banks."[10] To support his contention, Keehn offers data showing that in Wisconsin by the early 1880's the numbers and total assets of nonnational banks exceeded those of national banks, and that in most subperiods of years between 1870 and 1914—including the post 1900 years when national bank entry barriers were reduced by legislation—the rate of entry of nonnational banks exceeded the entry rates of national banks. In other words, while the national banking system may have suffered a retarded development because of legal entry barriers, the removal of note issue privileges from nonnational banks did not prevent them from developing rapidly along lines of pure deposit banking. A critical problem in this connection is the question of pure deposit banking. Keehn believes that soon after the Civil War it was easy for banks to operate profitably on a pure deposit basis: i.e., without note issue privileges, so that state and private banks could quickly negate the effects of legislative entry barriers faced by national banks. Keehn concludes, therefore, that in Wisconsin banking was generally competitive at least by 1880. His case against my entry-barrier hypothesis is that, "The ability of bankers to exercise substantial monopoly power was greatly restricted by the potential easy entry of new rivals."[11]

Keehn's tests of competition in Wisconsin banking, which consist in counting different types of banks and their assets, and calculating and comparing growth rates of these series over the years from the 1860's to 1914, do not confront the economic issues involved in the bank entry-barrier hypothesis I advanced. My own view is that the rise of pure deposit banking in the state and private sectors of the banking system, instead of being a cause of bank growth in these sectors, was rather a delayed result of the restrictive federal legislation which forced many areas of the United States to have pure deposit banking or no banking at all.[12] This is consistent with my conclusion that in many areas, including possibly Wisconsin as an agricultural state, monopolistic elements were present long after the Civil War.

How can one test to see whether Keehn's view or my own in the correct one? If Keehn is right, then the easy substitutability of nonnational deposit banks for national banks should have tended to produce competitive rates of return to bank capital in Wisconsin. If I am right that the federal laws restricted all and not just national banking development, then rates of return to bank capital will tend to be not at competitive levels but rather above competitive levels in an agricultural state like Wisconsin.

While arguing another issue in his paper, Keehn is helpful in providing us with data on returns to bank capital which allow us to see whether his view or mine is more realistic. Some writers, he notes, have argued that the restrictive features of

national banking worked to reduce the profitability of national in comparison with nonnational banks, and that this explains why the nonnational sector grew more rapidly than the national. This is a logical inference, and it appears to be supported by Wisconsin and other state data. But did either these restrictions on national banks or Keehn's postulated ease of entry for nonnational banks reduce the profitability of the national banks to competitive levels? Or, as I argued, did restrictions on national and nonnational bank entry tend to create monopoly returns? Keehn reports profit rates for country and Milwaukee national banks from 1871 to 1914. In his own words, the data indicate that "net returns to net worth in national banking appear to have been substantial throughout and above those available on alternative investment opportunities of comparable risk," and that "rates of return apparently were slightly lower in the years after 1900 than before 1890."[13] In short, Keehn's profit data are consistent with my entry-barrier hypothesis, even to the point of showing the effects of reduced legal entry barriers after 1900, and rather inconsistent with Keehn's own hypothesis that banking was essentially competitive in Wisconsin by 1880 or thereabouts.

How does Keehn handle the inconsistency of the bank profit data with his easy-entry hypothesis? He says that the bank profitability data

> are even more remarkable when it is remembered that this was a period of rapid entry of new national (and other) banks. High rates of return attracted an increasing number of entrants, but this did not substantially reduce average returns to net worth *because demand was also changing rapidly.* (Sylla: italics mine).[14]

There is little doubt that the demand for banking services grew in Wisconsin between 1870 and 1914. But is the lagging supply response indicated by bank profitability data over some four decades more in accord with an entry-barrier hypothesis or with Keehn's hypothesis of easy entry? Moreover, while Keehn offers no evidence on demand growth, I think he would be hard pressed to show that demand grew more slowly in the post 1900 years of prosperity when bank profitability in Wisconsin fell than during the Great Depression of the late nineteenth century when bank profitability was maintained at higher levels. All in all, the bank entry-barrier hypothesis seems to fit the Wisconsin facts much better than Keehn's all-encompassing easy-entry hypothesis.

Interest Rates from an Economic History "Rewriter"

In a wide-ranging and innovative study of the late nineteenth-century American economy published in 1974, Jeffrey G. Williamson devotes a chapter to the very issues raised by Davis in his seminal paper of 1965.[15] The chapter is entitled "Financial Intermediation, Capital Immobilities and Economic Growth," and in some ways it goes beyond the work of Davis and others to inquire into the national and regional economic effects of the capital immobilities implicit in large regional interest-rate differentials. Some words need to be said about Williamson's

methods since they are both exceedingly ambitious and as yet unconventional among economic historians. The basis of his analysis is a 72-equation general equilibrium model of the Northeastern and Middlewestern parts of the economy; the South and the Far West are excluded. The Northeast is taken to be exclusively industrial while the Midwest has both an industrial and an agricultural sector. The model is generally neoclassical in nature in that it assumes full employment of resources and deals with relative prices and real as opposed to monetary magnitudes. Williamson takes great pains to build regional interactions into his model, and this is how he is able to confront the issues posed by regional interest-rate differentials.

Williamson develops and uses his model in the following fashion. Parameters of the equations are estimated from selected empirical and conjectural materials; these remain fixed for the period 1870–1910. Some variables for this period— e.g., productivity, transport costs, the labor force, the land stock and relative commodity prices—are treated as exogenous and are given by their actual or estimated historical magnitudes. Other variables—notably input prices and the regional and sectoral distribution of outputs, inputs, savings and investment—are treated as endogenous, or in other words to be generated by the model. Given the parameters and a set of actual or presumably reasonable initial conditions for the exogenous and endogenous variables for the year 1870, Williamson can simulate the historical time paths of the endogenous variables by plugging in the exogenous variables for subsequent years and solving the resulting equation systems for the values of the endogenous variables.

The value of the exercise depends on the answers to two general questions posed by Williamson:

> Does the model fairly accurately reproduce fact or does it instead generate total fiction? Is the model capable of rewriting American economic history between [the Civil and First World] Wars?[16]

More specifically, the questions have to do with comparing the "predictions" of the model regarding the endogenous variables with their observed historical values. Does the predicted growth of output per worker from 1870 to 1910 match the observed figure? Do predicted structural changes as embodied in the regional and sectoral distributions of output and inputs over the period accord with reality? Do predicted factor prices behave as factor prices actually did over the period? Williamson answers these questions affirmatively. His simulation model, he feels, does "rewrite American economic history," and therefore it can be used both to explain historical trends which may have been differently explained by others and to explore counterfactual questions.

For issues of capital mobility and financial intermediation, the relevant data simulated by Williamson's economic history rewriter are three annual time series of real interest rates for the period 1870–1910, two referring to interest rates

("bond" rates) on industrial loans in the Northeast and the Midwest, and one series of interest rates ("mortgage" rates) paid by Midwestern farmers. Of the behavior of his simulated interest rates Williamson states, "There seems little doubt that our disequilibrium model replicates this aspect of American financial history very well."[17] Williamson has two grounds for this contention. One is that the levels and trends of his real Midwestern farm mortgage rate appear to follow levels and trends of real interest rates on Midwestern mortgages calculated from observed nominal rates at decade intervals, 1870–1910.[18] Second, with regard to the historically observed convergence of regional interest rates as reported by Davis, Williamson says, "The simulation produces a secular convergence in these rates over time, at least when the average Midwestern rate is compared with that prevailing in Eastern financial markets."[19] Williamson's grounds for feeling comfortable about the accuracy of his history rewriter's predictions are debatable, as I will argue below; but for now let us see how he uses his rewriter and its revelations to analyze the issues posed by financial intermediaries and capital mobility.

On the observed convergence of regional interest rates between 1870 and 1910, Williamson makes an interesting and valid theoretical point, and he also draws an empirical or historical conclusion based on his rewriter's predictions. His theoretical point is stated as follows:

> The financial historian has . . . observed a convergence of regional interest rates following the early 1870s. The convergence was sufficiently striking to warrant the term "national capital market integration." It should be apparent that this important phase of national capital market integration could have been generated by two forces: (i) a secular decline in the disequilibrating forces which produced the initial disequilibrium; and/or (ii) an expansion in existing intermediating activity which gradually removed the quasi-rents prevailing in 1870.[20]

In short, regional rate convergence could have resulted from either changes in regional demands for loans or from changes in supplies of loans offered *inter alia* by financial intermediaries. Williamson notes that financial historians like "Davis and Sylla prefer to stress institutional developments *endogenous* to the capital market in accounting for the convergence of regional interest rates."[21] He, on the other hand, draws the opposite conclusion. His rewriter, he holds, generates the convergence of regional rates—between the Northeast and Midwest regions in his work—through shifts in regional demands for capital without any appeal to supply-side effects such as institutional developments in intermediation.

Having satisfied himself as to the ability of his apparatus to "rewrite" American financial history between 1870 and 1910, Williamson turns to counterfactual questions. These involve supposing that instead of the regional and sectoral interest-rate differentials actually observed one dealt with a world of perfect capital mobility and rate equalization. He asks:

Would American post-Civil War development have been significantly different under conditions of perfect capital mobility? Would aggregate output growth have been raised? Was "market failure" in American capital markets serious? Did it inhibit or foster agricultural development in any important dimension?[22]

And he gives provocative answers to these questions. Under any of the conditions he specifies, the simulated effects of perfect capital mobility on total output per worker or income per capita are small; the gains from perfection are only on the order of one or two percent during the period 1870–1910. But "capital market imperfections did have a profound effect on the structural performance of the American economy."[23] And the effect, it may be added, is also a bit confusing. For, assuming (1) no technical change in either industry or agriculture, and (2) savings levels determined independently of interest rates, actual imperfections in the capital market lead to a situation where "too many resources are retained in agriculture," as compared with a counterfactual world of perfect capital mobility.[24] However, assuming (1) technical change as it actually occurred and (2) savings levels depending on interest rates, then "the employment share and the output share of agriculture would have been *higher* under perfect capital markets!"[25] Thus it appears that, depending on the assumptions Williamson makes and transmits to his rewriter, the counterfactual world of perfect capital mobility and financial intermediation is consistent with virtually any scenario of the relative balance between industry and agriculture as it might have developed between 1870 and 1910. One can only agree with Williamson when at the end of his chapter on intermediaries he says, "This analysis may tend to raise more questions than it answers."[26]

One such question is that of why Williamson's results are so confusing. I believe I have some answers. In the first place, the simulated real interest rates that come churning out of the rewriter to form the basis of his entire analysis of the roles of intermediaries and capital immobilities do not in fact converge at all, and it is only by a data manipulation that they can be made to appear to converge. Secondly, in addition to failing to converge, Williamson's simulated interest rates, in terms of overall levels and trends, are so at variance with historically observed interest rates that research results based on them in any factual or counterfactual way are highly suspect.

Let us first examine the issue of convergence. Williamson is able to show convergence of his simulated Northeastern and Midwestern real rates only by comparing the Northeastern "industrial" rate with an *average* of the Midwestern "industrial" and "agricultural" rates.[27] For two reasons this is a questionable procedure in the case at hand. First, an *average* Midwestern rate is irrelevant to economic behavior; lenders did not lend at it, nor did borrowers pay it when obtaining loans. Second, Williamson's use of the average Midwestern interest rate is suspect on technical grounds. One should not, of course, condemn the use of averages; often they are helpful in bringing a semblance of order to masses of data

even though it is well to remember that some information is lost in the process. In Williamson's case, however, the simulated Midwestern industrial and agricultural rates behave so differently in both their levels and trends that a question may be raised as to whether their average does not in fact cover up rather than reveal the essence of the Midwestern financial situation as simulated by Williamson. The two Midwestern rates are fairly close together in the 1870's, but they behave very differently from 1880 to the early 1900's when the real "industrial" rate is approximately 12 percent while the real agricultural rate is about 4 percent.

If, therefore, we do not accept Williamson's use of the average Midwestern rate as legitimate in this case and turn instead to the underlying rates used to compute the average, what do we find in regard to convergence? We find, as shown in Table 1, that the simulated individual rates underlying Williamson's finding of convergence tend themselves to *diverge* from one another over the period when historically observed interest rates *converge*. This is seen most clearly in the mean deviations of the two industrial rates, i_E and i_{IW}, from the farm mortgage rate, i_{AW}. In these two cases the divergence over the four decades is uniform and clear. Comparing the mean differences between the two industrial rates, there is a trend toward convergence over the first three decades but this is followed by a divergence large enough in the last decade to make the two rates farther apart in the 1900's than they were in the 1870's. It appears that Williamson's economic history rewriter performs rather more poorly than he lets on in generating a convergence of regional interest rates between 1870 and 1910.

Next let us examine the levels and trends in Williamson's simulated interest rates as compared with historically observed rates. This is not a straightforward task because Williamson's simulated rates are *real* rates and hence do not have any directly observable counterpart in historical data. It is possible, however, to derive approximate real rates from observed nominal rates, and *vice versa* for that matter. Indeed, Williamson shows us one method of performing the derivation, which consists of adjusting observed nominal rates by price-level changes in order to obtain approximate real rates.[28]

One may demonstrate the unreality of Williamson's real interest rates either by comparing them with real rates calculated by applying his method to observed nominal rates for the period 1870–1910, or by comparing the nominal rates implicit in Williamson's real rates with the historically observed nominal rates. Here I adopt the latter procedure. Some summary results are given in Table 2, which shows decadal means of the nominal rates implicit in Williamson's simulated real rates and, for purposes of comparison, decadal means of historically observed interest rates on railroad bonds and Middlewestern mortgages.

What do the comparisons show? They show that in American economic history, 1870–1910, nominal interest rates generally fell and were substantially lower in 1900–1910 than they were in the 1870's; while in the America of Williamson's economic history rewriter, 1870–1910, nominal interest rates generally rose and were very much higher in 1900–1910 than they were in the 1870's. Indeed, were

Table 1. Mean Differences by Period between Pairs of Williamson's Three Simulated Real Interest Rates, in Percentage Points

Interest Rate Pairs

Period	$(i_{AW}-i_{IW})$	$(i_{AW}-i_E)$	$(i_{IW}-i_E)$
1870–79	–0.8	0.6	1.4
1880–89	–2.4	–3.3	–0.9
1890–99	–6.3	–5.7	0.5
1900–10	–7.4	–5.7	1.7

Legend: i_{AW}– the real Midwestern agricultural interest rate.
i_{IW}–the real Midwestern industrial interest rate.
i_E–the real Northeastern industrial interest rate.

Source: Annual simulated interest rate data from Williamson (1974), p. 292. Differences between the interest rates were calculated annually and then the differences were averaged for the periods shown.

one to accept Williamson's simulated real interest rates as being in any way accurate, one would also have to believe that Northeastern and Middlewestern industrial and city borrowers had to pay nominal interest rates some two to three times higher in 1900–1910 than they paid in the 1870's. And that from 1890 to 1910, lenders in the Midwest were content to lend to farmers at interest rates that were only about one-half the rates they could have charged industrial and city borrowers.

Consequently, however stimulating and innovative is Williamson's analysis of other aspects of the late nineteenth-century American economy, with respect to new knowledge of historical trends in interest rates and the role of financial intermediaries it is rather disappointing. The methods of Williamson may be promising, but his results so far pose no serious challenge to earlier analyses that emphasized the role of financial intermediaries in forming a more perfect American capital market.

Did Interest Rates Really Converge?

In a recent paper Gene Smiley, after noting that the Davis and Sylla analyses are essentially alternative explanations of the convergence of regional short-term interest rates before 1914, then argues that "the question of rate convergence itself . . . has not been satisfactorily examined."[29] For the period 1888-1913, Smiley reestimates the loan interest rates implicit in national bank earnings and asset data in order to improve upon the Davis estimates. He then examines the relative dispersion of average individual state rates for nonreserve city banks and average

Table 2. Decade Means of Nominal Interest Rates Implicit in Williamson's Simulated Real Rates, and of Historically Observed Nominal Interest Rates, in Percent.

Period	Williamson's Implicit Nominal Rates			Actual Nominal Rates	
	i_E	i_{IW}	i_{AW}	Railroad Bonds	Middlewestern Mortgages
1870–79	5.3	6.7	6.1	7.1	8.9
1880–89	9.4	8.5	6.1	5.0	7.5
1890–99	9.1	9.7	3.5	4.4	6.5
1900–10	13.1	16.3	7.3 (7.7)*	4.0	(5.7)*

* Refers to years 1900–1904, for purposes of comparison, because the actual Middlewestern mortgage series ends with the year 1904.

Sources: Implicit Nominal Rates. Means for periods shown calculated from Williamson's simulated real rates (Williamson, 1974, p. 292) by using the formula and price-level data cited by Williamson in his computations of real rates (Williamson, 1974, Table 5.2, p. 97 and Table 7.2, p. 152).

Railroad Bond Rate. Means calculated from annual data appearing in U.S. Bureau of Census, *Historical Statistics of the United States, Colonial Times to 1957,* (1960), Series X332, p. 656.

Middlewestern Mortgage Rate. Means calculated from annual data appearing in Davis (September, 1965), Table 12, p. 384, the rate being that for Davis's Region IV, the Middlewest.

individual city rates for reserve cities, reaching what he calls "some surprising conclusions":

> First, for the non-reserve city national banks, no trend of rate convergence was found. The rates diverged during the 1890's depression and then converged through the end of 1913. The relative dispersion of rates, however, is about the same at the end of the period as at the beginning. For reserve city bank rates, if one does not make any adjustment for the continued appearance of new reserve cities, one finds a trend of rate divergence throughout the period. When a constant set of reserve cities is used rate convergence is found.[30]

While generally critical of Davis's paper, Smiley does give some support to Davis's argument that the development of a national commercial-paper market played a role in what minimal convergence of regional interest rates occurred, mainly in reserve cities, after 1900. But this development is said by Smiley to have

taken place much later than Davis supposed, most probably happening in the years 1907–1909.[31] My own hypothesis of declining entry barriers, particularly in country banking, receives little support according to Smiley, apparently because of the failure of the relative dispersion of country bank interest rates to decline between the beginning and end of the 1888–1913 period.

A minor problem with Smiley's conclusions is that they refer to the 1888–1913 period, whereas Davis's and my own conclusions were based on examining a period nearly twice as long. Some of the convergence of interest rates, judging by Davis's admittedly imperfect measures for the whole period 1870–1914, occurred before 1888. And while I did emphasize the Gold Standard Act of 1900 as providing a clear example of reductions in legal entry barriers, this was in no sense to argue that country banking was very monopolistic before 1900 and very competitive thereafter. Rather, it was to show by that one clear example applying to the whole nation that bank entry did in fact respond to reduced entry barriers after 1900, and that in consequence banking competition increased. My own view was and is that entry barriers were steadily eroded during the decades after the restrictive banking legislation of the 1860's, but that the response after 1900 indicated that entry barriers were still formidable up to that date.[32]

Nothing in Smiley's analysis persuades me to change these views. In terms of Smiley's own data, average country bank interest rates between the beginning and end of the 1888–1913 period do decline, and so does the relative dispersion of rates, albeit modestly enough that I would not argue with him that the relative dispersion of his country bank rates was about the same at the beginning and end of the period.[33] Moreover, there is a good reason, suggested by one of Smiley's own insights, to believe that his procedures minimize the decline in the relative dispersion of country bank rates over the 1888–1913 period.[34]

Even on its own ground, therefore, Smiley's evidence cannot be viewed as damaging to the bank entry-barrier hypothesis I advanced to explain short-term rate convergence between regions. Nor can it be viewed as damaging to Davis's empirical evidence, for when Smiley applies his methods for testing convergence to Davis's data the results turn out to be essentially the same as he obtains with his own data.[35] Thus, we may conclude that Smiley's "surprising conclusions" are not a function of his allegedly better data but rather are due almost entirely to his choice of methods of testing for rate convergence.

What then is Smiley's method? He uses a measure of relative dispersion, the coefficient of variation, rather than a measure of absolute dispersion such as the absolute rate differentials Davis implicitly and I explicitly used, to investigate whether regional bank interest rates converged. Smiley's measure would require him to conclude, for example, that no convergence of interest rates between Regions A and B occurs when rates in Region A fall from 10 to 5 percent while in the same period rates in Region B fall from 4 to 2 percent. In relative terms, at the beginning and end points, rates in A are two and one-half times rates in B. In

absolute terms, on the other hand, the initial interest differential between A and B is 6 percent while the terminal differential is only 3 percent.

Smiley's choice of a relative rather than an absolute measure of dispersion in testing for interest rate convergence is questionable. For a supply decision, such as the decision to supply banking services in Region A, a 6 percent absolute differential in the interest rate a banker could charge would provide a greater inducement to enter banking than would a 3 percent differential. For any given or projected bank, the 6 percent differential would yield both more dollars of earnings and a higher return on equity than the 3 percent differential. Hence, the existence of larger absolute interest rate differentials between U.S. regions at the beginning than at the end of the period 1870–1914 (or 1888–1914) may be taken as evidence of greater disequilibrium in the capital market, however caused. This would be true provided that higher costs of banking in Region A do not entirely offset the interest differential advantage. But the evidence for 1870–1914 indicates that regional cost differences cannot explain interest-rate differentials because banks in higher interest regions earned higher rates of return on bank equity.[36] These considerations provide a theoretical case, empirically buttressed, against Smiley's use of a measure of relative dispersion in testing hypotheses on regional interest rate convergence.

Smiley appears to recognize that his method is questionable, and so he attempts to justify it on two grounds.[37] One is that others have used the relative dispersion measure in testing for interest rate convergence, a precedential ground which might appeal to the legal profession but will not be very convincing to scholars. Smiley's second attempt at justifying his method addresses itself to a substantive issue but in it he misinterprets his own argument in such a fashion as to render his justification erroneous. He argues that the absolute dispersion of rates is the appropriate measure to test for convergence if the transactions costs that are always reflected in observed bank interest rates are an absolute or constant value, whereas if the transactions costs are themselves relative values tending to move with interest rates then the relative dispersion measure is the correct test of convergence. These propositions seem correct. But then Smiley cites as evidence for choosing the relative measure the fact, in itself unsurprising, that in the commercial-paper market "brokerage fees were generally stated as a percentage rate."[38] What Smiley seems to be unaware of is that a brokerage fee is customarily stated as a percentage of the value of a transaction, not as a percentage of the interest rate charged, e.g., on a loan transaction. The distinction is important. For a percentage brokerage fee on the value of a transaction becomes an *absolute* rather than a *relative* transaction cost when related to the interest rate on the loan transaction.[39] Smiley has therefore inadvertently provided a good argument for using absolute rather than relative differentials in regional interest rates to test for convergence over time.[40]

When one examines Smiley's regional interest rates in terms of absolute differ-

Table 3. Mean Absolute Differentials between Smiley's Regional Bank Interest Rates, 1888–1913, in Percentage Points.

	Regions					
Period	II	IIIA	IIIB	IV	V	VI

A. Differential between Nonreserve City Banks in Stated Region and Nonreserve City Banks in Region I.

Period	II	IIIA	IIIB	IV	V	VI
1888–99	.15	1.54	4.60	1.19	3.87	3.76
1900–13	.04	.80	4.11	.42	2.80	2.43

B. Differentials between Reserve City Banks in Stated Region and Reserve City Banks in Region I.

Period	II	IIIA	IIIB	IV	V	VI
1888–99	.70	1.31	3.72	1.70	3.45	3.28
1900–13	.38	.81	2.79	.55	1.62	1.51

C. Differentials between Nonreserve City Banks in Stated Region and Reserve City Banks in Region I.

Period	II	IIIA	IIIB	IV	V	VI
1888–99	1.57	2.96	6.02	2.61	5.29	5.18
1900–13	.76	1.52	4.83	1.12	3.52	3.15

Source: Calculated from annual regional interest rate data in Smiley (September 1975), Tables A-3 and A-4, pp. 613–614. Regions are defined by Smiley as follows:

I. Main, Vermont, New Hampshire, Massachusetts, Connecticut and Rhode Island.

II. New York, New Jersey, Pennsylvania, Delaware, Maryland and the District of Columbia.

IIIA. Virginia, West Virginia, North Carolina, Kentucky and Tennessee.

IIIB. South Carolina, Georgia, Florida, Alabama, Mississippi, Louisiana, Texas, Arkansas and Oklahoma.

IV. Ohio, Indiana, Illinois, Michigan, Wisconsin, Minnesota, Iowa and Missouri.

V. North Dakota, South Dakota, Nebraska, Kansas, Montana, Wyoming, Colorado and New Mexico.

VI. Washington, Oregon, California, Idaho, Utah, Nevada and Arizona.

entials, the conclusions reached turn out not to be at all surprising, but very much the same as those reached by earlier students. Using Smiley's Region I (New England), the region of generally lowest rates, as a base, I show in Table 3 the average absolute differences between rates in Smiley's Regions II through VI and

Region I rates both before and after 1900. The three sets of comparisons are for interest rate differentials (a) between nonreserve city banks in New England and the other six regions, (b) between reserve city banks in New England and the other regions, and (c) between reserve city banks in New England and nonreserve city banks in other regions. The results are similar to those I found in my earlier work using Lance Davis's interest rate data. Absolute rate differences between banks in every region and New England were lower, often sharply lower, in the period 1900–1913 than in 1888–1899. Rather than modifying or overturning Lance Davis's and my own findings and conclusions, Smiley's evidence relating to the quarter century before 1913 corroborates them.

Interest Rate Differentials and Risk

An issue not adequately dealt with in any of the aforementioned studies of secular trends in regional rate differentials is the possiblity that the observed differentials can be accounted for by differing exposures to risk on the part of banks in the various regions.[41] The issue is an important one. For if one assumes that banks were risk averse—i.e., that they required greater than average compensation for taking greater than average risks—then a greater exposure to risk in high interest regions could explain both the higher rates charged to borrowers and the greater rates of profit on bank equity earned in these regions. And a narrowing of risk differentials could provide an alternative explanation of regional interest rate convergence.

Two recent papers shed some light on the risk issue. Hugh Rockoff, measuring risk by bank failure rates among regions for various intervals of the period 1870–1914, finds evidence of positive correlations between the regional failure rates and regional rates of return on bank equity.[42] The correlations, however, are not very significant in the statistical sense. Moreover, the rates of bank failure, while varying among regions, are in general very very low—less than one percent in most of Rockoff's regions and intervals—while the rates of return to bank equity vary more widely, roughly from 6 to 12 percent. The overall impression is that bankers would have to have been extremely risk averse to require such large differences in profit rates to compensate for variable but in any case small risks of failure. Were one to compare the dollars of bank capital lost through failures with the added earnings implicit in the profit differentials of high interest regions, the "insurance premiums" that bankers paid themselves as "self-insurers" by charging their customers high interest rates would probably be revealed to have been extremely high. If so, different degrees of competitiveness would provide a more reasonable explanation of interest differentials.

A common characteristic of the aforementioned studies of interest rate convergence is that each emphasizes the importance of a single factor in accounting for historical trends. Davis, for example, emphasized changes in the supply of intermediating activity as the operative factor, while Williamson (and also Keehn)

argued that regional shifts in the demand for funds provide a more coherent explanation. Changes in monopoly power (Sylla), risk (Rockoff, and to a lesser extent, Smiley), and transactions costs (Keehn again) have been emphasized in a similar fashion. Perhaps this is the manner in which much scientific investigation proceeds. For the advancing and testing of one hypothesis is usually an exercising task in itself. After alternative hypotheses gain some support, however, a question naturally arises as to their relative importance. Too often a proponent of one hypothesis is willing to dismiss another hypothesis on purely conjectural grounds or on the basis of limited evidence of a contrary nature. A maturer approach is to attempt to incorporate several of the competing hypotheses into a systematic test.

A second recent paper dealing with the risk issue adopts the maturer approach to which I refer. John James develops a model of bank portfolio selection in which the average real rate of return on bank loans is determined by loss rates on loans, the variance of loss rates (a proxy for risk), and an index of the total number of banks per unit of population (a proxy for the degree of monopoly in banking).[43] Using average state and city bank data for the period 1893–1911 to estimate his model, James finds that variations in loss rates, risk, and monopoly power generally affected bank interest rates in the theoretically expected directions. But changes in monopoly power proved under *ceteris paribus* simulations to be the most important explanatory variable, accounting for almost all of the changes in interest rates in most states during 1893–1911. James concludes that his work confirms the importance of barriers to interregional capital mobility.

II. GERSCHENKRON ON BANKS IN THE INDUSTRIALIZATION OF EUROPE.

In his studies of the spread of the Industrial Revolution from country to country in nineteenth-century Europe, Alexander Gerschenkron gives a special emphasis to institutional aspects of the supply of capital to industry.[44] His hypothesis is that there are three characteristic institutional patterns of finance and that the one pattern which applies to any given country depends on that country's degree of economic backwardness at the time it began to industrialize. England, Germany and Russia are treated by Gerschenkron as providing examples of the three patterns relating institutional responses in finance to relative economic backwardness. In England, whose economy was relatively advanced, investment during the first industrial revolution was financed largely out of earlier accumulations of capital and the retained earnings of industrial enterprises themselves. Germany, in contrast, is viewed as a moderately backward country at the time of its later industrial revolution. Lacking the capital accumulations built up in England through commerce and empire in the years preceding the first industrial revolution, Germany substituted the funds and entrepreneurial activities of great banking institutions for the favorable elements of English economic history missing from German experi-

ence. Lastly, Russia, when it began to industrialize late in the nineteenth century, was even more backward than Germany had been on the eve of its industrial revolution. Consequently the burdens of industrial finance fell upon the policies and the budget of the Russian government because Russia lacked both the dynamic banks of Germany and the early capital accumulations of England.

Gerschenkron's seminal ideas on the relative importance of direct finance as compared with finance by either private or public financial intermediaries go well beyond the three examples he chose to exemplify his approach. He himself has used his tripartite model as a predictive and investigative insight, guiding research into the character and financing of initial spurts of industrial growth in other European countries—e.g., Italy and Bulgaria.[45] Other scholars, directly or indirectly influenced by Gerschenkron's ideas, have examined the role of banking in the economic modernizations of other European and non-European countries.[46] In addition, it would seem that Gerschenkron's approach could shed light on events as widely separated in time and space as the early nineteenth-century industrialization of the Northeastern United States, in which forms of direct finance along English lines appear to have predominated in a commercial economy similar to England's, and the underdeveloped economies of our own era, in which a substantial degree of economic backwardness is one factor that leads to an increased role for publicly operated financial intermediaries along Russian lines.

Most of the attention of those who have followed in Gerschenkron's footsteps has been directed, however, to the role of private intermediaries—especially banks—in modern economic history. It would be too ambitious here to attempt to examine critically the host of subsequent studies—e.g., those of Rondo Cameron and his collaborators, which are more or less in the methodological vein of Gerschenkron.[47] Rather, I will concentrate on some more recent studies which confront Gerschenkron on his own historical grounds but with the data and emphasis on hypothesis testing characteristic of the so-called new economic history.

The Gerschenkron Banking Hypothesis: A General Test

In a note published in 1973, David Good presents a formal quantitative test of Gerschenkron's banking hypothesis using data from eight countries—including England, Germany and Russia.[48] Good groups his eight countries into the three categories of relative economic backwardness according to the date at which each country is assumed to have entered upon its initial spurt of industrialization; the later the date, Good assumes, the more backward the country. To capture the banking influence, Good develops two measures: namely (1) the *level* of the ratio of bank assets to GNP in each country two decades after the commencement of its industrial spurt, and (2) the *rate of growth* of this ratio over the first two decades of the spurt. Support for Gerschenkron's intermediary hypothesis would follow from the two measures of banking influence being greater for the moderately backward

countries (France, Belgium and Germany) in Good's sample than for either advanced (England) or very backward economies (Denmark, Sweden, Russia and Italy).

The two measures, Good finds, give contradictory results. The Gerschenkron hypothesis is supported by the rate of growth of the bank asset/GNP ratio, which was substantially greater in moderately backward Belgium and Germany that it was in either the advanced or the backward countries. But in terms of the levels of the ratio, both England and the very backward countries had more bank assets in relation to GNP than the moderately backward economies. Good therefore argues that, depending on which measure of bank influence one feels is more important, one may either accept or reject Gerschenkron's hypothesis.

I am not so convinced that the balance for and against Gerschenkron's hypothesis is as equally weighted as Good implies. There are, of course, many problems with the data—both with regard to the dating of the industrial spurts and with regard to the measures of bank assets and GNP—which are very rough, different in their comprehensiveness, and subject to varying interpretations. There is also the further problem that a proper test of the hypothesis should relate the *industrial* lending of banks to *industrial* output, not total bank assets to broader output measures such as GNP.[49] These technical problems of testing the Gerschenkron hypothesis exist, but they do not necessarily imply that Good's results are biased against the hypothesis.

There is, however, a more important problem of interpretation raised by Good, an examination of which appears to me to result in a conclusion more favorable to the Gerschenkron hypothesis as Good himself tests it. Good's data on the levels of the bank asset/GNP ratio, which show the highest ratios for the very backward countries industrializing late in the nineteenth century, imply, he argues, that the penetration of banking into the various economies increased over time for reasons largely unconnected with industrialization. There are good reasons, I would add, for expecting this result. A basic trend of modern economic history seems to be the increasing extent of market relative to nonmarket activity, and a growing monetization of economic life. Banks are important agents in bringing about this trend through their provision of a growing proportion of the means of payment. Thus, it may not be surprising that even a backward economy of, say, 1900, would have a higher ratio of bank assets to GNP that would a less backward country in 1840 or 1780. I would argue, therefore, that the levels of bank asset/GNP ratios observed by Good over more than a century of European history are less meaningful as a test of the Gerschenkron hypothesis than are the rates of growth of the ratio during the several spurts of industrialization. On this interpretation I conclude that Good's work lends tentative support to Gerschenkron's generalization.[50]

The Gerschenkron Hypothesis: A Specific Test

Germany's joint stock *Kreditbanken* grew from small beginnings in the moderately backward economy at mid-century to become a dominant financial force in

industrialized Germany a half-century later. For their combining of commercial and investment banking with an entrepreneurial approach to the nurturing of industrial enterprise, the *Kreditbanken* have long been accorded a prominent position in Germany's rise to industrial eminence. Gerschenkron amplified this interpretation, but the essence of his contribution came in generalizing it to a proposition on the expected role of banking during industrializations taking place in conditions of moderate economic backwardness.

Hugh Neuberger and Houston Stokes have recently presented a formal econometric test of the Gerschenkon hypothesis on its German home ground.[51] The heart of their analysis is the specification and estimation of a production function for the nonagricultural part of the German economy during the period 1883–1913. The production function specifies German nonagricultural output as depending on inputs of labor and physical capital, on "time" in order to capture the influence of technological progess, and on a bank credit allocation variable— namely, the ratio of current-account credit extended by the *Kreditbanken* to their total extensions of credit, which consisted of current accounts, domestic and foreign bills of exchange, and security holdings. The emphasis of Neuberger and Stokes on the proportion of current-account credit as a shift term of the production function is based on several considerations. Current accounts were the largest part of *Kreditbanken* credits. In addition, most current-account credit went to industrial firms. And, perhaps most important of all, the current account, continual renewals of which disguised long-term credits as short-term loans, provided the banks with a commanding influence over the industrial enterprises they financed.[52] For these reasons Neuberger and Stokes hold that the ratio of current-account to total credit of the *Kreditbanken* is a proper shift variable to include in their production function for purposes of testing Gerschenkron's hypothesis. If the estimated coefficient of the current-account variable were to turn out to be positive and statistically significant, the implication would be that German nonagricultural output varied directly with current-account credit, and the Gerschenkron hypothesis would be supported.

The Neuberger-Stokes contribution is an important one in the interpretation of modern European economic history. It is both provocative and carefully executed. And by showing the potential of serious hypothesis testing with quantitative materials it represents a raising of the level of discourse to a higher-than-usual plane. Nevertheless, for a number of reasons their findings for Germany, which argue against the Gerschenkron hypothesis, are not altogether convincing as a test of that hypothesis. Their historical argument leaves out some important considerations; and their econometric results, solid in themselves, may possibly have resulted from a misspecified model.

In historical terms, while it is true that Gerschenkron and others before him placed great emphasis on the *Kreditbanken* and their current accounts, this does

not imply that quantitative tests should deal with the *Kreditbanken* to the exclusion of other banks. The emphasis of past historians on the *Kreditbanken* derived more from their entrepreneurial contributions to German industrialization than from explicit analyses of the quantitative importance of their credits. In making quantitative tests of the effects of bank-lending activity on industrialization, investigators must recognize that banking is a system and that what matters for industrial growth is the total amount of bank credit furnished to industrial enterprises. Stokes and Neuberger, in contrast, focus their attention on but one form of credit, the current account, of one group of German banks the *Kreditbanken*, and they relate their variable not to industrial production but to all nonagricultural output.[53]

In this exclusive emphasis on the *Kreditbanken*, do Neuberger and Stokes ignore any features of the German banking system that are pertinent to the Gerschenkron hypothesis? Their failure to bring in the *Reichsbank*, the German central bank, could constitute such an omission. The *Reichsbank* played an important role in the German financial system. Its liberal discounting policy pursued for most of the period studied by Neuberger and Stokes invariably aided the *Kreditbanken* in periods of financial stringency, and it thereby allowed the *Kreditbanken* to operate with minimal reserves and to invest short-term funds in long-term industrial investments. The *Reichsbank* also competed with other banks in the German bill market, holding a large and increasing proportion of all German bills of exchange over the period.[54] This bill policy of the *Reischsbank* may account for the secular rise, reported by Neuberger and Stokes, in the proportion of *Kreditbanken* credit taking the current-account form, and the fall in the proportion absorbed by domestic bills.[55] If so, the ratio of current-account credit to total *Kreditbanken* credit, which plays a key role in the findings of Neuberger and Stokes against the Gerschenkron hypothesis, was as much due to *Reichsbank* policy as to the allocative preferences of the *Kreditbanken* themselves.

The foregoing remarks are more in the nature of critical speculation than of criticism *per se* of the important work of Neuberger and Stokes. The suggestion offered here is that their specification be reformulated to measure, for example, the ratio of all industrial credits of German banks to all German bank credit, and to relate this ratio to total German output (to determine the allocative effects of concern to Neuberger and Stokes), or to German industrial output (to get at the point pertinent to the Gerschenkron hypothesis). The value of the approach taken by Neuberger and Stokes lies in part in the fact that such reformulation can be done by working with available data and in the context of their production-function model. Moreover, as they have subsequently demonstrated in findings more favorable to the Gerschenkron hypothesis, their general approach can be applied to other countries as well.[56] Thus, in challenging the traditional interpretation of German banking, Neuberger and Stokes have succeeded in opening up a whole new area of research based upon Gerschenkron's seminal insights.

III. Conclusion

The foregoing discussion should indicate why it is entirely proper to regard the contributions of Lance Davis and Alexander Gerschenkron as seminal ones in the historical study of financial intermediaries. Numerous students have devoted countless hours to exploring, amplifying, and also doubting the validity of their respective insights. Such attention is the sincerest form of academic flattery, and in the cases of Davis and Gerschenkron it is richly deserved. For on the whole it appears that their arguments, insights and conclusions continue to stand up rather well in the aftermath of the tremendous scrutiny to which they have been subjected.

That much said, it may also be added that the works inspired by Davis and Gerschenkron illustrate some very real problems that arise in attempts to provide quantitative tests of hypotheses offered to explain historical phenomea. One is the problem of quantitative versus nonquantitative explanations. Davis's hypothesis on why regional interest rates converged and Gerschenkron's on why banks play a critical role in industrialization under certain economic conditions are similar to one another in emphasizing institutional changes and in being essentially nonquantitative. Quantitative researchers are easily dissatisfied with hypotheses of this nature, and so they attempt either to provide alternative hypotheses which are amenable to quantitative testing or to transform the nonquantitative hypothesis into a quantitative one. Two questions may be asked about such efforts. First, does the success of an alternative quantitative hypothesis in explaining the data imply that a nonquantitative hypothesis is to be doubted? Second, do quantitative reformulations of originally nonquantitative hypotheses emphasize or suppress the essence of the latter? These questions are seldom confronted adequately in the literature.

When alternative quantitative hypotheses are advanced to account for the same historical observations, a second problem arises. Suppose each of two alternative hypotheses is supported by quantitative evidence. Should the researcher regard the hypotheses as mutually exclusive and try to make a case against one or another of them? Or should the support both hypotheses have gained lead to an inquiry into the relative importance of the two? Both tacks appear in the studies on intermediary history above examined. The second tack may appear preferable, but then the further question often arises of whether the available data can be fitted into an encompassing theory or model in order to make such complicated second-order testing feasible.

Finally, suppose there is agreement on the relevance of certain quantifiable concepts to the formulation and testing of a given hypothesis—e.g., on the relevance of risk or monopoly power to questions of interest rate convergence, or the relevance of the industrial lending of banks to hypotheses concerning the relation of banks to industrial growth. A serious problem remains. How should risk and monopoly power be measured? Which banks and which types of loans properly capture the bank effect? To go further, is interest rate convergence a

question of absolute or relative measures of rate differences? And are levels or rates of change of banking variables more relevant to questions of the importance of banking during industrial revolutions? Quantitative historians must face these thorny methodological and empirical problems if they wish their results to be accepted as significant within the on-going discussions of the historical problems they treat.

FOOTNOTES

*I thank D. N. McCloskey and P. K. O'Brien for helpful discussions of some of the issues dealt with here, and the National Endowment for the Humanities for financial support under Grant No. F-75-44.

1. Since the money question in recent economic history is dealt with by Anna J. Schwartz and Michael D. Bordo elsewhere in this volume, I shall devote my attention to works emphasizing intermediaries in the context of the savings-investment problem.
2. Davis (September 1965), pp. 355–399.
3. Gerschenkron (1962), ch. 1, pp. 5–30; and the Postscript, pp. 353–364.
4. Davis (September 1965).
5. See Sylla (December 1969), pp. 657–686.
6. See Keehn (Spring, 1974), pp. 1–27.
7. *Ibid.*, p. 21; see also pp. 2, 27.
8. *Ibid.*, pp. 21–22.
9. *Ibid.*, pp. 3–11. Two minor points of defense may be offered in reply. First, there would be no reason to expect that generalizations such as mine, based on aggregations of national and regional data, would be illustrated by *every* underlying individual observation at the state and city levels. Second, Keehn's unit of observation, Wisconsin, is in the East North Central region of the U.S. This region, made up of loyal and relatively settled states, was favored by the note issue allocations made under the early administration of the Civil War banking laws. So Wisconsin perhaps would not be an ideal state for studying the effects of legal and administrative entry barriers on bank competition.
10. *Ibid.*, p. 4.
11. *Ibid.*, p. 11
12. See Sylla (December 1969), pp. 662–663; and Sylla (1975), pp. 83–84.
13. Keehn (Spring 1974), pp. 12–13.
14. *Ibid.,* pp. 13–14.
15. Williamson (1974), Ch. 6.
16. *Ibid.*, p. 58.
17. *Ibid.*, p. 83.
18. *Ibid.*, Table 4.9, p. 84.
19. *Ibid.*, p. 84.
20. *Ibid.*, p. 127.
21. *Ibid.*
22. *Ibid.*, p. 134.
23. *Ibid.*, p. 137.
24. *Ibid.*
25. *Ibid.*, p. 145.
26. *Ibid.*
27. *Ibid.*, pp. 84–86.

28. *Ibid.*, Table 5.2, p. 97; and Table 7.2, p. 152. Denoting the real rate by r, the nominal rate by i, and the average annual rate of change in the price level over the preceding five years by p, Williamson's formula relating real to nominal rates is

$$r = \frac{i - p}{1 + p}$$

29. Smiley (September, 1975), p. 593.

30. *Ibid.*, p. 609.

31. *Ibid.*, pp. 607–609.

32. See Sylla (December 1969), pp. 662–664; (1975), pp. 47–78.

33. Using Smiley's data, I calculate that unweighted average country bank rates declined from 8.53 to 7.43 percent between 1888–1892 and 1909–1913, while asset-weighted average rates declined from 7.27 to 6.62 percent between the same periods. The average relative dispersion of the unweighted rates declines from .2589 to .2414, while that of the weighted rates declines from .2208 to .2200. The data are from Smiley (September 1975), Table A–5, p. 615.

34. Smiley found that rates diverged for all reserve cities between 1888 and 1913, but that they converged in the constant subsample of all cities that were reserve cities during the entire period. The reason for the anomaly is that many cities were transferred from nonreserve city status to reserve city status during the period. If adding new reserve cities to the list of reserve cities year by year is sufficient to turn a situation of actual convergence of reserve city rates into one of measured divergence, it is likely that removing these same cities from the country bank sample, which is what happens in the Comptroller's data, would have a similar effect on the measured dispersion of country bank rates. For the inclusion of a number of medium-sized cities where banking was relatively competitive in the nonreserve city sample in the early years of the 1888–1913 period would tend to narrow the relative dispersion of nonreserve city rates, while their exclusion from the sample after they became reserve cities would tend to increase the relative dispersion of remaining nonreserve city rates. Smiley's evidence supports this view. He finds that the relative dispersion of interest rates weighted by bank assets, which gives greater weight to cities and states with larger amounts of bank assets, is uniformly lower than the relative dispersion of the unweighted rates. Smiley (September 1975). pp. 615–616.

35. *Ibid.*, footnote 12, pp. 597–598.

36. See Sylla (December 1969); and Keehn (Spring 1974), pp. 11–12, 22–26.

37. Smiley (September 1975), footnote 13, pp. 599–600.

38. *Ibid.*, footnote 13, p. 600.

39. The point is easily demonstrated. A one-percent brokerage fee on a purchase of $10,000 of one-year commercial paper becomes a $100 *absolute* charge which must be subtracted from the stated annual interest yield to obtain the net interest return. If the stated rate is 9 percent, the gross one-year return is $900 and the net return is $800. If the stated rate is 2 percent, the gross return is $200 and the net return is $100. In each case the *percentage* brokerage fee becomes an *absolute* cost to be subtracted from the gross interest return in order to obtain the net return.

40. Smiley attempts further to bolster his erroneous justification of the relative dispersion measure by citing some evidence that percentage brokerage fees themselves declined between the 1870's and the 1900's. This is irrelevant to his point because brokerage fees are conventions unrelated to prevailing interest rates. What the decline of brokerage fees shows is that greater competition arose among commercial paper dealers, just as the absolute

decline of regional bank interest differentials shows that greater competition arose among bankers.

41. Smiley (September 1975, pp. 600–605) argues that risk, as measured by the ratio of loan losses to total loans and discounts, may have accounted for some of the relative divergence in regional rates during the cyclical depression of the 1890's. For Wisconsin, however, Keehn (Spring 1974, pp. 16–19) found that apart from the depression of the 1890's, the risk of banking, as measured by the ratio of losses to earning assets, was usually greater in Milwaukee than in the country banking sector despite the fact that country banks usually earned greater average returns on equity than Milwaukee banks.

42. Rockoff (1976).

43. James (1976).

44. Gerschenkron (1962), especially ch. 1, pp. 5–30; and the Postscript, pp. 353–364.

45. *Ibid.*, chs. 4 and 8.

46. See especially two volumes by Cameron and his collaborators (1967, 1972).

47. *Ibid.* For Cameron's good critique of Gerschenkron's work see his introduction to Cameron, *et al* (1972).

48. Good (December 1973), pp. 845–850.

49. During the early stages of industrialization the industrial sector of an economy is naturally quite small, and even though it may begin to grow rapidly the effects may not be very pronounced in terms of broader output measures.

50. The support is tentative because it depends on the proposition that an increasing monetization of economic activity occurred during the nineteenth century more or less independently of the degree of industrialization in the various European economies. I deem the proposition plausible, but it remains to be demonstrated.

51. Neuberger and Stokes (September 1974), pp. 710–731.

52. *Ibid.*, pp. 713–715.

53. Neuberger and Stokes (September 1974, p. 720), argue that their emphasis on nonagricultural output is correct for two reasons. The first is that the *Kreditbanken* did not lend to the agricultural sector. This is a dubious ground because their concern is with the overall allocative effect of the *Kreditbanken* on the growth of the German economy); to the extent that the *Kreditbanken* specialized in nonagricultural lending, they freed other German financial institutions to specialize on agricultural credit. Secondly, they argue that to relate *Kreditbank* operations only to the growth of heavy industry, as emphasized by Gerschenkron, would be to forego the opportunity to study the overall allocative effects of those operations. That may be the case, but if light industry was starved for credit by the *Kreditbanken*, as Neuberger and Stokes suggest, then the allocative effects should still appear when *Kredibanken* operations are related to total industrial output. Such a relation would be truer to the Gerschenkron hypothesis than their own emphasis on nonagricultural output, a much more comprehensive concept. One would need to know the correlations between industrial output, nonagricultural output and total German output in order to determine whether their econometric results are particular to the output concept Neuberger and Stokes select.

54. Data in a volume commemorating the 25th anniversary of the founding of the *Reichsbank* indicate that it held approximately 30 percent of all German bills in the 1870's, and close to 40 percent by the end of the century. See *Die Reichsbank, 1876–1900* (Jena, 1901), Table 55, p. 363.

55. Neuberger and Stokes, (September 1974), p. 714.

56. Neuberger and Stokes have applied their approach to Japan, using 1955–1967 data. They relate a measure of Japanese "gross enterprise national product" to several input variables and a bank credit-allocation variable, namely the ratio of manufacturing to total credit granted by *Zaibatsu* or "ordinary" banks. This is a more appropriately specified bank

variable than they used in the German study for purposes of testing the Gerschenkron hypothesis, and interestingly enough they find a positive and significant effect of bank credit allocation on Japanese output growth. This supports the Gerschenkron hypothesis, although Japan was far past its early period of industrialization in the period studied. Earlier work by Kozo Yamamura suggests, however, that a similar finding could well be expected for Japan in the 1920's. See Neuberger and Stokes (March 1975), pp. 238–252; and Kozo Yamamura, "Japan, 1868–1930: A Revised View," in Cameron et al. (1972), ch. 6.

REFERENCES

Cameron, Rondo, et al (1967), Banking in the Early Stages of Industrialization, New York: Oxford University Press.

————. (1972), Banking and Economic Development: Some Lessons of History, New York: Oxford University Press.

Davis, Lance E. (September 1965), "The Investment Market, 1870–1914: The Evolution of a National Market," Journal of Economic History, 25, pp. 355–399.

Gerschenkron, Alexander (1962), Economic Backwardness in Historical Perspective, Cambridge: Harvard University Press.

Good, David F. (December 1973), "Backwardness and the Role of Banking in Nineteenth-Century European Industrialization," Journal of Economic History, 33, pp. 845–850.

James, John A. (1976), "Banking Market Structure, Risk, and the Pattern of Local Interest Rates in the United States, 1893–1911," Review of Economics and Statistics.

Keehn, Richard H. (Spring 1974), "Federal Bank Policy, Bank Market Structure, and Bank Performance: Wisconsin, 1863–1914," Business History Review, 48, pp. 1–27.

Neuberger, Hugh, and Stokes, Houston H., (September 1974), "German Banks and German Growth, 1883–1913: An Empirical View," Journal of Economic History, 34, pp. 710–731.

————. (March 1975), "German Banking and Japanese Banking: A Comparative Analysis," Journal of Economic History, 35, pp. 238–252.

Rockoff, Hugh (1977), "Regional Interest Rates and Bank Failures, 1870–1914," Explorations in Economic History.

Smiley, Gene (September 1975), "Interest Rate Movement in the United States, 1888–1913," Journal of Economic History, 35, pp. 591–620.

Sylla, Richard (1975), The American Capital Market 1846–1917: A Study of the Effects of Public Policy on Economic Development, New York: Arno Press.

————. (December 1969), "Federal Policy, Banking Market Structure, and Capital Mobilization in the United States, 1863–1913," Journal of Economic History, 29, pp. 657–686.

Williamson, Jeffrey G. (1974), Late Nineteenth-Century American Development: A General Equilibrium History, London and New York: Cambridge University Press.

ISSUES IN MONETARY ECONOMICS AND THEIR IMPACT ON RESEARCH IN ECONOMIC HISTORY

Michael D. Bordo, CARLETON UNIVERSITY and

Anna J. Schwartz, NATIONAL BUREAU OF ECONOMIC RESEARCH

". . . [O]ne would hope that 'new economic history' will soon discover monetary theory." (Niehans, 1973)

Trends in research in economic history have long tended to reflect developments in subfields of economics. The rise of a specialized field of study—exemplified by the postwar creation of regional economics—sooner or later has led economic historians to apply the techniques of analysis used in that field to historical data.[1] Shifts in the subject matter of a subfield and in its treatment have, after some lag, been absorbed in subsequent research in economic history.

A profound change has taken place in recent decades in the lines of inquiry pursued in monetary economics. It will be the task of this chapter to review the extent to which the present state of monetary economics is reflected in recent work in economic history. A useful point of departure for this purpose is Wesley Clair Mitchell's essay on "The Role of Money in Economic History," (Mitchell, 1944), which serves to define a traditional approach to money that no longer characterizes recent work in monetary economics.

Monetary economics is the term that has come into current use to demarcate the field of study that has been known in the past as monetary theory and policy. The key variable the field deals with is the quantity of money. The contrast between this emphasis and an earlier view is highlighted by reference to Mitchell's essay. There he focused on money as meaning "making and spending money" (Mitchell, 1944, p. 67), in the sense of money income and money expenditure. Monetary economics does, of course, examine the effect of changes in the quantity of money on changes in money income and expenditure, but the reader of Mitchell's essay will find no reference to this relationship.

Mitchell's conception of the task of economic history with respect to the role of money was framed as a question: "Cannot economic history be organized most efficiently around the evolution of pecuniary institutions?" What he hoped economic historians would provide in response was

> the best account now feasible of the way men came to organize their dealings with one another on the basis of money payments, the way this scheme spread from one sphere to another, the material and cultural consequences to which it led, the rationalizations and condemnations it evoked, and the further changes it seems to be undergoing in our day. (Mitchell, 1944).

Monetary economists have been asking a rather different question. Why has society found use for money? They have sought to discover the economic forces that shape institutions and to establish the microfoundations of monetary economics. Some have constructed theories that center on the costs of acquiring information and executing transactions under barter conditions.[2] Money is an asset, on this view, that minimizes these costs and hence provides productive services by saving resources that would otherwise be allocated to search and acquisition of market information (Brunner and Meltzer, 1971; Niehans, 1969, 1971).

Such an approach provides a theoretical insight that is lacking in the question Mitchell set as a frame for the study of the role of money in economic history. The spread of the money economy viewed as the consequence of minimizing costs of information in a world of uncertainty is a subject for research in economic history consonant with the outlook of contemporary monetary economics.

To refer to a task of economic history at this juncture, however, is premature. What is first required is a guide to the analytic developments of recent years in monetary economics (section I). Next will follow a survey of the literature in economic history since the date of publication of Milton Friedman's restatement of the quantity theory of money (Friedman, 1956), to investigate the use of monetary theory in over 75 articles and books (section II). Finally, some views on the tasks of economic history in relation to issues in monetary economics will be in order (section III).

I. ISSUES IN MONETARY ECONOMICS

The flow of studies in monetary economics in recent years has been profuse, and the range of issues they have dealt with is wide in scope. No exhaustive coverage will be attempted here. The purpose of this section is to review the current state of knowledge with respect to a selected number of significant issues and to delineate the areas of substantial agreement and disagreement.

The central question debated in monetary economics has been whether changes in the quantity of money are the dominant independent determinant of cyclical changes in economic activity, and of trend changes in the price level. Though technical and theoretical formulations are at issue, the opposing views are fundamentally concerned with short- and long-run stabilization policy. The exchanges that have enlivened the debate have been oriented to current stabilization problems in the United States since the 1960's.

We begin by presenting the background of the debate (I.1). This is followed by a discussion of the specific topics on which the debate has turned (I.2): the definition of money (I.2a); the determinants of the supply of money and the possibility of controlling the quantity outstanding (I.2b); the determinants of the demand for money (I.2c); the role of interest rates (I.2d); and the role of financial structure (I.2e). The crux of the debate, how and with what potency monetary actions affect economic activity, is next covered (I.3): the transmission process (I.3a); fiscal vs. monetary policy (I.3b); aggregates vs. sectoral detail (I.3c); price vs. output change (I.3d). On all of these questions, both theoretical and empirical studies exist and are referred to. A miscellaneous group of questions is next taken up for discussion (I.4): money in a growth model (I.4a); monetary theory of the balance of payments (I.4b); the term structure of interest rates (I.4c). Considerable theoretical but as yet no empirical work has appeared in relation to the first topic, considerable theoretical work exists and preliminary investigations have been made on the second, while theoretical and empirical work on the final topic is extensive.

I. 1. Background of the Debate

The revival of interest in the quantity theory of money is the hallmark of work in monetary economics in the past two decades. To place this development in context, a review of intellectual history is appropriate.

Viewed from the Keynesian perspective that dominated monetary economics in the early 1950's, the quantity theory is a mere tautology that assumes full employment and is without substance, since velocity is unstable and hence can offset a change in the quantity of money (Kaldor, 1970). Autonomous spending— investment by the private sector and expenditures by government—not the quantity of money determines national income in that perspective. If autonomous expenditures change, so will national income, with the change affecting mainly

output, since prices tend to be highly rigid. Costs, mainly wages, determine prices, and wages are a heritage of the past. Another fixed conception in the Keynesian perspective was the interpretation of the root of the worldwide contraction that began in 1929. This was attributed to exhaustion of investment opportunities, leading to a catastrophic decline in business investment expenditures that the multiplier process transmitted in heightened degree to national income. Given an unstable marginal efficiency of investment and monetary policy impotent to cope with depression, fiscal policy emerged as the indispensable tool for economic stabilization. In this perspective the role of monetary policy was limited to its effect on credit and interest rates: low rates of interest were desirable to ease the burden of debt on the government budget and possibly to stimulate private investment.

The rehabilitation of the quantity theory began with a refutation of Keynesian criticisms. The quantity theory was restated (Friedman, 1956) as a theory of the demand for money (or velocity) rather than of prices or output (hence full employment is not assumed), and money was defined as an asset or capital good (hence the demand for money is a problem in capital theory). The restatement of the theory holds that velocity is stable in a functional sense, a proposition subject to empirical testing. Discussion of the detailed work on the demand function will be presented at a later point (I.2b). Here it suffices to say that the restatement of the quantity theory is to be distinguished from reformulations of liquidity preference theory along Keynesian lines during the past two decades. The restatement includes expected changes in the price level as a variable affecting the cost of holding money and other assets fixed in nominal terms, whereas in the reformula-tion of the demand for money as part of a more general theory of asset holding—the portfolio balance approach—prices are generally assumed to be stable. The importance of the distinction will be underscored in what follows.

The next stage in the rehabilitation of the quantity theory was a set of statistical tests of Keynesian conceptions vs. quantity theory. One was a comparison of the predictive performance of the velocity function (income to money) and the mul-tiplier relationship (income to autonomous expenditure). The test yielded results favorable to the quantity theory over the period 1897–1958 with the exception of the 1930's when neither the velocity function nor the multiplier relationship produced a good statistical fit (Friedman and Meiselman, 1963). A counterattack by Keynesian adherents came in response[3] (Hester, 1964; Ando and Modigliani, 1965). A subsequent statistical test of the relative power of fiscal actions and monetary actions to predict quarterly changes in GNP from 1952 I through 1968 II yielded results indicating that the response of economic activity to monetary actions, compared with that of fiscal actions, is larger, more predictable and faster (Andersen and Jordan, 1968). These results are still the subject of an ongoing controversy in monetary economics.[4]

Another challenge to Keynesian conceptions was based on historical studies of the role of money in U.S. economic history (Friedman and Schwartz, 1963;

Cagan, 1965). These studies argued that the severity of the economic decline that began in 1929 was a consequence of an unprecedented reduction in the quantity of money that the Federal Reserve System could have prevented. The conclusion that monetary policy was ineffective in 1930–1933 was based on a misreading of the facts: monetary policy was perverse. The historical studies also documented the often independent origin of monetary changes—they were not simply a reflection of changes in economic activity. This finding countered the criticism that the quantity of money supplied passively adjusts to the demand for it and has no independent role.

During the early years of the debate, Keynesians took the position that "money doesn't matter" since they alleged that any change in the growth rate of money would be offset by a change in velocity. Keynesians now readily acknowledge that "money matters"; "how much" is the critical issue that is still unsettled.

At this point, we turn from the background of the debate to the specific issues that have engaged participants.

I.2. Essential Elements of the Debate

I.2a. Definition of Money. How money should be defined has been a subject of theoretical and empirical interest. What assets held by whom should be counted as money? One general approach has been to define money on *a priori* grounds. Within this approach, different criteria have been suggested: whether the asset serves as a medium of exchange, whether it is an item of "net wealth," whether a payment is "neutral" in its effect on the asset and interest rate structure, whether the decisions of the public affect the monetary total, whether the asset possesses liquidity (Friedman and Schwartz, 1970). Conceptual ambiguities characterize each of these criteria. An alternative approach has been to define money empirically on the basis of: cross-elasticity of substitution of financial assets, discriminant analysis of time-series characteristics, stability of the relationship between the definition of money and aggregate nominal income (Feige, 1964; Kaufman, 1969). Empirical studies have not yielded a unique definition, although the choice is confined in the main between a narrow definition (coin, currency, and demand deposits held by the public) and a broader definition (including also time and savings deposits at commercial banks with the exception since 1961 of large negotiable certificates of deposit).[5]

From the modern quantity theory viewpoint, whichever definition of money is used, the results of economic analysis or interpretations of past events are generally the same (Meltzer, 1969). Money is a unique asset that justifies distinguishing commercial banks from the nonbank public, on this view. Opposition to this view has been prominent in the literature on the role of financial structure and financial intermediaries discussed below (I.2c). On the opposing view, money is not unique, it is but one of a large family of assets, so that only a broader aggregate, such as the total amount of credit outstanding or total liquidity—undefined—

merits attention. This view distinguishes financial intermediaries from the rest of the public.

Keynesians who may accept the narrow definition of money may, nevertheless, dispute its significance. Their analysis emphasizes credit rather than money. They regard the *source* of an increase in money as the crucial question (Tobin, 1965a). If holders of assets switch from Treasury bills to money, according to them, no further consequences need follow. However, if money is acquired through a loan transaction, the borrower will want to spend the money. Hence the definition of money is a mere exercise in taxonomy. What is important is credit conditions, availability of credit, whether interest rates are rising or falling, and the intermediary functions of financial markets.

I.2b. Determinants of the Quantity of Money Outstanding. What determines and who controls the size of the money stock have been questions under active discussion in monetary economics. The analysis has been concerned with the U.S. quantity of money, although applicable to any fractional-reserve banking system. A variety of approaches has been developed. One (Friedman and Schwartz, 1963) uses an identity that relates money broadly defined to three proximate determinants: high-powered money (H), the deposit-reserve ratio (D/R), and the deposit-currency ratio (D/C), expressed as

$$M = H \frac{D/R \ (1 + D/C)}{D/R + D/C}$$

The money stock can therefore be expressed as a product of a multiplier consisting of the two ratios and high-powered money. Other approaches (Brunner and Meltzer, 1964; Burger, 1971; Teigen, 1964) have developed money supply functions incorporating the same major determinants but with different behavioral assumptions.

The three proximate determinants reflect respectively the behavior of the monetary authorities—in the United States, the Treasury and the Federal Reserve System—the commercial banks and the public. The monetary authorities provide high-powered money—the sum of bank reserves and currency—that the banks and public divide between themselves in light of the factors influencing the two sets of ratios. For an open economy with fixed exchange rates, however, *H* is largely determined by balance of payments considerations. The deposit-reserve ratio is affected by legal reserve requirements, banks' expectations of currency movements into and out of their vaults, and interest rates. The deposit-currency ratio is affected by interest rates, income, and the public's preference for holding coin and currency.

With respect to the question of control of the quantity of money, the issue has been whether the quantity of money is a largely autonomous variable controlled by the monetary authorities, or an endogenous variable determined by the banks and

the public. Modern quantity theorists accord the central bank the dominant role based on empirical evidence that through control of the issue of high-powered money it can offset any undesired change by the other actors in some short-run. Economists of a Keynesian bent, relying mainly on abstract models, argue that changes in monetary growth may be due to the responses of the banks and the public, not primarily the actions of the central bank, and may not be subject to short-run control.

I.2c. Determinants of the Demand for Money.

While the modern quantity theory postulates that the nominal quantity of money is an exogenous variable under the control of the monetary authorities, the theory regards the quantity of real money balances, defined by the money demand function, as an endogenous variable not under the control of the monetary authorities. The demand for real money balances is assumed to be highly stable and determined by factors independent of those affecting the supply of nominal money balances. In the modern quantity theory formulation, the demand for real money balances is a function of bond and equity yields, the expected rate of change of the price level, real income, the ratio of nonhuman to human wealth, and a taste variable—a relation based on capital theory. Empirical testing of the demand for money has accounted for a large fraction of studies in monetary economics.[6]

The modern quantity theory of the demand for real balances is a statement of a portfolio approach to the demand for money. In that respect it has a similarity to Keynesian portfolio choice explanations of the composition of portfolios of assets. These models, like the modern quantity theory, assume that at the margin the rate of return on each asset in the portfolio is equated, allowing for risk and transaction costs. An increase in the supply of an asset in the economy will lower its price relative to that of all other assets and lead wealth holders to substitute the asset for which the price has fallen for those assets for which the price has not, in an effort to restore the equality of marginal rates of return. As wealth holders react to changing asset yields, a chain of substitution effects is induced.

Where the modern quantity theory differs from the Keynesian portfolio choice analysis is in the role assigned to money in the link to economic activity. In the Keynesian models, an increase in money may lead only to substitutions among financial assets with no real effects. These models require detailed knowledge of the financial system and of the effects of portfolio changes on the structure of interest rates, asset yields, and the availability of credit, before they can be used to analyze real effects.[7]

In Keynesian formulations, moreover, the nominal and real quantity of money are often used interchangeably. The Keynesian liquidity preference function does not determine explicitly the equilibrium quantity of real money balances. It posits a negative relation between the quantity of money held and the interest rate; an increase in the rate of monetary growth is said to require a reduction in interest rates to induce the community to hold the existing quantity. But it is the real, not the

nominal, quantity of money desired that is negatively related to interest rates. A higher rate of monetary growth necessarily raises the real stock to be held only if prices do not also rise at a correspondingly higher rate. Implicitly, therefore, the liquidity preference function assumes that prices are unaffected by the monetary change.

By abstracting from the price level, Keynesians interchange nominal and real variables and treat the nominal and real money stock as policy variables. The liquidity preference function determines the interest rate, whereas in the modern quantity theory, the demand for money, given the quantity of money available to be held, determines the equilibrium stock of real balances. The quantity theory emphasizes discrepancies between actual and desired real balances to explain movements in nominal income and in the price level, focusing on the nominal quantity of money as the policy variable. Keynesians assume a given price level, emphasize the discrepancies between actual and potential output, and focus on interest rates. Stabilization policy is therefore based on monetary growth in the quantity theory and on the level of interest rates in Keynesian analysis.

1.2d. Role of Interest Rates.   From the modern quantity theory viewpoint, Keynesian emphasis on interest rates is misleading. It encourages central banks to regard the purpose of open market operations as control over interest rates rather than control over the money supply. The traditional central bank effort to moderate interest rate fluctuations is made at the cost of excessive fluctuations in monetary growth. In addition, interest rates are a faulty indicator of whether monetary policy is restrictive or expansionary.

In Keynesian analysis it is taken for granted that an increase in the quantity of money lowers interest rates and a decrease raises them. No distinction is made between nominal and real rates of interest. In recent empirical studies (Cagan, 1972; Gibson and Kaufman,1968), it has been shown that the initial effects of higher or lower monetary growth rates are temporary; they are swamped by the ensuing increase or decrease in demand for credit as income changes in response to change in monetary growth rates. In addition, the effects of price anticipations on interest rates will introduce a discrepancy between real and nominal rates of interest. Thus an increase in the quantity of money may lower interest rates in the very short run but the income effect of the monetary growth will quickly restore them to their former level. If monetary growth at the higher rate is sustained, it will ultimately raise interest rates above their initial level as it produces inflation (Sargent, 1969; Yohe and Karnosky, 1969). To the extent that lenders and borrowers anticipate changes in the purchasing power of money, bond prices will tend to be lower and nominal yields higher when prices in general are rising than when prices in general are falling, since the decline (or the rise) in the real value of the principal is a deduction from (or addition to) the nominal interest paid.

Accordingly, the modern quantity theory stresses that central banks will be misled if they regard the level of or change in market interest rates as an indication

of whether their own actions are expansionary or contractionary. To make that determination, central banks would be better advised to concentrate on changes in the money supply, a variable that they control and that is a relatively unambiguous indicator of monetary conditions. A central bank that will interpret falling interest rates as an indicator of monetary ease and therefore maintain a low or negative monetary growth will prolong an economic downturn. Similarly, high interest rates are not necessarily an effect of current restrictive monetary policy. A central bank that will maintain a high monetary growth rate in the belief that its actions are contractionary because interest rates are high will accelerate inflationary tendencies.

Finally, the modern quantity theory stresses that changes in market rates may be an unreliable guide to changes in the expected real rate of interest and hence may not be the variable influencing investment and consumption. Keynesians, in this view, confound nominal interest rates with unobservable real rates, the variable relevant for economic decisions.

I.2e. Role of Financial Intermediaries. This issue has links with the appropriate definition of money, the efficacy of control of the quantity of money and the stability of the demand for money. The phenomenal growth of financial intermediaries since World War II directed attention to their liabilities, which are almost as liquid as commercial bank deposits (Goldsmith, 1958). One study argues that the liabilities of nonbank financial intermediaries are close substitutes for currency and commercial bank deposits, that such liabilities may be expected to grow secularly relative to currency and bank deposits, to move invertedly to bank liabilities over business cycles, to increase the interest elasticity of the demand for money, and thereby frustrate attempts by monetary authorities to affect the economy by controlling the quantity of currency and bank deposits (Gurley and Shaw, 1960).[8] Hence the quantity of money should be defined as a broader concept, including liabilities of nonbank financial intermediaries. On this analysis, financial structure and development are crucial issues for monetary theory and policy, and commercial banks are not a class of institutions to be sharply set off from nonbank financial intermediaries.

The latter proposition has come to be known as "The New View" (Tobin, 1963a). It emphasizes similarities between commercial banks and intermediaries on the ground that, for both, creation of liabilities is limited by the public's demand for liquid assets. Except that banks must operate with legal reserve requirements and a prohibition of interest payments on their demand deposits—controls not imposed on nonbank financial intermediaries—there are no differences between the two classes of institutions. Banks, like any other nonbank financial intermediary, merely borrow from the public what they issue.

The view that money is not a unique asset because there are many close substitutes is enshrined in the *Report* of the Radcliffe Committee on the Working of the Monetary System (Radcliffe, 1959). If there is a decline in the quantity of

money, the *Report* argues, it will be offset by an increase in other liquid assets, or by an increase in velocity. The demand for money is highly variable on this analysis, and monetary policy will merely change the composition of liquid assets. The emphasis here is on intermediation and disintermediation.

The foregoing propositions of the literature on intermediaries are all theoretical. Their authors have not themselves attempted to subject them to empirical testing, but others have (Friedman and Schwartz, 1970, pp. 180–185). The studies show that various assets are substitutes for one another in some degree, but the evidence indicates, contrary to the financial intermediary literature, a decline in the interest sensitivity of money demand alongside the growth of money substitutes (Cagan and Schwartz, 1975), a conclusion for which a theoretical explanation had been advanced long before the empirical evidence was available (Marty, 1961). The hypothesis that the effect on spending of changes in money is offset by opposite changes in velocity is also not substantiated by the evidence: velocity usually changes procyclically with a change in money, enhancing, not offsetting, the effect of the monetary change. Nor has there been evidence of an increase in the cyclical variability of velocity, as has been alleged in the financial intermediary literature.

The five topics discussed above set the stage for the main subject of the debate between Keynesians and modern quantity theorists, to which we now turn.

I.3. Effects of Monetary Disturbances

The key proposition of the modern quantity theory is that a change in the rate of growth of money will produce a corresponding but lagged change in the rate of growth of nominal income. The source of the change in the monetary growth rate may vary depending on the given circumstances—an increase in gold output, government issues of fiat currency, central bank open market purchases of domestic earning assets or of inflows of claims on foreigners—but the relationship with subsequent change in the growth rate of nominal income is consistently observed (Bordo, 1975a). The reality of the lag in effect of monetary change is widely accepted, but estimates of the length of the lag vary (Hamburger, 1974).

I.3a. Transmission Process.   Since an early stage in the development of the modern quantity theory, a sketch of the transmission of monetary change to income change has been available (Friedman and Meiselman, 1963; Friedman and Schwartz, 1963b). The process starts with the creation of a discrepancy between the actual balances the community holds and the money balances it wants to hold. The actions the community takes to try to eliminate the discrepancy serve as the link between monetary change and income change.

If the nominal quantity of money that people hold happens to correspond at current prices to a real quantity of money larger than that which they want, they will raise the volume of their expenditures and thus the community's receipts, leading to a bidding-up of prices and perhaps an increase in output. The initial

excess of money balances will be eliminated, either by a reduction in the real quantity available to be held as a result of the price rise, or by an increase in the real quantity desired as a result of the increase in output.

In the opposite situation, if nominal balances happen to correspond to a smaller real quantity of money than people would like to hold, they will lower their expenditures and the community's receipts, driving down prices or output. The initial deficiency in the amount of money balances will be eliminated either by an increase in the real quantity available to hold as a result of the price fall, or by a decline in the real quantity desired as a result of the reduction of output.

When actual and desired money balances are in disequilibrium, flows of every conceivable sort may be affected in the process of altering stocks of financial and nonfinancial assets to restore equilibrium. The particular mechanical sequence that Keynes outlined from money to bonds to interest rates to investment expenditures and thence to income is one, but only one, possible channel of transmission of monetary change to income change. There is no reason to suppose that it is exclusive. A discrepancy between actual and desired money balances may also be eliminated by a change in spending on all manner of goods and services including consumption goods.

In the event of redundant money holdings, the initial impacts of the rise in expenditures are diffused as the range of existing assets affected widens. As a result, potential creators of assets now more in demand are induced to offer both new financial assets as well as new nonfinancial assets to a receptive market. Such activities as capital goods production, manufacture of consumer durables, and housing construction therefore expand. Once existing asset prices are bid up, potential purchasers find new financial and nonfinancial assets more attractive. The rise in the price level of nonfinancial assets in turn tends to make the acquisition of services cheaper relative to the purchase of sources of services, at the same time that wealth is rising relative to income. This raises demand curves for current productive services both for producing new capital goods and for purchase of current output of services. Thus the adjustment to a change in monetary growth that produces a divergence between actual and desired money balances involves substitution between money, existing assets, new production of assets and of services of assets.

The range of substitution in the modern quantity theory version of the transmission process is much wider than in the Keynesian version. Moreover, in the Keynesian version the transmission may be halted at the very start if velocity declines when real money balances are increased. Another possible blockage of the transmission can occur in the Keynesian version if redundant balances are spent on financial assets, the prices of which rise. Only if the concomitant decline in interest rates induces spending on real goods and services will transmission not be truncated at this juncture. Hence only if a change in the monetary growth rate affects interest rates and only if the change in interest rates affects spending will the transmission process operate to change income. In the Keynesian version, the

transmission process would be described as operating through effects on interest rates rather than through the elimination of discrepancies between desired and actual money holdings. Both descriptions would theoretically provide the same answer provided that the rates of interest affected included some that cannot be observed in the market, such as imputed rates used internally by households and firms.

In the Keynesian version, furthermore, the role of money would be subordinated to that of credit. Even with no change in the quantity of money, an increase in loans financed by shifting money balances from a holder of idle balances to a borrower will have spending effects, on this view. Therefore to determine whether spending effects will occur, one needs to consider credit availability, how lenders and borrowers react to changes in the structure of interest rates, and how financial markets operate to bring lenders and borrowers together. From a quantity theory viewpoint, a shift of money balances from one holder to another, with no change in the quantity available to be held, is unlikely to have any net spending effect.

1.3b. Fiscal vs. Monetary Policy. If any issue seems to differentiate a modern quantity theorist from a Keynesian, it is the impact of fiscal actions. According to Keynesians, monetary effects are important only when money is created to finance government expenditures. According to modern quantity theorists, the effect of federal government expenditures with a constant quantity of money is positive for a few quarters but is zero in the long run. Only if a deficit is financed by money creation will nominal income rise. It is not the deficit that is responsible but the increase in the quantity of money. Keynesians, on the other hand, argue that fiscal actions will have a direct effect on nominal income, no matter how they are financed. The reason is that in the absence of money creation, interest rates will rise as the expansionary effects on income increase the public's demand for money. This in turn will lead to a rise in velocity which will make possible a higher level of spending and of nominal income. Modern quantity theorists, however, argue that in the absence of money creation, a deficit financed by the sale of bonds to the public will have no net effect on spending and nominal income. The public will have less available to spend when the government spends more. The reason is that lenders who would otherwise be financing private sector investment are financing the government deficit. The rise in interest rates as a result of the Treasury's increased supply of government bonds will reduce private investment to the extent that government spending increases (Tobin, 1974; Friedman, 1974).

1.3c. Aggregates vs. Sectoral Detail. The difference in approach between Keynesians and modern quantity theorists extends to another aspect of the controversy between them. For the modern quantity theory analysis of the effects of monetary change, disaggregation is not essential. The analysis can proceed directly from monetary change to nominal income change. In the Keynesian approach, however, an estimate of national income could not be constructed except

by adding up sectoral detail. Each of the expenditure functions that have become the convention in national income accounting has to be estimated.

The difference in approach is paralleled by the types of models favored by each analysis. The modern quantity theory favors simple models that seek to identify relationships with great explanatory power for few variables. Keynesians favor elaborate structural models that seek to provide detail on many sectors. Modern quantity theorists argue that complexity does not guarantee that the structure of the model corresponds to economic reality or that it yields reliable forecasts. Keynesians argue that quantity theorists fail to specify the analytic structural model which could generate their empirical results.

I.3d. Price vs. Output Change. Allocative detail does, however, concern the modern quantity theory for the determination of the division of the change in aggregate income between change in price and change in output. The issues that have received attention have been largely in response to Keynesian conceptions.

The Keynesian tradition essentially has developed nonmonetary theories of the absolute price level, deemphasizing aggregate demand as the source of inflation—though acknowledging its employment effects—and emphasizing costs and aggregate supply (Fand, 1969). Cost inflation models attribute inflation to rising wages, as a result of wage push by unions, markup pricing, sectoral shifts, and administered prices, due to market power and bargaining strength. During the 1950's, creeping inflation was associated with a reduction in aggregate supply due to rising factor costs or to shifts in demand. More recently, inflation has been attributed to special influences—a worldwide boom, shortages of basic materials, crop failures, fuel shortages, and depreciation of the dollar in foreign exchange markets. Policy recommendations have included efforts to control the behavior of wages and prices directly through wage-price guidelines, incomes policy, indicative planning, and supply management. Restrictive monetary policy was downgraded in the 1950's as ineffective in lowering prices—it accomplished only reduction in output. This was so because liquid assets that are close substitutes for money would increase to the extent of any reduction in the quantity of money and because aggregate demand was functionally related to the total volume of liquid assets, not one component only, the quantity of money. Even with stable aggregate demand, it was assumed that an autonomous rise in factor costs would cause a reduction in aggregate supply and a rise in prices. At the close of the 1950's, Phillips Curve analysis came into vogue for deriving a tradeoff function, relating the unemployment rate and the rate of price change. On this view, society could choose the degree of inflation it would accept to achieve the unemployment rate it regarded as tolerable (Phillips, 1958; Lipsey, 1960).

The quantity theory of course has always posited a direct link between monetary growth rates relative to changes in the demand for money and the long-run rate of change of the price level. It stresses a distinction between forces that cause prices to rise in specific markets and a monetary stimulus to aggregate demand. Relative

price changes signal a change in either demand or supply conditions in specific markets, but not a change in total demand for all goods and services.

Developments in monetary economics in response to Phillips Curve analysis have stressed the absence of a price anticipations variable in that analysis, and that the relation as initially formulated treated a nominal variable—money wages—as if it were a real variable. Hence the tradeoff between unemployment and inflation is temporary, lasting only as long as the inflation is unanticipated (Friedman, 1968).

Associated with empirical studies of the Phillips Curve incorporating a price anticipations variable, there has been a theoretical development of the microfoundations of employment and inflation. These studies start from the proposition that nominal income is determined by aggregate demand which in turn is determined by monetary growth. The division of nominal income into real output and the price level depends on the effect of unanticipated monetary change on the behavior of firms and workers. Their behavior is dominated by lack of perfect knowledge about prices relevant to their decisions. Firms are unable to distinguish relative from general price movements. An unanticipated acceleration of monetary growth will lead to increased spending. Firms facing unexpectedly high nominal demands will interpret the development as special to them and expand output and employment. Their workers and suppliers regard the increase in demand as temporary and special and do not alter their anticipations. Accordingly, output responds more quickly than prices. As anticipations begin to change, prices and interest rates rise. Firms realize that the rise in demand was a general price change not warranting an increase in output, and workers demand an increase in wage rates that cuts employment back to what it was initially.

Alternatively, an unanticipated deceleration of monetary growth will lead to reduced spending. Firms facing unexpectedly lower nominal demand will regard the reduction initially as a temporary or random change with no price response warranted until anticipations catch up and the decline is seen as reflecting a longer-lasting condition. Again output declines before price. In general, information costs and relocation costs as well as other factors have been suggested as explanations of unemployment of resources and simultaneous stickiness of prices (Laidler, 1974).

These are the main themes around which the debate between Keynesians and modern quantity theorists has developed. We now turn to some miscellaneous questions that have been investigated in monetary economics.

I.4. Miscellaneous Issues

I.4a. Money in a Growth Model. The role of money in a growing economy has been studied in a multiplicity of models (Tobin, 1965 b; Levhari and Patinkin, 1968; Stein, 1970).[9] The intent of the models is to display the difference between a monetary and a barter economy. The analysis deals with the neutrality of

money in the context of economic growth and the possibility of using monetary policy to influence the growth of the economy.

In one model, the distinguishing feature of a money economy in a growth context was that the introduction of money results in a lower value of the capital-labor ratio than characterizes a barter economy (Tobin, 1965 b.) In effect, people substitute money holdings for physical capital. The objection was raised that there would be no reason for a money economy to develop if a barter economy yields greater physical output under the same conditions. The model was adjudged faulty since it provided no rationale for holding money.

According to the model, when money and physical capital are substitutes in portfolios, alternative rates of growth of the money stock are not neutral. They affect both the speed of adjustment to balanced growth and the characteristics of the growth path. Thus, inflation, by making money holding less attractive, would increase the amount of real saving available for investment in the accumulation of physical capital and thus increase physical output on the steady-state equilibrium growth path of the economy. This conclusion was also challenged.

Other models account for the development of a money economy by treating money either as a consumer good or a factor of production. Money has been incorporated into real growth models by assuming that the reason wealth holders include real money balances in addition to physical capital in their portfolios is that money balances provide utility to consumers. The other assumption is that money balances enter the production function as a producer good. Money from this point of view is an asset held because it facilitates production; that is, it is productive.

An alternative model (Levhari and Patinkin, 1968) specified that the savings ratio depended on the respective rates of return which can be earned on the physical assets and real money balances in which savings can be held. Hence the capital-labor ratio in the steady state of the money economy is not necessarily less than the ratio in the barter economy. And even when it is, this does not mean that the individuals in the economy are worse off, for they may derive utility from real money balances as well as from physical consumption.

As for the role of inflation, two effects on real income that work in opposite directions have been distinguished: (1) a lower rate of pecuniary return as a result of inflation lowers the utility yield of money balances, thereby lowering the proportion of national income available for investment in physical capital—this is growth inhibiting; (2) a lower rate of pecuniary return lowers the ratio of real balances desired to income and hence lowers the proportion of any given amount of savings that has to be invested in the accumulation of real balances as opposed to the accumulation of physical capital. This is growth-enhancing. Hence the results are ambiguous with respect to differences in the rate of inflation monetary authorities choose (Johnson, 1969). This argument has been disputed in turn, on the ground that individuals who find the imputed utility yield of real balances reduced by inflation may indeed prefer to hold a larger stock of physical capital as a partial

substitute for the imputed yield of real money balances (Marty, 1969).

As for the alternative approach in which money is treated as a producer good, money holdings *per se* are assumed not to generate utility. Real money balances are held by the business sector and are like any other inventory which enters into the process of production. Money balances make possible increased output of commodities. With the same level of the capital-output ratio, the steady-state value of per capita output will be larger in a monetary than a barter economy. The direction of effect of changing rates of inflation when money is treated as a producer good is inconclusive.

No general model has yet been developed in which money is simultaneously a consumption good yielding utility to the household and a producer good in the production function of firms. Moreover, the conception of money incorporated in real growth models needs to be broadened. Economic growth may be more responsive to the presence of financial intermediation than to the introduction of money *per se*. Financial intermediation may be more important for the savings ratio and the accumulation of real capital than is money in the prevailing analysis of growth models.

I.4b. Monetary Theory of the Balance of Payments. The preceding account of the issues under discussion in monetary economics is addressed to the case of a closed economy. As a corrective to that orientation, the case of an open national economy has recently become the focus of analysis in the monetary theory of the balance of payments (Frenkel, 1971; Johnson, 1976; Mundell, 1971).

The theory states that for an open economy with fixed exchange rates, the national stock of money, rather than prices, adjusts to changes in the public's demand for money. Contrary to the Hume price-specie flow mechanism—which postulates significant lags in the adjustment of prices—according to the monetary theory, no lags are observed in the movement of world prices because of instant arbitrage. In the most rigid version of the theory, an increase in the demand for money cannot reduce prices because prices of internationally traded goods are determined in world markets and kept comparable in different countries by international arbitrage, and prices of domestic goods and services are kept in line with prices of internationally traded goods by domestic arbitrage. The reduction in the public's demand for goods and securities leads to reduced imports and ex-panded exports on the goods side, and to higher interest rates and capital imports on the securities side. The current account or the capital account or both move into surplus. To prevent appreciation of the currency, the monetary authority buys foreign exchange from its nationals, paying out newly created high-powered money. The increase in high-powered money leads to a multiple expansion of the domestic quantity of money which continues until the public's demand is satisfied.

In open economies on a fixed exchange rate, a once-for-all increase in the quantity of money in one country and a decrease in another would produce a balance of payments deficit in the first and surplus in the second and lead to a flow

of money to the second until equilibrium was reestablished. If a monetary authority in one country alone increased high-powered money, that would be equivalent to an increase in the world money supply. That country would experience a temporary balance of payments deficit until the world money supply was redistributed in proportion to the size of the country of issue, and the world price level would rise accordingly. In the long run, domestic monetary policy in a small country has a negligible influence on international prices, although in the short run the monetary authority can affect its price and income level by open market sales (purchases) equal to its balance of payments surplus (deficit) that will maintain the national money stock below (above) its equilibrium value. The closer the links among world commodity markets, the higher the degree of capital mobility, the less scope for independent monetary policy in the short run. The greater the elasticity of substitution between traded and nontraded goods, the less successful will such policy be. In the long run, however, independent monetary policy is inconsistent with fixed exchange rates.

The theory has been spelled out with respect to the effect of devaluations, tariffs, common currency areas, but empirical work has barely started (Connolly and Swoboda, 1973). Under floating exchange rates, no surplus or deficit in the balance of payments need occur. Exchange rates can float up or down to clear the foreign exchange market. The domestic price level then depends on the autonomously determined supply of money, the public's demand for real money balances, and real output. Since countries typically have intervened in the exchange market, the actual outcome in recent years has been a mixture of fixed and floating exchange rate systems. Little work has been done comparing price and output changes and capital flows in the international system under fixed and floating exchange rates and on the role of both in a mixed system.

I.4c. Term Structure of Interest Rates.   The term structure—the pattern of rates on loans of successively longer maturity, usually riskless securities, and typically government debt—is a subject that has received much attention in monetary economics in recent years. Three aspects of the theory of the term structure have been debated: (1) expectations concerning the spot rates that will prevail in the future; on this view the current term structure forecasts future short-term interest rates, so that current long-term rates are an average of expected short-term rates in the future; (2) liquidity preference, denying that the current term structure provides unbiased forecasts of future interest rates and implying that investors have an aversion to risk of capital loss, so that they must be compensated by a liquidity premium for holding long-term securities; (3) market segmentation, assuming that short- and long-term rates respond virtually independent of each other to changes in the stock of loans of different maturities outstanding, with no switching between maturities in response to changes in relative prospective yields because investors are said to match maturities of their assets to those of their liabilities.

Empirical work to confirm the expectations hypothesis was presented in a seminal study (Meiselman, 1962). Meiselman argued that the expectations hypothesis asserts that the market attempts to forecast future rates, not that it is successful. He provided a means of determining from measurable market phenomena how expectations would change from period to period if his hypothesis were valid. He did not attempt to specify how expectations are formed.

Later work on the term structure accepted Meiselman's procedures but questioned his conclusions. The thesis of one such study was that forward rates—today's rates for money to be delivered in the future for some specified period—should be viewed not as a pure expectations rate, as Meiselman did, but as an expected rate and a liquidity premium. In effect, the revision of forward rates cannot be explained wholly by the forecast error, so that other variables can be introduced to explain changes in forward rates.

The question of how the premiums vary over the business cycle is not settled. The leading explanations of the premium have opposite implications about the cyclical pattern. One theory views short-term securities as partial substitutes for money balances, performing to a degree the same functions in large portfolios (Kessel, 1966). These securities provide a nonpecuniary return, representing the value of the services they perform as substitutes for money holding. On the margin, this nonpecuniary return equals the liquidity premium yielded by higher earning long-term bonds. Suppose an expansion in business activity raises the level of interest rates. Because money is more expensive to hold, money is exchanged for liquid short-term assets until the marginal value of services of the remaining money balances rises to equal the foregone return available on nonliquid long-term bonds. Short-term yields are therefore held down relative to long-term yields. Although interest rates rise, the slope of the yield curve rises, independently of any change in expectations of changes in rates. Liquidity premiums are therefore large at peaks. Conversely, at business cycle troughs, money balances are less expensive to hold, and investors will purchase short securities then only if their yield is not too far below the return on long-term securities. Liquidity premiums at troughs are then comparatively small.

A belief that interest rates sooner or later gravitate toward a normal level provides an explanation of fluctuations in liquidity premiums which has different implications for variations in the premiums (Malkiel, 1966). If an average of past yields reflects what appears to investors as normal at any time, when interest rates are relatively low, long securities should have a higher yield relative to short securities, since long securities are especially subject to capital loss. This implies an opposite direction of fluctuations in premiums than that suggested by the first theory. When interest rates are high, the investor regards the currently high short rate as temporary, so he regards an extra large capital gain on long securities as probable, and buys long securities, so depressing the yields. Liquidity premiums are then low. When interest rates are low, the investor avoids long securities unless they carry an extra premium. Liquidity premiums are then high.

One study concludes that the money-substitute theory outperforms the normal level of the rate theory for the short end of the yield curve and possibly also at the long end, though here the results are more tentative (Cagan, 1969).

An attempt to find a relation between the composition of the federal debt and the term structure of rates isolated a negligible effect on the term structure (Modigliani and Sutch, 1967).

There is general agreement that opportunities for further research on the term structure are plentiful. In particular, the formation of and change in expectations need clarification and the effects of other variables that might influence expectations other than forecast error are still not well formulated.

The foregoing survey of issues that have occupied participants in the field of monetary economics has touched on the highlights. Its purpose is to provide a norm against which to check the economic history literature of the recent past for evidence of the intellectual influence of the work in monetary economics. We turn to this examination in section II.

II. A SURVEY OF THE APPLICATION OF MONETARY THEORY TO ECONOMIC HISTORY

In this section we examine a considerable number of articles in the economic history literature of the past two decades to ascertain the impact of the research in monetary theory described in section I. Our survey is concentrated in the main on articles in four journals: *The Journal of Economic History, Explorations in Economic History, Journal of Political Economy, and Journal of Money, Credit and Banking.*[10] In our survey we examine two types of articles in monetary history: those which directly apply recent developments in monetary theory, and those which use theory of an older variety but which yield evidence of importance to monetary economics—e.g., discussions of the effects of monetary disturbances. We examine few books, because most seminal ideas appear in journal articles and because of a time constraint. However, two books stand out because of their strong influence on the subsequent literature: *A Monetary History of the United States, 1867–1960* (Friedman and Schwartz, 1963), and *The Jacksonian Economy* (Temin, 1969).

The survey is focused largely on U.S. economic history, 1834–1933, because the vast majority of recent work has concentrated there; but we also examine studies done for other countries, especially Great Britain, Sweden, Canada and Japan, and studies for times as early as the middle ages.

The section is divided into five broad subheads, largely corresponding to items covered in section I. Section II.1 examines the influence of *A Monetary History of the United States* as background for subsequent studies. Section II.2 uses the classification scheme of section I.2 (except for financial intermediaries) in order to trace the influence of recent theory. Section II.3 surveys the literature examining the historical relationship between the quantity of money and real income and the

price level—and particularly the effects of monetary disturbances on these aggregates. Section II.4 looks at the historical literature on monetary disturbances under fixed and flexible exchange rates, on the Hume price-specie flow mechanism, and on the monetarist approach to the balance of payments (corresponding to section I.4b). Finally, section II.5 examines the literature on financial development. This encompasses three topics: money and economic growth (corresponding to I.4a), financial intermediation (I.2e), and the term structure of interest rates (I.4c).

II.1. Background

The most influential work in monetary history of the past twenty years has been *A Monetary History of the United States 1867–1960* (Friedman and Schwartz 1963). This study has set the tone for much of the subsequent literature in the United States and abroad. The book is a monumental study of the quantity of money and its influence on economic activity in the U.S. economy over nearly a one-hundred-year span, marked by drastic changes in monetary arrangements and in the structure of the economy.

The authors find that changes in the behavior of money are closely associated with the rate of change of nominal income, real income and the price level. Secularly they find a close relationship between the growth of money and nominal income and prices, independent of the growth of real income. Cyclically they find a close relationship between the rate of change of money and of subsequent changes in nominal income. As well, the authors find a number of remarkably stable relationships over the period. These include: (a) that velocity exhibits a steady secular decline of a little over one percent per annum until after World War II, a decline which is attributed to money being a luxury good; (b) that the relationship between U.S. prices and prices in other countries, adjusted for the exchange rate, changed little over the period, evidence of the strength of the purchasing power parity theory.

However, of most interest to us is the finding that the money-income relationship is invariant to changes in monetary arrangements and banking structure. These changes are captured in the arithmetic of the proximate determinants of the money supply. Over the long run, high-powered money (H) is the key determinant, then the deposit-reserve ratio (D/R) and the deposit-currency ratio (D/C); over the cycle the ratios become more important, expecially in severe contractions, when the D/C ratio dominates.

The different monetary arrangements since 1867 include: (1) the greenback episode, 1861–1878, when the United States had flexible exchange rates with the rest of the world and the money supply became an independent variable; (2) the gold standard period, 1879–1914, when the quantity of money became largely a dependent variable determined by the country's trading relationship with the rest of the world; (3) the gold exchange standard, from 1919 to 1934, when the quantity of M, though partly determined by external conditions, was also heavily

influenced by Federal Reserve monetary management; (4) the period since World War II of managed money under a dollar standard.

In addition, there were several important changes in the banking structure. These include: the establishment of the national banking system (1864); the establishment of the Federal Reserve (1914); and the institution of the F.D.I.C. (1934), which finally solved the problem of banking panics.

Finally the authors demonstrate that in most cases changes in M were independent in origin from changes in economic activity—the most notable examples being the gold discoveries in the 1890's, wartime issues of fiat currency, and the restrictive actions of the Federal Reserve in 1920–1921 and 1937–1938. Although they identify an influence from income to money over the business cycle, yet it is argued that the main influence both secularly and cyclically runs from money to income.

This book has spawned several types of research in the last thirteen years. These include:

a) A large number of articles extending the Friedman and Schwartz approach to other countries and other times, in identifying the proximate determinants of the money supply and examining the relationship between changes in money, prices and income.

b) Articles critical of their interpretation of particular historical episodes. For example, see Wicker (1965, 1966) for a reinterpretation of their explanation of Federal Reserve policy, 1919–1933. Also, see Duggar and Rost (1964), for a reinterpretation of the influence of Treasury cash on high-powered money in the 1880's; and Goodhart (1965) and James (1976), for a different explanation of the low issue of national bank notes, 1900–1913 and 1875–1900. Finally, see Aghelvi (1975) for a different explanation of how specie flows affected the money supply in the period 1879–1914.

c) Articles critical of the luxury good hypothesis. First, Timberlake (1974) argues that the secular fall in V can be explained by denominational shortages in the U.S. economy before 1879. He argues that V is downward biased because estimates of nominal income assume all real product is sold in the market, yet a significant nonmonetary sector existed in the nineteenth century U.S. economy. Over time, as the monetized sector increases, while money holding habits remain constant, measured V will decline, reflecting a bias. According to Timberlake, denominational shortages would encourage the continuation of barter. As the denominational constraints lessened after 1879, the cost of monetization fell and with barter reduced to a small fraction of income the downward trend in V ceased. Evidence of a significant increase in lower denomination money after 1879 supports his case.

Jonung (1976) finds that velocity in Sweden, as in the United States and Great Britain, exhibited a similarly declining trend in the nineteenth century. However, he attributes this trend to increased monetization of the Swedish economy and the spread of commercial banking.

Finally, Friedman and Schwartz have revised their interpretation of the decline in V (Schwartz, 1975). In a study comparing U.S. with U.K. velocity from 1879 to the present, Schwartz reports that before 1905 V in the U.S. falls much more rapidly than in the U.K.; after that date the series move parallel to each other. Friedman and Schwartz attribute the different behavior of the two series to increasing financial sophistication in the U.S. before 1905, and consequently adjust the U.S. velocity level series downwards, and the rate of change of velocity series upwards.

d)   Articles on the Great Depression. In *A Monetary History*, Friedman and Schwartz attributed the massive decline in prices and real output in the U.S. 1929–1933 to an unprecedented decline in the quantity of money (see section I.1). This fall in M was largely caused by bank failures in 1930–1931 and 1933, although they argue it could have been prevented by active monetary policy. Recently Temin (1976) has attacked the Friedman and Schwartz view by arguing that since there was no evidence of a rise in short-term interest rates 1929–1931 (short-term rates fell), then bank failures could not have caused the fall in the quantity of money. Rather, he argues, a fall in income produced by a decline in autonomous consumption expenditures led to a fall in the demand for money which, interacting with an interest-elastic money supply function, produced the fall in M and in short-term interest rates.

Unfortunately, Temin begins his analysis in August, 1929. Had it started in April, 1928, when the Federal Reserve sharply reduced the rate of monetary growth, he would have observed a rise in short-term interest rates between March, 1928, and September, 1929. Then as the lagged effects of monetary change affected prices and output in 1929, interest rates declined. Moreover, Temin neglects the distinction between nominal and real interest rates, misinterpreting the fall in interest rates as indicating monetary ease. Similarly, his emphasis on the rise in real money balances, 1929–31, as proof that the decrease in the stock of money could not have lowered the level of real expenditures overlooks the distinction between actual and desired money balances.

Other studies critical of Friedman and Schwartz include Kirkwood (1972), who uses a structural model similar to Temin's, and Gramm (1972), who presents evidence that a perverse real balance effect made the depression worse than it otherwise would have been.

II.2. Essential Elements in the Debate

Under this heading we briefly categorize the articles surveyed, according to their direct application of the new advances in monetary theory, discussed in section I.2.

Few pieces in the recent economic history literature are directly concerned with the debate between Keynesians and modern quantity theorists, and most of these focus on the interpretation of the Great Depression in the United States.

As noted above, Temin (1976) challenged Friedman and Schwartz's emphasis on the monetary origins of the contraction of 1929–1933. For "the money hypothesis," he substituted a modified version of "the spending hypothesis." According to the original version, a fall in income and prices was produced by the multiplier effects of a fall in autonomous spending (consumption and investment), supposedly caused by an oversupply of housing and by the stock market crash. In Temin's view, though the crash reduced consumption through adverse effects on the community's wealth, it was not crucial. Of greater importance to consumption expenditures was an agricultural depression originating abroad. Nevertheless, based on regression results, he argued that consumption declined much more than can be explained by the stock market crash and by poor harvests in 1930. Moreover he did not find evidence in favor of a massive decline in investment expenditures. Thus he concluded that an unexplained decline in autonomous consumption expenditure was the likely cause of the decline in economic activity, 1929–1931. After that period, following Kindleberger (1973), he regarded international forces as dominant.

A structural model of the U.S. economy, 1929–1939, following the Keynesian approach, has been constructed (Kirkwood, 1972). Simulations of the model lead to the conclusion that a liquidity trap existed, and hence monetary policy was impotent. This result runs contrary to the findings of the more careful demand for money studies of Brunner and Meltzer (1968) and Gandolfi (1974). In addition, for Kirkwood, the stock market crash was important in turning an excess capacity recession into a depression, and a fall in investment was responsible for the depression. In his view, massive government expenditure could have extricated the economy from the depression.

The real-balance effect during the depression has been studied (Gramm, 1972). It is alleged that a falling price level led to a perverse real-balance effect rather than the commonly accepted positive effect on consumer expenditures. The author argues, following Pesek and Saving (1967), that demand deposits can be regarded as part of the community's net wealth (see footnote 9). A fall in the price level reduced the deposit-currency ratio, *ceteris paribus*, because depositors perceived an increased probability of default on financial assets held by banks, reflecting their increased liability in terms of goods.[11] The fall in the D/C ratio induced banks to reduce their deposit-reserve ratio because of the increased probability of redemption. Thus the fall in the price level caused by a reduction in the money supply led to a further decline in the money supply by reducing the money supply multiplier. Tests of the model yielded negative effects of the price level on the D/C ratio and a negative wealth effect on consumption.

Finally a recent study asked whether the method by which money is introduced into the economic system matters (Bordo, 1975a). For Keynesians, the source of new money matters because of possible effects on the community's financial portfolio, whereas for the modern quantity theorists, first-round effects may exist but are considered to be unimportant (see I.2a, above). The author compares

different subperiods in U.S. monetary history, 1834–1914, which had different sources of monetary change, ranging from gold discoveries, to bank money, to silver, to fiat issues. Statistical tests revealed that the money-income relationship was not significantly affected by the source of monetary change.

II.2.a The Definition and Origin of Money.   In the literature surveyed there was little mention of the empirical approach to the definition of money. An *a priori* theory of the origins of money, with examples from the economic history of ancient Greece, has been presented (Hicks, 1970). Hicks argued that, with the development of exchange, merchants (middlemen) often became dealers in two types of commodities: a commodity in which the merchant specialized, and a commodity which was widely traded. This second good was usually one which was storeable, easily hidden and durable. Precious metals served this store of value function well. Soon after that, this general commodity served as a standard of value, if divisible and of uniform quality, and as a medium of exchange, if widely accepted. The government became involved with coinage once it was realized that taxes collected in the form of generalized purchasing power were more valuable than taxes collected in the form of specific commodities. In a similar vein, North and Thomas (1973), in their discussion of the economic development of Western Europe, analyzed the role of money as an efficient means of reducing the transactions costs of barter.

II.2b. Determinants of the Quantity of Money Outstanding.   Of numerous historical studies on the supply of money, most have followed the approach taken by Friedman and Schwartz (1963) and Cagan (1965). Cagan examined both the determinants and effects of changes in the quantity of money in the United States, 1875–1960. He found that changes in the public's currency-money ratio (C/M) contributed most to cycles in the rate of change in the money stock, equaling the contribution of high-powered money and the banking system's reserve ratio (R/D). This is in contrast to secular movements in M, which were largely explained by movements in H. He then isolated the sources of change in each of these determinants. Under the gold standard, the key source of change in H, both secularly and cyclically, was changes in the monetary gold stock, while under flexible exchange rates, 1861–1878, as well as since 1914 in periods of managed currency, it was the operations of the monetary authorities: the Treasury and the Federal Reserve Banks. The public's long-term desired currency-money ratio was explained by the net return on deposits, growth in real income, and urbanization; over cyclical periods, by expectations of financial stability. Finally, the key determinants of the banking system's reserve ratio in the long run were: legal reserve requirements and institutional changes in the monetary system that improved stability and lessened the need of banks for cash reserves; while cyclical movements in the ratio reflected changes in interest rates and in the demand for bank loans.

Studies that adopted the aforementioned approach cover the antebellum period in the United States (Stevens, 1971; Macesich, 1960; Temin, 1969); 1925–1934 (Courchene, 1969) and 1875–1958 in Canada (Hay, 1968); 1834–1844 in England (Adie, 1972); 1938–1954 in France (Meltzer, 1959); 1871–1972 in Sweden (Jonung, 1975b).

II.2c. Determinants of the Demand for Money. Only a few of the articles surveyed explicitly used and/or tested the modern theory of the demand for money, which views the quantity of desired real balances as a stable function of real income or wealth, the opportunity cost of holding money (the interest rate), price expectations, and other expectational variables (see I.2c, above).

A test of the stability of the demand for money in the United States during 1929–1933, using cross-section state data, showed the demand function to be stable with no evidence of a liquidity trap (Gandolfi, 1974).

Cagan's model of the demand for money in periods of hyperinflation (Cagan, 1956) was tested with data for the Soviet Union 1921–1926 (Pickersgill, 1968). The demand for real balances was expressed as a function of expected price change (based on black-market prices, adjusted for rationing) and real income. The author found coefficients of adjustment of actual to expected price change similar to those found by Cagan, in his study of seven European hyperinflations in the post-World War I period, and the demand function to be stable between periods of hyperinflation and in normal times.

A cross-section demand for money function was estimated across states for the years 1840, 1850 and 1860 (Rockoff, 1975). The author expressed real per capita balances as a function of real income per head, urbanization and a series of dummy variables, in an attempt to account for the impact on financial development of different state government regulations—free banking, usury laws and mutual savings bank regulations.

Finally, an estimate of the demand for money for the United States and the United Kingdom, 1878–1970, has been reported (Schwartz, 1975). Finding similar income and interest elasticities, Schwartz combined the data and found that the results of a common demand function suggest that the United States and the United Kingdom constituted a unified financial entity with respect to the behavior of velocity.

II.2d. Money and Interest Rates. One historical study deals directly with the relationship between money and interest rates (Harley, 1977), although in another study a Keynesian model of the money market in the antebellum era takes the interest rate as the only channel through which monetary forces affect the economy (Sushka, 1976).

Harley tested for Great Britain, 1873–1913, Fisher's explanation of the Gibson paradox, i.e., that sustained changes in the price level produce expectations of future price change that are incorporated in market interest rates with a lag. The

model expressed movements in the short-term interest rate as a function of: expected price change, the ratio of money to income (M/Y) (the liquidity effect), and a variable to account for short-term money market expectations—the ratio of gold in the Bank of England to total liabilities (BR). Harley found that in the period of secular deflation, 1873–1890, past movements in the price level (using geometrically declining weights) explained most of the variation in interest rates. His mean lag of 7.6 years is considerably smaller than that found by Fisher (1930). The other variables tested were also significant. The results for the period of secular inflation, 1897–1913, were similar. However, for the period of transition between deflation and inflation, 1890–1896, M/Y and BR become more important. The author concluded that the combination of expectations of deflation as well as the effects of new gold reduced the real rate of interest as well as the nominal rate. The decline in the real rate stimulated an economic boom in the 1890's which helped reverse price expectations and raise the nominal interest rate.

II.3. Monetary Disturbances and Economic Activity

At least 25 articles of those we surveyed deal with the effects of monetary disturbances on economic activity. We examine the evidence chronologically, first for the United States, then for other countries. Following this review, we examine the literature for studies dealing with issues discussed in section I.3, a-d.

As a preview, we note a study of the evidence on secular price change since ancient times (Schwartz, 1973). The author found a close association between changes in the price level and in the ratio of money per unit of real output in virtually every period examined. The only exception appears to be the Great Debasement in England, 1542–1551. In that episode, when money doubled, prices less than doubled; then when money declined by one third, prices did not change. Moreover, the money per unit of output-price relationship holds despite different sources of monetary change (gold in earlier times, bank notes and paper currency more recently).

II.3a. The United States.   U.S. monetary history is ripe with experiments for the monetary historian, from Colonial currency issues, to Revolutionary War paper issues, the Bank War, gold discoveries, the Civil War, Reconstruction, the gold standard, and now the dollar standard.

One of the earliest studies related monetary change to output over the period 1835–1885 (Warburton, 1958). Using relatively crude data, the author offered evidence that changes in M tend to precede changes in output in business cycles. His evidence also showed that changes in M, largely produced by changes in H, were independent of changes in income.

Monetary theory and the available evidence have been used to shed light on frequently raised issues about Colonial currency (Weiss, 1970). According to the evidence, currency issues as well as rates of price change varied markedly across the Colonies. Weiss argued, contrary to the accepted view, that significant infla-

tion, in terms of local currency, is evidence of overissue rather than dearth. Moreover, in his view, a successful flexible exchange rate system operated between the colonies.

Another study, based on a money supply series for the Jacksonian period, demonstrated that the monetary instability in the period 1834–1845 was not caused primarily by the Bank War and Jacksonian policy but rather was produced by external events (Macesich, 1960). The author argued that, given that the United States was part of the international specie standard, internal prices had to adjust to external prices, and how they did so did not matter. Macesich isolated the different determinants of monetary change and found that changes in the ratio of the public's holdings of deposits plus notes to specie and the ratio of the banks' liabilities to specie explained most of the change in M, reflecting uncertainty engendered by the Bank War.

A later study followed Macesich in arguing that the Bank War and subsequent Jacksonian policies were not responsible for the monetary instability of 1834–1843 (Temin, 1968, 1969). The approach was basically similar to Macesich's, but attached greater importance to changes in H, and less to the ratios, in explaining monetary movements. Temin argued, first, that the traditional view, that destruction of the Second Bank of the United States would encourage state banks to increase their lending, does not agree with the evidence, since the reserve ratio of commercial banks did not decline after 1834 in the South and West relative to the rest of the country, nor over the economy as a whole. He regarded the key source of change in the money supply in this period to be specie flows, but unlike Macesich did not attribute them to British capital inflows, but rather to Mexican silver.[12] He attributed the panic of 1837 to a fall in H, induced by a specie outflow to Britain, following a harvest failure there. The difference between Temin's and Macesich's interpretation of the events of 1834–1843 seems to stem from different methods used to construct their money supply series.[13]

Another study examined the economic impact of free banking (Rockoff, 1974). The author disputed the traditional view that free banking, which resulted from the destruction of the policing power of the Second Bank, led to wildcat banks and significant monetary instability. Rockoff found the incidence of wildcatting to be low, and serious in only one state, Michigan, 1837–1838; losses sustained by note holders were negligible. Finally, estimating the demand for money across states, he determined that the welfare loss, associated with the reduction in real balances, worked out to less than $1.00 per person in 1860.

U.S. monetary history, 1842–1861—a period characterized by free banking, the Independent Treasury and the California Gold discoveries—has also been reevaluated (Stevens, 1971). According to the evidence presented, the period of the gold discoveries exhibited a decline in the public's ratio of notes and deposits to specie, and a rise in the banks' ratio of monetary liabilities to specie. In the author's view, this contradicts the traditional view that the gold discoveries led to a

proportional expansion in bank money. The reason given for the perverse behavior of the ratios is that the public substituted higher quality (lower transactions and information cost) specie for bank money in a period when specie became more available. At the same time, the banks reduced their reserve ratios, because of improved investment opportunities, observed in a higher rate of interest.

Shetler (1973) disputed Stevens's results by critically examining the data sources on the outstanding specie stock.[14] He adjusted for errors in the California Mint figures, removed California from the sample, and excluded the Federal government from the definition of the public. With these revisions, the ratio of the public's holdings of bank money to specie did not decline nearly as much as Stevens alleged. Thus Shetler restored the traditional view of the effects of the gold discoveries.

Inflation in the Confederacy, 1861–1865,[15] and the conditions for a successful return to the gold standard following the greenback episode, 1862–1878, have both been analyzed (Lerner, 1955, 1956; Kindahl, 1961). The worst inflation in U.S. history occurred in the Confederacy, which financed the war mainly by printing money. Lerner showed that less money was created by banks in the South per dollar of money created by the Confederacy than by banks in the North per dollar of money created by the Union. Two other factors contributed to the accelerated rise of the ratio of money to output in the South. Holders of Confederate notes in occupied Southern territory shipped them to areas still under Confederate control, and at the same time the base of real output contracted. Moreover, velocity rose markedly in the South, and possibly not at all in the North. Hence inflation was eight times worse in the South.

The return to the gold standard after the war required restoring the former purchasing power parity with Britain and a reduction of the premium on gold to zero. Kindahl (1961) showed that the way in which resumption was achieved was through a passive monetary policy. (For a different view, see Timberlake, 1975). The government did not allow M to grow through increases in H, so that it was constrained to grow solely through increases in bank money. The slow growth in M, coupled with a decline in V and rapid growth in real output, allowed the price level to fall sufficiently to enable the United States to resume payments.

It is clear that the literature on monetary disturbances in the United States is abundant. We now turn to research on other countries.

II.3b. Canada.   To test the relationship between monetary growth and real output over the business cycle, Hay (1967) constructed Canadian money supply estimates from 1871 on. He found lags of business cycles behind money similar to those discovered in Friedman's study for the United States (Friedman, 1961). He then examined the linkage between the U.S. cycle in monetary growth and the Canadian monetary growth cycle, observing a close relationship in the downswing between U.S. and Canadian monetary growth but not in the upswing, when U.S. output growth appears to be more closely related to Canadian output growth.

II.3c. England. Was a decline in the quantity of money, or the Black Death responsible for the apparent recession in fourteenth- and fifteenth-century England? Miskimin (1964) argued that the Black Death led to an increase in the monetized sector and raised the amount of wealth per head. This led to an increase in expenditure on inputs, a balance of trade deficit, a specie outflow and an apparent shortage of money.

Closer to the present, the determinants of the English money supply for 1834–1844 have been analyzed (Adie, 1972). To derive the monetary series involves combining the liabilities of four types of institutions: a) the Bank of England, b) the London joint stock banks, c) issuing country banks and d) nonissuing country banks. Over the ten-year period, as well as for year-to-year changes, unlike the U.S. experience, the ratio of the public's holdings of bank liabilities to specie was the key determinant. Next in importance was the ratio of the banks' liabilities to specie, and then H. There was a weak association between changes in money and changes in nominal income, coupled with a much stronger one betwen monetary changes and changes in real income. For Adie, the state of the harvest is the key determinant of the public's monetary liability-specie ratio, low wheat prices leading to a high ratio, which raises M, and also reduces the demand for money. Simultaneously, a good harvest, by stimulating a favorable balance of payments,

Closer to the present, the determinants of the English money supply for 1834–1844 have been analyzed (Adie, 1972). To derive the monetary series involves combining the liabilities of four types of institutions: a) the Bank of England, b) the London joint stock banks, c) issuing country banks and d) nonissuing country banks. Over the ten-year period, as well as for year-to-year changes, unlike the U.S. experience, the ratio of the public's holdings of bank liabilities to specie was the key determinant. Next in importance was the ratio of the banks' liabilities to specie, and then H. There was a weak association between changes in money and changes in nominal income, coupled with a much stronger one between monetary changes and changes in real income. For Adie, the state of the harvest is the key determinant of the public's monetary liability-specie ratio, low wheat prices leading to a high ratio, which raises M, and also reduces the demand for money. Simultaneously, a good harvest, by stimulating a favorable balance of payments, leads to a rise in H and then M.

There is a test of the Keynesian view (Keynes, 1930) that falling prices and output in the United Kingdom in the 1920's reflected attempts to return to gold at the prewar parity (Lothian, 1972). A considerable slowdown in monetary growth, 1919–1921, came after prices had been rising at more than 10 percent per annum in the previous six years. All of the decline in nominal income that ensued, 1921–1925, first appeared in real output, then in prices. Also V fell as people began to adjust to deflation.[16] In 1925–1929, as in the period of resumption in the United States, money grew less than real output, allowing prices to fall. Lothian also found that H was the key determinant of monetary change, supporting the view that

the Bank of England followed a policy of conscious deflation to facilitate the return to gold. Finally, he used regression analysis to show that variations in money explain most of the variations in income, that the demand for money is a stable function of real income per head and the interest rate, and that M was exogenous in this period.

II.3d. Sweden. The simple quantity theory has been applied to early Swedish data (Eagly, 1967). Sweden has had a central bank since 1688. In the mid-eighteenth century the Swedish government used the central bank as an engine for economic development. As a result, the quantity of bank notes increased at greater than 10 percent per year, 1745–1762. Apparently this stimulated output, but it also led to rapid inflation and forced Sweden to go to a flexible exchange rate.

The rate of inflation in Sweden has been related to the growth of money per unit of output, over the period 1732–1972 (Jonung 1975a). A close relationship exists over long periods and in wartime—less so in other, shorter periods. Jonung observed a closer relationship between M and P also in periods of flexible exchange rates, when the central bank controlled H, than in periods of fixed rates, when foreign price changes determined domestic price movements.

II.3e. Other Countries: Nigeria, Japan and China. The cowrie shell currency, prevalent in West Africa from 1600 to 1895, satisfied all the properties of money (Nwami, 1975). It was portable, transferable and storeable. Also the cowrie was relatively scarce and had a nonmonetary use. As a result, it was for several centuries a stable commodity currency. The system broke down when European traders began to import cowries from Asia and Europe. This produced a massive inflation in the last half of the nineteenth century, reflected in the shilling-cowrie exchange rate.

From 1868 to 1897, while Japan was on a silver standard, the Bank of Japan could successfully pursue a policy of rapid monetary growth to stimulate development (Patrick, 1965). Then, when Japan adopted the gold standard in 1897, she ran into a conflict between internal and external policy goals (see II.4 below), which produced a balance of payments deficit and a reserve outflow. To offset this, the Japanese began allowing foreign investment into the country.

In China's bimetallic system, 1650–1830, both copper and silver circulated side by side as currencies with flexible exchange rates (Chen, 1974). Across regions, and even industries, preferences for one type of currency relative to the other differed, largely reflecting different income elasticities. High transport and transactions costs between regions also allowed the bimetallic rates to vary from place to place. Thus regional divergences in currency preferences, together with flexible bimetallic exchange rates, may have been equivalent to flexible exchange rates among currency areas. The system broke down between 1800–1850, with increased importation of opium leading to a silver outflow. This produced an economy-wide deflation (although it would have been worse if the economy had been on a pure silver standard), as well as social unrest, since all taxes were fixed in

terms of silver, and most low-income people received their incomes in copper. According to Chen, attempts to impose a unified currency area using paper money backed by silver would probably not have succeeded, because of the government's inability to conduct proper monetary management.

II.3f. Issues in the Determination of Monetary Effects. We turn from this review of the literature on the effects of monetary disturbances to studies bearing on specific issues involved in their determination . We were unable to find any research that attempts to trace out the transmission mechanism by which monetary change affects economic activity within a country (I.3a). Only two studies of the Great Depression directly compare fiscal and monetary policy (Kirkwood, 1972; Temin, 1976). With respect to the level of aggregation, several papers adopt the Keynesian structural model approach (Kirkwood, 1972; Aghelvi, 1974). Aghelvi has tested a structural model of the U.S. balance of payments under the gold standard. Perhaps the lack of reliable data in earlier times has deterred the large-scale model builders. Finally, the tradeoff between prices and output has been examined in a historical context—namely, the period of the Napoleonic Wars in Great Britain, which was characterized by rapid inflation and significant unemployment (Savin and Mokyr, 1976). According to the authors, a series of unanticipated shocks (harvest failures, the continental blockade and increased government expenditures) led to a shift of resources from the nonagricultural to the agricultural sector. Unemployment occurred, because the labor force was not completely mobile nor wages completely flexible. At the same time the price level rose, because of a fall in real income, a rise in velocity (as government debt increased at the expense of desired real balances), and an increase in M.

II.4. The Open Economy

We next examine the literature on the effects of monetary disturbances on prices and output in the open economy—an important issue for most countries in the world today and in preceding centuries. Then we examine the literature on the transmission mechanism of monetary changes between countries. Finally, we briefly discuss the issues of unified currency area formation, the monetary approach to balance of payments theory, and monetary policy under the gold standard.

II.4a. Monetary Disturbances in the Open Economy. It is widely accepted that under fixed exchange rates a small economy has little control over its domestic money supply and that its price level is determined by its relationship with the outside world. It is only when a country is on a flexible exchange rate that the money supply can be treated as an independent variable and domestic prices and economic activity can be insulated from foreign monetary disturbances.

Both Macesich (1960) and Temin (1969) argued, using a model of a small open economy under fixed rates, that U.S. monetary disturbances were largely caused

by events abroad, which precipitated specie flows, and/or adjustment of the D/C or D/R ratios, to produce a money supply consistent with purchasing power parity at the fixed dollar price of gold (see II.3a, above). However an alternative view of this period and of the whole nineteenth-century U.S. experience under the gold standard has been offered (Williamson, 1961, 1963). Williamson disagrees with Macesich on the issue of external influences on the adjustment under the specie standard. He argued that we must consider the balance of payments in a general equilibrium context. According to his theory, it is the long swing cycle in the growth of real output that determines specie and capital flows. Increased real growth leads to both an excess demand for goods (a balance of trade deficit), an excess supply of bonds (a capital inflow), and an excess demand for real balances. The excess demand for money is satisfied by a specie inflow, with little change in the price level, while at the same time we observe a long swing in capital inflows. Moreover, he argued, the external balance is both a cause as well as a reflection of the long swing, since in the 1830's it was British demand for U.S. cotton that was the key source of the long swing in output, the increased output of which then induced British investment in railroads and canals. The important question that arises is whether Williamson is describing an income effect which increases the speed of adjustment to external disturbances or a different causal ordering.

In a similar vein, it has been argued that the truth lies somewhere between the Macesich and Williamson approaches (Willett, 1968). For Willett, during the free banking era, in the short run, banks could satisfy their excess demands for money without importing specie, because an increase in the demand for money would call forth an increase in bank-created money. This apparent extension of the real bills doctrine produces the modern result that the banking system can temporarily sterilize specie flows.

In contrast to the fixed exchange rate (specie standard) case, U.S. experience with flexible exchange rates in the greenback episode may be considered (Kindahl, 1961; Wimmer, 1975). Kindahl described the mechanism by which the government, acting as an independent authority, engineered the return to gold parity (see II.3a). Wimmer, on the other hand, illustrated the operation of the exchange market under flexible exchange rates by analyzing the events of Black Friday, September 24, 1869. Traditionally, this episode has been viewed as an example of destabilizing speculation. The evidence, however, is consistent with Friedman's view that speculation under flexible rates is stabilizing (Friedman, 1953), as Wimmer showed.[17]

II.4b. Currency Areas.   Two papers discussed the problems of formation in earlier times of unified national currency areas—areas which use a common currency (i.e., have perfectly fixed exchange rates between regions) and in which factors of production and goods are mobile (Fraas, 1974; Chen, 1974).

Fraas looked at the operation of the Second Bank of the United States from the mid-1820's to the Bank War. The preceding decade was characterized by regional

flexible exchange rates between the East and West. Price trends diverged markedly between the regions and western bank notes circulated at a considerable discount in the East. The Second Bank succeeded, in the mid-1820's, in creating a unified currency area across the country, by limiting credit in its western branches relative to the East and forcing all its correspondent banks to redeem their notes in specie. This policy quickly reduced the discount on western notes and led to a convergence of the two price levels.

Chen analyzed the operation of flexible bimetallic exchange rates within China, 1600–1850 (see II.3e). He argued that the system persisted so long, despite its apparent cumbersomeness, because it might have been an example of a system of optimum currency areas (Mundell, 1968). During a period of low factor mobility between regions, when government influence was weak, flexible bimetallic exchange rates between silver and copper could have served the function of arranging currency areas along regional and industry groupings.

II.4c. Monetary Theory of the Balance of Payments.

One attempt has been made to use historical data to test the monetary theory of the balance of payments (see I.4b) (Zecher and McCloskey, 1976). The authors used a model that assumes arbitrage in world commodity and local markets to explain movements in the U.K. and U.S. balance of payments under the gold standard, 1880–1913. The model also assumes that traded goods (e.g., wheat) and nontraded goods (e.g., haircuts) are close substitutes; assumes full employment, and that growth of real output is independent of the growth of the money supply.

Implications of the model for the classic gold standard included: (a) in each country the money supply was determined by the demand for money; (b) world prices were determined by the world money stock and each country could affect its price level only to the extent that it affected the world money stock; (c) central bankers in the nineteenth century ignored the rules of the game—to facilitate gold inflows by procyclical monetary policy—because the rules were inconsequential; (the central banks could control only the composition of H, not its total amount); (d) no lags are observed in the movement of world prices, because of instant arbitrage.[18]

The authors tested the arbitrage assumption by examining correlations among price changes between countries, and between regions within countries. For traded goods, such as wheat, they found synchronous correlations equally high between regions as between nations, unlike the case of nontraded goods, such as labor services and bricks. They also found evidence in favor of capital market arbitrage.

Finally, they tested their model by comparing gold flows—predicted by a simple demand for money function less the money supply produced by domestic credit expansion—with actual gold flows, and found a very close relationship.

The approach adopted by Zecher and McCloskey may be compared with the one Williamson used (see II.4a, above). There are evident similarities.

II.4d. Monetary Policy Under the Gold Standard. An unpublished paper reported a test of whether the Bank of England prevented gold flows from affecting the domestic money supply, hence violating the rules of the gold standard (Pippinger, 1974). Using both spectral analysis and OLS, the author found little relationship between variations in the monetary gold stock and high-powered money in short-run (weekly, monthly and quarterly) data, but a significant relationship in semiannual and annual data. Apparently, the Bank of England acted passively with respect to gold flows, but fluctuations in British government deposits at the Bank tended to weaken, in the short run, the link between gold and high-powered money. This tended to sterilize the effects of the gold flows.

II.5. Financial Development

The literature on the development of financial institutions in different countries includes some attempts to relate financial development to the growth of economic activity. Here we limit our review to articles concerned with financial intermediation (see I.2.e, above), money and economic growth (I.4a), and the term structure of interest rates (I.4c), which is related to the development of financial markets.

II.5a. Financial Intermediation. There are basically two themes in this literature. The first attempts to explain the development of a unified capital market in the United States in the post-Civil War period. The second uses recent developments in portfolio theory and the demand for money to explain the growth and behavior of financial institutions in the nineteenth-century U.S. economy.

(1) The Unified Capital Market

The persistence of high interest differentials between regions in the United States in the nineteenth century has been regarded as evidence of an imperfect capital market (Davis, 1965).[19] Davis argues that barriers to short-term capital mobility were gradually eliminated by the spread of a national market for commerical paper, while barriers to long-term capital mobility were reduced by the expansion of intermediaries such as mortgage and life insurance companies. In short, institutional change removed the differential.

Another interpretation of the persistence of the differentials is that the national banking act, by erecting significant barriers to entry—minimum capital requirements and prohibition of loans against mortgages—was responsible for creating local monoplies in the South and West (Sylla, 1972). Country national banks price-discriminated between the local market (where the elasticity of demand was low) and the reserve city money market (where it was close to infinite), where they held reserves. Sylla argued that the country bank monopolist would lend at home (price discriminate within the local market) until the marginal loan rate in the local market equalled the rate in the reserve city, its remaining funds then being lodged as bankers' balances in New York. The result of this practice was a continuing interest differential between regions and, at the same time, the pooling of substan-

tial funds in New York. Finally, according to Sylla, the practice broke down when the Gold Standard Act of 1900 removed the barriers to entry.

Both Davis's and Sylla's explanations for capital market imperfection, as well as Stigler's hypothesis that the capital market was perfect except for risk and information costs (Stigler, 1961), have been subjected to a test (James, 1975). Using a Tobin-Markowitz model of portfolio selection based on risk and return, James ran both cross-section and time series regressions to explain movements in local interest rates between cities. He found the evidence inconsistent with both the Stigler and Davis approaches but not with that of Sylla. He argued that it was competition by state banks that eroded the potential monopoly power of the national banks—i.e., that state bank minimum capital requirements were the key variable explaining cross-section differentials in interest rates. This variable also explained the time-series decline in interest differentials. Thus institutional change, which encouraged the growth (reemergence) of state banks, was the key force explaining the growth in efficiency of the capital market.

The persistence of the differentials has also been explained by different rates of bank failure (Rockoff, 1977). High failure rates lead to high interest rates by increasing risk and by creating barriers to entry—high interest rates may represent returns to a scarce form of capital, a reputation for soundness. As evidence, Rockoff cited a significant correlation between regional failure rates and profit rates.

(2) The Use of Portfolio Theory and the Demand for Money in Financial Development

The theory of money demand and portfolio selection has been applied to analyze the behavior of nineteenth-century financial institutions (Rockoff, 1975; Hinderliter and Rockoff, 1973, 1975).

Rockoff tested the hypothesis that a laissez-faire policy toward financial intermediaries tends to deepen financial development and accelerate economic growth (see McKinnon, 1973). He examined the period 1840–1860, when there was no federal government regulation of banking, and assessed the impact of financial development of free banking, usury laws, and mutual savings bank laws, using real balances per head as an indicator of financial development. Rockoff ran cross-section demand-for-money equations, including, in turn, a dummy variable to represent sound versus unsound banking, the rate of usury across states, and a dummy to account for restrictive mutual savings bank laws. None of these variables improved the explanation of variations in real balances already provided by real income per head and urbanization.

Hinderliter and Rockoff used the Tobin-Markowitz model to analyze the reserve behavior of 82 banks in 3 eastern cities, in the period between the collapse of the Second Bank of the United States and the advent of the national banking system. According to the Tobin-Markowitz theory of portfolio selection, banks are assumed to choose their portfolios so as to maximize utility, where utility is a

function of expected portfolio returns and risk. Three types of variables are used to explain interbank variation in liquid asset ratios: structure of liability variables—to account for risk; earnings variables; and attitude variables. The authors obtained significant results, especially for the risk variables, which suggested that banks behaved in both a rational and responsible manner in the absence of a central bank.

Later, Hinderliter and Rockoff used the same approach to analyze the portfolio behavior of banks in the world's leading financial centers (New York, London and Paris) in the heyday of the late nineteenth-century gold standard. London banks had higher liquid asset ratios than did those in Paris and New York. Hinderliter and Rockoff explained this conservative behavior by the less conservative policy of the Bank of England compared to that of the Bank of France, and the fact that U.S. national banks had required reserve ratios.

II.5b. Money and Economic Growth.

In our survey of the literature we were unable to find any articles explicitly using or testing recent models of money and growth. However several pieces are concerned with the linkages between the growth of bank credit and economic development.

One approach is to examine the effects of banking on U.S. economic development in the nineteenth century (Sylla, 1973). Rather than continuing in the tradition of Redlich (1951), who emphasized "soundness," Sylla followed Tobin (1963) in looking at the effects of banks as financial intermediaries. He distinguished three effects of the intermediary function: a) the credit creation effect, b) the fund concentration effect, and c) the pure intermediary effect. All three effects reflect the view that financial intermediaries allocate resources efficiently.

The credit creation effect is a variant of the forced saving argument. Bank money, used to finance new projects, bids resources away from other uses, raises their prices, and forces other users of these resources to save what the firm invests. If the project succeeds, the firm repays the loan, the economy has a larger flow of goods and services, and prices fall. Sylla argued that there is evidence that frontier banks economized on scarce capital—that local bank money served as a substitute for a national loan market. Evidence that bank reserve ratios, especially in the West, declined in periods of boom and rose in periods of depression is consistent with the hypothesis.

The fund creation effect occurred with the development of the national banking system, which provided a pool of funds in New York sufficient to finance large-scale investments. Finally, the pure intermediation effect, whereby the saver gets a more attractive risk return package and the borrower pays a lower interest rate, is observed both in the evidence of declining interest differentials in the ninteenth century and in the growth of new types of intermediaries.

A test has been conducted of Gerschenkron's hypothesis that the German Universal, or Credit Banks, through the method of current account advances (a combination demand deposit and line of credit), raised German growth in the

period 1883–1913 over and above what it would have been with just an increase in outstanding bank credit (Gerschenkron, 1966; Neuberger and Stokes, 1974). Neuberger and Stokes tested for the substitution effect of current account advances—substitution should occur since the banks extended long-term credit to particular industries at short-term rates, so that some industries received loans at less than free market rates while others paid a higher rate—by seeing whether the ratio of current account credit to total credit produced an upward shift in the aggregate nonagriculture production function. Including the current account advance variable in a simple Cobb-Douglas production function produced a significant negative coefficient, which implied that the German Universal banks led to an inefficient allocation of capital.[20]

The authors conducted the same test for Japan in the post-World War II era, since Japan, like Germany, experienced belated development (Neuberger and Stokes, 1975). A few large banks have played a key role in Japanese industrial growth since World War I, and these banks used a long-term credit scheme similar to that used by the German banks. The authors included the same credit account variable in their regression, as well as a variable to account for payments made for imported technology. They found a positive and significant credit substitution effect. They concluded that the Gerschenkron effect occurred in Japan rather than Germany because: a) Germany had to develop most of its own technology, while Japan borrowed it from the West; b) industries promoted in Germany might have been more important for national defense than growth.

II.5c. The Term Structure of Interest Rates. Only one paper surveyed examined the term structure: an analysis of the effects of price expectations on British interest rates 1873–1913 (Harley, 1975). The author used Meiselman's expectations theory of the term structure (Meiselman, 1962); i.e., the yield on consols (long-term bonds) can be viewed as the expectation of future short rates. Empirically, the long rate was predicted by assuming it to be dependent on the expected short rate, where expectations of the short rate are generated by a geometrically weighted distributed lag of past short rates. The regressions produced a mean lag of the influence of the short rate on the consol rate of 5.25 years and the result that a sustained one percent rise of the short rate would result in a rise of the long rate by three quarters of one percent.

III. AN ASSESSMENT AND SOME SUGGESTIONS FOR FURTHER RESEARCH

To conclude this paper, it is in order to take stock of the contributions historians have made using the recent tools of monetary economics, the ones that have not been made and, finally, some suggestions on topics of merit.

As our survey in section II has shown, much work has concentrated on the subject of monetary disturbances. As more data become available for earlier times

and diverse countries, we expect the subject will continue to attract economic historians. Second, there have been many studies of the supply of money in various countries and historical periods. Third, the open economy, the adjustment to international disturbances, has received much attention. Fourth, financial development, a traditional subject in economic history, has continued to be popular but now is treated with the more sophisticated tools of Tobin and Markowitz.

Most of the other topics discussed in section I have received very little attention, indeed. One topic, in particular, the demand for money, has been investigated in only a few studies. This appears to us to be a most shocking lacuna in the historical literature, since it has been, and continues to be, the most important topic in current monetary economics. Surely the widespread existence of money supply, population, price, interest rate, and real output data for a large number of western countries from the last quarter of the nineteenth century could be exploited in additional studies of the demand for money.

Other surprising gaps are research on the origins of money, the use of money in growth models, detailed analysis of periods of secular inflation and deflation, and analysis of the breakdown of changes in nominal income into changes in real output and prices.

The absence of historical studies bearing on the Keynesian-modern quantity theory debate is understandable since most of the issues in the debate have derived from the use of economic policy in this century. Examples of the use of discretionary fiscal and monetary policy before 1914 do not leap to the mind, although research should definitely be encouraged on those examples that do exist.

At this juncture, we propose a menu of topics ripe for examination by monetary historians:

(1) The question of the origins of money. The origins of exchange should be systematically examined with historical data. Did the use of money in the early middle ages or in ancient China arise primarily as a record-keeping device or as an adjunct to the development of organized markets?

(2) The effects of money on growth. Much work has focused on money and financial intermediaries in the context of economic development, but there has been no application of the recent literature introducing money into growth models. Does the introduction of money increase or decrease capital intensity? the savings ratio?

(3) The transmission mechanism following monetary change. Considerable work has been done demonstrating the consequences of monetary disturbances on prices and real output, but there has been virtually no work tracing out the dynamic effects of monetary changes through different markets (both financial and real).[21]

(4) Expected inflation and deflation. Recent developments in the theory of expectations (Muth, 1961) could be tested using historical data. The Bailey (1956) and Friedman (1971) framework to measure the welfare cost of inflationary finance in early wartime inflationary episodes could be extended. Finally, periods of

deflation, such as 1869–1896, could be examined within the framework of Friedman's optimum quantity of money (Friedman, 1969).

(5) The breakdown of changes in nominal income into changes in real output and prices. The tradeoff could be examined using historical data. It would be interesting to see if the theory and testing by Lucas and Rapping (1969), Lucas (1973) and others would hold up in earlier times. Work by Sargent and Wallace (1975) on rational expectations may be applicable to explaining periods such as the so-called "Great Depression" in England, 1873–1896, when prices fell, real output rose, and contemporary observers complained of economic disaster.

(6) Money and interest rates. Further work of the type done by Harley (1975) should be encouraged. It may be interesting to use time-series analysis to see whether nineteenth-century capital markets perfectly incorporated all available information.[22]

(7) Stabilization policy. Recent analysis of stabilization policy could be applied to the behavior of the Bank of England in the nineteenth century, to the New York banks in the nineteenth century, and to the U.S. Treasury before 1914 (Friedman, 1953; Karaken and Solow, 1963; Kochin, 1974).

In sum, much interesting ground remains to be covered in monetary history. If the pace of research activity of the past several years continues at the same or even a faster rate, we expect much of it will be accomplished.[23]

FOOTNOTES

1. In the case of regional economics, it was sooner: e.g., North (1955) examined the relevance of the theory of regional economic growth to the historical development of the American economy; Williamson (1965) examined regional development across many countries and over long periods of time within individual countries.

2. Harry Johnson suggests that this is the wrong approach, on the ground that "reliance on the use of money for economic organization is an unusual and possibly transitory form of social organization, so that the problem may well be to explain its use in spite of its disadvantages, rather than the advantages of its use" (Johnson, 1974, p. 216). He does not make clear the basis for his belief that the use of money is "unusual." The basis for his belief that it is "transitory" is his conjecture that "the use of money as we know it might virtually disappear" (Johnson, 1974, p. 217), thanks to the credit card, the charge account and, more generally, the advance of computer technology. But this is irrelevant. The stock of money would certainly not disappear—payments would simply be automated. Money would not be any the less useful for the change; it might be more useful.

Johnson's theory is that in a primitive economy "credit would be necessary to efficiency of production but money would be unnecessary and absent" until trade with foreigners, war against foreigners, and technical change occurred. The need for money would arise only with an increase in uncertainty, change and personal mobility. (See also Pierson, 1972).

3. Harry Johnson suggests that Keynesians were ineffective in countering the test results because they accepted the rules under which the test was conducted: evidence based on tests of simplified hypotheses is meaningful; behavioral relationships should be invariant to institutional and historical change; statistical tests can be relied on to define and measure the concepts Keynesian theory stresses for which there are no exact empirical counterparts

(Johnson, 1970). He believes Keynesians should have rejected the first rule, on the ground that evidence should have been based on "the full structure of a general equilibrium model in the detail necessary to produce an adequately good statistical 'fit'" (Johnson, 1970, p. 87), possibly the second rule, and in practical application the third rule. Finally, he believes Keynesians could have interpreted the inconclusive results for the 1930's "as confirming the master's insight."

4. A one-day conference on monetarism was held at Brown University in November 1974 with the aim of specifying an analytical framework which would generate the empirical results of this test. For the papers and discussion, see Jerome Stein (1976).

5. These findings apply to the contemporary U.S. economy. An empirical definition clearly would vary with the degree of financial maturity of an economy.

6. Various definitions of the variables and various combinations of variables have been tested (Laidler, 1969). The expected rate of change of prices has been isolated as an important determinant of the demand for money in European hyper-inflations, post-World Wars I and II, in the inflation in the U.S. Confederacy, and in recent Chilean inflationary experience (Cagan, 1956; Lerner, 1956; Deaver, 1970). It has not been possible to assign a similar role to expected price change in the U.S. demand for money, probably because demand studies testing the variable covered a period when the U.S. price level was relatively stable.

7. In the most elaborate portfolio choice model (Tobin, 1963), there are five financial assets plus real capital (Keynes limited the choice to money and bonds) and substitutability is imperfect (Keynes assumed perfect substitutability). In the model, monetary wealth—currency, unborrowed bank reserves, plus government securities—is distinguised from money. Monetary wealth may increase without a change in money, and money may increase without a change in monetary wealth. An increase in monetary wealth, whatever happens to money, changes its ratio to real physical assets, lowers the supply price of capital and stimulates investment expenditures. An increase in money is expansionary only if it leads to a desired reduction in the ratio of monetary wealth to real assets.

8. This pioneering study proposed a framework in which to examine the role of financial intermediaries. (An empirical analysis that was to follow has not appeared.) Financial development in this framework proceeds apace with real development. Starting with a rudimentary economy in which there is only one financial institution, a government bank, and one financial market, only for government-issued money, financial development advances through stages, including the introduction of a market for long-term primary securities issued by private firms to finance development, that the public and the government bank buy, until the final stages of the emergence of nonbank financial intermediaries and a private banking system controlled by a central bank. Nonbank financial intermediaries purchase primary securities and issue their own liabilities to the private sector, tailored to give asset holders the short-term securities they desire in their portfolios, and the profit-making private banks issue money.

9. Much model-building in monetary economics has been devoted to establishing the conditions under which the effects of monetary change on the real economy—the real rate of interest, the choice between present and future consumption, the growth rate of output—would be neutral or nonneutral. One line of inquiry has been analysis of the consequence of changes in the ratio of inside money—money produced by the private banking system—to outside money—money produced by the monetary authorities. Initially, inside money was not regarded as wealth, on the ground that the banking system acquired debts and assets of equal value so that aggregate net worth did not change. Outside money was, however, regarded as net wealth (Gurley and Shaw, 1960). A change in the community's holdings of government debt was then interpreted as affecting the stock of real assets held by the public, with effects on the willingness to save and the equilibrium interest

rate. Subsequent developments questioned the attribution of a net wealth effect to government debt, on the ground that debt implied tax liability to pay interest or redeem the debt, which when capitalized equaled the community's holding of the debt (Johnson, 1962).

A later study argued that increases in inside and outside money have the same effect on wealth and that both are part of net wealth (Pesek and Saving, 1967). Inside money, provided it is not interest-bearing, is net wealth since the banks earn income through their operations and wealth increases by the capitalized value of the banks' earnings. Outside money is also net wealth. Corresponding to a reduction in the private sector's holding of government debt as a result, say, of an open market purchase, which increases outside money, there is a reduction in the income stream, since the government now needs to pay less interest on its outstanding debt. Therefore it takes less in taxes to finance interest payments and the capitalized tax liability of the public is lower, so the increase in outside money is net real wealth.

Critics of the latter study agree that demand deposits represent net wealth, but only because the charters granted to banks are the source of net worth—demand deposits merely serve as a proxy for the value of bank charters. Were there free entry and no prohibition on the payment of interest on demand deposits, the value of the monopoly charter would disappear; hence, inside money would not be a component of net wealth (Brunner, 1971; Johnson, 1969; Patinkin, 1969).

10. The choice of these journals was dictated partly by a time constraint, but also on the ground that most papers in economic history explicitly using theory have appeared there. We avoided purely institutional pieces, which is why we do not include any items from the *Economic History Review*.

11. One problem with this approach is that in concentrating on the quantity of real balances Gramm ignored the decline in real services, which is crucial to any analysis of wealth effects.

12. Rockoff (1971), however, argued that more important than the inflow of Mexican silver was the fact that Britain was exporting capital to the United States. This allowed her to run a larger trade deficit without a contraction in prices than otherwise could have been maintained.

13. Schwartz (1971) would attach more importance to movements of the ratios than does Temin, tending to add support to the Macesich position. Engerman (1970) demonstrated that the destruction of the Second Bank, by increasing the share of specie in total money, and hence tying up greater resources in commodity money, imposed a welfare loss of only .15% of U.S. annual GNP over the period 1834–1860.

14. Apparently Temin and Stevens used the same sources.

15. Wesley Clair Mitchell's thesis (Mitchell, 1903) that the Civil War inflation redistributed income from workers to profit earners because of a wage lag has been challenged (Kessel and Alchian, 1959). Kessel and Alchian argue that Mitchell's evidence of a fall in the real wage is not sufficient to confirm the hypothesis. They explain the fall in the real wage by real forces: a decline in the terms of trade of the North, increased taxation and import duties, and special circumstances of the base year (1860) used in Mitchell's study. Moreover, in their view, these forces would have led to a decline in other factor incomes.

Acknowledging that Kessel and Alchian are correct in the long-run, the authors of another study argue that in the short-run a wage lag is possible if workers do not adjust their wage expections to inflation fast enough (Decanio and Mokyr, 1975). They set up and test a model of the labor market in the Civil War period which shows that in the long-run wages are neutral with respect to prices and that real forces dominate; however, in the short-run there exists a wage lag. Moreover, they find that the wage lag accounts for approximately one half the decline in income experienced by wage earners during the Civil War.

16. Kochin and Benjamin (1976), in an unpublished paper, argue that persistently high

levels of unemployment in the 1920's in Great Britain can be largely explained by a large increase in the ratio of unemployment insurance benefits to wages in 1920, and an extension throughout the decade of eligibility requirements to the majority of the labor force.

17. Jay Gould attempted to bid up the dollar price of gold in order to depreciate the dollar. This depreciation would, he later testified, help move an abundant wheat crop (whose price in the United States would otherwise have fallen), help relieve a recession, and incidentally stimulate business for his railroad. His plan was to raise the premium on gold from its equilibrium value of $1.30 to $1.45, and hence devalue the dollar from $6.32 to $7.05 per £, which required the creation of an excess supply of foreign exchange. Wimmer demonstrated that Gould could have absorbed the excess supply generated by the current account surplus, but not the excess supply in the capital account, assuming speculation to be stable, because eventually there would have been a massive short-term capital inflow. As it happened, the foreign exchange market resisted for several weeks Gould's attempt to bid up the price. Finally, the public purchased gold, when led to believe that the government backed the scheme. Within two days the premium was bid up to $1.62. It fell back within two hours to its original level, when it became known that the government disapproved the scheme. Even if the government had not intervened, massive specie flows from abroad, arriving within two weeks, would have cleared the market.

18. The implication of the specie flow mechanism indentified with Hume's name is that the lag in response of prices is significant. An increase in U.S. M first raises domestic prices, leading to a balance of payments deficit, and a specie outflow. Because of an increase in U.S. demand for U.K. lower-priced exports, the U.K. balance of trade moves into surplus. The resulting specie inflow leads to an increase in the U.K. money stock and subsequently to an increase in U.K. prices.

19. See comments on a later version of the paper in Schwartz (1975b).

20. The Neuberger-Stokes approach has been challenged (Fremdling and Tilly, 1976), and a rebuttal offered (Neuberger and Stokes, 1976).

21. See John Cairnes, "Essays on the Austrialian Gold Discoveries," in his *Essays on Political Economy* for one of the few lucid treatments of the dynamic effects of monetary disturbances on prices and output behavior in different sectors of the economy, consequent upon the gold discoveries, 1849–1873. For a discussion of Cairnes's essays on gold, see Bordo (1975b).

22. See Roll (1972), who demonstrated, using the capital asset pricing model, that the Civil War bond markets were efficient, in that bond prices quickly reflected changes in the premium on gold, as well as all information on military events.

23. More than half of the items surveyed have appeared since 1970, and the rate of growth of the monetary history literature since then has been accelerating.

REFERENCES

Adie, D.K. (Winter 1971–1972), "The English Money Stock 1834–1844," *Explorations in Economic History*, 9 pp. 112–143.

Aghelvi, B.S. (March 1975), "The Balance of Payments and the Money Supply Under the Gold Standard Regime: U.S. 1879–1914," *American Economic Review*, 65, pp. 40–58.

Andersen, L. C. and Jordan, J.L., (November 1968), "Monetary and Fiscal Actions: A Test of Their Relative Importance in Economic Stabilization," Federal Reserve Bank of St. Louis, *Review*, 50, pp. 11–23.

Ando, A. and Modigliani, F., (September 1965), "Velocity and the Investment Multiplier," *American Economic Review*, 55, pp. 692–728.

Bailey, M. (April 1956), "The Welfare Cost of Inflationary Finance," *Journal of Political Economy*, 64, pp. 92–110.

Bordo, M.D., (December 1975a), "The Income Effects of the Sources of Monetary Change: An Historical Approach," *Economic Inquiry, 13,* pp. 505–525.

——. (Fall 1975b), "John E. Cairnes on the Effects of the Australian Gold Discoveries, 1851–73: An Early Application of the Methodolgy of Positive Economics," *History of Political Economy, 7,* pp. 357–379.

Brunner, K. (March 1971), "A Survey of Selected Issues in Monetary Theory," *Schweizerische Zeitschrift für Volkswirtschaft und Statistik, 107,* pp. 317–324.

Brunner, K. and Meltzer, A. H. (May 1964), "Some Further Investigations of Demand and Supply Functions for Money," *Journal of Finance*, 19, pp. 240–283.

——. (January/February 1968), "Liquidity Traps for Money, Bank Credit, and Interest Rates," *Journal of Political Economy,* 76, pp. 1–37.

——. (December 1971), "The Uses of Money: Money in the Theory of an Exchange Economy," *American Economic Review*, 61, pp. 784–805.

Burger, A.E. (1971), *The Money Supply Process,* Belmont, California: Wadsworth Publishing Company.

Cagan, P. (1965), "The Monetary Dynamics of Hyperinflation," *Studies in the Quantity Theory of Money* (edited by Friedman, M.) pp. 25–117, Chicago: University of Chicago Press.

——. (1965), *Determinants and Effects of Changes in the Stock of Money, 1875–1960,* New York: Columbia University Press.

——. (1969), "A Study of Liquidity Premiums on Federal and Municipal Government Securities," *Essays on Interest Rates* (edited by Guttentag, J.M. and Cagan, P.,) Vol. 1, pp. 107–142, New York: National Bureau of Economic Research.

——. (1972), *The Channels of Monetary Effects on Interest Rates,* New York: National Bureau of Economic Research.

Cagan, P. and Schwartz, A.J. (May 1975), "Has the Growth of Money Substitutes Hindered Monetary Policy?" *Journal of Money, Credit and Banking,* 7, pp. 137–159.

Cairnes, J.E. (1973), *Essays on Political Economy,* London: Macmillan.

Chen, C. (August 1975), "Flexible Bimetallic Exchange Rates in China, 1630–1830," *Journal of Money, Credit and Banking,* 7, pp. 359–376.

Clower, R. (December 1967), "A Reconsideration of the Microfoundations of Monetary Theory," *Western Economic Journal,* 6 (1), pp. 1–8.

Connolly, M.B. and Swoboda, A.K., (eds.) (1973), *International Trade and Money,* London: George Allen and Unwin.

Courchene, T.J. (May/June 1969), "An Analysis of the Canadian Money Supply: 1925–34," *Journal of Political Economy,* 77, pp. 363–391.

Davis, L. (September 1965), "The Investment Market, 1870–1914: The Evolution of a National Market," *Journal of Economic History,* 25, pp. 355–399.

Deaver, J.V. (1970), "The Chilean Inflation and the Demand for Money," *Varieties of Monetary Experience* (edited by Meiselman, D.), pp. 9–67, Chicago: University of Chicago Press.

Decanio, S. and Mokyr, J. (1975), "Inflation and the Wage Lag During the American Civil War," Northwestern University Discussion Paper.

Duggar, J.W. and Rost, R.F. (September 1969), "National Bank Note Redemption and Treasury Cash," *Journal of Economic History,* 29, pp. 512–520.

Eagly, R. (December 1969), "Monetary Policy and Politics in Mid-Eighteenth Century Sweden," *Journal of Economic History,* 29, pp. 739–757.

Engerman, S.L. (July/August 1970), "A Note on the Economic Consequences of the Second Bank of the United States," *Journal of Political Economy,* 78, pp. 725–728.

Fand, D.I. (September 1969), "Some Issues in Monetary Economics," Banca Nazionale del Lavoro *Quarterly Review*, 90, pp. 215–247.

Feige, E.L. (1964), *The Demand for Liquid Assets: A Temporal Cross-Section Analysis*, Englewood Cliffs, N.J.: Prentice-Hall.

Fisher, I. (1930), *The Theory of Interest*, New York: Macmillan.

Fraas, A. (June 1974), "The Second Bank of the United States: An Instrument for an Inter-regional Monetary Union," *Journal of Economic History*, 34, pp. 447–467.

Fremdling, R., and Tilly, R. (June 1976), "German Banks, German Growth, and Econometric History," *Journal of Economic History*, 36, pp. 416–424.

Frenkel, J.A. (May 1971), "A Theory of Money, Trade, and the Balance of Payments in a Model of Accumulation," *Journal of International Economics*, 1, pp. 159–187.

Friedman, M. (1953a), "The Effects of a Full Employment Policy on Economic Stability: A Formal Analysis," *Essays in Positive Economics*, pp. 117–132, Chicago: University of Chicago Press.

———. (1953b), "The Case for Flexible Exchange Rates," *Essays in Positive Economics*, pp. 157–203, Chicago: University of Chicago Press.

———. (1956), "The Quantity Theory of Money: A Restatement," *Studies in the Quantity Theory of Money*, (edited by Friedman, M.), pp. 3–21, Chicago: University of Chicago Press.

———. (October 1961), "The Lag in Effect of Monetary Policy," *Journal of Political Economy*, 69, pp. 447–466.

———. (March 1968), "The Role of Monetary Policy," *American Economic Review*, 58, pp. 1–17.

———. (1969), *The Optimum Quantity of Money and Other Essays*, Chicago: Aldine.

———. (July/August 1971), "Government Revenue from Inflation," *Journal of Political Economy*, 79, pp. 846–856.

———. (1974), "Comments on the Critics," *Milton Friedman's Monetary Framework* (edited by Gordon, R.J.), pp. 137–148, Chicago: University of Chicago Press.

Friedman, M. and Meiselman, D. (1963), "The Relative Stability of Monetary Velocity and the Investment Multiplier in the United States, 1897–1958," *Stabilization Polices*, (by Commission on Money and Credit) pp. 167–268, Englewood Cliffs, N.J.: Prentice-Hall.

Friedman, M. and Schwartz, A.J. (1963a), *A Monetary History of the United States 1867–1960*, Princeton: Princeton University Press.

———. (February 1963b), "Money and Business Cycles," *Review of Economics and Statistics*, 45, (1, Supplement), pp. 165–268.

———. (1970), *Monetary Statistics of the United States*, pp. 104–146, New York: National Bureau of Economic Research.

Gandolfi, A. (September/October 1974), "Stability of the Demand for Money During the Great Depression, 1929–33," *Journal of Political Economy*, 82, pp. 969–983.

Gerschenkron, A. (1966), *Economic Backwardness in Historical Perspective*, Cambridge: Harvard University Press.

Gibson, W.E. and Kaufman, G.G. (May/June 1968), "The Channels of Monetary Effects on Interest Rates," *Journal of Political Economy*, 76, pp. 472–478.

Goldsmith, R.W. (1958)), *Financial Intermediaries in the American Economy since 1900*, Princeton: Princeton University Press.

Goodhart, C.A.E. (October 1965), "Profit on National Bank Notes, 1900–1913," *Journal of Political Economy*, 79, pp. 515–522.

Gramm, W.P. (June 1972), "The Real-Balance Effect in the Great Depression," *Journal of Economic History*, 32, pp. 499–519.

Gurley, J.G. and Shaw, E.S. (1969), *Money in a Theory of Finance*, Washington, D.C.: Brookings Institution.

Hamburger, M.J. (1974), "The Lag in Effect of Monetary Policy: A Survey of Recent Literature," *Monetary Aggregates and Monetary Policy*, pp. 104–113, New York: Federal Reserve Bank of New York.

Harberger, A.C. (1963), "The Dynamics of Inflation in Chile," *Measurement in Economics, Studies in Mathematical Economics and Econometrics in Memory of Yehuda Grunfeld*, pp. 219–250, Stanford: Stanford University Press.

Harley, C. (forthcoming, 1977), "Prices and the Money Market in Britain, 1873–1913," *Explorations in Economic History*. 14, No. 1, pp. 69–89.

Hay, K.A.J. (June 1967), "Money and Cycles in Post Confederation Canada," *Journal of Political Economy*, 75, pp. 262–273.

———. (1968), "Determinants of the Canadian Money Supply 1875–1958," Carleton Economic Papers.

Hester, D.D. (November 1964), "Keynes and the Quantity Theory: A Comment on the Friedman-Meiselman CMC Paper," *Review of Economics and Statistics*, 46, pp. 364–368.

Hicks, J. (1969), *A Theory of Economic History*, London: Oxford University Press.

Hinderliter, R.H. and Rockoff, H. (Fall 1973), "The Management of Reserves by Ante-Bellum Banks in Eastern Financial Centers," *Explorations in Economic History*. 11, No. 1, pp. 37–54.

———. (June 1976), "Banking Under the Gold Standard: An Analysis of Liquidity Management in the Leading Financial Centers," *Journal of Economic History*, 36, pp. 379–398.

James, J. (April 1975), "The Development of the National Money Market," Madison, Wisconsin: Cliometrics Meetings.

———. (April 1976), "The Conundrum of the Low Issue of National Bank Notes," *Journal of Political Economy*, 84, pp. 359–367.

Johnson, H.G. (June 1962), "Monetary Theory and Policy," *American Economic Review*, 52, pp. 335–384.

———. (February 1969), "Inside Money, Outside Money, Income, Wealth, and Welfare in Monetary Theory," *Journal of Money, Credit and Banking*, 1, pp. 30–45.

———. (1970), "Recent Developments in Monetary Theory," *Money in Britain, 1959–1969* (edited by Croome, D.R. and Johnson, H.G.), pp. 83–114, London: Oxford University Press.

———. (July 1974), "Major Issues in Monetary Economics," *Oxford Economic Papers* (New Series), 26, pp. 212–225.

———. (1976), "The Monetary Approach to Balance-of-Payments Theory," *The Monetary Approach to the Balance of Payments* (edited by Frenkel, J.A. and Johnson, H.G.), pp. 147–167, Toronto: University of Toronto Press.

Jonung, L. (May 1976), "The Behavior of Velocity in Sweden, 1871–1913," UCLA: paper given at Workshop in Monetary Economics.

———. (1975a), "Money and Prices in Sweden 1732–1972," *World Inflation* (edited by Parkin, J.M. and Zis, G.), Manchester: Manchester University Press.

———. (1975b), "Studies in the Monetary History of Sweden," UCLA, unpublished Ph.D. Dissertation.

Kaldor, N. (July 1970), "The New Monetarism," *Lloyds Bank Review*, 97, pp. 1–18.

Karaken, J. and Solow, R. (1963), "Lags in Fiscal and Monetary Policy," *Stabilization Policies* (by Commission on Money and Credit), pp. 14–96, Englewood Cliffs, N.J.: Prentice-Hall.

Kaufman, G.G. (March 1969), "More on an Empirical Definition of Money," *American Economic Review*, 59, pp. 78–87.

Kessel, R.A. (1965), *The Cyclical Behavior of the Term Structure of Interest Rates*, Occasional Paper 91, New York: National Bureau of Economic Research.

Kessel R.A. and Alchian, A. (October 1959), "Real Wages in the North During the Civil War: Mitchell's Data Reinterpreted," *Journal of Law and Economics*, 2, pp. 95–113.

Keynes, J.M. (1930), *A Treatise on Money*, Vol. II, London: Macmillan.

Kindahl, J.K. (February 1961), "Economic Factors in Specie Resumption," *Journal of Political Economy*, 59, pp. 30–48.

Kindleberger, C. (1973), *The World in Depression 1929–39*, Berkeley: University of California Press.

Kirkwood, J.B. (November 1972), "The Great Depression: A Structural Analysis," *Journal of Money, Credit and Banking*, 4, pp. 811–837.

Kochin, L. (1974), "Judging Stabilization Policies," University of Chicago: unpublished Ph.D. dissertation.

Kochin, L. and Benjamin, D. (June 16, 1976), "Searching for an Explanation of Unemployment in Interwar Britain," UCLA: paper presented at Workshop in Monetary Economics.

Laidler, D.E.W. (1969), *The Demand for Money*, Scranton, Pennsylvania: International Textbook Company.

———. (1974). "Information, Money and the Macroeconomics of Inflation," *Swedish Journal of Economics*, 76 (1), pp. 26–41.

Lerner, E. (February 1955), "Money, Prices, and Wages in the Confederacy, 1861–65," *Journal of Political Economy*, 63, pp. 20–40.

———. (1956), "Inflation in the Confederacy, 1861–65," *Studies in The Quantity Theory of Money* (edited by Friedman, M.), pp. 163–175, Chicago: University of Chicago Press.

Levhari, D., and Patinkin, D. (September 1968), "The Role of Money in a Simple Growth Model," *American Economic Review*, 58, pp. 713–753.

Lipsey, R.G. (February 1960), "The Relationship Between Unemployment and the Rate of Change of Money Wage Rates in the United Kingdom, 1862–1957," *Economica*, 27, pp. 1–31.

Lothian, J. (February 1972), "A Monetary Interpretation of the United Kingdom in the Nineteen Twenties," Report 7172-9, University of Chicago: Workshop in Economic History.

Lucas, R., and Rapping, L. (September/October 1969), "Real Wages, Employment, and Inflation," *Journal of Political Economy*, 77, pp. 721–754.

———. (June 1973), "Some International Evidence on Output-Inflation Tradeoffs," *American Economic Review*, 63, pp. 326–334.

Macesich, G. (September 1960), "Sources of Monetary Disturbances in the United States, 1834–45," *Journal of Economic History*, 20, pp. 407–434.

McKinnon, R. (1973), *Money and Capital in Economic Development*, Washington, D.C.: Brookings Institution.

Malkiel, B.G. (1966), *The Term Structure of Interest Rates*, Princeton: Princeton University Press.

Marty, A.L. (February 1961), "Gurley and Shaw on Money in a Theory of Finance," *Journal of Political Economy*, 69, pp. 56–62.

———. (May 1969), "Some Notes on Money and Economic Growth," *Journal of Money, Credit and Banking*, 1, pp. 252–265.

Meiselman, D. (1962), *The Term Structure of Interest Rates*, Englewood Cliffs, N.J.: Prentice-Hall.

Meltzer, A.H. (June 1959), "The Behavior of the French Money Supply: 1938–54," *Journal of Political Economy*, 67, pp. 275–291.

———. (March 1969), "Money, Intermediation, and Growth," *Journal of Economic Literature*, 7, pp. 29–40.

Miskimin, H. (December 1964), "Monetary Movements and Market Structure—Forces for Contraction in Fourteenth-and Fifteenth-Century England," *Journal of Economic History*, 24, pp. 470–490.

Mitchell, W.C. (1903), *A History of the Greenbacks*, Chicago: University of Chicago Press.

———. (December 1944), "The Role of Money in Economic History," *Journal of Economic History*, 4, pp. 61–67.

Modigliani, F., and Sutch, R. (August 1967), "Debt Management and the Term Structure of Interest Rates: An Experimental Analysis of Recent Experience," *Journal of Political Economy*, 75, pp. 569–589

Mundell, R. (1968), *International Economics*, New York: Macmillan.

———. (1971), *Monetary Theory*, Pacific Palisades, California: Goodyear.

Muth, J. (July 1961), "Rational Expectations and the Theory of Price Movements," *Econometrica*, 29, pp. 315–335.

Neuberger, H.M. and Stokes, H.H. (June 1976), "German Banks and German Growth: Reply," *Journal of Economic History*, 36, pp. 425–427.

———. (September 1974), "German Banks and German Economic Growth 1883–1913: An Empirical View," *Journal of Economic History*, 34, pp. 710–731.

———. (March 1975), "German Banking and Japanese Banking: A Comparative Analysis," *Journal of Economic History*, 35, pp. 238–252.

Niehans, J. (November 1969), "Money in a Static Theory of Optimal Payments Arrangements," *Journal of Money, Credit and Bankin̄⌐   ⁻06–726.

———. (December 1971), "Money and Barter in Ge   ⌐quilibrium with Transactions Costs," *American Economic Review*, 6, pp. 773–783.

———. (February 1973), "Introduction," The Universities-National Bureau Conference on Secular Inflation, *Journal of Money, Credit and Banking*, 5, (1, Part II) p. 238.

North, D.C. (June 1955), "Location and Regional Economic Growth," *Journal of Political Economy*, 43, pp. 243–258.

North, D.C. and Thomas, R. (1973), *The Rise of the Western World*, New York: Cambridge University Press.

Nwami, O. (February 1975), "The Quantity Theory in the Early Monetary System of West Africa with Particular Emphasis on Nigeria, 1850–1895," *Journal of Political Economy*, 83, pp. 185–194.

Ostroy, J. (September 1973), "The Informational Efficiency of Monetary Exchange," *American Economic Review*, 63, pp. 597–610.

Patinkin, D. (December 1969), "Money and Wealth: A Review Article," *Journal of Economic Literature*, 7, pp. 1140–1160.

Patrick, H. (June 1965), "External Equilibrium and Internal Convertibility: Financial Policy in Meiji Japan," *Journal of Economic History*, 25, pp. 187–213.

Pesek, B. and Saving, T. (1967), *Money, Wealth and Economic Theory*, New York: Macmillan.

Phillips, A.W. (November 1958), "The Relation Between Unemployment and the Rate of Change of Money Wage Rates in the United Kingdom, 1861–1957," *Economica*, 25, pp. 282–299.

Pickersgill, J.E. (September/October 1968), "Hyperinflation and Monetary Reform in the Soviet Union, 1921–26," *Journal of Political Economy*, 71, pp. 1037–1048.

Pierson, G. (August 1972), "The Role of Money in Economic Growth," *Quarterly Jounal of Economics*, 86, pp. 383–395.

Pippinger, J. (1974), "Bank of England Operations 1890–1908," unpublished paper, Santa Barbara: University of California.

(Radcliffe) Committee on the Working of the Monetary System (1959), *Report*, Cmd. 827, London: HMSO.

Redlich, F. (1951), *The Molding of American Banking: Men and Ideas*, New York: Hafner Publishing Company.

Rockoff, H. (1971), "Money, Prices and Banks in the Jacksonian Era," *The Reinterpretation of American Economic History* (edited by Fogel, R. and Engerman S.), New York: Harper and Row.

———. (May 1974), "The Free Banking Era: A Re-Examination," *Journal of Money, Credit and Banking*, 6, pp. 141–168.

———. (March 1975), "Varieties of Banking and Regional Economic Development in the United States, 1840–1860," *Journal of Economic History*, 35, pp. 160–181.

———. (1977), "Regional Interest Rates and Bank Failures, 1870–1914," *Explorations in Economic History*, (forthcoming).

Roll, R. (June 1972), "Interest Rates and Price Expectations During the Civil War," *Journal of Economic History*, 32, pp. 476–498.

Sargent, T.J. (February 1969), "Commodity Price Expectations and the Interest Rate," *Quarterly Journal of Economics*, 83, pp. 127–140.

Sargent, T.J., and Wallace, N. (April 1976), "Rational Expectations and the Theory of Economic Policy," *Journal of Monetary Economics*, 2, pp. 169–183.

Savin, N., and Mokyr, J. (April 1976), "Stagflation in Historical Perspective: The Napoleonic Wars Revisited," Northwestern University Discussion Paper.

Schwartz, A.J. (June 1970), "Review of P. Temin, *The Jacksonian Economy*," *Journal of Economic History*, 30, pp. 476–479.

———. (March 1975a), "Monetary Trends in the United States and the United Kingdom, 1878–1970: Selected Findings," *Journal of Economic History*, 35, pp. 138–159.

———. (1975b). "Comment: The Evolution of the American Capital Market, 1860–1940: A Case Study of Institutional Change, *Financial Innovation* (edited by Silber, W.L.) pp. 45–51, Lexington, Massachusetts: Heath.

———. (February 1973), "Secular Price Change in Historical Perspective," *Journal of Money, Credit and Banking*, 5, Part II, pp. 243–269.

Shetler, D. (November 1973), "Monetary Aggregates Prior to the Civil War: A Closer Look," *Journal of Money, Credit and Banking*, 5, pp. 1000–1006.

Stein, J.L. (March 1970) "Monetary Growth Theory in Perspective," *American Economic Review*, 60, pp. 85–106.

Stevens, E. (February 1971), "Composition of the Money Stock Prior to the Civil War," *Journal of Money, Credit and Banking*, 3, pp. 84–101.

Stigler, G. (June 1961), "The Economics of Information," *Journal of Political Economy*, 69, pp. 213–225.

Sushka, M. (December 1976,) "The Antebellum Money Market and the Economic Impact of the Bank War," *Journal of Economic History*, 36, pp. 809–835.

Sylla, R. (December 1969), "Federal Policy, Banking Market Structure and Capital Mobilization in the U.S. 1863–1913," *Journal of Economic History*, 29, pp. 657–686.

———. (Winter 1971–1972), "American Banking and Growth in the Nineteenth Century: A Partial View of the Terrain," *Explorations in Economic History*, 9 (2), pp. 197–227.

Teigen, R. (October 1964), "Demand and Supply Functions for Money in the United States: Some Structural Estimates," *Econometrica*, 32, pp. 476–509.

Temin, P. (March/April 1968), "The Economic Consequences of the Bank War," *Journal of Political Economy*, 76, pp. 257–274.

———. (1969), *The Jacksonian Economy*, New York: W. W. Norton.

———. (1976), *Did Monetary Forces Cause the Great Depression?* New York: W. W. Norton.

Timberlake, R. (September 1974), "Denominational Factors in Nineteenth Century Currency Experience," *Journal of Economic History*, 34, pp. 835–850.

———. (July 1975), "The Resumption Act and the Money Supply," *Journal of Monetary Economics*, 1, pp. 343–354.

Tobin, J. (1963a), "Commercial Banks as Creators of Money," *Banking and Monetary Studies*, (edited by Carson, D.), pp. 408–419, Homewood, Illinois: Richard D. Irwin.

———. (1963b), "An Essay on Principles of Debt Management," *Fiscal and Debt Management Policies* (by Commission on Money and Credit), pp. 143–218, Englewood Cliffs, N.J.: Prentice-Hall.

———. (June 1965a), "The Monetary Interpretation of History," *American Economic Review*, 55, pp. 646–685.

———. (October 1965b), "Money and Economic Growth," *Econometrica*, 33, pp. 671–684.

———. (1974), "Friedman's Theoretical Framework," *Milton Friedman's Monetary Framework* (edited by Gordon, R.J.), pp. 77–89, Chicago: University of Chicago Press.

Warburton, C. (September 1958), "Variations in Economic Growth and Banking Developments in the United States from 1835 to 1885," *Journal of Economic History*, 18, pp. 283–297.

Weiss, R. (December 1970), "The Issue of Paper Money in the American Colonies, 1720–1724," *Journal of Economic History*, 30, pp. 770–784.

Wicker, E. (August 1965), "Federal Reserve Monetary Policy, 1922–33: A Reinterpretation, *Journal of Political Economy*, 73, pp. 325–343.

———. (June 1966), "A Reconsideration of Federal Reserve Policy During the 1920–21 Depression," *Journal of Economic History*, 26, pp. 223–238.

Willett, T. (March 1968), "International Specie Flows and American Monetary Stability, 1834–60," *Journal of Economic History*, 28, pp. 28–50.

Williamson, J.G. (September 1961), "International Trade and United States Economic Development: 1827–1843," *Journal of Economic History*, 21, pp. 372–383.

———. (January 1963), "Real Growth, Monetary Disturbances and the Transfer Process: the United States, 1879–1900," *Southern Economic Journal*, 29, pp. 167–180.

———. (July 1975), "Regional Inequality and the Process of National Development: A Description of Patterns", *Economic Development and Cultural Change*, 13, Part II.

Wimmer, L. (April 1975), "The Gold Crisis of 1869," *Explorations in Economic History*, 12, pp. 105–122.

Yohe, W.P. and Karnosky, D.S. (December 1969), "Interest Rates and Price Level Changes," Federal Reserve Bank of St. Louis, *Review*, 51, pp. 19–36.

Zecher, R. and McCloskey, D. (1976), "How the Gold Standard Worked, 1880–1913," *The Monetary Approach to the Balance of Payments* (edited by Frenkel J. and Johnson, H.G.), pp. 357–385, Toronto: University of Toronto Press.

POPULATION ISSUES IN AMERICAN ECONOMIC HISTORY: A SURVEY AND CRITIQUE

Richard A. Easterlin,* UNIVERSITY OF PENNSYLVANIA

The dearth of work on population by American economic historians can only be a source of wonder. From 1790 through 1860, and for a century or more before 1790, the American population growth rate averaged close to 3 percent per year, a figure that doubles population in only 23 years. By contrast, in Europe in the nineteenth century—the period of highest population growth there—no country had a growth rate even half as high for as much as two consecutive decades. Despite the uniqueness of American population growth, questions of the nature, causes or economic effects of this growth have been largely neglected by American economic historians. Economic history textbooks have rarely devoted more than a few pages to the subject—an early exception being the text authored by Herman E. Kroos, to whom the present volume is dedicated.[1] Indeed, foreigners—a Japanese, a Briton and two Australians—are responsible for several of the most important research contributions in the last two decades.[2] And American economic historians have virtually ignored exciting new work on colonial demography by their colleagues in social history.[3]

In contrast, in European economic history, population growth has always been a major subject of concern.[4] Moreover, with the advent in recent years of the technique of family reconstitution, the subject has taken on new excitement and vitality.[5] Nor can the general lack of vital statistics records for the U.S. before 1900 serve as an excuse for neglect of the subject by American scholars. The historical censuses of American population are perhaps the best in the world, and there are

other pertinent data available, including some that lend themselves to the family reconstitution technique.[6]

Fortunately, there is enough recent work on American population to make it possible for this survey to be more than a mere statement of research needs. In the hope of stimulating further work, the following discussion centers on several major issues which have emerged in the areas of mortality, fertility and immigration. Brief mention at the end of the article is made of some other important issues as well.

I. DID AMERICAN MORTALITY AND LIFE EXPECTANCY IMPROVE IN THE 80 YEARS BEFORE 1880?[7]

American economic historians are indebted to three young scholars for extending the concerns of the discipline to a subject previously treated only by demographers—namely, the trend in American mortality. Meeker and Higgs have focused on the span from 1850 or 1870 to 1920; Vinovskis, on the colonial period to 1860.[8] The main conclusions of this work have been brought together and expanded in a recent survey piece by Meeker, who states: "It is evident that late in the ninteenth century the United States underwent a vital revolution, one which occurred in both urban and rural areas."[9] In like manner, Higgs, whose work focused on rural mortality, asserts that "[i]n the half century after 1870 nothing less than a 'vital revolution' occurred in the American countryside."[10]

The issue.   There is general agreement in the demographic literature that American mortality improved markedly from sometime around the end of the nineteenth century onward (let us say 1880, since this is the pivotal date in Meeker's analysis). This development characterized Western European nations as well and might in and of itself be termed a "vital revolution."[11] What is uncertain, however, is the nature of the trend prior to 1880—was American mortality fairly constant, rising or declining (perhaps at a slower rate than after 1880)? Vinovskis' survey of Massachusetts mortality from the seventeenth century through 1860 tentatively concludes that "death rates remained relatively constant throughout the entire period, especially for the smaller agricultural towns."[12] Meeker's view, which relates to the entire U.S., is qualified, but he clearly suggests the possiblity of no improvement before 1880. In his first article he states that "average mortality and life expectancy improved little, *and very likely worsened*, [in the three decades] prior to 1880. . . ."[13] In his later piece a longer time span is encompassed: "The changes in mortality and life expectancy which occurred during the 40-year period after 1880 represented the most significant—*and possibly the only*—sustained improvement in the health of Americans since early colonial times."[14] One might also point to recent work by historians in colonial historical demography which indicates that American mortality conditions were better than

those in Europe in the eighteenth century.[15] This would be consistent with the view that the American mortality trend was level over the period up to 1880, and that Western European countries, which are known to have shown improved life expectancy before 1880,[15a] were catching up with the U.S. On the other hand, one of the mortality determinants often cited as responsible for both the earlier European improvement and the post-1880 American advance, a rising level of living, was clearly operating in the U.S. before 1880, and should have had a positive impact on American life expectancy. Higgs's vital revolution in the American countryside after 1870 is attributed almost wholly to the level of living.[16] Would not a similar mortality improvement have been expected to occur before 1870, since there was a significant improvement in rural living conditions before that date?

Thus, the issue is posed: did American mortality and life expectancy improve before 1880? The discussion that follows takes up first the evidence and then the causes of mortality change. Both raise doubts about the view that there was no improvement in American life expectancy before 1880. This is not meant to detract, however, from the contribution that these authors have made in extending the interests of American economic history to the important subject of mortality. And if it ultimately is established that there was an earlier uptrend in life expectancy, the present writer must share in the stigma for error, for he too is on record as saying that ''there may have been little improvement [in mortality conditions] for a good part of the nineteenth century.''[17]

The evidence.   Of the data used by Meeker in his mortality study, there are two sets that permit comparisons of experience before and after 1880—life expectancies for Massachusetts and estimates of crude death rates for the whole United States. Table 1 enables one to compare the change in Massachusetts life expectancy in two thirty-year periods before and after 1880, and in the sixty-year period prior to 1850 (the selection of dates is constrained by the limited availability of data before 1880). Expectation of life advances not only in the period after 1880 but in the two early periods as well.[18] The rate of improvement increases in each successive period, with the advance being most marked after 1880.

Although Massachusetts has the best mortality data, especially for the period from the 1840's on when vital registration began, its representativeness is subject to question because of the disproportionate importance of urbanization and immigration in the state. Table 2 gives Meeker's national crude death rates for periods of equal length before and after 1875–1885. These data are derived partly from census survival rates, but also involve extrapolations based on English life table trends for persons under ten. The extent to which they fully reflect U.S. experience is therefore uncertain. For what they are worth, they show a picture like that in Table 1. Mortality is improving both before and after 1880, but at a faster rate in the later period. Both sets of data are consistent with the view that the rate of

Table 1.   Expectation of Life at Birth, White Population, by Sex, Massachusetts, 1789 to 1909–11

Date	Level		Change per Decade since Preceding Date	
	Males	Females	Males	Females
1789	34.5	36.5		
1850	38.3	40.5	0.6	0.7
1878–1882	41.7	43.5	1.1	1.0
1909–1911	49.3	53.1	2.5	3.2

Source: Thompson, Warren S., and Whelpton, P.K. (1969), *Population Trends in the United States*, p. 240, New York: Gordon and Breach Science Publishers.

Table 2. Crude Death Rate, White Population, 1850–60 to 1900–10

Period	Level	Decline since Preceding Date
1850–1860	21–23	
1875–1885	19.6	1.4–3.4
1900–1910	15.6	4.0

Source: Meeker, Edward (Summer 1972), "The Improving Health of the United States, 1850–1915," *Explorations in Economic History, 9*, p. 362.

improvement after 1880 was "the most significant" that had yet occurred. They are not, however, consistent with the notion that the period after 1880 witnessed "possibly . . . the only sustained improvement in the health of Americans since early colonial times," nor with the statement that "average mortality and life expectancy improved little and very likely worsened, [in the three decades] prior to 1880."[19] However, much more documentation is needed on the facts of mortality change before 1880.

Causes.   What about the causes of mortality change? Do they show a pattern consistent with the notion of lack of improvement before 1880? Meeker centers his attention on four determinants of mortality:

   1. Improvement in levels of living (especially in diets and housing).
   2. Changes in the proportion of the population living in the higher mortality urban areas.

3. New public health practices.
4. Advances in medical science.[20]

Focusing first on the decline from 1880 to 1920, Meeker argues:

> This reduction is largely attributable to improvements in both levels of living (especially in diets and housing) and public health practices. (Prior to World War I these primarily consisted of the provision of sanitary sewers and water treatment plants, and the enforcement of smallpox vaccination statutes.) In addition, changes in the proportion of the population living in urban areas affected aggregate mortality; infectious disease can spread more easily in an agglomerated setting. Finally, although dramatic advances in medical science were made during the last two decades of the 19th century, their impact was felt primarily in the area of public health.
>
> The effect of improved living standards on health is readily seen in rural America, where public health was virtually nonexistent: death rates there declined strikingly between 1880 and 1910. On the other hand, in urban areas, which had the benefit of both public health and improved living standards, the decline in mortality was even more dramatic.
>
> An explanation of health improvement based on rising living standards and better public health fits well the actual trend of mortality experience. Before 1880, the beneficial aspects of increased living standards on aggregate mortality were offset by the adverse effect of urbanization. Public health was nearly unknown prior to 1880; however, after that date cities rapidly began to install sanitary sewers and improved water works. . . . These public health measures reduced the negative impact of urban living on health, and the combination of continuing improvement in living standards and new public health projects resulted in the downward trend in overall mortality that began late in the 19th century. . . .
>
> While modern medicine has unquestionably led to a decline in the overall death rates, this reduction bears no comparison with that due to the combined effect of public health measures and improvements in the living standards. The overall decline in the death rate which took place prior to 1920 exceeds that which has occurred since. Almost none of the former reduction in the death rate, and only part of the latter, is attributable to medical practice.[21]

Although the argument seems reasonable, little evidence is presented on the various mortality determinants, except for public health, to support it. Hence in Table 3 a crude attempt has been made to assemble pertinent measures. If real national income per capita can be taken as a reasonable proxy for the trend in level of living, one finds that this rose almost as rapidly in the forty-year period before 1880 as after (line 1, cols. 6,7). The rise in the proportion urban, which has a negative impact on mortality, is greater in the forty-year period after 1880 (line 2, cols. 6,7). If the beneficial effects of increased living standards were offset by the adverse effect of urbanization before 1880 this would appear to be even more the case from 1880 to 1920, unless public health advances reduced the urban-rural mortality differential to negligible size very shortly after 1880, an unlikely event. If

one moves back to the 1800–1840 period, urbanization is much lower than after 1840, so its adverse effect would be much smaller, while the admittedly debatable figures on real national income per capita show a substantial rise, although less than after 1840. All in all, the impression one gets from this brief look at key mortality determinants is that it raises doubts about the case for a lack of improvement before 1880.

One problem with Table 3 is that the changes in mortality determinants are not translated into their mortality effects, so that their comparative weights can be accurately assessed. Table 4 represents a rough attempt to do this, though it should be viewed as no more than illustrative of research needs. The details of the procedures appear in the notes to the table; the general rationale follows.

Consider first the theoretical relationship between life expectancy and real NNP per capita with other factors—public health, medical arts, urbanization and virulence of pathogens—held constant. For reasons spelled out by Auster and others, the effect of given absolute increments in income on life expectancy should be positive but at a diminishing rate—in effect, a diminishing marginal productivity of income in terms of life expectancy—until a point is reached where further increments in income have zero effect on life expectancy.[22] Preston has estimated such a relationship using international cross-section data for the 1930's and 1960's[23]. For application to the nineteenth century, the levels of Preston's curves are undoubtedly too high, because they have been shifted upward by medical and public-health advances. Moreover, the controls for other variables are not perfect. But if one assumes that the shape of the 1930's curve in the relevant income range remained fairly constant between the nineteenth century and the 1930's, then one can form some tentative notion of the differential advance in life expectancy implied by the observed increments in U.S. per capita income in the three forty-year periods after 1800. The results, shown in line 1 of Table 4, show rather similar orders of magnitude, with the smallest advance occurring in the period after 1880. The similarity among the periods reflects two offsetting factors—a larger absolute growth in income in each successive period making for greater advance in life expectancy, and the "diminishing returns" effect making for a progressively smaller impact from any given absolute income change.

To estimate the effects of urbanization and public-health changes, the framework presented in Higgs's Appendix is employed.[24] The national average life expectancy at any given time is viewed as an average of urban and rural life expectancies, weighted respectively by urban and rural shares of total population. In Table 4 the effect of urbanization in a given period is estimated by multiplying the average differential in urban-rural life expectancy during the period by the change in the proportion of the population urban. The effect of public-health advances in a given period is obtained by weighting the differential gain in urban over rural life expectancy by the average proportion of the population urban.

The effect of urbanization on life expectancy, shown in line 2 of Table 4, is, of course, negative. The order of magnitude of the urbanization effect is considerably

Table 3. Values of Key Determinants of Life Expectancy, Specified Dates 1800–1920

	units of measurement	(1) Level 1800	(2) 1840	(3) 1880	(4) 1920	units of measurement	(5) Change 1800– 1840	(6) 1840– 1880	(7) 1880– 1920
1. National income per capita	1963 dollars	205	306	542	985	percent/year	1.00	1.44	1.50
2. Proportion of population urban	percent	6.1	10.8	28.2	51.2	percent points	4.7	17.4	23.0
3. Public health							negligible		substantial

Sources And Methods:

Line 1. Indexes of net national product (in decade averages centered on specified date) for 1840, 1880, 1910 and 1920 from Davis *et al.* (1972), *American Economic Growth*, p. 34, were converted to per capita terms using total population as given in U.S. Bureau of the Census (1960), *Historical Statistics of the United States: Colonial Times to 1957*, Series A p. 72. For 1800–1840, Gallman gives a crude estimate of the per capita rate of change in Gallman, (1975), "The Agricultural Sector and the Pace of Economic Growth: U.S. Experience in the Nineteenth Century," p. 54, which permitted the NNP per capita index to be extended from 1840 back to 1800. The index values were then converted to 1963 dollar values using Preston's figure for national income per head in 1904–1913 as the absolute value for 1910 (Preston, (July 1975) "The Changing Relation between Mortality and Level of Economic Development" p. 245.

Line 2. U.S. Bureau of the Census (1964), *Characteristics of the Population.*

Table 4. Guesses at Change in National Life Expectancy Implied by Changes in
Key Determinants, Three Periods, 1800–1920
(years)

Determinant	1800–1840	1840–1880	1880–1920
1. National income per capita	+6.5	+7.5	+5.0
2. Proportion of population urban	–0.4	–1.7	–1.4
3. Public health	0	0	+3.0
4. Net	+6.1	+5.8	+6.6

Sources And Methods

Line 1. For the initial and terminal dates of each period, life expectancies corresponding to the national income per capita values in Table 3, cols. 1–4,
were read from the "1930's" curve in Preston, "The Changing Relation
. . . ," p. 235, and differenced to obtain the change over each period.

Line 2. Computed from $(e_0^u - e_0^r)$ $(\Delta\mu)$, where the first term is the average shortfall
of urban compared with rural life expectancy in a given period, and the
second is the change in the proportion of the population urban as given in
Table 3, cols. 5–7. The first term was assumed to be 10 years in the first
two periods, an order of magnitude suggested by nineteenth-century
figures in Vinovskis (March 1972), "Mortality Rates . . . ," Tables 6 and
8, and Yasuba (1962), ch. III, and 1900 data in Thompson and Whelpton,
p. 242, and Taeuber and Taeuber (1958) *The Changing Population of the
United States*, p. 274. For the third period it was assumed to average 6.25
years, implying a decline in the rural-urban differential, 1880–1920, of
7.5 years (see explanation in next section).

Line 3. In 1900, life expectancy at birth of white males was 10 years higher in rural
than urban areas; by 1939 this differential had been reduced to about 2.5
years (Taeuber and Taeuber, 1958, pp. 274–275). This differential gain of
urban over rural areas of 7.5 years was assumed to be true also for the
period 1880 to 1920, though it is almost surely an overestimate. This gain
was assumed to reflect the differential impact of public health on urban
areas, and was multiplied by the average percentage urban in this period,
around 39.7 (Table 3, cols. 3 and 4) to obtain the implied change in
national life expectancy.

less than for the income effect, reflecting the fact that even with a 10-year urban-rural life expectancy differential, a shift in a 40-year period of about one-fifth of the population to urban areas will produce only a two-year decline in national life expectancy. The adverse effect of urbanization is smaller from 1880 to 1920 than from 1840 to 1880, despite the larger population shift in the later period, because the average urban-rural life expectancy differential is assumed to be lower in the later period, due to public-health advances.

The effect of public-health changes, shown in line 3, is by assumption zero before 1880. For the period 1880 to 1920, a very large diffential gain of urban compared with rural mortality, equal to 7.5 years, has been assumed, but since the urban population averages only about 40 percent of the total population in this period, the effect on national life expectancy on public-health changes is reduced to a gain of three years.

Summing the effects of income, urbanization and public health in the three periods, one finds that the "predicted" changes in national life expectancy are about the same order of magnitude, thus casting doubt on the notion of a lack of improvement before 1880. Despite the fact that gains from public health are absent in the first two periods, income change yields substantial gains in all periods and its effect is somewhat greater before 1880.

Several qualifications to Table 4 should be noted. First, while an attempt was made in developing the estimates to make reasonable assumptions, the appropriateness of using Preston's curve for the 1930's to estimate the effect of income on life expectancy in the nineteenth century is seriously in doubt. Second, the growth in national income per capita for 1800–1840 is highly conjectural. Some authors have estimated that growth may have been negligible; others, that is was virtually as high as after 1840.[25] A relevant finding, implying that for mortality analysis the estimate in Table 4 may be too high, is Gallman's inference that there was little improvement in the American diet between 1775 and 1840, although there was a marked advance thereafter.[26] Third, the state of public health in cities may have worsened in the period from 1800 to 1860, in which case negative entries might be appropriate in columns 1 and 2 of line 3.[27]

These last two considerations suggest that the estimated gains in life expectancy in the first two periods, and especially that for the 1800–1840 period, may be high relative to the gain for the third period. Nevertheless, one is hardly left with the impression of a level life expectancy trend before 1800, especially in view of the sizeable growth of income between 1840 and 1880. More plausible, perhaps, is an inference like that which Stolnitz made for Western European countries in his study of life expectancy trends from the 1840's to the 1940's—an uptrend throughout the period, but at a considerably higher rate after the 1890's.[28] Clearly much more work is needed on both the nature and causes of American mortality trends before this issue can be satisfactorily resolved.

II. WAS THE HISTORICAL DECLINE IN AMERICAN FERTILITY DUE TO INDUSTRIALIZATION AND URBANIZATION?

The Issue.   In Western European countries other than France the "demographic transition" in fertility—a shift from high to low birth rates—commences in the latter part of the nineteenth century. It is typically linked with a "vital revolution" in mortality rates and associated by scholars in a general way with the ongoing process of industrialization and urbanization.

Students of the American fertility decline have come increasingly to question an interpretation stressing so heavily industrialization and urbanization. The pioneering study was by Yasukichi Yasuba, a doctoral dissertation done under Simon Kuznets at Johns Hopkins University.[29] As was true of most who had previously studied nineteenth-century fertility, Yasuba used as a measure of fertility the "child-woman ratio," the ratio of children under 10 (or under 5) to women of reproductive age, computed from published census data on the sex and age distribution of the population. Working with child-woman ratios for states, calculated from the federal censuses from 1800 to 1860, Yasuba found (as had others) much higher fertility in newer western states than in older eastern states, both in the North and South.[30] He also noted a repeated pattern of declining fertility as a state aged. In seeking to explain these patterns, Yasuba found that the most important factor associated with fertility differences and trends was population density—the higher the density, the lower the child-woman ratio. In his analysis density was measured as the ratio of current population to 1949 arable land. Yasuba interpreted this density measure as an index of the availability of land, and argued that:

> . . .[In] a community where the supply of land is limited, the value of children as earning assets is low and hence the demand for children may not be so great as where there is plenty of open land nearby. The increased cost of setting up children as independent farmers and fear of the fragmentation of family farms may further encourage the restriction of family size in densely populated areas.[31]

Subsequently, Potter examined Yasuba's analysis and found it "not very convincing. in the first place, high density is itself correlated with high urbanization. . .; secondly, the terms 'availability' and 'ease of access' are ill defined."[32] Potter argued that if there was a decline in the birth rate in this period, "it seems to have been heavily concentrated in the urbanized counties and above all in the industrializing areas of the Northeast; the decline elsewhere may have been so slight as to be negligible."[33] He concludes that "the evidence still seems to support the view that industrialization and urbanization, with the accompaniment of higher living standards and greater social expectation (but possibly also higher infant mortality), were the main reasons for the declining rate of population

growth, either through postponement of marriage or the restriction of family size."[34]

Thus the issue is joined—were urbanization and industrialization at the bottom of the American fertility decline? If not, was the cause of the decline bound up with decreasing "land availability"?

The evidence. Since Potter's critique, new work has been done following up Yasuba's hypothesis, some of which is supportive and some not. The most extensive study is by Forster and Tucker, who were particularly interested in evaluating Potter's views on the importance of urbanization and industrialization.[35] Because of this, they focused especially on fertility data relating to rural areas. In addition, they explored how sensitive Yasuba's results were to the methodology employed, and found them quite robust. Addressing themselves particularly to Potter's statement, quoted above, that the birth-rate decline was concentrated in urbanized and industrializing areas of the Northeast, they conclude:

> This has too many things against it:. . . the downward trends appear to have been much more general, affecting largely rural states and territories as well as more highly urbanized states in the northeast; Yasuba's failure and our own to obtain close inverse associations between refined birth ratios and urban proportions by means of "standardized rank correlation" or Kendall's coefficient of partial rank correlation . . .; our failure to obtain significant coefficients of partial linear correlation between refined birth ratios and urban proportions after logarithmic transformation of the explanatory variables . . .; [and] the generally downward trends of the *rural* white refined birth ratios of states and territories during the period 1800–1840. . . .[36]

Further, they factor the absolute decline from 1810 to 1840 in children aged 0–4 per 1,000 women 20–44 for the total population into three components, with the following results:[37]

Component	Percentage share in decline
Decline in rural birth rates	78
Decline in urban birth rate	11
Rural–to–urban shift of population	11
All components	100

Again they are led to the conclusion that the rural fertility decline is the fundamental source of the decline for the total population.

Vinovskis, in a multivariate analysis of child-woman ratios in 1850 and 1860 for

states other than those in the American West, introduced a new factor into the picture, education.[38] His results are summarized as follows:

> This study confirmed the value of including more independent variables in the analysis. Yasuba's and Forster and Tucker's investigations confined themselves mainly to examining the effects of urbanization and land availability, ignoring such potentially important factors as education. In fact, this analysis discovered that the percentage of the white adults who were illiterate was the best predictor of fertility differentials in 1850 and 1860.[39]

Leet and McInnis extended Yasuba's approach to a lower level of aggregation—namely, counties within a state or province—the first to Ohio in 1850 and 1860 and the second to the Canadian provinces of Ontario and Quebec in the census years 1851–1881.[40] Like Yasuba and Forster and Tucker before them, they found high correlations between child-woman ratios and land availability. Unlike Vinovskis, Leet found that the introduction of an education variable did not alter the central importance of land availability.

A common problem with the studies discussed so far, whether pro or con the Yasuba hypothesis, is their reliance on published census data.[41] Because of this, differences between old and new states shown by child-woman ratios might be caused by differences in the composition of the population, by, say, marital status, age and place of residence. For example, the child-woman ratio might be lower in older compared with newer states because of a lower proportion of females married or because of a larger share of lower fertility urban-industrial persons in the population. As has already been suggested by the discussion above, the authors of these studies were well aware of these influences, and attempted to test for them, with most success in the case of rural-urban residence. Recently, an opportunity has arisen to resolve these questions more definitively, by use of the massive sample of rural households taken from the 1860 manuscript censuses by Fred Bateman and James D. Foust.[42] The sample covers all households living on farms or in rural villages in each of 102 townships scattered across sixteen northern states from New Hampshire to Kansas. In total there are 20,664 households, and over half of the household heads live and work on farms.

This sample has been used by Easterlin, Alter and Condran to address the problems of possible compositional influences in the published census data.[43] They single out households in old and new areas living on farms and in which the wife is a given age—in her thirties, say—and living with her husband. The results, shown in line 2 of Table 5, show clearly that there were real fertility differences between farm households in old and new areas. Nor can this finding be attributed to differences in the ethnic mix of the population. As shown in line 3 there was little variation between old and new areas in the foreign-born proportion of the population. Lines 5 and 6 suggest that wives in older areas not only started their

Table 5. *Mean Value of Specified Item for Farm Husband-Wife Households with Wife Aged 30–39, by Settlement Class, Bateman-Foust Norhtern Farm Sample, 1860*

Line Item	All classes	Farm Settlement Class[a]				
		I(Old)	II	III	IV	V(New)
1. Number of households	2,870	757	766	470	565	312
2. Children 0–49	2.11	1.77	2.01	2.40	2.42	2.22
3. Percent of heads born abroad	15	13	11	17	16	28
4. Age of wife	34.3	34.5	34.2	34.2	34.2	34.2
5. Age of mother at first birth	22.7	23.3	22.8	21.8	21.9	23.7
6. Age of mother at latest birth	29.6	28.9	29.2	30.2	30.3	29.9
7. Percent literate:						
a. Husbands	94	96	96	93	89	93
b. Wives	91	97	96	87	84	86
8. Percent of migrants with all children born in state of residence[b]	74	—	87	84	79	35
9. Growth of constant dollar value of land and buildings per farm acre, percent per year	1.8	1.3	1.6	2.0	2.0	2.2

[a] Households were grouped according to the farm settlement class of the township in which they reside. Settlement classes, consisting of quintiles from zero to 100 percent, are established by computing for each county containing a sample township the percentage of everimproved agricultural land not improved by 1860.

[b] For migrants with at least two children and head born in northcentral or southern states.

Source: Lines 1–8, Easterlin (forthcoming), "Factors in the Decline of Farm Family Fertility in the United States: Some Preliminary Results." Line 9, from worksheets underlying Easterlin, "Population Change and Farm Settlement in the Northern United States," *Journal of Economic History*

child-bearing later but probably terminated it earlier, presumably, at least for some wives, by the deliberate limitation of fertility.

Vinovskis's emphasis on literacy as a key factor in the fertility differentials is also called into question. In these farm households, literacy was generally high (line 7). While literacy does show a negative relation with fertility, of the type found by Vinovskis, the variation in literacy between old and new areas is small and accounts for only a small proportion of the total fertility variation. As was true in Leet's more aggregative study, the authors find that when education and a land-availability measure are both used as explanatory variables, land availability is much more important.

One novel finding in this study is the somewhat intermediate level of fertility shown by households in the very newest area (line 2, last column). The authors suggest that the reason for this is that, in contrast to the other areas, many of the residents of the newest area had started child-bearing under the less favorable fertility conditions in the older areas from which they had migrated. Evidence consistent with this hypothesis is shown in line 8 of Table 5.

Causes of the fertility decline. The evidence for the United States clearly calls into question the usual explanation of the secular fertility decline based on industrialization and urbanization. But if this explanation does not hold, there remains the problem of explaining why fertility did decline—in particular, why families show declining fertility as an area becomes more settled.

One way of trying to salvage the urbanization thesis is to argue that there was a diffusion of new knowledge about contraception from urban to rural areas. Potter states, for example: "One can do no more than suggest the possibility that, from about the 1820's the deliberate limitation of family size through contraception was beginning in certain parts of the northern states. If this were indeed a significant factor, then both the growth of towns and the improvement of communications must be granted an important role in facilitating the spread of knowledge."[44] While Potter is thinking primarily in terms of the sources of declining fertility in urban areas, a similar argument might be advanced for farm areas as well, on the grounds that contraceptive knowledge spread from urban to rural areas.

The problem with this argument is that the means of fertility limitation within marriage that appears most likely to have been used by farm families is coitus interruptus, and use of this practice is hardly contingent upon new information. Moreover, since so many of the high-fertility households in newer areas had migrated from older areas, one can hardly suppose that those in older areas were privy to knowledge not available to those in newer areas. It seems highly doubtful, therefore, that the secular fertility decline can be attributed to the diffusion of new fertility-control knowledge.

The most plausible explanations for the decline in farm-family fertility link it to economic pressures that arise as an area becomes settled. It is such pressures that Yasuba had in mind (as is clear from the quotation above), as well as other scholars

who obtained similar findings. One source of these pressures may be connected with the value of child labor. The argument is that children are especially valuable in new areas because of the demands for breaking and clearing new land, on the one hand, and a shortage of sources of labor supply, on the other. Hence there is an incentive to high fertility which diminishes as an area becomes settled. The evidence for this argument, however, is uncertain. For example, the argument implies that wage rates for young farmhands would be systematically higher in newer than older areas. In fact, this does not seem to have been true throughout much of the nineteenth century.[45]

Another explanation emphasizing economic pressures centers on farmers' concerns for giving their children a start in life. These concerns, suggested by previous scholars, have been developed more fully in recent work.[46] If one assumes that a farmer wishes to provide for each of his children at least as well as he himself was provided for, then the number of children he can "afford" will depend on the outlook for multiplying his capital during the course of his lifetime. If, for example, he can anticipate a six-fold multiplication of his capital, he will be able to provide for six children; if he can only expect a doubling of his capital, he can afford no more than two children. Since the prospective growth of capital declines with the stage of settlement of an area, pressures for limiting fertility grow correspondingly. As an area is initially settled, farmers anticipate high economic returns and a rapid increase of their capital, which means little problem of giving their offspring a proper start in life. As an area ages, however, the prospective rate of return declines (in part because of the opening up of newer areas), and the outlook for continuing to increase one's capital at the same rate correspondingly diminishes. Hence, a farmer in an old area, as the number of his offspring grows, will become increasingly concerned about his ability to give his children a proper start in life, and feel pressure to prevent further additions.

There are ample indications of lower economic returns in eastern compared with western farm areas in the nineteenth century, as, indeed, economic theory would say were necessary to induce the westward movement of population that was taking place. The competition caused by the opening up of new areas in the West was in part responsible for the dimming of the outlook in the East. The abandonment of farms in some eastern areas and the need in others to take up new lines of actitivity such as dairying and market gardens attest to the pressures that were being felt in the East. Another indicator, although an imperfect one, of differences between older and newer areas in economic returns is the growth in farm-acreage values that actually occurred. These data are given in line 9 of Table 5 and show, as hypothesized, a positive relation with fertility. The only exception is the newest area; but, as has been mentioned, a large proportion of the children enumerated in this area were conceived and born in the less favorable fertility environments of the settlers' areas of origin.[47]

Factors similar to those operating in farm areas may have been at work in urban

areas too. In cities the prospective return from child labor was lower than on farms, and became increasingly restricted by child-labor laws. Moreover, the costs of childrearing were higher, since food, housing and the opportunity-cost of a wife's time, the dominant elements in child cost, were typically higher than in rural areas. In addition, concerns about educating one's children—an investment in human capital much like the farmer's interest in the provision of material capital for his offspring—may have served as a deterrent to unrestricted fertility.

The issue posed at the start of this section can not be viewed as fully resolved, although we do know more about the facts and possible explanatory factors. But there remains a distressing lack of information on inheritance arrangements in nineteenth-century America, on the manner in which farms and farmland passed from hand to hand in the course of the settlement process, and on the extent to which parents felt responsible for giving their children a start in life, whether in farming or not. If this gap in knowledge could be bridged, it would help not only to clarify trends and differentials in family-building in nineteenth-century America, but also to provide new insight into the mechanisms shaping our social structure.

III. DID NINETEENTH CENTURY IMMIGRATION RAISE THE RATE OF POPULATION GROWTH? OF PER CAPITA OUTPUT GROWTH?

The issue. For the most part economic historians have left to their colleagues in history the pleasures of extolling the virtues of immigration. Of course, if "immigration" is taken to include all inflows of persons since the discovery of America there can be no issue about its importance. Or if attention is focused on cultural or political contributions, then the question lies outside the economic historian's competence. But if, as is sometimes the case, the problem centers on the contributions of immigration to American economic growth in a specific period—say, the nineteenth century,—then a relevant issue is posed. Would America's rate of economic development have been noticeably different in the absence of the massive nineteenth-century immigration that made America the "melting pot of the world?"[48]

Since immigrants came in great numbers, especially from the 1840's on, and their locations, jobs and (less accurately) rates of pay can be fairly well identified in historical records, it is possible to point to such evidence, as historians do, as a record of accomplishment. But this leaves some troubling questions unanswered. Did immigration merely take the place of native population growth which would otherwise have occurred, a possibility suggested almost a century ago by Francis A. Walker and since termed "the Walker effect?"[49] If so, then the jobs and incomes held by the foreign-born might in the absence of immigration have been held by native-born. Of course, if immigration did not supplant native population growth—if there were no "Walker effect" and the total growth of the American population had been no more, say, than the actual increase of the colonial stock of

1790—then the expansion in labor force would have been less, and growth of *total* output smaller. But what of output growth *per capita*? To say that the total size of the American economy would have grown less rapidly is not to say that the living levels of the native-born descendants of the colonial stock would have moved forward at a slower pace. Thus, two issues are raised: in the absence of nineteenth-century immigration, would American population growth have been less? And did immigration raise or lower the rate of growth in America's per capita output?[50]

Analysis. Although inquiry into such issues has been surprisingly scarce, there has been some work of relevance. A recent paper by Albert W. Niemi, Jr., addresses itself to the role of immigration in United States commodity production since 1869.[51] It concludes that "as much as 14 percent of the United States 1909 per capita commodity production would have been lost in the absence of immigration."[52] The methodology is described as follows:

> The generation of the estimates of the contribution of foreign born labor to total commodity output is rather simple: (1) estimates are made of employment in the commodity producing sectors of agriculture, manufacturing, mining and construction for the total labor force and for foreign born labor; (2) a commodity output series is estimated, by sector, for 1869–1929; (3) average labor productivity for each commodity producing sector is constructed for the total labor force; (4) the product of average labor productivity of the total labor force and immigrant employment, by sector, is taken to yield estimates of commodity output produced by the foreign born labor force.[53]

The key to the result obtained is that immigrants are disproportionately concentrated in commodity-producing industries with above average output per worker. The "marginal productivity" of a typical immigrant worker is thus taken to be higher than that of a native worker, so that addition of an immigrant raises per capita commodity output more than that of a native-born worker.

An important problem with this procedure is that it does not provide a *ceteris paribus* estimate of the effect of immigration. The contribution attributed to immigration is a composite of numerous factors. As noted, the calculated contribution stems from the higher than average productivity level in industries in which immigrants were concentrated. But suppose there had been no capital accumulation or technological progress in these industries after 1869? Then the expansion of the work force of these industries (from immigration or any other source) with *all other factors held constant* would have quickly lowered the marginal productivity of labor to that prevailing in other industries. With a zero productivity differential among industries, the differential contribution of subsequent immigration to per capita output, all other things being equal, would also have been zero. Thus, one cannot accept the results of the calculation as a plausible estimate of the contribution of immigration *per se* to per capita output.

A more ambitious assessment of the effect of immigration on economic growth, covering the period 1790–1912, appears in a paper by Neal and Uselding.[54] The authors assume that the "Walker effect" existed in full, that is, that in the absence of immigration the rate of natural increase of the American population would have been equal to the actual rate of population growth. This assumption, they believe, understates the gains to the economy from immigration derived by their estimating procedure.

The source of the gains to the economy which Neal and Uselding seek to estimate is a more rapid accumulation of physical capital brought about by immigration. They argue that immigration freed resources from the production of consumer goods that would have been required to rear children in a population wholly dependent on natural increase as its source of growth. Some proportion of the resources so released was devoted to capital goods production that would not otherwise have occurred. Employing variant assumptions, they estimate that by 1912 "between 13.2 and 41.9 percent of the total capital stock could be attributed to the accumulated effects of immigration."[55] To put it differently, if the United States had had to rely solely on natural increase to achieve the observed population of 1912, capital equipment per worker at that time might have been as much as 42 percent lower than it actually was.

The authors do not estimate the likely effect of lower capital per worker on output per worker, although they imply that it would have been susbstantial. In most attempts to account for the factors underlying per capita output growth, however, the source that is found to be important is not the growth of capital or other factor inputs per capita, but the productivity of the factor inputs.[56] This raises some doubt about the importance of their results for per capita product growth.

An analysis by Easterlin comes to more skeptical conclusions about the economic significance of nineteenth-century immigration.[57] With regard to the effect of immigration on population growth, the Walker effect is rejected. In his view it is doubtful that high immigration caused lower fertility, because declines in American fertility are observed in times and places not only where immigration was high but also where immigration offered little or no competition. Fertility turned down early in the nineteenth century, before any substantial influx of immigrants occurred. Moreover, fertility declines occurred not only in the areas of immigration but in others as well, notably the American South. What seems to be a common feature of the areas where fertility declines set in is not that workers in these areas were experiencing competition from foreign immigrants, but that the process of settlement was completed. Moreover, without immigration to supply the labor demands of industrial cities, the workers for American industrial expansion would have been drawn more from rural areas than was actually the case. This means that the native-born population would have been less involved in new settlement and more engaged in urban activities—that is, more exposed to a low-than a high-fertility environment. This implies that in the absence of immigration, fertility might have been even lower than that actually observed. Thus, it is

doubtful that American population growth would have been unaltered if immigration had been prevented. On the contrary, in the absence of immigration, American population growth would have been lower in the nineteenth century. The analysis then turns to the effects of lower population growth on output growth. If one assumes that there had been no immigration after 1790 and that natural increase of the 1790 colonial stock would have been the same as it actually was (implying no effect of immigration, positive or negative, on native fertility), then the white population of 1920 would have numbered 52 million, about half the actual population. With population growth halved, total output growth would have undoubtedly been lower. But what of output growth per capita?

The author turns first to the evidence on growth rates of per capita output and population to see whether there is any association between trends in the two magnitudes. The answer is no. Each magnitude shows a long period of secular stability during which the other changes markedly. Prior to 1860 the secular growth rate of population was high and fairly stable, while the secular growth rate of GNP per capita was rising. After 1860, the pattern shifts. The growth rate of GNP per capita remains high with little evidence of a secular trend, but the growth rate of population moves downward.

Theoretical arguments about the effects of immigration are then considered, among them whether immigration added special skills or entrepreneurial abilities to the labor force. The author points out that while there were immigrants who succeeded as entrepreneurs and others who had special labor skills, the foreign-born are underrepresented among the industrial leaders of the nineteenth century. The great bulk of the "captains of industry" were native-born, and the mass of immigrants filled manual jobs which could have been done by native workers.

As for whether immigrants were exceptionally motivated, the point is made that vigorous pursuit of material gain is apparent in American towns and rural areas as early as the seventeenth century, and was the despair of early religious leaders. The story of land speculation seems much the same whether one is looking at Puritans in seventeenth-century New England or their descendants in the nineteenth-century Midwest.

The critical question in the author's view is whether the growth and spread of modern technology would have occurred as rapidly in the United States in the absence of substantial nineteenth-century immigration. Pointing to the first half of the nineteenth century, a period in which immigration played a small role in population growth, the author notes that it was during this period that the "American System of Manufacturing" came into being, a system so distinctive that at mid-century the world's leading industrial nation, Great Britain, sent a special commission to study it. Most of the leaders in the development of the American machine-tool industry were native Americans. This suggests that even before immigration rose markedly in the nineteenth century, the United States was well started on the transformation of its economy to modern technology. This was probably because Americans shared a common cultural heritage with the leading

people in the process of modern economic growth, the English; were in close touch with developments in that country; were strongly oriented toward material gain; and were operating within a framework of institutions that favored economic mobility. Moreover, the American colonial population was an especially favorable selection from the English population. In England, Nonconformist groups provided entrepreneurs of the Industrial Revolution far out of proportion to their numbers. In the United States, the much higher representation of English Nonconformists in the population provided an unusually favorable basis for modern economic growth.

Finally, it is noted that in Europe, and especially northwestern Europe, high *emigration* did not prevent the development and adoption of modern technology. In the United States between 1840 and 1957 real per capita product multiplied 4.6 fold; in the major European countries, the corresponding figure was as follows:

United Kingdom, 1850's to 1950's	3.7
West Germany, 1870's to 1960's	5.2
France, 1840's to 1960's	5.2

In the author's view it is doubtful that in the absence of heavy immigration the relative standing of the United States would have been significantly reduced, because the same processes that raised per capita product so markedly in the European countries were also operating in the United States, even before immigration became substantial.

IV. OTHER ISSUES

The discussion above has sought to focus attention on some key issues in the relation between population and economic development in nineteenth-century American history—issues regarding the causes of mortality and fertility change and the effects of immigration. Any such survey of the literature is necessarily selective and reflects the author's biases and interests. In conclusion, brief note should be made of several other subjects in the population area that have attracted considerable scholarly interest in recent years.

The first is the causes, rather than the effects, of international migration. In particular, the relative importance of "push" versus "pull" factors as causes of migration has been a subject of controversy. For example, Brinley Thomas, in a pioneering work published shortly after World War II, viewed the nineteenth-century surges in American immigration as arising from European development, such as the potato famine in Ireland or accelerated natural increase.[58] In contrast, Easterlin saw these movements as primarily responses to swings in labor demand in the United States.[59] The analysis of this question and more generally of the causes of migration—trends, differentials, and fluctuations in the United States

and elsewhere—has produced a number of contributions in the last two decades. A recent article by Jeffrey A. Williamson provides a valuable summary and critique of this work.[60]

The second subject is that of swings in population growth and the relation of population swings to similar movements in economic growth. Concern with such questions, particularly in connection with building cycles, goes back a long way.[61] It was Simon Kuznets, however, who focused new attention on the subject in the post-World War II period by presenting new evidence of waves in population growth and linking them to more general movements in the rate of economic growth.[62] Easterlin, following Kuznets and Abramovitz, sought to develop a causal model of economic-demographic interrelations during long swings, and to link earlier swings in immigration to the post-World War II swing in fertility.[63] Other writers have expressed reservations about the reality of these movements, or have attempted to formulate and test more rigorous formal models.[64]

Finally, the recent flood of interest in slavery has engendered a spate of articles on the black population both before and after the Civil War. Although this research has involved some attention to questions of causality, most of its has focused on establishing the facts of change—fertility, mortality and the movement of persons, both internal and external. In view of the fact that the historical record for the white population is only imperfectly known and that data on the black population are much more inadequate, this emphasis on establishing facts seems well placed. A recent article by Edward Meeker provides a helpful bibliography.[65]

At the outset of this article, it was pointed out that by comparison with scholars interested in European economic history, researchers in American economic history have been backward in their attention to population. Nevertheless, the impression with which one comes away from this survey is that there is a burgeoning of interest and scholarship in the area that augurs well for the future.

FOOTNOTES

*The research on which this paper is based is supported by NICHD grant 1-R01-HD 05427. Valuable assistance has been provided by Robert Cohen, Stacy Hinck, Neil Weintraub, and Katheryn Wisco.

1. Krooss (1955), chapter 4. See also Gilboy and Hoover (1969), pp. 247–280; Niemi, Jr. (1975), chapter 13. The fullest recent treatment is in Davis *et al*, (1972), chapter 5. For a helpful survey of population in history textbooks, see Landes (1972), pp. 23–42.

2. Yasuba (1962); Potter (1964), pp. 631–688; Forster and Tucker (1972).

3. Demos (April 1965), pp. 264–286; Demos (1968), pp. 40–57; Greven (April 1966), pp. 234–256; Henretta (January 1965), pp. 75–92; Lockridge, (1966), pp. 318–344. Exceptions to the statement in the text are Higgs and Stettler, III (April 1970), pp. 282–294; and Stettler, III (1970), pp. 17–27.

4. Drake (1969); Eversley (1965), Section VII; Glass and Eversley (1965); Habakkuk (1971); Wrigley (1971).

5. For valuable discussions see Mendels (April 1970), pp. 1065–1073; Tilly and Tilly (March 1971), pp. 190–191; Tilly (forth coming), chapters 1, 9 and Bibliography; Kantrow and van de Walle (October 1974), pp. 611–623; Wrigley (1966); Hollingsworth (1969).

6. Kantrow (1976); Wells (Autumn 1971), pp. 273–282; Wells (March 1971), pp. 73–82.

7. The analysis in this section has benefitted a great deal from discussions with Gretchen Condran and Eileen Crimmins-Gardner, who are currently engaged in studying long-neglected census data on mortality. See Condran and Crimmins-Gardner (April 29, 1976).

8. Higgs (Winter 1973), pp. 73–195; Meeker (Summer 1972), pp. 353–374; Vinovskis (March 1972), pp. 184–219.

9. Meeker (forthcoming), pp. 6–7.

10. Higgs (Winter 1973), p. 182.

11. Stolnitz (July 1955), pp. 24–55.

12. Vinovskis (March 1972), p. 212.

13. Meeker (Summer 1972), p. 353. (Italics mine.)

14. Meeker (forthcoming), p. 4. (Italics mine).

15. Lockridge (1966), p. 332; Demos (April 1965), pp. 270–272; Greven (April 1966), pp. 237–240; Norton (November 1971), pp. 440–441; Smith (March 1972), pp. 167–169.

15a. Stolnitz (July 1955).

16. Higgs (Winter 1973), pp. 189–194.

17. Davis et al, (1972), p. 145.

18. Vinovskis argues that the 1789 figure is too low, but the only numerical adjustment he makes raises the 1789 figure by about one year, which would still imply an increase in life expectancy between 1789 and 1850. (Vinovskis, September 1971, pp. 570–591).

19. Meeker (forthcoming), p. 4.

20. Higgs adds the possibility of a decline in the virulence of pathogens. He concludes that this factor probably accounts for "less than one-sixth of . . . the decline in the rural crude death rate [in the half century] before 1920." (Higgs, Winter 1973, p. 188).

21. Meeker (forthcoming), pp. 7–9.

22. Auster, Leveson and Sarachek (Fall 1969), pp. 411–436.

23. Preston (July 1975), pp. 231–248.

24. Higgs (Winter 1973), appendix, p. 195.

25. David (1973); Gallman (1971); Gallman (1975); and Martin (1939).

26. Gallman (1971), pp. 71–77.

27. Gore (September 1903), pp. 30–56; Yasuba (1962), chapter 3.

28. Stolnitz (July 1955).

29. Yasuba (1962).

30. Grabill, Kiser and Whelpton (1958), chapter 1; T'ien (January 1959), pp. 49–59.

31. Yasuba (1962), p. 159.

32. Potter (1965), p. 677.

33. Ibid., p. 676.

34. Ibid., p. 678.

35. Forster and Tucker (1972).

36. Ibid., p. 88.

37. Ibid., p. 90.

38. Vinovskis (forthcoming). Another recent study which raises doubts about Yasuba's results is that by Modell (1971), pp. 615–634. However, his failure to obtain supporting results is probably due to his concentration on frontier counties. There are no "older areas" in his analysis.

39. Vinovskis (forthcoming), mimeograph manuscript p. 11.

40. Leet (1975), pp. 138–158; Leet (April 1974); McInnis (April 1972). See also Bloomberg, Fox, Warner and Warner, Jr. (Fall 1971), pp. 26–46.

41. McInnis did draw a sample from the manuscript censuses which, though more limited in size than that reported on here, yielded similar results. (McInnis, forthcoming).

42. Bateman and Foust (January 1974), pp. 75–93.

43. Easterlin, Alter and Condran (forthcoming).

44. Potter (1965), p. 678.

45. Easterlin (March 1976), p. 61.

46. *Ibid.* pp. 45–83.

47. In a new and wideranging theoretical and empirical study, Lindert explores some of these questions for a later period, arriving at results which are in some respects similar. See Lindert (forthcoming). A recent study examining economic pressures on fertility in coal mining areas is Haines (July 1975).

48. Contributions by historians to this subject are, among others, Handlin (1954); Hansen (1964); Handlin and Handlin (1955), pp. 17–48.

49. Walker (August 1891), p. 638.

50. Useful earlier studies bearing on these questions are Gilboy and Hoover (1961); Spengler (1958), pp. 17–51; and Thomas (1955), pp. 166–174.

51. Niemi, Jr. (June 1971), pp. 190–196.

52. *Ibid.*, p. 196.

53. *Ibid.*, pp. 191–192.

54. See Neal and Uselding (1972), pp. 68–88. A related paper by Uselding is concerned with correcting Corrado Gini's old estimates of the human capital provided by immigration; that is, in transforming the figures on foreign-born labor force by occupation into wealth estimates using earnings data. See Uselding (Fall 1971), pp. 49–63.

55. Neal and Uselding (1972), p. 84.

56. The pioneering studies were Abramovitz (May 1956), pp. 5–23; and Solow (August 1957), pp. 312–320. Gallman provides the most up-to-date analysis, but for total, not per capita, GNP. If his results are converted to per capita terms, the contribution of productivity growth is greatly enhanced. See Davis *et al* (1972), p. 39.

57. See Davis *et al.* (1972), pp. 173–181.

58. Thomas (1954), pp. 116–118. An up-dated and expanded version has recently been issued. (See Thomas, 1972).

59. Easterlin (April 1961), pp. 331–351.

60. Williamson (Summer 1974), pp. 357–391.

61. Silberling (1943); Hansen (1941); Isard (November 1942a) pp. 149–158; and Isard (November 1942b) pp. 90–110.

62. Kuznets (February 1953); pp. 25–52; and Kuznets (1961), chapters vii, viii.

63. Easterlin (1968); Abramovitz (April 1961), pp. 225–248.

64. Denton and Spencer (1975); Franks and McCormick (June 1975), pp. 295–343; Klotz and Neal (August 1973), pp. 291–298; and Neal (1974), pp. 34–43.

65. Meeker (January 1976), pp. 13–42. See also Fogel and Engerman (1974), Vol. 1, pp. 23–29, 79–84, and 124–126.

REFERENCES

Abramovitz, Moses (May 1956), "Resources and Output Trends in the U.S. since 1870," *American Economic Review, Papers and Proceedings,* 46, pp. 5–23.

———.(April 1961), "The Nature and Significance of Kuznets Cycles," *Economic Development and Cultural Change,* 9, pp. 225–248.

154 RICHARD A. EASTERLIN

Auster, Richard, Leveson, Irving and Sarachek, Deborah, (Fall 1969), "The Production of Health, An Exploratory Study," *The Journal of Human Resources*, 4, p. 411–436.

Bateman, Fred and Foust, James D. (January 1974), "A Sample of Rural Households Selected from the 1860 Manuscript Censuses," *Agricultural History*, 48, pp. 75–93.

Bloomberg, Susan E., Fox, Mary Frank, Warner, Robert M. and Warner, Jr., Sam Bass (Fall 1971), "A Census Probe into Nineteenth Century Family History: Southern Michigan, 1850–1880," *Journal of Social History*, 5, pp. 26–46.

Coale, Ansley J. and Zelnik, Melvin (1963), *New Estimates of Fertility and Population of the United States*, Princeton, N.J.: Princeton University Press.

Condran, Gretchen and Crimmins-Gardner, Eileen (April 29, 1976), "The United States Population in the Nineteenth Century: Mortality," Montreal: paper presented at the annual meeting of the Population Association of America.

David, P.A. (1973), "New Light on a Statistical Dark Age: U.S. Real Product Growth before 1840," *New Economic History* (edited by Temin, Peter), Baltimore: Penguin Books, Inc.

Davis, Lance E. *et al.* (1972), *American Economic Growth*, New York: Harper & Row.

Demos, John (January 1968), "Families in Colonial Bristol, Rhode Island: An Exercise in Historical Demography," *William and Mary Quarterly*, 25, pp. 40–57.

———. (April 1965), "Notes on Life in Plymouth," *William and Mary Quarterly*, 22, pp. 264–286.

Denton, Frank T. and Spencer, Byron G., (1975), *Population and the Economy*, Boston: D.C. Heath.

Drake, Michael (1969), *Population in Industrialization*, London: Methuen and Co.

Easterlin, Richard A. (December 1976), "Factors in the Decline of Farm Family Fertility in the United States: Some Preliminary Research Results," *Journal of American History* 63, pp. 600–614.

———. (April 1961), "Influences in European Overseas Emigration before World War I," *Economic Development and Cultural Change*, 9, pp. 331–351.

———. (March 1976), "Population Change and Farm Settlement in the Northern United States," *Journal of Economic History*, 36, pp. 45–83.

———. (1968), *Population, Labor Force, and Long Swings in Economic Growth*, New York: National Bureau of Economic Research.

Easterlin, Richard A., Alter, George and Condran, Gretchen A. (forthcoming), "Farms and Farm Families in Old and New Areas: The Northern States in 1860," *Demographic Processes and Family Organization in Nineteenth Century American Society* (edited by Hareven, Tamara K. and Vinovskis, Maris A.), Princeton, N.J.: Princeton University Press.

Eversley, D.E.C., ed. (1965), *Third International Conference of Economic History*, Munich 1965, Section VII, Paris: Mouton & Co.

Fogel, Robert William and Engerman, Stanley L. (1974), *Time on the Cross*, Boston: Little, Brown & Co.

Forster, Colin and Tucker, G.S.L. (1972), *Economic Opportunity and White American Fertility Ratios, 1800–1860*, New Haven: Yale University Press.

Franks, Charles M. and McCormick, William W. (June 1971), "A Self-Generating Model of Long Swings for the American Economy, 1860–1940," *The Journal of Economic History*, 32, pp. 295–343.

Gallman, Robert E. (1975), "The Agricultural Sector and the Pace of Economic Growth: U.S. Experience in the Nineteenth Century," *Essays in Nineteenth Century Economic History: The Old Northwest* (edited by Klingaman, David C. and Vedder, Richard K.), Athens, Ohio: Ohio University Press.

————. (1971), "The Statistical Approach: Fundamental Concepts as Applied to History," *Approaches to American Economic History*, (edited by Taylor, George Rogers and Ellsworth, Lucius F.), Charlottesville, Va.: The University Press of Virginia.

Gilboy, Elizabeth W. and Hoover, Edgar M. (1961), "Population and Immigration," *American Economic History* (edited by Harris, Seymour E.), pp. 247–280, New York: McGraw-Hill.

Glass, D.V. and Eversley, D.E.C. eds. (1965), *Population in History*, London: Edward Arnold.

Gore, John K. (September 1903), "On the Improvement in Longevity in the United States During the Nineteenth Century," *Proceedings of the Fourth International Congress of Actuaries*, pp. 30–56, New York.

Grabill, Wilson H., Kiser, Clyde V. and Whelpton, P.K. (1958), *The Fertility of American Women*, New York: John Wiley and Sons, Inc.

Greven, Philip J. (April 1966), "Family Structure in Seventeenth Century Andover, Massachusetts," *William and Mary Quarterly*, 23, pp. 234–256.

Habakkuk, H.J. (1971), *Population Growth and Economic Development since 1750*, New York: Humanities Press.

Haines, Michael (July 1975), *Fertility and Occupation: Coal Mining Populations in the Nineteenth and Early Twentieth Centuries in Europe and America* occasional paper No. 3, Ithaca, N.Y.: Cornell University Western Societies Program.

Handlin, Oscar, ed. (1959), *Immigration As a Factor in American History*, Englewood Cliffs, N.J.: Prentice-Hall, Inc.,

Handlin, Oscar and Thomas, Brinley, eds. (1955), *The Positive Contribution by Immigrants*, Paris: United Nations Educational, Scientific and Cultural Organization.

Handlin, Oscar and Handlin, Mary F. (1955), "The United States," *The Postivie Contribution by Immigrants* (edited by Handlin, Oscar and Thomas, Brinley), pp. 17–48, Paris: United Nations Educational, Scientific and Cultural Organization.

Hansen, A.H. (1941), *Fiscal Policy and Business Cycles*, New York: W.W. Norton.

Hansen, Marcus Lee (1964), *The Immigrant in American History*, New York: Harper & Row.

Henretta, James A. (January 1965), "Economic Development and Social Structure in Colonial Boston," *William and Mary Quarterly*, 22, pp. 75–92.

Higgs, Robert (Winter 1973), "Mortality in Rural America, 1870–1920: Estimates and Conjectures," *Explorations in Economic History*, 10, pp. 177–195.

Higgs, Robert and Stettler III, H. Louis (April 1970), "Colonial New England Demography: A Sampling Approach," *William and Mary Quarterly*, 27, pp. 282–294.

Hollingsworth, T.H. (1969), *Historical Demography*, Ithaca, N.Y.: Cornell University Press.

Isard, Walter (November 1942a), "A Neglected Cycle: The Transport Building Cycle," *Review of Business and Statistics*, pp. 149–158.

————. (November 1942b), "Transport Development and Building Cycles," *Quarterly Journal of Economics*, pp. 90–110.

Jacobson, Paul H. (April 1957), "An Estimate of the Expectation of Life in the United States in 1850," *The Milbank Memorial Fund Quarterly*, 35, pp. 197–202.

————. (July 1964), "Cohort Survival for Generations Since 1840," *The Milbank Memorial Fund Quarterly*, 42, pp. 36–53.

Jones, E.F. (October-December 1971), "Fertility Decline in Australia and New Zealand: 1861–1936," *Population Index*, 37, pp. 301–338.

Kantrow, Louise (1976), "The Demographic History of a Colonial Aristocracy: A Philadelphia Case Study," Ph.D. dissertation in demography, University of Pennsylvania.

Kantrow, Louise and van de Walle, Etienne (October 1974), "Historical Demography vs. Demographic History," *Population Index*, 40, pp. 611–623.
Kelley, Allen C. (September 1965), "International Migration and Economic Growth: Australia, 1865–1935," *The Journal of Economic History*, 25, pp. 333–354.
Klotz, Benjamin and Neal, Larry (August 1973), "Spectral and Cross-Spectral Analysis of the Long-Swing Hypothesis," *Review of Economics and Statistics*, 60, pp. 291–298.
Krooss, Herman E. (1955), *American Economic Development*, chapter 4, Englewood Cliffs, N.J.: Prentice-Hall, Inc.
Kuznets, Simon (1961), *Capital in the American Economy: Its Formation and Financing*, Princeton, N.J.: Princeton University Press.
———. (1965), *Economic Growth and Structure, Selected Essays*, New York: W.W. Norton and Co., Inc.
———. (February 1953), "Long-Swings in the Growth of Population and in Related Economic Variables," *Proceedings of the American Philosophical Society*, 102, pp. 25–52.
Landes, David (1972), "The Treatment of Population in History Testbooks," *Population and Social Change*, (edited by Glass, D. V. and Revelle, Roger), pp. 23–42, London: Edward Arnold.
Leet, Don R. (1975), "Human Fertility and Agricultural Opportunities in Ohio Counties: From Frontier to Maturity, 1810 to 1860," *Essays in Nineteenth Century History: The Old Northwest*, (edited by Klingaman, David C. and Vedder, Richard K.), pp. 138–158, Athens, Ohio: Ohio University Press.
———. (April 26–28, 1974), "The Determinants of the Fertility Transition in Antebellum Ohio," paper presented at the annual meetings of the Population Association of America.
Lindert, Peter (forthcoming), *Fertility and Scarcity in America*, Princeton: Princeton University Press.
Lockridge, Kenneth (1966), "The Population of Dedham, Mass., 1636–1736," *Economic History Review*, 19, pp. 318–344.
Martin, Robert F. (1939), *National Income in the United States, 1799–1938*, New York: National Industrial Conference Board, Inc.
McInnis, R. Marvin (April 13–15, 1972), "Birth Rates and Land Availability in Nineteenth Century Canada," Toronto: paper presented at the annual meeting of the Population Association of America.
———. (forthcoming), "Childbearing and Land Availability: Some Evidence from Individual Household Data," *Population Patterns in the Past*, (edited by Lee, Ronald D.), New York: Academic Press.
Meeker, Edward (January 1976), "Mortality Trends of Southern Blacks, 1850–1910: Some Preliminary Findings," *Explorations in Economic History*, 13, pp. 13–42.
———. (forthcoming), "Public Health and Medicine," *Dictionary of American Economic History*, New York: Charles Scribner's Sons.
———. (Summer 1972), "The Improving Health of the United States, 1850–1915," *Explorations in Economic History*, 9, pp. 353–374.
Mendels, Franklin F. (April 1970), "Recent Research in European Historical Demography," *American Historical Review*, 75, pp. 1065–1073.
Modell, John (1971), "Family and Fertility on the Indiana Frontier, 1820," *American Quarterly*, 23, pp. 615–634.
Neal, Larry (1974), "Structural Breaks, Shifting Harmonics, or Random Effects?: Spectral Results of the Death of the Long Swing," *Proceedings of the American Statistical Association*, pp. 34–43.

Neal, Larry and Uselding, Paul, (1972), "Immigration, A Neglected Source of American Economic Growth: 1790–1912," *Oxford Economic Papers*, 24, pp. 68–88.

Niemi, Jr., Albert W., (June 1971), "The Role of Immigration in United States Commodity Production, 1869–1929," *Social Science Quarterly*, 51, pp. 190–196.

————. (1975), *U.S. Economic History: A Survey of Major Issues*, chapter 13, Chicago: Rand-McNally.

Norton, Susan L. (November 1971), "Population Growth in Colonial America: A Study of Ipswich, Massachusetts," *Population Studies*, 25, pp. 433–452.

Okun, Bernard (1958), *Trends in Birth Rates in the U.S. since 1870*, Baltimore: Johns Hopkins Press.

Potter, J. (1965), "The Growth of Population in America, 1700–1860," *Population in History*, (edited by Glass, D.V. and Eversley, D.E.C.), pp. 631–688, London: Edward Arnold.

Preston, Samuel H. (July 1975), "The Changing Relation between Mortality and Level of Economic Development," *Population Studies*, 29, pp. 231–248.

Silberling, N.J. (1943), *The Dynamics of Business*, New York: McGraw-Hill.

Smith, Daniel S. (March 1972), "The Demographic History of Colonial New England," *The Journal of Economic History*, 32, pp. 165–183.

Solow, Robert M. (August 1957), "Technological Change and the Aggregate Production Function," *The Review of Economics and Statistics*, 39, pp. 312–320.

Spengler, J. J. (1958), "Effects Produced in Receiving Countries by Pre-1939 Immigration," *Economics of International Migration* (edited by Thomas, Brinley), pp. 17–51, London: Macmillian.

Stettler, III, H. Louis (1970), "The New England Throat Distemper and Family Size," *Empirical Studies in Health Economics: Proceedings of the Second Congress on the Economics of Health*, pp. 17–27, Baltimore: Johns Hopkins Press.

Stolnitz, George J. (July 1955), "A Century of International Mortality Trends: I," *Population Studies*, 9, pp. 24–55.

Taeuber, Conrad and Taeuber, Irene B. (1958), *The Changing Population of the United States*, New York: John Wiley.

————. (1971), *People of the United States in the 20th Century*, Washington, D.C.: Bureau of the Census.

Thomas, Brinley (1954), *Migration and Economic Growth*, Cambridge: Cambridge University Press.

————. (1972), *Migration and Urban Development*, London: Methuen & Co.

————. (1955), " The Economic Aspect," *The Positive Contribution by Immigrants*, (ed. Handlin, Oscar and Thomas, Brinley), pp. 166–174, Paris: United Nations Educational Scientific and Cultural Organization.

Thompson, Warren S. and Whelpton, P.K., (1969), *Population Trends in the United States*, New York: Gordon and Breach Science Publishers.

T'ien, H. Yuan (January 1959), "A Demographic Aspect of Interstate Variation in American Fertility, 1800–1860, *Milbank Memorial Fund Quarterly*, 37, pp. 49–59.

Tilly, Charles, ed. (forthcoming), *Historical Studies of Changing Fertility*, chapters 1, 9 and Bibliography, Princeton, N.J.: Princeton University Press.

Tilly, Charles and Tilly, R. (March 1971), "Agenda for European Economic History in the 1970's," *Journal of Economic History*, 31, pp. 184–198.

Uhlenberg, P.R. (November 1969), "A Study of Cohort Life Cycles: Cohorts of Native-Born Massachusetts Women, 1830–1920," *Population Studies*, 23, pp. 407–420.

U.S. Bureau of the Census (1964), *Characteristics of the Population*, Washington, D.C.: Government Printing Office.

————. (1960), *Historical Statistics of the United States, Colonial Times to 1957*, Washington, D.C.: Government Printing Office.

Uselding, Paul (Fall 1971), "Conjectural Estimates of Gross Human Capital Inflows to the American Economy: 1790–1860," *Explorations in Economic History*, 9, pp. 49–63.

Vinovskis, Maris A. (forthcoming), "A Multivariate Regression Analysis of Fertility Differentials in Massachusetts Towns in 1860," *Historical Studies of Changing Fertility* (edited by Tilly, Charles), Princeton, N.J.: Princeton University Press.

————. (March 1972), "Mortality Rates and Trends in Massachusetts Before 1860," *The Journal of Economic History*, 32, pp. 184–214.

————. (September 1971), "The 1789 Life Table of Edward Wigglesworth," *The Journal of Economic History*, 32, 570–591.

Walker, Francis A. (August 1891), "Immigration and Degradation," *The Forum*, 11, p. 638.

Wells, Robert V. (Autumn 1971), "Demographic Change and the Life Cycle of American Families," *Journal of Interdisciplinary History*, 2, pp. 273–282.

————. (March 1971), "Family Size and Fertility Control in Eighteenth Century America: A Study of Quaker Families," *Population Studies*, 25, pp. 73–82.

Williamson, Jeffrey G. (Summer 1974), "Migration to the New World: Long Term Influences and Impact," *Explorations in Economic History*, 11, pp. 357–391.

Wrigley, E.A., ed. (1966), *An Introduction to English Historical Demography from the Sixteenth to the Nineteenth Century*, Cambridge Group for the History of Population and Social Structure, Publication No. 1, London: Weidenfeld and Nicolson.

————. (1971), *Population and History*, New York: McGraw-Hill Co.

Yasuba, Yasukichi (1962), *Birth Rates of the White Population in the United States, 1800–1860*, Baltimore: Johns Hopkins Press.

STUDIES OF TECHNOLOGY IN ECONOMIC HISTORY

Paul Uselding, UNIVERSITY OF ILLINOIS

Herman Krooss carried a gentle, probing sense of irony with him in his rounds as an economic and business historian, much as a good carpenter carries a ruler.For most of his professional life economic history was a "small" discipline. The *cognoscenti* were relatively few in number, and the volume of first-rate literature in the field could be fitted into the reading schedule of nearly all. In the late 1950's exponential growth came to the profession of economic history and shortly thereafter its literature expanded enormously. One does not have to have Herman's perspicacity to realize that an individual scholar can no longer cover everything under the rubric of economic history and be as widely informed of the developments in all the sub-branches of the discipline as it was once possible to be. Today we are specialists, we know more of a particular thing, but less of the generality. Those who knew Herman will always remember his wit. It stabbed and darted about a roomful of academicians like the incandescence from a Leyden jar—in brilliant but never fatal pulses of energy. Perhaps it was his persistent and ever gentle reminder that we were, as specialists, becoming a duller lot than we had any right to be? Whatever the case may be, Herman knew that the "knowledge explosion" had hit economic history and was bringing in its train vertical disintegration, specialization of function and division of labor, that ever familiar trinity in the annals of economic and business history. He envisioned a series of monographs, built upon review articles written by specialists, as a way of coping with

the rapid accumulation of essays and monographs in the field, to improve the total flow of information and keep all economic historians abreast of developments outside the areas of their special competence. It is especially fitting that the structure of Herman's own memorial volume should bear so clearly the influence of his own observation.

As economic historians are fond of empirical proofs, let me offer my findings on the possibilities for conveniently reviewing all the recent studies of technology that bear upon economic history. Even in the generous format herein provided, the task is hopeless. By confining my review mainly to U.S. studies since the apperance of H. J. Habakkuk's epic work in 1962 it is possible to keep the task within barely manageable bounds. Even with this severe organizing principle, not even the barest coverage of the major monographs can be given; British experience is given only the briefest coverage, and Continental and nonindustrial aspects must be virtually omitted. One can only assume that similar problems of inclusion would confound attempts at longish reviews in other areas of economic history. Having pursued the subject of technology in economic history for over a decade, and having read everything within bibliographic purview, I still had enormous difficulty in pulling together even the recent literature. If its subsets are that large, it must be the case that the recent literature of economic history proper must be beyond the reading range of a single individual. This report is hardly an independent discovery, but rather a confirmation of what Herman already knew: the paradox of the literature management and assimilation problems, usually associated with whole fields of learning, in what is customarily regarded as "an area" of economics proper. The paradox runs at many levels: the "large" field problems being visited upon a "small" one such as economic history, the rapidity of structural change in a field that had been accustomed to a traditional mode, a dilemma usually associated with the sciences appearing to bedevil historians, and historians writing collectively more than they can read individually in several lifetimes. Herman loved that sort of thing!

I. HABAKKUK AND HIS INTERPRETERS

The appearance of H. J. Habakkuk's celebrated *American and British Technology in the Nineteenth Century* in 1962 gave rise to a stream of interpretive literature attempting either to refine or elaborate upon the themes he set out.[1] Practically all work on American technology in the 19th century appearing in print since 1962 has been influenced by Habakkuk because the work is so inclusive and wide-ranging in its scope. Yet the very nature of Habakkuk's argument has led to no little misunderstanding, and a certain degree of controversy.

The central problem contained in Habakkuk's work concerns the explanation of why Americans had, by the time of the Crystal Palace Exhibition in 1851, evolved a mechanical technology which the British had not. The story of American prowess

at the Crystal Palace, the displays of the Colt Revolver, the McCormick Reaper, the Singer Sewing Machine—all embodying the principle of interchangeability —is now a familiar tale. The explanation of how American mechanics and entrepreneurs evolved these special methods of production known to contemporaries as "the American System" is one of the central features of Habakkuk's book. Many elements are brought into play: 1) labor scarcity and the choice of technique, 2) the rate of investment, 3) market inperfections, 4) the trade cycle, 5) demand factors and 6) the general level of economic development, including the role of agriculture.

Habakkuk adduces a set of general equilibrium characteristics and attempts to weave them into a mutually consistent set of explanatory forces. However, this exercise by its very nature is beset with several problems. First, the historical and economic conditions which are sufficient to explain the emergence of a distinctive industrial sector in New England are not necessarily the same factors that can suitably explain the "inducement to mechanise" in the New England context. Because of the manner of presentation of the argument it is not always entirely clear what factors are intended to explain the level and structure of economic development, as distinct from the nature of the particular line of evolution displayed in the choice of mechanical techniques in the industrial sector. There is no rigorous partitioning of the technological as opposed to the economic development aspects of the emergence of an American industrial sector exhibiting high rates of technical progress and labor productivity growth.

The second difficulty present is common to most work in economics attempting to deal with technology, the tension between the purely economic definitons, such as "a shift in the production function" or "a set of long-range planning blueprints embodying all scientific and productive knowledge currently available," and the need of the historian to come to grips with productive arrangements and artifacts as they actually existed. What do we mean by terms such as technological change? Technology? If, for example, you were sent to Houston, Texas, with the assignment of writing a report on technology, where would you begin to look for evidence of technology? Almost automatically one would begin to think of looking for specific, concrete, observable "things" and to describe them. But the "thing" is merely a manifestation of cultural, social and economic forces that have brought it into existence. These forces, which influence the existence and evolution of the thing-aspect of technology, are difficult to isolate and describe. If one comes at the problem from the vantage point of a particular discipline, that produces a kind of monodimensional view of the terrain. Hence, we get purely economically determined explanations of technological evolution, social theories, political explanations, or even the internalists' view that "technology has its own logic and dynamic." Beyond that the social, political and economic influences on technology do not act in their respective force fields without mutually influencing each other, hence making the task of isolation of pure effects more difficult.

There are really three questions involved in a work such as Habakkuk's: a) How do we describe or define the state of technology that is of interest? b) How does "the state of technology" evolve to some predetermined point? c) How do we measure or describe the consequences of a particular sequence of technical events? At all points the tension between the economic and historical view of the problem exists.

The third kind of difficulty in an analysis of Habakkuk's type relates to the spirit of the inquiry, and whether or not the method of inquiry is appropriate to what is at issue—in this case, the reasons for differential evolution of technology in Britain and America. The spirit of Habakkuk's approach is definitely historical, concerning itself with the classic historical problem of change over time. The method of analysis is neoclassical, best suited to a description and explanation of behavior in an invariant economic structure. At most, neoclassical analysis permits the description of an economic system in different equilibrium states by the method of comparative statics as a way of handling change over time. Structural change of an evolutionary nature cannot be handled within neoclassical models, as is wellknown. These models conveniently describe such things as the consequences of a shift in the production function, but do not explain what it is that gives rise to the shift itself. As such, explanations of phenomena like technological change are confined principally to effects, like labor productivity measurement, measures of the factor bias in technical advance and other familiar descriptions of the consequences of an alteration in the productive arrangement. Moreover, when the facts adduced are handled from the vantage point of economic consequences it is generally the case that only economic influences are admitted into the analysis. The model, neoclassical in Habakkuk's case, preselects only certain salient features of historical experience as relevant to the problem at hand. But beyond this, the very nature of the problem chosen is heavily influenced by the explanatory range of the model and its underlying rationale. The formal dissonance in Habakkuk's work reflects his choice of an historical problem, the comparative evolution of technology; and his attempt to handle it in part by standard economic-historical explanation and in part by the comparative static analysis of neoclassical economics. In short, the nature of the problem Habakkuk chose to analyze is much broader and more evolutionary in character than the spirit of the formal explanatory apparatus he employed. Comparative statics has no purchase on the problem of structural change.

While Habakkuk spoke of two distinct concomitants of labor scarcity—factor intensity within a given technology and technological change—most of the subsequent work has focused on factor substitution within a given technology, for the simple reason that this part of Habakkuk's problem is most readily amenable to direct analysis by models cast in the neoclassical framework. Peter Temin set out ". . . to reexamine the statements of the British visitors of the 1850's and the labor-scarcity explanation of American conditions to see if they can be formulated

in terms of modern concepts and if they are supported either by logical inferences or by empirical evidence.''[2] Since Temin's 1966 essay did not offer any empirical evidence, its contribution must be seen in the light of any clarification it provided on the issues raised by Erwin Rothbarth and their subsequent expansion and restatement by Habakkuk.[3]

As Temin has pointed out, Rothbarth's model contains two sectors: agriculture and manufacturing. Agriculture uses only labor and land in production, while manufacturing uses only labor and capital. Temin argues that this specification is a fair interpretation of the Rothbarth-Habakkuk version of the labor scarcity hypothesis and that, "Despite its obvious shortcomings this model appears to be implicit in all discussions of this problem."[4] Using this two-sector, two-factor specification and the maintained hypothesis of a common technology between Britain and America, Temin derives the factor-price dual of the common production function, i.e., factor-price frontier. Since both countries had identical factor-price frontiers, and since the frontier is convex to the origin and negatively sloped, it follows that a higher American interest rate (which evidence is adduced by Temin from information outside the formal model) would be consistent with an American wage rate that was lower than the corresponding wage rate in Britain. Temin thus concluded that the factor substitution interpretation of the labor scarcity hypothesis was not tenable and that if Americans were, in fact, using more capital per worker the reasons for it must be sought in explanations which emphasized the economic differences which led to the divergence in the technology of the two countries.

Temin's attempt to come to grips with both aspects of Habakkuk's argument ("more machines" and "better machines" per worker) foundered because of several errors in execution. First, the maintained hypothesis under which Temin derives the common factor-price frontier implies two economies which are structurally identical in every economic respect. This is so because Britain and America share a common technology and form for the production function in Temin's formulation. Strictly speaking, the formal requirements of the model imply that the economies were identical and this purely internal characteristic of the argument would not permit the interest rates to diverge between the two economies. The evidence of the higher American interest rate is brought to bear as a brute fact of history; but formally it is inadmissable as evidence since the relatively higher American interest rate would have had to have been generated in a real world setting that did not conform in the slightest to the formal properties of the model, i.e., identical economies in every respect. Temin's procedure constituted an injudicious mixing of exogenous historical information that, in itself, was inconsistent with the maintained conditions under which the model was derived, and the internal implications of the model itself. Second, by too readily accepting the implied specification of the agricultural and manufacturing production functions suggested by Rothbarth, Temin ruled out too quickly the possibility that a variant

of the traditional version of the labor scarcity hypothesis could be consistent with the factor substitution interpretation under the maintained assumption of common technologies.

Robert Fogel turned his attention to this second problem and quickly reestablished the dual scarcity version of the labor scarcity hypothesis[5]; namely, that both the American interest and wage rates exceeded their British counterparts. This respecification led to the logical conclusion that dual scarcity would be consistent with the "more machines per worker" interpretation of the economic effects of labor scarcity. Fogel accomplished this objective by giving the manufacturing production function a more "realistic" specification. Land, in the form of agricultural output, was included in the production function of the manufacturing sector. This enabled Fogel to use the price of agricultural output as a shift parameter which, because of the adduced lower relative price of American agricultural commodities, moved the American factor-price frontier outward and everywhere above the British. This divergence in the factor-price frontiers of the two countries, with the American frontier everywhere above the British, was sufficient to establish the possibility of dual scarcity.

In 1970 I set out to explore the formal properties of the "more machines" vs. "better machines" analysis of the labor scarcity issue explored by Temin and Fogel[6]. While accepting Fogel's more inclusive specification of the manufacturing production function, I showed that the dual scarcity argument would be consistent with American factor proportions being either more or less capital intensive than the British. This showed that the question of relative capital intensity could not be established by merely ordinal estimates of the British and American interest rate positions on the ordinate of the factor-price frontier graph, as Fogel had attempted to do in his earlier essay.

As a further extension in the direction of "realism," I introduced two types of labor, skilled and unskilled, into the manufacturing production function. The effect of the introduction of unskilled labor into the manufacturing production function was to create another shift parameter, whose influence on the position of the American factor-price frontier relative to the British was ambiguous. This was so because the shift parameter arising from the introduction of unskilled labor into the production function tended to move the American factor-price frontier toward the origin, counter to the tendencies imparted by the other two shift parameters, the real prices of manufacturing and agricultural commodities.

In addition to that exercise, I also derived the factor-price frontier for the two economies from an agricultural production function in which unskilled labor, land and capital entered as independent variables. Since, under competitive assumptions, one would expect that competition between the two sectors, manufacturing and agriculture, would equalize the unskilled wage rate between them, I felt that it was necessary to show that American frontiers derived from both sectoral production functions would give equivalent answers, under plausible assumptions about

the relative magnitudes of agricultural and manufacturing prices. The question asked was whether or not the American unskilled wage rate would remain consistently above the British. The finding was that the manufacturing frontier implied an American unskilled wage rate greater than the British, consistent with available evidence and contemporary comment. However, when approached from the direction of the comparison of agricultural frontiers, the model implied that the American unskilled wage rate was below the British.

The conclusion of this exercise was that the two-sector models employed by Temin and Fogel, in conjunction with historical facts, do not give answers that are consistent with their own internal assumptions, i.e. competition between the two sectors for unskilled labor tending to bring about an intersectoral equalization of the unskilled wage rate in the American economy. The point of this exercise was to show that the conjectural estimates of the relative magnitudes of the shift parameters, based on the perceived, exogenous experience of some real, historical economies whose structure and behavior may not have conformed to the assumptions and implications of the theoretical model, could not establish results that were consistent with the internal logic of the model itself. If these adventures did not serve to resolve the "more machines" vs. "better machines" issues in the Rothbarth-Habakkuk analysis, they did serve a purpose in demonstrating rather strikingly that historical reality cannot be pulled rabbitlike from some theoretical hat.

In 1971, Peter Temin once again entered the lists in a further attempt at sharpening his earlier analysis of the labor-scarcity hypothesis[7]. According to Temin the following passage from Rothbarth contains the elements of the "Basic Theorem of the Labor Scarcity Hypothesis":

> In any country where land is readily available in large quantities, labour is likely to be expensive. For the income of the industrial worker must be sufficiently high to present an attractive alternative to his cultivating the land for his own profit. Thus the high productivity of labour in American industry at the beginning of this century can be explained by the fact that industry had to install labour-saving equipment and to economise in the use of labour until its productivity was sufficiently far higher than it was in agriculture to enable relatively attractive wages to be paid in industry[8].

Temin reformulates this statement into the two-part statement of the Basic Theorem:

(1.1) If one country has a higher ratio of land to labor than another, all other things being equal, then this country will use *more* machinery for each worker in manufacturing than the other country.

(1.2) If one country has a higher ratio of land to labor than another, all other things being equal, then this country will use *better* machinery for each worker in manufacturing than the other country.[9]

Temin then argues that only when land and labor are used to produce agricultural commodities, and only labor and capital are used to produce manufactures, will variant 1.1 of the Basic Theorem hold. This conclusion does not follow from the logic of an explicit factor-price frontier analysis. For if it were the case that the land-abundant country were also the country in which interest rates were high (which is not precluded by anything in Temin's specification), then the relatively land-abundant country would also have *less* machines per worker! Where ''less machines per worker'' is taken to mean a lower capital-labor ratio.

The second version, 1.2, of the Basic Theorem is analyzed by Temin under less restrictive assumptions; namely, that all three factors of production are used in both manufacturing and agriculture. He concludes that this variant cannot be applied to the American case, because it is necessary to show that the United States could not or would not levy tariffs to promote manufacturing at a given level of technology.[10] He also claims, quite legitimately, that it is not known that conditions in America in the 19th century were such as to preclude manufacturing under a regime of free trade. While this last point is formally acceptable, it does not answer the question of whether or not the qualitative and quantitative composition of the American manufacturing sector that was achieved by, say 1850, under actual historical circumstances could have emerged under free trade and the absence of technological change. Thus Temin adduces the conditions under which manufacturing could exist, in the absence of improvements in mechanical technology (better machines), and has modifid his statement of the 1.2 variant of his Basic Theorem to the point where it is no longer a proposition relating to the conditions under which technological change will occur.

Temin's schema has provided a useful way to summarize the dilemma of all writers dealing with the Habakkuk thesis. Versions of the labor scarcity hypothesis similar in spirit to Temin's 1.1 Theorem are amenable to treatment by the methods of comparative statics in a neoclassical framework. Even here, the use of exogenous information not consistent with the logical structure of the model can in certain instances render even this procedure tenuous in the extreme, as has been mentioned above. The second variant of the hypothesis, relating to technological change, is really an evolutionary proposition that requires a reasonably complete, even if less than formally rigorous, handling of all elements bringing about structural change in the manufacturing sector. Whether the Habakkuk thesis is really either one or both propositions of Temin's Basic Theorem is of interest only insofar as it relates to the purely formal properties of the argument. To understand in what respect American technology diverged from the British it remains necessary to go out and look at the facts, however they might be perceived. This is the domain of the historical as opposed to the deductive method.

Since the facts of Habakkuk's analysis were in dispute, and could not be deduced by available theory, this gave rise to a considerable industry founded on the accumulation of available wage data for various occupational groups in Britain

and America, which continues to the present day. The principal studies were carried out by Nathan Rosenberg, Donald Adams and Jeffrey Zabler.[11]

At this writing the final word on the interpretation of the Rothbarth-Habakkuk thesis has been written by Paul David.[12] The principal thrust of David's argument is to demonstrate the advantages of the "localized learning" formulation of technological change introduced by Atkinson and Stiglitz.[13] This view, being non-neoclassical in spirit, makes no attempt to distinguish between factor substitution and technological progress. Rather it views innovations as a series of specific changes in observable production methods. Focusing as it does on the possibilities for reducing production costs at a particular point in the set of available techniques, it is very much in keeping with Habakkuk's argument that technical possibilities are richest at the capital-intensive end of the production possibility spectrum. Moreover, the view holds that there are minimal "spill-over effects" from innovations or discrete changes in production processes taking place, at a given level of factor intensity, to on-going progress in some other significantly removed area of the factor intensity spectrum.

By initiating the process of technological progress at a particular level of factor proportions, the succession of technical advances proceeding over time has a Hicks neutral character when viewed at close range. Globally, the cumulative effect of localized change proceeding along Hicks neutral or quasi-neutral lines will acquire a particular factor-saving bias, reflecting the initial endowment point dictated by relative factor prices and their continuing influence with the passage of time. The essential notion is that localized learning possibilities carry producers down their available process ray (a ray from the origin to a particular point on the available process frontier, APF, which resembles the "kinky" von Neuman type production function, i.e. a linear combination of Leontief functions, which reflect the discrete nature of technological possibilities, rather than a spectrum of smoothly continuous production points as in the neoclassical world). This movement of the APF toward the origin constitutes technological progress in David's model. Further, the localization of specific, discrete improvements to existing technology is ensured by the existence of "elastic barriers" which bound the available process ray. Technological progress is likened to a random walk within these elastic barriers. Intuitively, the barriers arise from some unspecified amalgam of social, legal and political constraints which "bound" innovative possibilities. Moreover, they are plausible because much of technological history attests to the presence of purely embodied technological constraints—past capital accumulations—which force new technologies to conform to preexisting sequences of machines or processes. Such considerations may also be found in the economic development literature concerning "the advantages of borrowing and the penalty of taking the lead."

The main implication of David's conceptualization of the non-neoclassical view of technological progress is the nonseparability of resource inputs in the fundamen-

tal production functions of agriculture and industry. This means, according to David, that techniques that were relatively capital-intensive could also be resource intensive. There are a number of examples of this correspondence in the recent-literature of economic history which we will review below, so we will defer discussion of the authors David marshals in support of his proposition.

As a generalization of David's argument it should be pointed out that as more factors, other than capital and labor, enter the production function there are more "wedges" that loosen the direct dependence of the respective marginal productivities of capital and labor on the capital-labor ratio. Thus, depending on how inclusive one wants to be in specifying the righthand side of the production function, one can find all kinds of correlates that presumably "explain" or rather are consistent with capital intensity and labor-saving bias. What provides the historically appealing connection between resource-using technologies and capital-intensity is the work of Edward Ames and Nathan Rosenberg on the development of American woodworking technology, exogenous historical information, not the formal implications of David's model.[14] The localized learning model developed by David has the nice virtue of being consistent with the known facts of technological history, as written for the most part by economic historians. Whether or not it can provide an independent guide to new discoveries on why things developed technologically as they did in the American case remains an open question.

II. THE AMERICAN SYSTEM

While earlier studies by Duncan Burn in 1935 and John Sawyer in 1954 had brought to the attention of economic historians some of the main elements in the story of America's rise to prominence in the metal- and wood-working industries, Habakkuk's work renewed interest in this subject and gave rise to a number of subsequent studies dealing with various aspects of "the American System."[15] The term American System was an expression used by comtemporaries to denote the novel elements in America's mechanical technology. The main elements of machines or products falling under this rubric were: 1) standardization or rendering uniform the product to be manufactured, 2) division of labor and specialization of function, 3) uniformity of work method and 4) mechanization of the routinized and standardized work tasks. The first three elements were not, in themselves, dissimilar from the level of sophistication achieved in the latter stages of the handicraft system in America, or for that matter, in the Birmingham gun industry in England at mid-nineteenth century. What distinguished the American System of manufacturing was the use of special-purpose machinery, very often exhibiting the use of self-acting mechanisms in the workpiece feed and disengage modes of operation. Moreover, this special-purpose machinery was sufficiently accurate so that common piece parts produced by machining would be so close in dimensional tolerance as to permit assembly with a minimum of time for fitting, or mating the

connected parts of an assembly by the use of hand labor augmented by hammers, files, chisels, rasps, etc.

Although England held a considerable lead over the Americans in the purely technical aspects of what might be termed machine design and machine building, the English had not taken the possibilities of machine production and adaptation, in an economic sense, as far as the Americans by mid-nineteenth century. It is well to remember that an Englishman, Marc Isambard Brunel, had, by 1804, developed the Portsmouth block machinery, which in most respects duplicated the famous woodworking machinery (ultimately, 17 separate machines for turning gunstocks) of the American, Thomas Blanchard. And further, Brunel was in advance of Blanchard by almost a full two decades! Yet the mechanical principles embodied in the Portsmouth machinery never spread to the remainder of British industry, owing to the particular economic and cultural circumstances of the British economy in the early part of the nineteenth century. The failure of the British to adopt widely the essential principles found in the American System, was the focus of Habakkuk's inquiry.

In 1968, Nathan Rosenberg published the *Report of the Committee on the Machinery of the United States (1855)* and the *Special Reports of George Wallis and Joseph Whitworth*, in his *The American System of Manufactures*.[16] Rosenberg's introductory essay is a masterful exposition in three acts. First, Rosenberg recounts the impact the American exhibitors at the Crystal Palace Exhibition in 1851 had on the eminent mechanical engineers in England. Colt's revolvers, achieving practical interchangeability, and the factory in which he produced them were of special interest to the Board of Ordnance. The advantages of interchangeability were readily apparent, and the regularity and volume of production anticipated from an armory established according to the principles of the Colt works were sought by initiating inquiries into the requirements for establishing a Royal Arsenal at Enfield.

The second part of Rosenberg's essay recounts the role played by John Anderson, superintendent of machinery to the War Department, in bringing about the transfer of American-made special purpose machinery to Enfield. Rosenberg also redresses the balance of historical judgment by pointing out that the entire section of the report written by the Committee on Machinery (1855) relating to the production methods then in use in the United States was written by Anderson.[17]

The remainder of the essay pulls together the available information on specific items transferred to Enfield from the United States. Notable among them were the Lincoln miller, the Ames recessing machine and gun-stocking machinery of the Blanchard-Buckland type. The Enfield Arsenal experience was an example of English awareness of their lag in precision manufacture; it showed government determination to remedy the perceived shortcoming in small arms procurement, and it was the first direct transplantation of uniquely American machine processes to the supposedly more advanced economy of England. For counterpoint, Rosenberg also analyzes the state of the arms procurement industry in England, with

special reference to the Birmingham gunsmiths and the metal trades generally in the Birmingham district. Because of the wide variety of source material used by Rosenberg, including both British and American government reports and official documents directly relating to small arms production and machine technology, this essay would be a good reference point for anyone beginning an investigation of more specialized topics on the American System.

As an outgrowth of this work, Rosenberg collaborated with Edward Ames in a 1968 study of the implications of the Enfield Arsenal experience for production theory, as used by economic historians.[18] The essential point of this article was that conventional neoclassical production theory does not admit the use of historically significant categories and structures in characterizing production processes. "It is not possible to talk about Blanchard lathes and carpenters' tools in the context of homogenous capital."[19] The fact that America had, by verifiable evidence, evolved a set of machines qualitatively different from the English machines can only be analyzed by qualitative means, in the Ames-Rosenberg view. This aspect of "Habakkuk's problem" (referred to earlier in this essay as the evolutionary-historical part) is precisely where attempts at formalization of the issues along neo-classical lines have met with little success in adding to our understanding of how and why the production methods of the two countries diverged. As Ames and Rosenberg argue, it is meaningful, at the level of generalization where historical research proceeds, to speak of production functions differing, say, as between two countries, if their arguments are qualitatively different. Alternatively, production functions also differ, on this view, if some elements (milling machines) enter the list of predetermined variables of the historically defined function of one country and not the other. Hence, the presence or absence of certain specific, qualitative elements cannot be lightly dismissed as not fitting neatly into preconceived categories of homogeneous labor or capital inputs, since the qualitative elements may contain the essence of the phenomena under investigation.

In the subsequent work by Paul David, referred to in the preceding section, we saw how important the Ames-Rosenberg emphasis on the close historical connection between resource-intensive and labor saving technology was. The resource abundance of the American economy provides part of the key to understanding America's precociousness in adopting labor saving machinery. Interpreted in the Ames-Rosenberg spirit, the presence of "raw materials" in the historical production function, as well as other qualitatively different inputs, means that the marginal productivities of the homogeneous factors, "labor" and "capital," do not depend exclusively on the ratio of those factors. The bias of technical progress thus comes to depend on the presence (or absence) of third (wood), fourth (iron) . . . nth inputs. Moreover, the presence of multiple inputs, each qualitatively different, alters the pair-wise elasticity of substitution of the respect inputs, among them the homogeneous capital for homogeneous labor substitution rate; and this

fact will have implications for the homogeneous capital intensity of the production process. The Ames-Rosenberg work on the Enfield Arsenal was an early example of the dissatisfaction with the neoclassical theory of production as a means of characterizing technological change. Beyond that, it is a prime example of the impressive intellectual gains to be obtained from collaborative work in economic theory and history following the rules of division of labor and specialization of function. One may even go so far as to see in this work a premonition of the growing interest in evolutionary economic theory, just coming into vogue in recent years.

An essential feature of the difference between American metal machining and English practice was the fact that Americans had developed the process of metal removal by milling sometime before 1818. By the 1830's, milling machines were a rather common adjunct to many American metal working establishments. The transfer of American machinery to Enfield after 1854 included some milling machines; but notwithstanding this fact, milling machines did not become widely used in British industry until the 1890's. Because milling by machine methods was so distinctly an American practice throughout most of the nineteenth century, and because, according to popular legend, the origins of milling machines were linked to the inventive genius of Eli Whitney, there has been a great deal of interest in recent years in pinning down the exact lineage of this machine tool. Moreover, early writers had credited Whitney with practically inventing every aspect of the American System itself.

In 1960, Robert Woodbury, writing in *Technology and Culture*, effectively debunked most of the claims advanced for Whitney.[20] Although Woodbury accomplished this by the use of direct written evidence, his case would have to be considered circumstantial, since no direct patent claims or artifact evidence could be obtained. Woodbury's case against Whitney as the true inventor of the milling machine is made up of several parts. First, Whitney's celebrated contract of 1798 stipulated the production of a stand of 10,000 arms made by the principle of interchangeability, as it was then understood, and called for delivery by September of 1800. The contract was not actually fulfilled until January of 1809. Whitney's motivation for entering into the contract of 1798, which was unusual by prevailing standards, since very few private arms contractors could achieve a delivery rate of more than 500 arms per year at that time, much less arms that had interchangeable parts, was financial. As Woodbury documents, Whitney's most pressing concerns were with the litigation of suits involving infringements on his patent for the cotton gin. These legal interests kept him away from Connecticut a great deal of the time prior to 1806. Further, tests performed on actual surviving arms produced under the contract of 1798 proved that they were not interchangeable in all their parts. Moreover, documentary records attest to the fact that Whitney used a large number of files, which suggested to Woodbury that the "uniformity principle" employed by Whitney consisted of filing parts of the musket lock to shape with the aid of

pattern jigs. A final bit of evidence against the claim for Whitney as the inventor of the milling machine is the fact that he visited John Hall's rifle manufactory at the Harpers Ferry Armory after 1817 to see the "new system being adopted there." It is known that Hall began work on interchangeable manufacture before 1811, and began installing his system at Harpers Ferry by 1817. There is also documentary evidence that knowledgeable mechanics in the employ of the federal government, as arms inspectors, considered Hall's production machines to be the most advanced in use in America in the early 1820's.

Woodbury had established that Whitney was not likely to have been the sole inventor of the milling machine, that his uniformity system did not rest exclusively on metal removal by machines (as we know it today), and that Hall was more likely than Whitney to have been first in milling by machinery. In 1966, Edwin Battison, examining a Whitney arm in the Smithsonian collection, manufactured sometime between 1812 and 1824 on Whitney's second contract, concluded on the basis of physical evidence that Whitney did not use true milling practice during this period.[21] True milling requires metal removal by cutting as opposed to abrasion. Battison pointed out that Whitney probably used hollow milling performed by a vise-held rotary file and that the component parts of Whitney locks were marked prior to case hardening—a solid indication that they were mated uniquely in one assembly and therefore not interchangeable from one lock assembly to the next, as would be required if true interchangeability had been achieved at a practical level. Battison's findings were important in that the earlier physical evidence on which Woodbury based his argument was drawn from extant arms manufactured by Whitney before 1809. Woodbury's physical evidence still left open the possibility that Whitney might have invented the milling machine sometime between 1810 and 1818. Tending to undermine Battison's findings was the fact that the sample arm he used could have been drawn from a production batch made before Whitney invented the milling maching, anytime between 1812 and 1818. Additionally, the sample size was sufficiently small (perhaps one) so that the arms examined might well have all come from the 1812–1818 period. Nevertheless, Battison's findings tended to narrow the ground upon which the claim of Whitney's priority in inventing the milling machine could stand.

Further investigation into the origin of the milling machine was reported by Merritt Roe Smith in 1973.[22] Smith found documentary evidence consisting of the testimony of Simeon North, taken in 1852, that he invented the milling machine about the year 1816.[23] In addition, the testimony of Robert Johnson, a leading private contractor who, like North, was located in Middletown, Connecticut, said that North was the first person ". . . who milled his work generally in carrying on the business of a gunsmith."[24] Even though Johnson's testimony was recorded in 1852, well after the stated date of invention of 1816, it is an important corroborative finding. According to Smith, the second stage of milling development proceeded at the Harpers Ferry armory between 1819 and 1826 under the principal

direction of John Hall. From Harpers Ferry, milling technology was transmitted to the armsmakers of the Connecticut Valley by the migration of mechanics who had worked on Hall's machinery. Specific individuals and their destinations are adduced by Smith in his essay. While Smith's work is important for what it adds to our knowledge of the specific names, places and dates relating to the evolution of milling, it should be pointed out that North's and Johnson's testimony could have referred to the process of hollow milling, in the context of what could be construed to embrace the definition of a "machine" in 1816. Beyond that, however, Smith's essay establishes quite clearly that there were many individuals involved, some relatively obscure mechanics, in the development of modern milling practice. In this sense, Smith's finding fits more closely with the Usherian view of gradual evolution and multiple influence in technological progress, than with the Schumpeterian concept of dramatic discovery and personal ingenuity.

In 1973, Edwin Battison reported the results of in-progress research on the origins of the milling machine.[25] Several points emerge from Battison's latest research. First, by the time of Whitney's third government contract in 1822, he was making plans to acquire designs and ideas from more advanced armories. Battison further concludes that the "Whitney machine" of 1818 was probably a popularized version of John Hall's "straight cutting machine." Moreover, the popularly accepted date, 1818, of the Whitney machine is based on a highly circumstantial statement made by a technical writer, E.G. Parkhurst, writing in the March 8, 1900, issue of *American Machinist*.

Second, Battison points out that the possibility cannot be ruled out that some intermediate phase of milling development occurred elsewhere between the time of North's purported invention in 1816 and the date (1826) by which Hall's "straight cutting engine" was seen at Harpers Ferry. It should also be mentioned in this connection that Merritt R. Smith has not established conclusively that Hall's work was influenced by North, on the basis of available documentary or artifact evidence. Battison concludes by withdrawing his earlier claim for Robert Johnson as the probable inventor of the process of machine milling, and alluding to John Hall as the main progenitor of modern milling practice, as typified by the Whitney machine of 1818, the earliest surviving artifact.

It would be in order at this point to enter a *caveat*, that these findings, even resting as they do on very careful historical scholarship, cannot be taken as conclusive in the absence of direct artifact or patent-claim evidence. It is also possible that further work may uncover other aspects of milling development that have not yet been brought to light. It would also be interesting to learn the results of examinations of the North muskets manufactured between 1815 and 1820, and whether or not the component parts display evidence of manufacture by true milling (chip removal) methods. Careful and exhaustive as has been the work of scholars such as Battison and Smith, there is much interesting research waiting to be conducted in this fascinating corner of the history of technology. Work of this

kind provides economic historians with most of what they know about the detailed historical aspects of the American System of manufacturing.

In addition to the emphasis on milling machine evolution in the United States as one of the central and distinctive aspects of the American System, some research has emphasized the importance of metal-working operations prior to milling. In a 1974 essay, I brought out the importance of the development of die forging for precision manufacturing, and chronicled the role played by Elisha K. Root, the superintendent of Samuel Colt's gun factory in Hartford, Connecticut.[26] By means of available patent designs for Root's inventions pertaining to the forging of axe polls made while he was in the employ of the Collinsville Axe Company, it could be established that Root's extensive use of die forging in Colt's factory owed much to the prior experience he had obtained in the production of axes—a case of transfer of technique from one industry to another. The argument was also presented that the precision milling required in a system of interchangeable manufacture was more efficiently accomplished if the workpiece had been taken as close as possible to its final dimensional tolerances by die forging. Milling, on light-framed machines, is not a particularly efficient way to remove large amounts of metal from workpieces. The developments and improvements in duplicate die forging were thus seen as an example of one metal-working process, forging, being substituted for another, heavy milling cuts. In terms of the evolution of the American System, the development of die forging was seen as the innovation of a new form of metal-working technology, substituting for another as diminishing returns (in an economic sense) had set in on processes employing the earlier technological practices. When diminishing returns to inventive activity within the framework of a given technology set in, the perceived payoff to seek further improvements within that particular technological framework (milling) declines. This signals inventors and innovators to begin searching for alternative technologies (forging) that are substitutes for certain classes of metal-working operations.

Russell Fries examined the reasons for the failure of the British small arms industry to adopt the methods of production used in America after 1850.[27] His first finding is that the British response was diversified. In those sectors of the domestic and foreign small-arms market where it was profitable to do so, the British generally adopted the machine processes, achieving interchangeability. In addition to the variegated British market for small arms, the structure of production itself is seen by Fries as an important explanatory component in understanding the failure of the military arms contractors generally to adopt American machine methods. In briefest terms, the subdivided nature of the contract system for military arms, as typified by the practices prevalent in the Birmingham district, precluded individual piece part fabricators from reaping the full benefits of mechanization. Cost reductions attributable to manufacture along interchangeable lines are held by Fries to be mainly achieved in the assembly stage. Secondly, the

other principal benefit of interchangeability is the possibility of quick repair of a damaged arm through the use of duplicate replacement parts. This benefit occurs in use, not in production. Fries raises the interesting economic point that, in an industrial structure organized along subcontract lines, many of the benefits of mechanization and interchangeability will be external to individual subcontractors; and, further, that piece part producers will not receive any of the use benefits deriving from the improvement in the final product, i.e., improvements in product quality are mainly captured by consumers as part of their surplus. While there is merit, in a broad conceptual way, to this argument, such an absolute partitioning of the incidence of benefits, in production and end use, would seem unwarranted. It is likely that transfer prices between subcontractors and prime contractors would reflect improvements in product quality and reductions in assembly cost made possible by interchangeable manufacture at the subcontract stage. Further, if mechanization reduced production costs for subcontractors, by any amount, then these low prime costs would serve to widen the margin of profit between cost of production and transfer selling price.

Fries outlines in extensive fashion the nature and size of the domestic and export markets of the British small-arms manufacturers. In summary, their perceived need to produce arms tailored to the needs of particular market "niches" precluded the product standardization and volume production required to make widespread adoption of American style mechanization economically feasible in the British context.

An article appearing in 1966 by John Murphy highlights important developments in American manufacturing methods that took place in the clockmaking industry.[28] Clockmaking was an important industry from the standpoint of developing mechanical technology along the lines of precision machining and interchangeable manufacture. By 1814, Eli Terry was manufacturing clocks made of cherry-wood parts, by methods which could be classified an interchangeable manufacture. Murphy uncovered six patents for machinery issued to Terry on August 22, 1814, which establish this.[29] One patent was for a multiple gear-cutting arbor arrangement which mounted several cutting wheels on one axis, permitting the simultaneous cutting of teeth on several gear blanks. As Battison noted in his 1966 essay, gear-cutting during the early part of the 19th century was accomplished by means of indexing a circular gear blank around the cutting axis of what was essentially a circular saw. The formal similarly between gear-cutting by means of a circular saw and the operations of slitting and plain milling is striking, thus suggesting the possibility of a close connection between machining practices well-established in clockmaking before the probable time of invention of a Whitney-type machine in 1816, and the basic machining principles embodied in the early form of the milling machine. This is another example, admittedly conjectural but strongly suggestive, of how machining technology evolved as principles and practices appearing in one branch of manufacturing were transmit-

ted and adapted to production problems in another. Murphy also outlines how the economic incentive to alter existing craft methods of production was provided by the peddling system and subsequent marketing networks for clocks, which reached out to tap the larger rural market, thus creating the volume demand for a standardized product necessary to justify the relatively large fixed investment in special purpose machinery undertaken by such clock manufacturers as Terry.

Another paper by David Jeremy, in 1973, reported on the technological details of the major American adaptive innovations that appeared in the textile machinery originally used in the British System of textile manufacturing.[30] Jeremy analyzes the developments of these American modifications in the period between 1812 and 1840 within the framework of nine laborsaving principles: 1) large-scale production, 2) production of standardized low- or medium-quality goods, 3) vertically integrated manufacturing, 4) flow production, 5) maximum use of inanimate power, 6) high operating speeds, 7) mechanical vertical integration, 8) maximum mechanical control and work performance and 9) automatic fault detection.[31] The study is especially important for what it adds to our knowledge of the specific technical details of textile machinery evolution in the United States before 1840 under categories 8) and 9). In a general way, this study concludes that market pressures were mainly responsible for the large-scale production of cheap, standardized low-quality goods during the initial phase of the mechanization of the textile industry. The direction of innovation was influenced by the shortage of unskilled labor in America, but Jeremy concludes that labor shortage does not go far in explaining the narrow range of improvements made under the Rhode Island system as against the broader range of innovations achieved under the Waltham form of organization. The Rhode Island form of organization developed around horizontal specialization and provided a focusing device for mechanical innovations at the preparatory and spinning stages only. Under the Waltham plan, vertically integrated manufacturing corporations allowed the concentration of resources and processes so that a fuller range of engineering skills could be brought to bear on the solution of problems arising from the general shortage of unskilled labor and product adaptation to market dictates. Like the study by Fries, Jeremy's work underscores the importance of industry organization as a critical determinant of the pace and direction of technological change.

In 1974, R.C. Floud set out to review the impact of American engineering exports on Britain, with special reference to their timing during the last half of the nineteenth century.[32] Duncan Burn's earlier work had stressed the notion that: "The view that England was industrially without a serious rival till quite late in the nineteenth century needs more qualification than it usually receives."[33] Burn's view was that between 1850 and 1870 British manufacturers frequently adopted American engineering equipment, and further, that this was a sign of "mature" engineering competition from America as early as 1850. S.B. Saul offered a reinterpretation of Burn's work in 1967.[34] Here Saul argues for a more compli-

cated view than Burn advanced, hinging on the diversity of experience from one segment of British industry to another. Textile machinery from the United States was quickly adopted while improvements in the construction and design of agricultural implements and railroad locomotives were not. In general, Saul found that the domestic customers for British engineering products were not interested in new methods and would not buy new machines, hence there was no incentive for British engineers to adopt such methods.

Floud used export data on engineering goods from the United States to Great Britain to provide tests or checks of these views on American engineering competition. The trend and level of exports of engineering machinery are found to be generally consistent with the interpretations of Burn and Saul. Yet certain features of the export statistics are difficult to reconcile with the Burn-Saul view. Chiefly, it is the boom in American engineering exports in the 1890's that does not square with either the view that American products provided significant competition for their British counterparts before 1890, or that only by this later date did British engineers realize fully the superiority of American engineering machinery. Floud argues that the America machine-building sector grew up, during the last half of the ninteenth century, behind a protective tariff wall as high as that of any major economy of the time. The tariff rate on machinery entering America was 45% *ad valorem* from 1868–1869 onwards to the period of the 1890's. This tariff in America prevented British firms from entering the American machinery market and made American machines comparatively more expensive to potential British customers than home-produced items. According to Floud, only in areas of the British market where nonprice competition was the rule did American machinery exports enter in quantity before the 1890's. Behind this protective tariff wall, domestic American machinery prices had been trending downward from 1870 on so that by 1890 they were sufficiently attractive to British customers to bring about the American export boom in machinery.

Floud's comparative analysis of British and American machinery tariffs is not complete, in that it does not take demand elasticity in the two countries into account, nor is evidence adduced on the relative level of the machinery tariffs in the respective countries. Neither does Floud explain the quick relative fall in American machinery prices. Likewise the role of relative factor costs remains in the background in Floud's analysis, not being treated explicitly for lack of sufficient evidence. New work on this question will, one may hope, take into account some of these conceptual and empirical omissions. Nevertheless, Floud provided a sharper frame of reference within which to consider the question of American engineering competition during the last decades of the nineteenth century.

R.A. Church, writing in 1975, explores the reasons why the American and Swiss clock and watch manufactures superceded the British in the nineteenth century.[35] Church's study is in the spirit of Habakkuk's inquiry on the distinctive

aspects of American technology. Church stresses the British manufacturers' attachment to craft traditions of high quality and artisanship and their disdain for cheap American clocks and watches as an example of the kind of social and institutional impediments accounting partly for the British failure to mechanize. While the Swiss studied the export market very closely and sent technical teams to America to study production methods, the British producers appeared to be content to sell to the traditional market, emphasizing hand-built quality and craftsmanship. By mid-century the Swiss were even selling American-style watches, according to Church, in New York! Church does not hold much stock with the relative factor cost explanations of technological divergence in this comparative context. Instead, he argues that watch-making machinery, embodying the principles of interchangeable precision work and self-acting mechanisms, was invented not so much to abridge the shortage of labor as to create, in effect, a new product. This view is very important because it stresses the possibility of demand-induced invention and innovation as opposed to the preponderant emphasis in the literature on supply side (relative factor cost) explanations. In addition, Church points out that the flow of information between Britain and America was asymmetrical. The failure of technical knowledge to flow to Britain, Church holds, was attributable to a "lack of enthusiasm" on the part of British producers for competing in the low- and medium-price market for clocks and watches. Studies such as this help in building a fund of case materials and specific examples in which the economic historian can see how well general explanatory variables fit individual industry situations, and aid in providing familiarity with additional factors that must be taken into account in interpretations of the causes of technological divergence between countries, or even industries within a particular country.

III. TECHNOLOGY TRANSFER AND DIFFUSION

A seminal article on the development of American manufacturing in the nineteenth century was written by Nathan Rosenberg in 1963.[36] It is of considerable importance in understanding how advances in metal-working technology were diffused throughout the industrial sector. Rosenberg brings to the fore the role of the machine-tool industry in the process of diffusing mechanical information. Capital-goods using industries, machine-tool customers, coming to the specialized engineering firms with specific, technical problems, obtained solutions that were embodied in particular configurations of machine-tool design. As these configurations became standardized, they were produced in enough volume to move the machine-tool industry out of the "to order," custom-order style of marketing operation. Since the problems brought to the machine-tool firms from one industry contained elements of technical similarity with problems in some other branch of manufacturing, solutions to them embodied in standardized machine tools could be quickly diffused from one industry to the other. Presumably, the standardiza-

tion of machine-tool design in America enabled some production economies to be achieved in their manufacture and concomitantly lowered final selling price, thereby further hastening the diffusion of innovation. Rosenberg points out that the historical experience of the machine-tool industry might well suggest that technological change enters the economy "through a particular door" rather than appearing with equal likelihood in any sector of the economy. The term which Rosenberg attaches to the process of focusing problems on a particular industrial sector, machine tools, for subsequent diffusion elsewhere in the economy is *technological convergence*. Its simplicity tends to belie the crucial significance of Rosenberg's interpretation for understanding the actual historical-technological process by which mechanical technology was diffused widely throughout the American economy in the nineteenth century.

A somewhat related theme was pursued by Edward Ames and Nathan Rosenberg in a 1965 study on the implications of industrial specialization for the economic development process generally.[37] Ames and Rosenberg elaborate on an earlier theme by George Stigler, based in turn on Adam Smith's famous dictum that the division of labor is limited by the extent of the market.[38] Initially, as economies enter the early industrial phase, manufacturing firms must be fully integrated, as the market for their inputs is too small to support a periphery of specialized supplier firms. As final demand for industrial goods grows, and with that growth, the size of the industrial sector, a sufficient demand for producer durables and other producer inputs rises to induce specialized supplying firms to be organized. The movement from the earliest phase of industrialization to the second phase constitutes a movement from vertical integration to a collection of "disintegrated" firms. As industrialization proceeds into its later stages, vertical integration will again appear as the specialized producing units are recombined under one organizational entity, the third stage. As a final stage, one might add, that horizontal merger of fully integrated and partially integrated firms, as typifies the present industrial structure, constitutes a later fourth stage of the progression of industrial structure as the economy develops. From a technological standpoint, Ames and Rosenberg conclude that development policy and technical assistance programs should reflect the fact that the level and qualitative character of the industrial structure of a particular economy will be a function of its state of economic development. From this it follows that direct transplants of technology from mature industrial countries to LDC's will not be successful due to the imbalance of industrial structures between transmitting and receiving country and the kinds of economic incentives that flow from the respective patterns of industrial organization.

In a 1970 essay, Rosenberg continued the theme of the relationship of technology to economic development.[39] The nature of this essay was to suggest problems and obstacles to the international diffusion of technology that are suggested by a consideration of specific historical examples and episodes. Although this wide-

ranging essay does not lend itself readily to summarization, the main points covered may be indicated. Rosenberg considers such events as: 1) the role of the capital-goods producing industry, 2) the nature of consumer demand and the structure and generation of individual preferences within a particular social context, 3) the nature of administrative and managerial response to technological change, 4) public versus private initiatives, 5) institutional arrangements and 6) the importance of invoking technical distinctions between the necessary and sufficient conditions for technical transfer in an industrial, as opposed to agricultural, environment. In sum, the essay is in keeping with Rosenberg's traditional emphasis on the evolutionary and gradual view of technological phenomena, and draws many examples from his previously cited work. In 1972, Rosenberg continued to develop this theme of technology transfer by exploring the factors responsible for diffusion.[40] The 1972 article continued the Rosenberg tradition of interpretive synthesis by use of historical example and economic analysis and examines the implications of technological and economic factors for the nature of diffusion intra- and internationally. What emerges from Rosenberg's treatment is not so much a conclusion as a perspective on the nature of technological processes. The main point of this essay is that new processes replace old ones only very slowly, which accounts for the historical *apparentness* of the slowness of a technological diffusion phenomenon. Among the factors accounting for "slowness" of diffusion treated by Rosenberg are: 1) the continuous nature of inventive activity, 2) the gradual improvement to inventions after their initial introduction, 3) development and diffusion of technical skills among users, 4) the development of machine-making skills, 5) the role played by technical complementarities and past accumulations of capital, which represent older, embodied technologies, 6) improvements in "older" technologies as a retardant of the adoption of new inventions and 7) the institutional context in which diffusion takes place.

Technology transfer in agriculture and its relationship to economic development is the subject of a 1973 article by Vernon Ruttan and Yujiro Hayami.[41] The authors begin by pointing out that there are a number of different disciplinary approaches to the study of transfer: anthropology, economics, geography, sociology, as well as several other disciplines. Most of these models, though they all focus on different aspects of transfer and diffusion phenomena, are of only limited relevance for the international transfer of technology in agriculture. Typically, in the Hayami-Ruttan view, these models take the attributes of technology and potential adopters as given. This sharply limits their applicability in the international agricultural setting, where ecological variations as well as factor endowments limit direct transfer. Hayami and Ruttan hold Griliches' well-known studies of the diffusion of hybrid seed varieties as the exception to this general bill of indictment.[42] What makes the Griliches studies unique is the incorporation of the behavior of public research institutions and private agricultural supply firms into the model. Another virtue of Griliches' approach is the presence of a mechanism

which allows for local adaptation to innovation in the interregional transfer of technology.

The authors delineate three phases in the international diffusion as: a) material transfer, b) design transfer and c) capacity transfer. They then illustrate these concepts by reference to specific examples drawn from experiences in the transfer of sugarcane varieties throughout the world and tractorization in Russia and Japan, drawn from the earlier writings of Robert Evenson and Dana Dalrymple.[43] The implications of technology transfer for agricultural trade are discussed by Ruttan and Hayami in the framework of Raymond Vernon's product-cycle model.[44] Briefly stated, Vernon's model analyzes the innovation-investment-trade sequence between large, technically advanced countries and less technically developed ones. An innovation first appearing in a country like the United States, because the domestic market provides the appropriate kinds of interrelationships between innovative efforts and market response, eventually assumes a standardized design configuration and is produced in sufficient quantity to achieve economies of scale. In the next phase of the cycle, export of the commodity in question from the United States enlarges the size of the foreign market. As the foreign market grows, foreign producers will begin to out-compete United States producers, as they achieve not only the scale economies made possible by the standardized product design and production technology, but labor-cost advantages. The cycle is completed when foreign producers, on the basis of lower labor and/or resource costs, begin to enter the American market as well.

An example that fits rather well into the Vernon product-cycle framework is the diffusion of new high-yielding varieties (HYV) of rice and wheat in the tropics. After discussing the history of the development and diffusion of HYV's, Ruttan and Hayami conclude that several severe obstacles to diffusion are present in most LDC's: 1) inadequate marketing capacity and the tendency to sharp increases in marketable surpluses after the adoption of HYV's, 2) complementary input and credit supply constraints, 3) the tendency to widening income differences among farmers after adoption of HYV's, 4) wage and price effects in nonagricultural industries and 5) foreign-exchange management problems.

The *Tasks Issue* of the 1974 *Journal of Economic History* contains five essays on the subject of agricultural technology and economic development. Yujiro Hayami explores the roles of adaptive research and land infrastructure in the process of diffusion of agricultural technology in Japan, Taiwan and Korea. These developments are contrasted with the experience in South and Southeast Asia heralded as the "green revolution," and found to be similar in that in each case two common features were found: a) adaptation of a biological technology to different environmental conditions, and b) assimilation of the adapting environments to those in which the technology originated.[45] Robert Evenson, in a preliminary survey, discusses various models of diffusion of agricultural technology, outlining the problems of applying these models and using the case of sugarcane technology

transfer as an illustrative example.[46] He also develops and tests a "diffusion-cum-discovery" model for cereal-grain technology in the post-World War II period. The exploratory nature of the essay precludes any specific summary of findings. Andrew Watson summarizes his findings on the Arab agricultural revolution from the 8th through the 12th centuries.[47] The spread of Islam into three continents during the 7th and 8th centuries was coupled with the diffusion of new crops and irrigation technology. A central role is ascribed to Islamic law, culture and philosophy in accounting for the innovation and diffusion of hydraulic technology throughout the empire. An essay by Keith Aufhauser on the relationship of slavery to technological change begins by dividing technical progress into two types: 1) changes in techniques in existing economic activities, and 2) changes in the mix of economic activities.[48] He examines two specific cases: the use of the plow to hole sugar in Jamaica and Barbados and the vacuum pan for distillation of sugar syrup in Brazil. The evidence adduced by Aufhauser goes against the view that, on either of the two definitions of technical progress, slavery (in these particular national contexts) led to technological retardation. Alexander Eckstein et al. provide an interim research report on the pattern of development in Manchuria between 1860 and 1960, applying the staple theory of growth to Manchurian conditions.[49] The study is of interest because Manchurian experience contrasts so sharply with the development pattern in China Proper; yet over the period studied by Eckstein, Manchuria's importance in the Chinese economy as a whole rose steadily. During 1860–1930, the period of expansion of Manchuria's agricultural frontier, economic growth was propelled by the mutual interaction of population growth, expansion in arable and the rapid rise in staple exports. After 1920, however, the increasing domination of Manchurian economic policy by the Japanese shifted the basis of growth more toward industrialization.

A number of recent diffusion studies have focused on the textile industry. In 1966, Irwin Feller brought to test the proposition, quite common in histories of the New England textile industry, that the Draper loom was adopted too slowly in the years between 1894 and 1914 because of conservative management practices on the part of mill owners.[50] Using available data on loom sales by state, Feller reached the following conclusions: 1) in the early 1890's the Draper loom had only limited applicability to the output produced by the New England textile industry, 2) the cost savings obtainable through adoption of the Draper loom by the New England branch of the textile industry were not sufficiently great to warrant, on economic grounds, general adoption, 3) the Draper loom was not superior to newer forms of non-automatic looms until roughly 1910–1911, and 4) adoption of the Draper loom in New England, by itself, could not have reduced costs of textile production in New England to the level achievable in the South.[51] In short, survival of the New England industry was not dependent on the adoption of the Draper loom. In 1968, Lars Sandberg questioned the handling and representativeness of the data used by Feller to calculate weaving costs by Draper and non-

automatic looms.[52] Feller replied to Sandberg's "comment," that the data he used were in fact appropriate for the calculations he performed.[53] As in any empirical issue, we must leave this question with a certain degree of indeterminateness. In general, however, Feller's conclusions appear to pass through, well within the acceptable margins of measurement error.

In a 1974 essay, Feller picks up the same theme of diffusion and location in the American cotton-textile industry.[54] Looking at the period from 1890–1970, Feller finds similarities in the experience of the American industry in international markets after the 1930's and the shift in interregional comparative advantage from North to South in the period between 1890 and 1920. Feller's findings are strongly suggestive of the applicability of Raymond Vernon's product-cycle model to the case of either the North-South migration of the cotton textile industry or the shift in comparative advantage to non-American producers. Both instances are suggestive of the shift of comparative advantage in the manufacture of a standardized product from the locus of initial invention and innovation, which is also a high-wage area, to lower-wage countries or regions, which benefit from the adoption of the advanced and standardized technology on the basis of the prior existence of a market sufficient to generate the economies of scale in production inherent in the newer technology.

Lars Sandberg examines in a 1969 article the reason why ring spinning became dominant in the United States as early as 1870, whereas it was so slowly adopted elsewhere, especially in Britain.[55] The British lag in ring spinning has usually been taken as a sign of technological backwardness, but Sandberg investigates the proposition of whether or not the ratio of mule to ring spinning in Great Britain was justified by differing factor costs, institutional arrangements and market conditions. The relative efficiency of ring and mule spindles is a function of the count of the yarn being produced. Armed with this proposition, Sandberg computes comparative production costs in the United States and Great Britain, varying yarn count in order to determine the comparative differences in the benefits derived from replacing mules with rings in the two countries. A technological fact adduced by Sandberg, conformable to the Ames-Rosenberg emphasis on raw material inputs as possible explanatory factors in technological innovation, is that ". . . for a given count of yarn, ring spinning required a longer cotton staple than did mule spinning."[56] Moreover, the per pound price of cotton rises with staple length. Putting these propositions together with available data on labor, capital and raw material costs, Sandberg then finds that rings were preferable for warp and weft production for yarn counts below the low 40's in Great Britain, but were never more profitable than mules for higher count yarns in the period immediately preceding World War I. In the United States ring-spun yarn achieved a higher cost saving per pound than in Britain at a count of 40, and the cost saving per pound of yarn rose with count up to 120. Taken in light of the available evidence, the failure of British cotton-textile producers to adopt a similar ratio of rings to mules as the

United States cotton-textile industry is seen as an understandable market response, not a case of technological conservatism or economic irrationality.

D.C. Coleman investigates the transfer of the "New Draperies" to the English textile industry in the 16th and 17th centuries through the agency of the migration of Dutch Protestant artisans in his 1969 article.[57] Several implications emerge from the study of the transfer of the New Draperies: 1) the use of the term "new product" needs careful definition, 2) there was no clear or deliberate search for cost reduction in the English industry leading to invention or innovation, 3) the example under examination is but one of a sequence of transfers from one national context to another i.e., no innovations are ever entirely new and 4) in the specific case of the New Draperies the transfer of artisans had to be brought about by noneconomic forces, war or persecution, to insure movement of skills on a large enough scale to establish the new industry firmly. Coleman's study is of interest because these points can easily be "transferred" to the economic history of diffusion phenomena in other time periods and technological contexts.

In a 1973 study, David Jeremy outlines the features of British textile technology transmission to the Philadelphia region between 1770 and 1820.[58] The study is divided into a history of American efforts to acquire Britain's new textile technology, in the face of legal and economic constraints, and the methods of transfer. Jeremy illustrates how and why so many elements of textile machine design and construction were "nonverbal," i.e., could not be transferred readily by written words or blueprints. The nonverbalness of mechanical technology generally meant that textile machine technology had to be transferred by the migration of individual artisans during the early period of the establishment of that portion of the American textile industry based on machine methods.

Gary Saxonhouse's 1974 study of technological diffusion in the Japanese cotton-textile industry during the Meiji Period finds evidence of a surprising level of uniformity of technique and managerial practice among firms.[59] The principal reason adduced for this is the high degree of technical cooperation among firms in the industry. Saxenhouse's finding is not surprising in view of the fact that the Japanese development policy, with reference to cotton textiles, utilized the "pilot firm" technique to gather, focus and diffuse new practices throughout the industry; in contrast to, say, the American use of a high tariff to protect the "infant-industry" in a blanket fashion.

Diffusion of techniques in the American iron industry is the subject of a 1964 essay by Peter Temin.[60] Temin extends Louis Hunter's earlier analysis of the relationship between the nature of demand for iron and the choice of technique in Western Pennsylvania.[61] Two points formed the core of Hunter's argument: 1) the abundance of wood in the United States did not have a major influence on the price of iron made from charcoal, as labor was the principal cost component in charcoal production, and 2) coke iron was inferior to iron made with charcoal. These

factors, according to Hunter, account for the slowness with which the American iron industry adopted coke in blast furnaces. By way of comparison, as early as 1810 over 90 percent of the blast furnaces in Great Britain utilized coke, whereas only 10 percent of American furnaces used coke on the eve of the Civil War. Temin finds that anthracite iron sold for the same price as charcoal iron in eastern Pennsylvania, since the anthracite deposits of that region were relatively free of the principal element that made bituminous coal inferior to charcoal—sulphur. In order for coked iron to be produced in western Pennsylvania, its price had to rise relative to other types of iron. Yet only if the quality of iron made from coke improved would this be likely to occur. As Temin points out, the discovery of the Connellsville deposit, containing a chemically pure form of bituminous coal, paved the way for the output expansion of coked iron in western Pennsylvania. It is more than coincidental that the exploitation of the Connellsville field dates from 1859, the date of introduction of the first blast furnace in Pittsburgh designed specifically for the use of this coal. Temin also indicates that the growth in demand for iron rails may have stimulated the production of low-cost pig iron made from coke. Here again we have an example of specific factors relating to geography, market conditions and the pattern of relative input costs conditioning the rate of adoption and diffusion of a specific technique. This forms a recurrent theme in the economic-historical literature on technological diffusion.

In 1973, Charles Hyde examined the adoption of coke-smelting in the British iron industry during the 18th century.[62] Hyde found that the reason why coke iron was not generally produced in the British industry before the 1750's may be found in the economic variables affecting entrepreneurial decision-making: costs, prices and profits. By the late 1750's the total cost of producing pig iron with coke had fallen below the variable cost of producing charcoal iron. The main cost component accounting for this differential was fuel cost. By comparing "best-practice" coke furnace with "best-practice" charcoal furnaces, Hyde found a difference in fuel costs per ton of pig iron of almost £3 in the 1760's, as compared with a selling price of £5–6 in this period. Hyde studied the question of technological change in the British wrought-iron industry between 1750 and 1815 in a 1974 article.[63] Here Hyde found that the traditional view of the discontinuity of technological change in the wrought-iron sector is not borne out. He argues that the key innovation, before 1790, was the "potting and stamping" process. It accounted for over half the bar iron output of the British industry by 1788 and enabled the refining sector to expand output and increase its share of the domestic bar iron market during the period before 1790. Hyde also finds that Cort's puddling process had little impact on the iron industry until the mid-1790's, after considerable modification of the original puddling process.

Peter Temin assesses some generalizations on the diffusion of steam power in America in the early 19th century in his 1966 essay.[64] Temin's first conclusion is that the American use of high-pressure steam, as contrasted with the British

preference for lower-pressure engines, was more ". . . a matter of style than economy."[65] Watt was "conservative" whereas the Americans lacked "fear of explosions." Comparing the costs of steam versus water power Temin finds that for two groups of New England cotton mills, about 1840, the costs of the two types of power were about equal. The locational advantage of steam became important as industry moved westward after 1840. Before that date Temin finds that stationary steam engines served as a substitute for land transportation by bringing power to raw-material supplies. After 1840 the steam engine was used to supply transportation directly.

In 1974, Eric Robinson outlined some of the reasons for the slow and spasmodic diffusion of the steam engine outside of England.[66] Robinson focuses on three elements in explaining this phenomenon: a) entrepreneurial failure, b) inefficiencies in the steam engine itself and c) unfavorable resource endowments. Historical examples drawn from a variety of national and regional contexts are utilized to explore the applicability of these various elements to specific situations.

James Brittain examines a number of cases dealing with the international diffusion of electrical power in the period 1870–1920 in a 1974 article.[67] The examples, analyzed in the framework of the history of technology, are: the Gramme dynamo, the Edison dynamo, the revolving-field alternator and the Alexanderson alternator. Brittain recounts the importance of wars, specific creative acts of individual engineers and inventors, international exhibitions, the role of government action and corporate policies in each case. An intriguing suggestion offered by Brittain is the notion of the persistence of "national or regional technological styles," which are not attributable to different governmental policies or market conditions. While style is a difficult concept to specify precisely for purposes of economic measurement, and is never defined in Brittain's essay, it may prove to be a useful organizing principle in technological history.

Diffusion of technical knowledge in ocean shipping in the period 1675–1775, with special reference to colonial waters, is the focus of a 1970 article written by Gary Walton.[68] Walton found evidence of roughly a 1% annual increase in total factor productivity over the principal commodity routes during the period.[69] In colonial shipping, two factors account for most of the observed productivity improvement: a) better market organization and b) reduction of piracy on the main trade routes. Improved market organization reduced in-port times and reduced the ratio of idle port time to productive sea time over the course of any given year. The decline of piracy reduced armament and crew size requirements per ship and paved the way for the adoption of the Dutch flyboat, a commercially superior vessel. Walton lists five factors that affected the rate of diffusion of the flyboat in colonial waters: 1) the extent of cost saving before and after the elimination of piracy, 2) uncertainty about the operating characteristics of the flyboat immediately after its initial introduction, 3) English government policy 4) the influence of Dutch factor costs on the early configurations of the flyboat, 5) the effects of London guilds on the adoption of new architectural designs and practices in ship construction.

Charles Harley investigated the shift from sail to steam in ocean transport in a 1971 publication.[70] He concludes that the principal reason why the transition took so long was that the steamship had to transport its own fuel. This meant that factor inputs and costs of steamship transportation varied directly with the length of the voyage from a given coal source. Harley hypothesizes that steam should have replaced sail on the shorter routes close to coal sources first, and only then spread to the longer routes. Empirical tests confirm this hypothesis. Only after the 1890's did improvements in steamship design lead to the displacement of the sailing ship by the steamship on the longest voyages. Thus Harley concludes that one must look principally to other explanations than the diffusion of the steamship to explain the observed 19th century decline in ocean freight rates.

In 1973, Harley also studied the persistence of wooden shipbuilding in North America during the second half of the 19th century.[71] Although technological factors dictated that ocean steamships had to have metal hulls, sailing ships could be made with either metal or wooden hulls. Thus, Harley's study concentrates on the building of sailing ships. Differential rates of factors cost and technological change in iron and wooden shipbuilding account for the downward shift in the British supply curve of iron ships in the 1870's and 1880's, while the Canadian supply curve for wooden ships was relatively more inelastic, according to Harley's calculations. This was because of the immobility of labor and other factors employed in wooden shipbuilding in Maine and British North America. Competitive ship prices were set by supply and demand conditions in the British shipbuilding industry, leaving North American wooden shipbuilders in the position of having to respond to downward price adjustments for iron ships over the period. Because of their greater relative inelasticity in supply-side response the North American wooden shipbuilders "persisted," even in the face of greater technological change in iron shipbuilding.

James Mak and Gary Walton offer a different view of the causes of the persistence of an "old" technology in their 1973 study of the persistence of flatboats on western rivers after the introduction of the steamboat.[72] The introduction of the steamboat was accompanied by improvements in the navigability of western rivers, which also benefited flatboat transport. One immediate effect of the introduction of steamboats was the elimination of the long, arduous upriver journey by land for flatboat crewmen. Subsequent improvements in steamboat technology benefited flatboating by reducing the opportunity costs of labor. Mak and Walton measure the change in total factor productivity in flatboating between 1815–1860 and find it to be 2.2% per annum, compared with roughly 1.5% for steamboat haulage. The Mak-Walton analysis suggests that external benefits arising from the introduction of new technologies may accrue to older technologies, either through the reduction of factor costs or improvements in the "operating environment." On this view, it is not necessary to appeal exclusively to the fact that older technologies undergo successive improvement subsequent to the introduction of new, competitive modes of production to explain their persis-

tence. In the case of flatboating there was little, if any, direct technological improvement after the introduction of the steamboat on western rivers, yet flatboating not only persisted, but expanded, due to the externalities which attended the introduction of steamboats. This approach should be a potentially fruitful one for examinations of other technological case histories.

In a 1963 essay, Norman Wilkinson outlined four specific areas of manufacturing activity in the Brandywine Valley that were technologically dependent upon "borrowings" from European practice[73]: 1) textiles and textile machinery, 2) tanning, 3) black powder mills and 4) papermaking. Wilkinson outlines the backgrounds of individuals involved in the technical transfers and provides much needed historical data on the technological origins of several important industries in the Brandywine region. A study in a vein similar to Wilkinson's is my 1970 piece on the contributions of Henry Burden, an immigrant Scot, to the evolving American metal-working technology in the early 19th century.[74] In this essay I trace Burden's role as a consulting engineer to American arms contractors in both the areas of hydraulic engineering and iron rolling. Burden's part in introducing the rolling of barrel scalps and welding barrels by rolling is outlined, and later aspects of Burden's career as a successful industrialist and inventor are brought out, including his contributions to the evolving American system.

Mira Wilkins offers a classificatory scheme in her essay, published in 1974, on the role of private business in the international diffusion of technology.[75] Wilkins lists eight ways in which a private company can transfer (export) technology across national boundaries: 1) export of product, 2) transfer of patents, 3) export of technical knowledge and assistance, including direct investment, and 4) extension of the firm itself into another country. By considering firms as recipients, she obtains a counterpart list to the one given above, thus yielding her eight modes of corporate transfer. In addition, Wilkins considers the distinction between the "imitation lag" and the "absorption gap," the first being the time it takes for actual transfer to take place, the second, the rate at which technology is effectively incorporated and assimilated into a receiving country. Specific historical examples are used to illuminate each of the concepts employed by Wilkins. There is also some discussion of the obstacles to diffusion of technology by private business.

IV. CHOICE OF TECHNIQUE AND INNOVATION

Paul David's celebrated 1966 essay on the innovation and subsequent diffusion of the mechanical reaper in midwestern agriculture during the 1850's demonstrates both the strengths and weaknesses of microeconomic modeling, along neoclassical lines, in economic history.[76] David wishes to calculate the threshold farm size (wheat acreage to be harvested per farming unit) that was minimally necessary to justify the purchase of a mechanical reaper. He estimates that in the period 1849–1853 the threshold farm sizes were 48 and 35 acres for hand-rake and

self-rake reapers, respectively. By 1854–1857 the threshold farm sizes had fallen to 35 and 25 acres for hand-rake and self-rake reapers, respectively. In David's formulation of the estimating equation for threshold farm size, the dependent variable is a direct and positive function of the annual rates of interest and depreciation and the purchase price of a reaper. Threshold farm size is inversely related to the wage rate paid to harvest labor and the number of man-days of labor saved by mechanization of the cutting operation per acre harvested. Historically viewed, the fall in the cost of reapers relative to the wage rate of harvest labor reduced threshold farm size and hastened the adoption of the reaper in midwestern agriculture. The rising price of grain in the decade of the 1850's also hastened the adoption and diffusion of the mechanical reaper.

Several possible shortcomings in the analysis may be suggested. First, David assumes that there was no possibility of "custom" reaping or cooperative purchase, hence each decision to adopt by an individual farmer must be on the basis of his ownership unit bearing full costs and benefits. Second, no attention is paid to horse prices, complementary inputs, over the period as a possible factor hastening or retarding adoption of an innovation that required the tractive effort of horsepower. Third, harvesting (cutting of grain from the field) is not taken in the context of its relationship to threshing (separation of grain from the plant). But it is well-known that in a structured, vertically integrated, sequence of productive activities the improvement of one element in the chain will affect related productive operations, so that the decision for improvement must take this interrelatedness into account.

A 1975 essay by Alan Olmstead reexamines some of the issues raised in Paul David's essay on the adoption and diffusion of the mechanical reaper.[77] Olmstead provides evidence that sharing and contracting of reapers was widely practiced. This finding knocks out one of the maintained hypotheses under which David specified his threshold model, i.e., no sharing or contracting. The second type of evidence adduced by Olmstead is that many improvements in reaper design and function affected the machine's productivity, and, hence, diffusion rate. In addition, the sensitivity of David's calculated threshold size to changes in interest and depreciation rates is investigated. Olmstead argues that more realistic estimates of both rates would put the threshold size close to double the levels actually calculated by David. This finding implies (if we accept Olmstead's evidence in conjunction with David's threshold function) that few if any midwestern farmers could have rationally adopted the reaper in the 1850's. Olmstead concludes that this result arises from the incorrect premises on which David's comparative static threshold function was specified.

Further work on the mechanization of reaping was undertaken by Paul David in his 1971 investigation of the factors governing the relatively slow rate of mechanical reaper adoption in English agriculture.[78] In this essay David employs a more detailed and complex form of the threshold model to account for the special details

of terrain and crop mix in the English case, in order to estimate the rate of return to adoption of the mechanical reaper. Two features of English cereal farming affected the rate of reaper adoption: a) the character of the terrain—uneven field surfaces in "ridge and furrow" land, and b) the size, shape and arrangements of the field. The principal overall finding is the importance of considering technical interrelatedness between a potentially adoptable technology and past accumulations of physical capital, in this instance farm land. David considers this finding in the framework of the "penalties of an early start," since the renovation of ridge and furrows lands to create an optimal terrain for the adoption of the reaper, or, alternatively, the adoption of mechanical reaping on less-than-optimal terrain, would tend to depress the anticipated economic rate of return from adoption. From a purely methodological point of view this essay marks an early turning point away from strictly neoclassical analysis by a leading practitioner of cliometric history. David's analysis of the effects of the landscape on the adoption of the reaper is in keeping with the emerging evolutionary mode of analysis, in its explicit recognition of the idea that ongoing economic processes (agricultural capital accumulation in land of a particular configuration) bring about irreversible changes in institutional arrangements that condition (neoclassically conceived) microeconomic decisions in the current period.

A 1971 essay by Nathan Rosenberg explores the relationship among the elements of technical interrelatedness, economic interdependencies and the environment.[79] The arguments are arranged under three headings: 1) the urban context, 2) the ecological context and 3) the poor-country setting. Rosenberg explores technological innovation in each of these particular contexts, emphasizing the historical, technical and evolutionary elements affecting innovation.

The above essays by David and Rosenberg relate to earlier research by Edward Ames and Nathan Rosenberg published in 1963 on the subject of whether or not countries that have been innovators incur a "penalty for taking the lead."[80] Ames and Rosenberg argue that the latecomer thesis has three logical variants: 1) the *weak* thesis, which holds that latecomers will pass through any sequence of development more rapidly than early starters, 2) the *moderate* thesis, which asserts that latecomers will ultimately reach higher levels of development than early starters, even though the latter do not cease developing, and 3) the *strong* thesis, which states that latecomers will surpass early-starters, in part because the latter will cease to develop.

Each of these versions of the latecomer thesis has certain defects: a) the *weak* thesis depends on the propositions that latecomers can avoid past mistakes of early starters, will make no more current mistakes than early starters, and that mistakes do not contain useful experience for those who make them; b) the *moderate* thesis is based in part on the assertion that early starters are subject to a form of retardation that does not affect latecomers; and c) the *strong* thesis rests on the nature of transition costs, for if the cost of moving from a lower to a higher

technology is an increasing function of the level of technology already reached, the rate of development will slow down as a country develops. Ames and Rosenberg also enumerate a variety of empirical questions, the resolution of which tends to affect the validity of the three variants of the latecomer hypothesis. They conclude that all published latecomer theories contain logical defects and unresolved empirical questions, which, from a more formal point of view, render them no more than tantalizing suggestions.

Wayne Rasmussen offers a 1968 case study that relates, concretely, to the themes set out by the David (1971) and Rosenberg (1971) essays, mentioned above.[81] Rasmussen traces the development of mechanical tomato harvesting as an example of the "package" or systems approach in agricultural technology. Among the elements that have to be considered simultaneously in agricultural innovations are: machines, seed development, tillage, fertilizer, water use, and control of weeds, fungi and pests by chemical means. According to Rasmussen, the development of the mechanical tomato harvester resulted from the systems approach, combining the joint efforts of mechanical engineers, horticulturalists, agronomists, irrigation specialists, plant geneticists, and many others. The key to the development and successful introduction of mechanical harvest in tomato production lay in developing varieties of tomatoes that could be handled by machine, while at the same time exhibiting satisfactory yields and uniform ripening characteristics. Rasmussen's account is clearly written and a fascinating modern example of the relationship between scientific research and technological innovation.

A 1971 article by Yujiro Hayami offers a historical perspective on the "green revolution" in Asia since 1965.[82] Hayami's point of departure is that the development and subsequent diffusion of high-yielding varieties of rice (HYV's) in Asia represents a process similar to the transmission of improved rice varieties from Japan to Taiwan and Korea in the 1920's and 1930's. The forces that induced the technology transfer in both cases are hypothesized to consist of: a) factor and product price relationships favorable to the development of new strains, b) responses of national and international agencies (utilizing crop-breeding research and high caliber scientists) to the favorable price relationships, and c) bias in the new agricultural technology towards facilitating the substitution of an increasingly abundant factor (fertilizer) for an increasingly scarce one (land).

A crucial element in Hayami's analysis is the response of public agencies to economic incentives, rather than the response of individual profit-maximizing firms. The distinguishing technological feature of Hayami's analysis is that HYV's (and most plant hybrids) are highly fertilizer-responsive. In both cases, declining fertilizer-rice price ratios brought about continuous adjustments in the form of the creation and diffusion of fertilizer-responsive rice varieties, and provided the inducement mechanism that gave a particular factor-saving bias (land) to technological innovation in this agricultural sector.

Research published in 1969 by Nathan Rosenberg a sort of historical reconnaissance mission to illuminate why technological problems are posed in a certain way at a certain time. X^3 Inducement mechanisms and focusing devices, as Rosenberg terms them, arise in three ways. First, Rosenberg argues, along lines similar to Paul Mantoux's treatment of technical imbalances in the relationship of various spinning opeations, that complex technologies create internal compulsions and pressures that initiate exploratory activity in paticular directions. X^4 This idea is elaborated by examples drawn from automobile manufacture, machine tool development, steel production, and even medieval siege machinery. Second, the refractory nature of labor in certain historical eras led to an interest in the means of its abridgement. The threat of strikes and other disruptions, lowering perceived rates of future profitability by factory owners, is pursued in a Marxian framework. Finally, the third source of inducement and focusing is the disruption of an accustomed source of supply of an input and the unavailability of alternative sources of supply or close substitutes. At any point in the life of a firm it will tend to attack what appears to be the most restrictive constraint. Rosenberg thus suggests a reformulation of the microeconomic approach to technical change, in terms of a bottleneck analysis. These ideas should prove useful in future studies of technology in an economic-historical context.

Using recent advances in learning theory, Paul David investigates, in his 1973 essay, short- and long-run learning effects in the Lawrence Mill #2 of the Lawrence cotton-textile company in Lowell, Massachusetts.[85] The Lawrence Mill #2 is chosen for analysis because from its erection in 1834 until 1857 there was no expansion of the mill's capacity, nor was there any investment in new machinery. Such a facility is well suited to the empirical study of such forms of disembodied technological change as comprise the "Horndal-effect". The term "Horndal-effect" derives from an experience at a Swedish steelworks at Horndal built in 1935–1936. Although no additional new investment was undertaken for a period of fifteen years after its construction, output per man hour rose continuously at a rate of about 2% per annum over the period. This form of endogenous improvement in productivity, arising from increased efficiency in the workforce and in the operation of the mill itself is the phenomenon of learning-by-doing.

David finds that over the 22-year period studied, average labor productivity rose at a rate of about 1.95% per annum, which is close to the 2.25% per annum average rate of increase in cloth output per manhour over the same period he measured in an earlier study of integrated mills owned by a sample group of six leading New England textile firms. In fitting the short-run learning curve, David points out that it is appropriate to focus attention on the minimum levels for real labor cost (input) per yard of cloth, since fluctuations in the labor productivity index will arise from variations in capacity utilization over the course of a typical business cycle, and, hence, not reflect the true course of technical progress at full capacity levels of operation. Not all observations of labor cost per unit of output over a long period of

time, 22 years in this case, should be accorded equal weight for this reason. By connecting successive minima, David finds the implied labor productivity growth rates for three peak-to-peak intervals to be: 1839–1846, 3.37% per annum; 1846–1851, 2.35% and 1851–1856, 0.29%. The pattern of continuous retardation in labor productivity change over time is consistent with what might be expected when improvements in efficiency are based on the accumulation of production experience, i.e., learning by doing. By econometric estimation, using "elapsed time" as the relevant measure of learning experience, David finds that the estimated learning coefficient implies a reduction of real unit labor costs by roughly 15% for each doubling of the mill's operating life. This study, along with David's earlier 1970 piece, which is taken up in a later section, is "must" reading for any economic historian interested in disembodied technological change.

An interesting 1974 essay by Charles K. Harley examines the observed slowness of British industry to adopt capital-using, labor saving methods of production in the decades before World War I.X[6] Harley's point of departure is Habakkuk's suggestion that British choice of technique and trade flows reflected the available relative supplies of labor and capital. Harley interprets Habakkuk to refer to *homogenous* labor and *homogenous* capital. Harley's task is to show that the simple two-factor models using simple definitions of labor and capital, discussed in an earlier section of this essay, are inadequate for explaining British choice of technique or trade flows during the Edwardian period.

Harley examines machine processes in four industries as instances of a substitution of machines for labor skill. The industries discussed are: shipbuilding, iron and steel, textiles and engineering. The Leontief Paradox arose from the finding that the mid-twentieth century trade pattern of the United States exhibited capital-intensive imports and labor-intensive exports, exactly opposite to the factor intensity of trade that would be predicted by the Heckscher-Ohlin model for a capital-intensive country. The resolution of the Paradox in the American case was attained with the finding that adjustments to the simplified form of homogeneous labor, by explicit accounting for labor quality and skill, redefined the factor-intensity in United States production so that the observed trade pattern was consistent with the factor endowment specified in commensurable "efficiency units." Harley strongly suggests that the British neglect of new machine techniques came about because of the abundance of skilled labor in the economy, a point overlooked in two-sector models or in the naive interpretation of Habakkuk's theoretical propositions. Such comparative advantage as England possessed rested upon the craft skills of her industrial labor force. This stylized fact also conditioned the choice of technique and makes the slow rate of adoption of machine technology in Edwardian industry appear to be dictated by prevailing factor endowments, not by economic irrationality, entrepreneurial failure or technological "backwardness." Harley's investigation bears on issues discussed in the first section of this essay, dealing with the Habakkuk model.

A 1969 essay by Clive Trebilcock takes exception to the generally negative assessments of the technological prowess exhibited by the 19th century British armaments industry offered by such economic historians as Habakkuk, Landes, Saul and Nef.[87] Trebilcock looks at the British armaments industry after 1870 in terms of its contribution, through transfer of productive techniques and disembodied forms of technology, to civilian industries. The phenomenon of technology transfer from the military to the civilian sector is often termed "spin-off." The greater importance of spin-off for diffusing techniques after 1870 is attributed to the greater availability of government contracts after this date. Especially important was the rapid development of the British armaments industries after the late 1870's. Although accepting Habakkuk's proposition that the armaments industries did not act as "learning centres" during the first three-quarters of the nineteenth century in Britain, Trebilcock holds that spin-off effects became a reality during the last quarter of the century. Trebilcock outlines the relevant aspects of British armament industry developments between 1870 and 1914 to show that spin-off effects, though a term applied to modern economies, were present in late nineteenth-century Britain, as improved technologies developed in the military sector were partly transferred to general, civilian industries.

In 1971, Donald Paterson commented on Trebilcock's essay, and Trebilcock replied.[88] Paterson used the example of the Anglo-French nickel cartel to argue, by example, that the existence of certain marketing mechanisms acted as a barrier to the transfer of militarily developed technologies for steel making to the civilian sector. Moreover, Paterson argued that, on the basis of the example adduced, the spin-off process was attended with inefficiencies, since the relative prices for inputs (among them nickel), derived from a bargaining situation in which a monopsonist buyer in the government military sector confronted an oligopolistic cartel, would not hold for users of induced technologies in the civilian sector. In short, Paterson raised the more general point of whether or not effective relative factor prices in the military and civilian sectors of the economy are sufficiently close so as not to significantly impede the transfer of technology *a la* spin-off. Trebilcock's riposte argued that whereas he had adduced eighteen examples of spin-off, Paterson had offered only one exception. Moreover, he argued that Paterson had not "proved" his case for a divergence in relative factor prices between the two sectors. We may conclude by noting that a divergence in effective relative factor prices may be taken as a possible retardant in the transfer of militarily developed technologies to general industrial use. The importance of this case remains an empirical issue.

A 1967 essay by Richard Du Boff examines the introduction of electric power into American manufacturing.[89] Du Boff raises the interesting point that the spread of electrification for industrial uses was dependent upon the growth of the electric utility industry, which in turn depended in part on the growth of nonindustrial demand. Though this implication is not pursued further, it may be a promising area

for future research. The essay discusses the chief economic and technological forces underlying the introduction of electric power in manufacturing. Du Boff also explores the longer run implications and effects of electrification, with special reference to the manufacturing processes it transformed. Du Boff finds that the inherent potential of electric motors to support small-scale manufacturing enterprise was never realized in practice, as electric power served to support the forces leading to industrial concentration in the post-1900 period.

Ramon Knauerhase investigated the productivity effects of the introduction of the compound marine steam engine in the German merchant fleet between 1871 and 1887, in research reported in 1968.[90] Knauerhase finds that for the German merchant fleet as a whole, productivity, as measured by total clearings per man, rose 94% over the period 1873–1887. Of this total productivity change in the industry, consisting of steam and sail, the introduction and diffusion of the compound steam engine accounted for 52% of the increase, improvements to the steam engine itself after 1873 accounted for 16% of the change, and improving efficiency within sailing accounted for 15%.

Gary Walton commented on Knauerhase's measure of productivity in 1970.[91] Walton's point was that clearings-per-crewman was an inadequate productivity indicator, tending to overstate the efficiency of steam relative to sail. Walton argues that tonnage cleared does not reflect the distance hauled, hence one cannot accept Knauerhase's unqualified finding for the superior productivity of steamship haulage versus sail in the late nineteenth century.

V. MEASURES OF PRODUCTIVITY, TECHNICAL CHANGE AND THEIR BIASES

Douglass North investigated the sources of productivity change in ocean shipping during the period from 1600 to 1850 in an article appearing in 1968.[92] Dividing the two and one-half century span into two subperiods, North finds that the annual rate of growth of total factor productivity in ocean shipping was .45% in the period 1600–1784 and 3.30% in the period 1814–1860. During the earlier period, falling labor costs and declining port time account for most of the growth of productivity, while during the later period increasing ship size and improved load factors account for the measured productivity increase. North's findings lead him to conclude that changes in technology of a disembodied type and externalities are principally responsible for the productivity improvement in ocean shipping. Since the dominant sailing ships in terms of payload and performance characteristics were of designs similar to the Dutch flute, North concludes that what needs explaining is the length of time necessary for ships of the flute configuration to spread to all the commodity routes, once they had entered the Baltic and the English coal trade in the first half of the seventeenth century. Ships of the flute type were optimal only where piracy had been eliminated, thus obviating the need for

carrying heavy armament. In North's view, the elimination of piracy and privateering and the development of markets and the growth in trade volume were the primary factors accounting for the growth of shipping efficiency over the two and one-half century period.

In 1967, Gary Walton published some of the results of his larger research on American colonial shipping in an essay dealing with the sources of productivity change in shipping in colonial trade routes between 1675 and 1775.[93] Walton's findings for the American colonial trade are similar to Douglass North's results for ocean shipping generally. Both North and Walton use similar proxies for the productivity index. The reciprocal of the freight-rate index is used in Walton's work, because of the stability of input prices over the period he studied. Walton's research isolates the decline in crew size as the major determinant of declining costs over the period. This decline was made possible by the elimination of piracy and armaments-manning requirements. The decline in idle port time to productive sea time is also a source of productivity improvement over the period. Finally, like North, Walton finds that most of the productivity improvement in shipping cannot be traced to the influence of technological changes to ships themselves. Rather he points to the disembodied aspects of improved cargo handling organization and marketing arrangements in accounting for the reduction of idle port time. Likewise, externalities, in the form of the elimination of piracy, are also figured prominently in this analysis.

Following his earlier article, Walton published his findings on productivity change in American colonial shipping in a 1968 study.[94] The sources of productivity improvement discussed in the 1967 essay were measured using the same indirect productivity index as in the earlier study. Walton found an overall increase in total factor productivity in American colonial shipping of around 1.35% per annum from 1675 to 1775. In addition, considerable variation in the annual rate of productivity change by commodity route was found, with the per annum productivity change ranging from 0.6% to 3.1%. The study does not report reasons for the differential productivity advance by commodity route, and presumably this question might provide an interesting basis for further work.

A 1972 study by James Mak and Gary Walton investigates the advance in total factor productivity in United States river transportation between 1815 and 1860.[95] Employing a productivity index composed of the ratio of input to output prices, Mak and Walton find that the increase in total factor productivity over the period ranged between 4.6 and 5.5% per annum, depending on the choice of base year weights for the productivity index. Here the authors find that changes in the physical characteristics of vessels account for the major portion of productivity improvement. Increases in the carrying capacity per measured ton, increases in the navigation season and improved passage times resulted from improvements in steamboat design. Reduced cargo collection times also aided productivity advance, but in this case the reduction of cargo collection time is traced to the growth in the size of the market and improvements in commercial organization.

In 1972, I explored some of the implications in the literature on the bias of technical change by fitting data taken from the operations of the Springfield Armory between 1820 and 1850 to various econometric models.[96] The findings were that the principal source of productivity improvement arose from disembodied technical change, which on different variants in estimating form and procedure accounted for between 83% and 94% of the proportional shift in the production surface. Among the disembodied improvement factors, labor quality augmentation played a significant role. While over the entire period 1820–1850 the bias of technical change was found to be labor saving, the behavior of estimates of bias in the subperiods raised certain questions. In the subperiod 1820–1831, a "capital-saving" bias was found, while in the period 1831–1841 no consistent bias could be detected. Since relative factor price "pressure" did not result in a labor saving bias before 1841, this finding casts doubt on the importance of factor scarcity explanations of the bias of technical advance. Three variants of the Ames-Rosenberg hypothesis are offered, yet only one is tested due to data limitations. This version of the A-R hypothesis, which states that the presence of a third, or "material," variable in the production function will display significantly non-negative out put elasticities, is confirmed by the estimates, subject to the usual econometric reservations, owing to the presence of some intercorrelation between the material and labor input variables in some of the estimating forms.

An extension of the version of the A-R hypothesis, advanced above, was offered by David Klingaman, Richard Vedder and Lowell Gallaway in 1974.[97] In a rejoinder I pointed out ˙that in the K-V-G measure, the dependent variable employed tended to give an upward bias to the estimate of the output elasticity of material, which was the basis of their claim that under the gross output definition of the dependent variable, stronger support was lent to the A-R formulation.[98]

The 1972 contribution of Ephraim Asher measures factor-saving bias in technical change in the American and British textile industries during the nineteenth century.[99] Asher's estimating approach is based on the method of Paul David and Theo van de Klundert.[100] David and Klundert used a CES production model for the U.S. private economy over the period 1899–1960. They measured the Hicksian bias of technical change by estimating econometrically the absolute difference in the respective growth rates of the labor-efficiency and capital-efficiency parameters, where technical change comes about through factor augmentation. In the Hick's definition of factor-saving technical change, inventions are designated neutral, labor saving, or capital-saving, according to whether they leave the marginal productivity of labor relative to that for capital unchanged, lower it, or increase it, respectively, for a given capital-labor ratio. In Asher's formulation of the CES production function, when the elasticity of substitution is less than unity, if the proportionate time rate of growth of the marginal productivity of labor is greater than the proportionate growth of capital's marginal productivity, then the bias of technical change is labor saving, in a Hicksian sense.

Using data for the American cotton and wool industries over the years 1850–

1900, and for the British industries from the years 1820–1880 (cotton) and 1850–1900 (wool), Asher finds the bias of technical change in the wool and cotton industries of both countries was labor saving. Contrary to expectation, Asher also found the labor saving bias of technical change in Britain to be greater than in America. While certain sensitivity questions remain regarding Asher's findings, they suggest the further need for reinterpretation of the naive version of Habakkuk's model. It should also be pointed out that Asher's data measure both capital and labor in highly aggregate units, so that the results should not be accepted as definitive.

My 1972 study of factor substitution and labor productivity growth in American manufacturing over the period 1839–1899 posed two questions: 1) what proportion of the observed change in labor productivity could be accounted for by the substitution of capital for labor, and 2) what was the level and rate of change of factor intensity in manufacturing production over the period?[101] Using a method first introduced by W.E.G. Salter, in conjunction with well-known data series provided by Robert Gallman, Stanley Lebergott, Solomon Fabricant, Simon Kuznets, etc., it was found that over the period between 38 and 50 percent of the measured increase in labor productivity could be accounted for by the substitution of capital for labor alone. This finding calls into question the simple interpretation of Habakkuk's writings that factor substitution alone, or capital intensity, accounted for the productivity growth in the American manufacturing sector over the last six decades of the nineteenth century. Direct estimates of the capital per worker ratio are presented which show that, with the exception of the decade ending in 1869, the capital per worker ratio rose over the period, but that this alone could account for no more than one-half of the observed increase in labor productivity.

My 1973 study with Bruce Juba attempted to measure the factor-saving bias in the American manufacturing sector over the last six decades of the nineteenth century.[102] Using decadal data developed by Gallman, Lebergott and others, it was found that the overall bias of technical change was labor saving throughout the nineteenth century in American manufacturing, on the assumptions that the underlying manufacturing production function was not Cobb-Douglas, that technical progress itself was non-neutral, and that the elasticity of substitution of homogeneous labor for homogeneous capital was less than .9. For certain decades, the 1840's, 1870's and 1890's, technical progress was found to be capital-saving in a Hicksian sense, which raises the possiblity that the short-run pattern of factor-saving bias may be a cyclically induced response, notwithstanding the broad long-run tendency toward labor saving bias in technical progress.

Moses Abramovitz and Paul David explore the causes of economic growth in the United States over the course of the nineteenth and twentieth centuries in their 1973 study.[103] They offer the historical view of the growth process as being less a case of steady accumulation of capital and other factors of production leading to

output expansion along some equilibrium growth path than ". . . a sequence of *technologically induced traverses*, disequilibrium transitions between successive growth paths . . ."[104] Drawing on econometric investigations of others, as well as results obtained in the course of their own research, Abramovitz and David conclude that the observed 1.9% increase per annum in total factor productivity, during the period 1927–1967, measured using conventional definitions of the factors, drops to 1.3% per annum on a more "refined" measure. The refined measure arises from adjustments to the conventionally measured inputs, owing to changes in the quality-mix of capital and labor. The authors argue that, by accounting more fully for capital inputs, the "residual" measure of factor productivity might well be placed in the neighborhood of 0.6% per annum, far below even the refined measures of total factor productivity in the period 1927–1967. They also go on to point out that the 0.6% per annum increase in factor productivity is a lower-bound measure of ". . . our ignorance of the process of economic growth," and that it is impossible to apportion the growth rate of per capita product between the contributions of "invention" and "accumulation" in a mutually exclusive way because we cannot, given the present state of knowledge, specify the interactions between technical and social innovations on the one hand and the availability of factors of production on the other. On this view, they find no warrant for arguing that the role of invention and innovation in the process of economic growth (as opposed to capital accumulation and deepening) has altered during the course of transition from the nineteenth to the twentieth centuries, evidence of an upward adjustment in the size of the measured residual between these time periods notwithstanding.

William Parker and Judith Klein studied productivity growth in United States grain production between 1840–1860 and 1900–1910 in their 1966 essay.[105] They set out to investigate the proportionate contributions of westward expansion and technological changes to the growth in grain-farming productivity over the period. By using a factorial index number they examine changes in the combined and separate effects of regional shift, preharvest, harvest and postharvest labor requirements per unit of output and per acre, between the base period, 1840–1860, and the terminal period of indexation, 1900–1910. The statistical procedures employed should be of interest to economic historians, as factorial design has received little attention in recent work in economic history. The number of combinations of the indexes employed by Parker and Klein defy simple summarization. However, the idea of their work may be conveyed by stating that their statistical analysis proceeds along three lines: 1) westward movement of agriculture without technological change, 2) technological change without westward movement and 3) westward movement and technological change as they actually occurred between base and terminal periods. Their findings are, qualitatively stated, that without technological change (mainly mechanization) westward expansion would have been accompanied by only a modest rise in agricultural

productivity. Since much of the technological change actually taking place in agriculture over the period was made possible by the westward shift in production, confinement of agriculture (with technological change) to the eastern region of the country under alternative 2) would not have resulted in the actual growth in grain productivity observed. Here, of course, the path of technological change, induced by eastern factor proportions and institutional arrangements, would likely have brought about a different type of technology. As Parker and Klein point out, such a technology would have to have been land-saving, and they judge that the state of scientific knowledge in the nineteenth century would not have created as productive a land-saving technology, as the labor saving, land-using technologies developed for western agriculture.

In a 1968 study, Fred Bateman analyzes the changes in yield per animal in American dairying, between 1850 and 1910, that resulted from improved breeds, feeding and care.[106] Since dairying over the period did not experience any mechanical improvements comparable to the mechanization of reaping (so prominently featured in the Parker-Klein study), Bateman confines his reserach to the yield per animal measure, rather than the total factor productivity measurement. Bateman finds that the 50% observed increase in dairy yields over the period is directly attributable to three factors: 1) lengthening of the annual milking season, which by itself accounted for 54% of the increase in milk yields; 2) increase in the daily yield, which accounts for 38% of the observed yield increase (at a constant 1850 milking season); and 3) the combined effect of these two sources of improvement, accounting for the remainder of the observed yield increase. Bateman's overall conclusion is that the diffusion of existing dairying techniques, rather than the invention of new ones, is the principal cause of improved yields per animal.

Following the above study, Bateman investigated labor productivity in American dairying in work published in 1969.[107] The inquiry proceeded along two avenues: a) the changes in average annual dairy-labor requirements per animal and b) the relationship between labor requirements and annual milk yields. Bateman finds that while average annual yield per animal rose over the period, labor requirements rose more than proportionately to the increase in output, resulting in a decline in dairy-labor productivity, measured in milk output per manhour of labor time. Bateman's conclusion is that farmers focused attention on increasing milk yields per animal rather than upon the overall efficiency of the dairying enterprise. Further, the gains in yield per animal were partly obtained by more labor-intensive dairying methods, arising from the fuller utilization of the under-employed labor on family farms. Some of the ramifications and implications of Bateman's estimates were discussed in an exchange with Gerald Gunderson.[108] While not altering Bateman's basic conclusions, the exchange did serve to provide a clearer picture of the quality of the data sources, their handling, and some of the conceptual underpinnings of Bateman's analysis.

Roderick Floud investigates the labor productivity experience of one machine-tool firm, Greenwood and Batley, between 1856 and 1900 in an article published in 1971.[109] Floud finds that embodied technical change raised labor productivity for the firm considerably faster than the average for British industry as a whole. Moreover, Floud finds little evidence of factor substitution accounting for the observed increase in labor productivity over the period. Greenwood and Batley's labor productivity was found to rise 2.4% per annum, as contrasted with the growth in labor productivity for the British economy as a whole of 0.6% per annum over the period 1870–1913. This leads Floud to the conclusion that there were still areas of British industry that could yield adequate returns to investment in new, productivity-raising machinery.

Donald McCloskey's 1971 investigation of the labor productivity differences between the British and American coal and steel industries starts from the proposition that large and persistent differences in productivity between the two economies are contradicted by two principal considerations: 1) that technical information and practice were easily transferred by the late nineteenth century and 2) that persistent differences of production possibilities between the two economies would imply an irrational foregoing of profits by British entrepreneurs.[110] By making cross-sectional comparisons for Britain and America in the first decade of the twentieth century, McCloskey finds no significant difference in productivity performance of the coal and steel industries of the two economies. He concludes by suggesting that his evidence is not consistent with the traditional emphasis on the loss of managerial and entrepreneurial vigor and technological "backwardness" as explanations of the slower overall growth of output in Britain.

A 1968 paper by Robert Solo discusses a wide range of conceptual issues involved in the attempt to measure such causes of economic growth as productivity changes.[111] The purpose of the paper is to illuminate the relationship of technology to its cultural context. In addition, Solo discusses, among other considerations too numerous to detail, the economic-conceptual difficulties of arriving at general-purpose productivity indices, measuring inputs (and outputs) to the production process in a consistent way, and excluded outputs and inputs. Solo's general conclusion is that the notion of economic progress is too multidimensional to be successfully measured.

A 1971 essay by Gerald Flueckiger offers a radical departure from the existing literature on methods of measuring technological change.[112] Flueckiger characterizes technological change as a qualitative, observable set of attributes in productive processes, and he defines technological change as ". . . any change in the lists of commodity names at a given level of resolution."[113] A "level of resolution" is the definition of the productive entity. It can be *fine*, as in observing a subassembly of a particular machine, or *coarser*, when the productive entity is taken as, say, the entire assembly line. Flueckiger offers a symbolic taxonomy of his system and uses it to develop measures of technological change for the process of iron-making

over the eighteenth and nineteenth centuries. He also demonstrates how the qualitative measure varies as the "level of resolution" is varied. While offering an ingenious way of viewing the phenomenon of technological change, Flueckiger's analysis raises several questions. First, how can a qualitative-technical measure (which is binary) be used to reveal underlying economic behavior? Second, how can one apply measures of significance to a qualitative index? These reservations aside, technological historians may profit from a careful study of Flueckiger's analysis.

VI. LEARNING BY DOING

Paul David's 1970 study on the existence of long-run learning effects in the antebellum cotton-textile industry deals with the question of whether or not the high protective tariff enjoyed by American manufacturers between 1816 and 1860 was justifiable.[114]

Almost a half century ago, F.W. Taussig argued that the protective tariff on textile imports in the antebellum period was unjustified because, by as early as 1824 and no later than 1832, the industry had reached a position of maturity where it could meet foreign competition on even terms. David suggested that the protective tariff might be justified on the ground that there were "learning effects" accruing to production experience, effects that were external to any individual firm. Learning effects accruing in the form of externalities are presumed to have social benefits, by making technical knowledge, skills and institutional arrangements (i.e., production experience) available to new firms as well as established ones. Where learning effects can be internalized to the firm, this social benefit is largely absent. Yet even where external, long-run learning effects are present, it makes a difference how "production experience" is accumulated. If the experience cannot be transferred to other firms, but must be generated *de novo* by each entrant through a repetition of the relevant learning experience, then the basis for infant industry protection is largely absent. Also tending to weaken the case for blanket protection is the possiblity of establishing pilot plants in the nascent industrial sector, which can be used to accumulate the production experience and disseminate production knowledge and skills to new entrants.

David's econometric study is aimed at that portion of the cotton-textile industry's historical experience that, according to the Taussig view, offered no justification for the high protective tariff on infant-industry grounds. The findings may be briefly summarized. On the basis of his econometric findings, David argues that learning by doing in the cotton-textile industry was not dependent on cumulated output. Since learning measures based on elapsed time as a measure of production experience performed uniformly better than cumulated output, according to David, this finding, coupled with the absence of scale economics, weakens considerably the case for protective tariffs. Over the period 1833–1839, total factor

productivity rose at a rate of 2.6% per annum. Of this increase, learning by doing accounted for almost 80% of the change in total factor productivity. Toward the end of the antebellum period in the quinquennia 1855–1859, the rate of increase in total factor productivity had attenuated to 1.17% per annum, with learning by doing accounting for about 45% of the measured increase in factor productivity. The retardation in the contribution of learning by doing to total efficiency growth toward the end of the antebellum period is attributed to the reduced rate at which effective additions were made to the collective production experience of the sample group of firms. On the basis of this and other evidence, David concludes that the blanket tariff protection offered the American cotton-textile industry after 1824 was unjustified on the learning by doing formulation of the infant industry argument.

In 1972 an exchange ensued between Paul David and Jeffrey Williamson over some econometric issues raised in David's 1970 essay on learning effects.[115] While David had found (on the basis of a neoclassical model with Cobb-Douglas specification) evidence of constant returns to scale, robust learning effects, a significant rate of disembodied technical progress and strong rates of labor quality augmentation over the sample period, Williamson set out to illustrate the difficulties of discriminating among these sources of productivity improvement. Williamson points out that it is formally impossible to distinguish between an embodiment and disembodiment model of technical change strictly on the basis of historical evidence, hence the prior specification of a disembodiment model by David strongly influenced his findings. Further, the magnitude of measured learning effects in such a model will be larger than in one where a positive rate of growth of embodied technology is presumed to take place. The crucial issue, according to Williamson, is the desirability of constraining the estimates of the parameters in the learning function by assuming constant returns to scale. Williamson argues that since so much econometric work on nineteenth-century manufacturing has found constant returns to scale, this evidence should not be ignored in the estimation procedure. Finally, Williamson argues, on the basis of qualitative knowledge of the technological history of the American cotton-textile industry, that the nature and magnitude of technical progress was quite different before and after the 1840's, and that this discontinuity should also be reflected in the estimating procedures. By David's model, Williamson finds no basis for discriminating between the two alternative versions of the learning hypothesis: a) production experience measured by cumulated output or b) production experience measured by elapsed time from the inception of productive activity, for the period 1834–1860 as a whole. Williamson finds, on the basis of his constrained estimates, that the rate of disembodied productivity improvement is insignificantly different from zero under either an elapsed time or cumulative output specification of the learning variable, and that the proportionate contribution of learning effects to productivity growth, while still relatively large, is significantly reduced in size when the

exogenous rate of disembodied progress is set equal to zero by prior restriction. In the 1830's and 1840's, Williamson finds that slightly less than two-thirds of productivity growth can be attributed to learning, while in the decade and a half before the Civil War, learning effects make no contribution to explaining observed productivity growth. Beyond this, Williamson's specification enlarges the explanatory role of capital-augmenting technical progress in productivity advance, which source accounts for one-sixth of the overall productivity growth over the period.

David's response concerns the appropriate use of prior information. The essence of his position is that Williamson's constrained estimates are unfounded because the use of a prior restriction of constant returns to scale, where the prior has been drawn from work on the macro level, is inappropriate for micro-level analysis. Likewise, he argues that the observed steady rate of embodied technical progress in the macro economy cannot be transferred to micro level studies in the form of constrained estimation procedures. While David's point, that econometric work in economic history cannot proceed solely on the basis of assumptions drawn as priors from previous empirical or qualitative work, is well taken, the fact remains that procedures such as those employed by Williamson are quite often necessary to get any results in econometric history. The case at hand appears to indicate that the geometric progression of econometric sophistication does not inevitably lead to conclusive results. Whether or not one accepts Williamson's assumptions is, in the final analysis, a matter of taste. In the end, the ability of econometric analysis to distinguish between such things as disembodied and embodied technical change, alternative measures of learning experience, the strength and presence of learning effects, and similar conceptual magnitudes turns upon such questions as one's degree of belief with respect to propositions about the prior existence of scale parameters of a given magnitude in the underlying industry production function, sharp changes in the size and qualitative character of technical progress itself and a host of other matters.

In 1973, Tsuneo Ishikawa sharpened the attack on David's learning by doing formulation.[116] Two broad issues are taken up. The first is the basis for David's choice of elapsed time as the measure of production experience. The second is the cogency of his case of pilot firms as generating centers for relevant production experience. On the first point, Ishikawa examines the econometric evidence which led David to conclude that the elapsed time formulation constituted a superior explanation, when in fact both measures of production experience produced about equal statistical results.

On the pilot firm issue, Ishikawa pointed out that David failed to distinguish between the conceptualization of learning by doing as: a) the *discovery* of new technical and managerial "know-how" and b) the *transmission* of know-how. The failure to distinguish clearly which type of learning is relevant to the case at hand confuses David's discussion of the relevant learning *entity*, according to Ishikawa.

So long as learning is transferable, repetitive discoveries (of the very same information) become redundant, and tariffs designed to encourage such repetitive discoveries are grossly inefficient. Ishikawa points out that David did not offer a persuasive discussion as to how and why pilot firms bring about all potentially significant discoveries. Since discovery as a form of learning is a probabilistic activity—it occurs by chance—Ishikawa believes it is reasonable to suppose that this form of learning is a direct function of the number of relevant learning entities, i.e., the greater the number of firms (or some other measure of the learning entity) the greater the chance of productively effective discovery taking place. By confining his attention exclusively to the transferability of technical and managerial know-how as the essence of learning activity, David overlooks the importance of the size and number of learning entities in the textile industry as an important source of learning.

Managerial Behavior and Technical Change

Relatively few studies in economic history have dealt with technological change as the outcome of purposive decision-making on the part of industrial managers and entrepreneurs within a framework of economic rationality. An exception is Jeffrey Williamson's effort published in 1971.[117] Williamson's purpose is to develop a model of replacement behavior that is consistent with the economic environment in Britain and America in the 1820's and 1830's. The optimal useful life of capital goods is postulated to be a function of the rate of embodied technical progress, the money rate of interest, the wage of unskilled labor, and the price of investment goods relative to the price of final output. The sensitivity of the economically useful life of capital goods with respect to these variables is examined. Williamson finds evidence of a higher replacement rate in the United States than in Britain in the 1820's and similar replacement rates in the 1850's. This result is explained by the convergence of the rates of embodied technical progress between the two economies over the last four decades of the antebellum period. In Williamson's model, American interest rate behavior had an effect opposite to that of differentials in embodied technical progress. The higher the rate of interest, the longer is the optimal useful life of capital goods. Thus the higher American interest rate during the antebellum period did not require a complete closing of the gap between British and American rates of embodied technical progress to equalize replacement cycles between the two economies. Williamson employs models of both neutral and labor saving technical change. When technical progress is neutral, the replacement rate for capital goods is a positive function of the wage rate. Thus the higher American unskilled wage meant that the replacement rate for capital goods in America was greater—i.e., the optimal useful life of capital goods was shorter than in Britain. Where technical progress is labor saving, wages have no effect on the replacement rate. For this reason, Williamson finds Habakkuk's argument to be inconsistent, since Habakkuk holds that technical

change was labor saving, American wage rates were relatively high, and the American replacement cycle was relatively short. According to Williamson, these three conditions cannot exist simultaneously.

When the tariff rate is introduced into the model, the effect of the high American tariff is to raise the price of consumption goods relative to investment goods. The replacement rate is a positive function of the final output price in the model, so the effect of the tariff is to raise the American replacement rate. Also, since the optimal life of investment goods is a positive function of their price, anything which tends to reduce the price of capital goods raises the replacement rate, which is the reciprocal of the optimal useful life.

An exchange between David Denslow and David Schulze and Jeffrey Williamson on an issue raised in the latter's 1971 article took place in 1974.[118] Denslow and Schulze showed that when it is assumed that entrepreneurs expect wages to rise at the same rate at which labor saving technical change occurs, Williamson's findings—that 1) the unskilled wage rate has no effect on the replacement rate, 2) the Habakkuk interpretation is inconsistent, and 3) a tariff structure that raises the prices of consumption goods relative to investment goods raises the replacement rates—do not follow. Williamson's reply was that the historical experience of the period could not possibly have led entrepreneurs to expect that wage increases and technical advances would move together, much less at equal rates.

A 1973 essay by D.L. Brito and Jeffrey Williamson explores the reasons for the divergence in the capital intensity of manufacturing between Britain and America.[119] They modify the naive interpretation of Habakkuk's propositions on the effect of the price of homogeneous labor on factor proportions and construct a model that features heterogeneous labor inputs. The nexus between capital intensity and skilled labor lies in the proposition that skilled labor is required to maintain, repair and schedule capital intensive production processes. In the Brito-Williamson model, the firm selects capital and skilled labor inputs in a combination that minimizes the cost of capital services. Second, the firm chooses the level of capital services and unskilled labor that maximizes profit for a given level of output. Brito and Williamson also point out that it is incorrect to use the money rate of interest as an accurate index of the price of capital services facing the firm. The rental rate of capital is, after all, the relevant variable (along with the real wage rate) in decisions governing factor proportions. The effect of the high American tariff was to lower the relative price of capital and, hence, the relative service price of capital. Moreover, the rate at which capital goods are utilized affects the price of capital services. These considerations suggest that there is no simple connection between the money rate of interest and the price of capital services.

Brito and Williamson find, in the context of their model, that American manufacturers would have employed higher rates of capital replacement and utilization and more capital intensive techniques than their British counterparts, owing to the

greater American possibility of substituting skilled labor for capital. If technical progress is fully embodied, then the average age of the capital stock reflects the rate at which new technologies have been adopted. Thus higher American depreciation rates, resulting from higher utilization and replacement rates, would be consistent with a more youthful vintage of investment goods embodying a greater proportion of "best practice" technology. By moving away from the practice of specifying production conditions where only homogeneous factors are used, Brito and Williamson demonstrate the theoretical plausibility of many of Habakkuk's propositions, although these issues are not tested empirically in their work.

My 1973 study examined the evolution of industrial management techniques and their relationship to technological innovation at the Springfield Armory between 1794 and 1850.[120] The first task that had to be accomplished in this establishment (one of advanced metal working complexes in America in the antebellum period) was to create a system of discipline for assimilating the labor force to the regimen of the factory form of organization. The second task involved the evolution of a method of account-keeping that could record and monitor industrial task performance. Allied to the accounting function was the establishment of regular procedures for inspecting work and controlling raw, semi-finished and finished materials inventories and flows, and coordinating these stocks and flows with the machine processes. In this study, early attempts at technological innovation are seen as evolving partly from the need to control labor. Contemporary statements and the examples of cost and benefit calculations of innovations like the Blanchard gun-stocking machines show that these innovations did not cover costs nor compete effectively with earlier hand methods of production for nearly a decade after adoption. It is argued that the rationale for adoption must be sought elsewhere—in the taming or house-breaking of the labor force—than in narrow calculations of economic costs and savings. This research offers a case example of the unfolding sequence of events that led to disembodied technical progress and paved the way for embodied technical innovation.

VII. SUMMARY

These studies of technology in the recent lierature of economic history cover a variety of topics and methods. Because of this a simple, straightforward summarization is hardly possible. Yet there appear to be certain recurring themes and tendencies in these studies that presage areas toward which new research efforts may be directed.

H.J. Habakkuk's, *American and British Technology in the Nineteenth Century*, as we have seen in the preceding pages, was responsible for many of the essays appearing since 1962. In many respects Habakkuk's work is like John Hicks' celebrated *Value and Capital*, in that it has a certain kaleidoscopic quality. Certain changes in perspective reveal an endless variety of possibilities for viewing

technological events, their causes and consequences. Economists are fond of saying "It's all in Adam Smith," and one is tempted to remark that for economic historians concerned with technological events, "It's all in Habakkuk."

Habakkuk deserves pride of place because he paved the way for such able and influential students of the technological dimension in economic history, as Paul David and Nathan Rosenberg. Rosenberg's work individually, as well as jointly with Edward Ames, has done much to advance the evolutionary, historical understanding of the economics of technology. By skillful use of economic reasoning, Rosenberg has revealed much of the substructure and implications of technological events. Mention should also be made of Rosenberg's excellent book, *Technology and American Economic Growth* (1972), as a good introduction to the Rosenberg style of analysis and the larger issues evolving out of his research. Rosenberg's principal contributions consist of his analysis of the importance of market structure and industrial organization for the dissemination of effective technical information via the mechanism of *technological convergence,* along with his emphasis (jointly with Edward Ames) on the historically-specified production function, including qualitative differences in heterogeneous inputs. Perhaps the most distinguishing hallmark of Rosenberg's work, in general, is the continual emphasis on the question of why a particular, observable technology appears in a specific context at a given time. The approach here is as much to understand as to describe. It is evolutionary in execution and faithfully historical in its final form.

Paul David's recent work has been important in two respects. First is the introduction of the concept of localized learning effects as a disembodied medium of technological change. Historically, this idea has considerable appeal, for it is consistent with the numerous studies in the history of technology that call attention to the large, cumulative impact of the small improvements made to existing processes by many individual mechanics and workers. If learning by doing as a source of technological change is not entirely the negation of the hero-inventor approach, it is an important, if not overshadowing, adjunct. David, in moving away from the "smooth and continuous substitutability" of the neoclassical world, has offered significant insights to the economic historian into how microeconomic events may be handled where technology displays "discreteness", and, further, is advancing the evolutionary approach by his essays dealing with the effect of past, embodied accumulations of capital, institutional arrangements, and technical interrelatedness on current period microeconomic decisions.

Our review of the literature on the American System of manufacturing has revealed some recent gains in our understanding of the specific historical sequence of observable developments, like the work of Edwin Battison and Merritt Roe Smith on the origins of the milling machine. Yet a great deal of information has not yet come to light, especially on the disembodied aspects of the American System: plant layout, scheduling procedures, inspection, etc. It also is the case that much work on technology is confined to the antebellum period in America. One thing we

learn from David Landes's masterful book on technological change in Western Europe from 1750 to the present, *The Unbound Prometheus*, is the difficulty of handling technological events in a narrowly focused, exact context in the late 19th and early 20th centuries. The number of inventions and innovations, and their diversity, in this period complicates the task of handling the technological element well in some meaningful historical sense. The Industrial Revolution in England and the antebellum industrial development in America provide epochs oriented around technological phenomena few enough in number and complexity so that, if they are not always well understood, they are at least "well-behaved" in economic historical explanation. In good part, this accounts for the concentration of work in these periods. Much remains to be done, not only in examining the technology of the late 19th century, but in understanding how it fits into the larger social context.

The work of Douglass North and Gary Walton reminds us that externalities play a large role in conditioning the adoption and diffusion of innovations. Yet one may broaden the economically determining effects of externalities, such as the elimination of piracy or the improvement of navigation, to include mutual influences between some concrete technological phenomenon and the operating environment, defined inclusively. Such an approach is illustrated in the work of the Annales School, in the writings of such scholars as Lucien Febvre and Marc Bloch. Beyond economic determinants of technological change one may glimpse the mutual interactions of custom, culture and law with technical events. Marc Bloch's essays, "Technical Change as a Problem of Collective Psychology," "Medieval 'Inventions'" and "The Advent and Triumph of the Watermill," reprinted in *Land and Work in Medieval Europe* (1969), would be a good starting point for those interested in this approach. Lucien Febvre and Marc Bloch cannot be mentioned without calling to mind the fascinating studies by Lynn White, *Medieval Technology and Social Change* (1968) and Carolo Cipolla, *Guns, Sails and Empires* (1965). These are subtle works dealing with the philosophical, psychological and cultural impulses in Western Europe in the Middle Ages that led to the expansionist phase of development, made possible by the unleashing of science and technology from its customary restraints. In turn, the unfolding technological sequence reacts back upon society, in these mutually interactive studies. One can only speculate on the delights of the sumptuous feasts to be prepared by scholars working within these frameworks on technological and economic materials of more modern periods.

Two additional ideas that should play important roles in future work are Raymond Vernon's product cycle model and Nathan Rosenberg's notion that innovations enter the economy "through a particular door." Both views offer important organizing principles for studies dealing with adoption and diffusion of innovations, both interregionally and internationally.

To the familiar trinity in the diffusion literature—geography, market, and relative input costs—industrial structure should be added. The essays by Russell

Fries and David Jeremy, and the above-mentioned work of Rosenberg, reveal the crucial role played by the organization of the industrial sector in affecting the incentives to adopt new technologies.

Supply side considerations have been featured prominently in most of the recent work on technical choice and innovation. Yet the essays of D.C. Coleman and R.A. Church remind us that much innovation was demand-induced. The economic history of technology would be well-served if more work were done in this area of demand-induced innovation, paying special attention to the definition of the term "product." For most economic historians, technological change has been equated with a "shift in the production surface." But an entirely different form of change takes place as new or technically improved products enter the consumption possibility set of a society.

The introduction of heterogenous labor into the production function in the work of Jeffrey Williamson, Charles Harley, Dagobert Brito, Edward Ames and Nathan Rosenberg has resulted in a refinement of the role of relative factor price in technical choice. Measures of technical progress employing heterogenous inputs will probably be of considerable importance in future work.

While some work on the disembodied aspects of technological change *vis a vis* the diffusion of managerial and technical know-how has been done by Paul David, Jeffrey Williamson and Tsuneo Ishikawa, most economic historians have focused their studies on the hardware aspects of technology. The essays by Brito and Williamson and myself have provided an initial exploration of this area and make the point that the productive system, in a technical sense, cannot be understood independently of the system of managerial control. Because of its significant microeconomic orientation and its growing emphasis on the evolutionary approach emphasizing disembodied improvement factors, recent studies of technology in economic history are beginning to exhibit features and characteristics of that somewhat neglected antecedent taproot of economic history—business history! Herman Krooss, whose questions always had a certain pertinence about them, could often be heard to remark in after-hours conversation, "What ever happened to business history?" One might reply that the micro-orientation and evolutionary approach now being exhibited in technological studies in economic history may be a recrudescence of the old spirit! One of the beauties of historical work is its exemption from the Second Law of Thermodynamics. Facts and elements of earlier approaches are recombined under the "focusing devices and inducement mechanisms" of contemporary questions to produce new work. For the economic historian, analytical ability improves and the factual horizons expand over time. As a consequence of this, a relabeling takes place, but something long-standing and fundamental endures. There is an ecological quality about historical-economics that insures this conservation of intellectual energy.

FOOTNOTES

1. Habakkuk (1962).
2. Temin (September 1966), p. 277.
3. Rothbarth (September 1946), pp. 383–390.
4. Temin (September 1966), p. 285.
5. Fogel (September 1967).
6. Uselding (June 1970), Chapter 1.
7. Temin (Winter 1971).
8. *Ibid.*, p. 252.
9. *Ibid.*, p. 253
10. *Ibid.*, p. 262.
11. A representative collection would include: Rosenberg (June 1967), pp. 221–229; Adams (September 1970), pp. 499–520; Adams (September 1968), pp. 404–426; Zabler (Fall 1972), pp. 109–117; Adams (Fall 1973), pp. 89–99.
12. David (1975), chapter 1.
13. Atkinson and Stiglitz (September 1969).
14. Ames and Rosenberg (December 1968).
15. Burn (1936), pp. 292–311; Sawyer (1954), pp. 361–379. These essays by Burn and Sawyer are reprinted in Coats and Robertson (1969), pp. 150–164 and 278–292, respectively.
16. Rosenberg (1969), pp. 1–i6.
17. *Ibid.*, p. 51.
18. Ames and Rosenberg (December 1968).
19. *Ibid.*, p. 841.
20. Woodbury (1o60). (Reprinted in Coats and Robertson, (1969), pp. 49–69; and in Kranzberg and Davenport (1972), pp. 218–236.)
21.cBattison (Summer 1966), pp. 9–34.
22. Smith (October 1973), pp. 573/591.
23. *Ibid.*, p. 576.
24. *Ibid.*, p. 576.
25. Battison (October 1973), pp. 592–598.
26. Uselding (October 1974), pp. 543–568.
27. Fries (July 1975), pp. 377–403.
28. Murphy (June 1966), pp. 169–186.
29. *Ibid.*, p. 175.
30. Jeremy (January 1973), pp. 40–76.
31. *Ibid.*, p. 48.
32. Floud (February 1974), pp. 57–71.
33. Burn (1936), p. 292.
34. Saul (April 1967), pp. 111–130.
35. Church (November 1975), pp. 616–630.
36. Rosenberg (December 1963), pp. 414–443. (Reprinted in Coats and Robertson, 1969, pp. 166–186; and *Purdue Faculty Papers in Economic History*, 1956–1966, pp. 405–430.)
37. Ames and Rosenberg (July 1965), pp. 363–383. (Reprinted in *Purdue Faculty Papers*, 1967, pp. 345–362.)
38. Stigler (June 1951), pp. 185–193.

39. Rosenberg (October 1970), pp. 550–575.

40. Rosenberg (Fall 1972), pp. 3–34.

41. Ruttan and Hayami (April 1973), pp. 119–151.

42. Griliches (October 1957), pp. 501–522; (July 1960), pp. 275–280.(The second essay is reprinted in Fogel and Engerman (1971), pp. 207–213.) Griliches' work sparked several exchanges with sociologists: Brandner and Straus (December 1959), pp. 381–383; Griliches (September 1960), pp. 354–356; Rogers and Havens (September 1962), pp. 330–332; Griliches (September 1962), pp. 327–330; Babcock (September 1962), pp. 332–338; Klonglan and Coward, Jr. (March 1970), pp. 77–83.

43. Evenson (1969); Dalrymple (July 1966), pp. 187–206.

44. Vernon (May 1966), pp. 190–207.

45. Hayami (March 1974), pp. 131–148.

46. Evenson (March 1974), pp. 51–73.

47. Watson (March 1974), pp. 8–35.

48. Aufhauser (March 1974), pp. 36–50.

49. Eckstein et. al., (March 1974), pp. 239–264.

50. Feller (September 1966), pp. 320–347.

51. Ibid., p. 346.

52. Sandberg (December 1968), pp. 624–627.

53. Feller (December 1968), pp. 628–630.

54. Feller (October 1974), pp. 569–593.

55. Sandberg (February 1969), pp. 25–43.

56. Ibid., p. 35.

57. Coleman (December 1969), pp. 417–429.

58. Jeremy (Spring 1973), pp. 24–52.

59. Saxonhouse (March 1974), pp. 149–165.

60. Temin (May 1964), pp. 344–351. (Reprinted in Fogel and Engerman (1971), pp. 116–121.)

61. Hunter (February 1929), pp. 241–281. (Reprinted in Coats and Robertson, 1969, pp. 87–112.

62. Hyde (Summer 1973), pp. 397–419.

63. Hyde (May 1974), pp. 190–206. See also his essay on the adoption of specific techniques in the British iron industry (Hyde, Spring 1973, pp. 281–294).

64. Temin (June 1966), pp. 187–205.

65. Ibid., p. 191.

66. Robinson (March 1974), pp. 91–104.

67. Brittain (March 1974), pp. 108–121.

68. Walton (Winter 1970–1971), pp. 123–140.

69. Ibid., p. 124.

70. Harley (1971), pp. 215–234.

71. Harley (June 1973), pp. 372–398.

72. Mak and Walton (June 1973), pp. 444–451.

73. Wilkinson (Winter 1963), pp. 1–13. (Reprinted in Kranzberg and Davenport (1972), pp. 337–350.)

74. Uselding (June 1970), pp. 312–337.

75. Wilkins (March 1974), pp. 166–188.

76. David (1966), pp. 3–39. (Reprinted in Fogel and Engerman, 1971, pp. 214–217; and David, 1975, pp. 195–232.)

77. Olmstead (June 1975), pp. 327–353.

78. David (1971), pp. 145–204. (Reprinted in David, 1975, pp. 233–280.)

79. Rosenberg (October 1971), pp. 543–561.

80. Ames and Rosenberg (March 1963), pp. 13–31. (Reprinted in *Purdue Faculty Papers in Economic History, 1956–1966*, pp. 363–382.)

81. Rasmussen (October 1968), pp. 531–543. (Reprinted in Kranzberg and Davenport, 1972, pp. 255–270.)

82. Hayami (Summer 1971), pp. 445–472.

83. Rosenberg (October 1969), pp. 1–24.

84. Mantoux (1948).

85. David (Winter 1973), pp. 131–150. (Reprinted in David, 1975, pp. 174–194.)

86. Harley (Summer 1974), pp. 391–414.

87. Trebilcock (December 1969), pp. 474–490.

88. Paterson (August 1971), pp. 463–464; and Trebilcock (August 1971), pp. 464–468.

89. DuBoff (December 1967), pp. 509–518.

90. Knauerhase (September 1968), pp. 390–403.

91. Walton (June 1970), pp. 435–442.

92. North (September/October 1968), pp. 953–970. (Reprinted in Fogel and Engerman, 1971, pp. 163–174.)

93. Walton (April 1964), pp. 67–78.

94. Walton (August 1968), pp. 268–282.

95. Mak and Walton (September 1972), pp. 619–640.

96. Uselding (Spring 1972), pp. 291–316.

97. Klingaman, Vedder and Gallaway (Spring 1974), pp. 315–316.

98. Uselding (Spring 1974), pp. 315–316.

99. Asher (June 1972), pp. 431–442.

100. David and van de Klundert (June 1965), pp. 357–394.

101. Uselding (September 1972), pp. 670–681.

102. Uselding and Juba (Fall 1973), pp. 55–72.

103. Abramovitz and David (May 1973), pp. 428–439.

104. *Ibid.*, p. 429.

105. Parker and Klein (1966), pp. 523–579. (A condensed version of this essay is reprinted in Fogel and Engerman, 1971, pp. 175–186.)

106. Bateman (June 1968), pp. 255–273.

107. Bateman (June 1969), pp. 206–229.

108. Gunderson (September 1969), pp. 501–505; Bateman (September 1969), pp. 506–511.

109. Floud (1971), pp. 313–337.

110. McCloskey (1971), pp. 285–304.

111. Solo (July 1968), pp. 389–414.

112. Flueckiger (Winter 1971–1972), pp. 145–178.

113. *Ibid.*, p. 159.

114. David (September 1970), pp. 521–601. (Reprinted in David, 1975, pp. 95–168.)

115. Williamson (September 1972), pp. 691–705; and David (September 1972), pp. 706–727.

116. Ishikawa (December 1973), pp. 851–861.

117. Williamson (November/December 1971), pp. 1320–1334.

118. Denslow and Schulze (May/June 1974), pp. 631–637; and Williamson (May/June 1974), pp. 638–640.

119. Brito and Williamson (Spring 1973), pp. 235–252.

120. Uselding (1973), pp. 51–84.

REFERENCES

Abramovitz, Moses and David, Paul (May 1973), "Reinterpreting Economic Growth: Parables and Realities," *American Economic Review*, 93, pp. 428–439.

Adams, Donald, (September 1968), "Wage Rates in the Early National Period: Philadelphia, 1785–1830," *Journal of Economic History*, 28, pp. 404–426.

———. (September 1970), "Some Evidence on English and American Wage Rates, 1790–1830," *Journal of Economic History*, 30, pp. 499–520.

———. (Fall 1973), "Wages in the Iron Industry: A Comment," *Explorations in Economic History*, 11, pp. 89–99.

Ames, Edward and Rosenberg, Nathan (March 1963), "Changing Technological Leadership and Industrial Growth," *Economic Journal*, 73, pp. 13–31.

———. (July 1965), "The Progressive Division and Specialization of Industries," *The Journal of Development Studies*, 1, pp. 363–383.

———. (December 1968), "The Enfield Arsenal in Theory and History," *Economic Journal*, 78, pp. 827–842.

Asher, Ephraim (June 1972), "Industrial Efficiency and Biased Technical Change in American and British Manufacturing: The Case of Textiles in the Nineteenth Century," *Journal of Economic History*, 32, pp. 431–442.

Atkinson, Anthony B. and Stiglitz, Joseph E. (September 1969), "A New View of Technological Change," *Economic Journal*, 79.

Aufhauser, Keith R. (March 1974), "Slavery and Technological Change," *Journal of Economic History*, 34, pp. 36–50.

Babcock, Jarvis M. (September 1962), "Adoption of Hybrid Corn: A Comment," *Rural Sociology*, 27, pp. 332–338.

Bateman, Fred (June 1968), "Improvement in American Dairy Farming, 1850–1910: A Quantitative Analysis," *Journal of Economic History*, 23, pp. 255–273.

———. (June 1969), "Labor Inputs and Productivity in American Dairy Agriculture, 1850–1910," *Journal of Economic History*, 29, pp. 206–229.

———. (September 1969), "Issues in the Measurement of Efficiency of American Dairy Farming, 1850–1910: Reply," *Journal of Economic History*, 29, pp. 506–511.

Battison, Edwin A. (Summer 1966), "Eli Whitney and the Milling Machine," *Smithsonian Journal of History*, 1, pp. 9–34.

———. (October 1973), "A New Look at the Whitney Milling Machine," *Technology and Culture*, 14, pp. 592–598.

Brandner, Lowell and Straus, Murray A. (December 1959), "Congruence versus Profitability in the Diffusion of Hybrid Sorghum," *Rural Sociology*, 24, pp. 381–383.

Brito, D. L. and Williamson, Jeffrey (Spring 1973), "Skilled Labor and Nineteenth Century Anglo-American Managerial Behavior," *Explorations in Economic History*, 10, pp. 235–252.

Brittain, James E. (March 1974), "The International Diffusion of Electrical Power Technology, 1870–1920," *Journal of Economic History*, 34, pp. 108–121.

Burn, Duncan L. (1936), "The Genesis of American Engineering Competition, 1850–1870," *Economic History* (supplement to *Economic Journal*), 55, pp. 292–311.

Church, R. A. (November 1975), "Nineteenth-Century Clock Technology in Britain, the United States and Switzerland," *Economic History Review*, second series, 28, pp. 616–630.

Coats, A. W. and Robertson, R. M. (1969), *Essays in American Economic History*, London: Edward Arnold.

Coleman, D. C. (December 1969), "An Innovation and its Diffusion: The 'New Draperies'," *Economic History Review*, second series, 22, pp. 417–429.

Dalrymple, Dana G. (July 1966), "American Technology and Soviet Agricultural Development, 1924–1933," *Agricultural History*, 40, pp. 187–206.

David, Paul and van de Klundert, Theo (June 1965), "Biased Efficiency Growth and Capital-Labor Substitution in the U.S. 1899–1960," *American Economic Review*, 55, pp. 357–394.

David, Paul (1966), "The Mechanization of Reaping in the Antebellum Midwest," *Industrialization in Two Systems* (edited by Rosovsky, Henry), pp. 3–39, New York: John Wiley and Sons.

———. (September 1970), "Learning by Doing and Tariff Protection: A Reconsideration of the Case of the Antebellum Cotton Textile Industry," *Journal of Economic History*, 30, pp. 521–601.

———. (1971), "The Landscape and the Machine: Technical Interrelatedness, Land Tenure and the Mechanization of the Corn Harvest in Victorian Britain," *Essays on a Mature Economy* (edited by McCloskey, Donald), pp. 145–204, London: Methuen.

———. (September 1972), "The Use and Abuse of Prior Information in Econometric History; a Rejoinder to Professor Williamson on the Antebellum Cotton Textile Industry," *Journal of Economic History*, 32, pp. 706–727.

———. (Winter 1973), "The 'Horndal Effect' in Lowell, 1834–1856: A Short-Run Learning Curve for Integrated Cotton Textile Mills," *Explorations in Economic History*, 10, pp. 174–194.

———. (1975), "Labor Scarcity and the Problem of Technological Practice and Progress in Nineteenth-Century America," *Technical Choice Innovation and Economic Growth*, chapter 1, London: Cambridge University Press. (Most of the essays by David listed above are reprinted in this volume.)

Denslow, David and Schulze, David (May/June 1974), "Optimal Replacement of Capital Goods in Early New England and British Textile Firms: A Comment," *Journal of Political Economy*, 82, pp. 631–637.

DuBoff, Richard (December 1967), "Introduction of Electric Power in American Manufacturing," *Economic History Review*, second series, 20, pp. 509–518.

Eckstein, Alexander, *et al.* (March 1974), "The Economic Development of Manchuria: The Rise of a Frontier Economy," *Journal of Economic History*, 34, pp. 239–264.

Evenson, Robert (1969), "International Transmission of Technology in the Production of Sugarcane," University of Minnesota Agricultural Experiment Station Scientific Journal Paper No. 6805, Saint Paul.

———. (March 1974), "International Diffusion of Agrarian Technology," *Journal of Economic History*, 34, pp. 51–73.

Feller, Irwin (September 1966), "The Draper Loom in New England Textiles, 1894–1914: A Study of Diffusion of an Innovation," *Journal of Economic History*, 26, pp. 320–347.

———. (December 1968), "The Draper Loom In New England Textiles: A Reply," *Journal of Economic History*, 28, pp. 628–630.

———. (October 1974), "The Diffusion and Location of Technological Change in the American Cotton-Textile Industry, 1890–1970," *Technology and Culture*, 15, pp. 569–593.

Floud, R. C. (1971), "Changes in the Productivity of Labour in the British Machine Tool Industry, 1856–1900" *Essays on a Mature Economy* (edited by McCloskey, Donald), pp. 313–337, London: Methuen.

———. (February 1974), "The Adolescence of American Engineering Competiton, 1860–1900," *Economic History Review*, second series, 27, pp. 57–71.

Flueckiger, Gerald (Winter 1971–72), "Observation and Measurement of Technical Change," *Explorations in Economic History*, 9, pp. 145–178.

Fogel, Robert (September 1967), "The Specification Problem in Economic History," *Journal of Economic History*, 27, pp. 283–308.

Fogel, Robert W. and Engerman, Stanley L., eds. (1971), *The Reinterpretation of American Economic History*, New York: Harper & Row.

Fries, Russell I. (July 1975), "British Response to the American System: The Case of the Small-Arms Industry after 1850," *Technology and Culture*, 16, pp. 377–403.

Griliches, Zvi (October 1957), "Hybrid Corn: An Exploration in the Economics of Technological Change," *Econometrica*, 25, pp. 501–522.

———. (July 1960), "Hybrid Corn and the Economics of Innovation," *Science*, 132, pp. 501–522.

———. (September 1960), "Congruence versus Profitability: A False Dichotomy," *Rural Sociology*, 25, pp. 354–356.

———. (September 1962), "Profitability versus Interaction: Another False Dichotomy," *Rural Sociology*, 27, pp. 327–330.

Gunderson, Gerald (September 1969), "Issues in the Measurement of Efficiency of American Dairy Farming, 1850–1910: A Comment," *Journal of Economic History*, 29, pp. 501–505.

Habakkuk, H. J. (1962), *American and British Technology in the Nineteenth Century*, Cambridge, England: University Press.

Harley, Charles K. (1971), "The Shift from Sailing Ships to Steamships, 1850–1890: A Study in Technological Change and Its Diffusion," *Essays on a Mature Economy: Britain after 1840* (edited by McCloskey, Donald N.), pp. 215–234, London: Methuen and Co., Ltd.

———. (June 1973), "On the Persistence of Old Techniques: The Case of North American Wooden Shipbuilding," *Journal of Economic History*, 33, pp. 372–398.

———. (Summer 1974), "Skilled Labour and the Choice of Technique in Edwardian Industry," *Explorations in Economic History*, 11, pp. 391–414.

Hayami, Yujiro (Summer 1971), "Elements of Induced Innovation: A Historical Perspective for the Green Revolution," *Explorations in Economic History*, 8, pp. 445–472.

———. (March 1974), "Conditions for the Diffusion of Agricultural Technology: An Asian Perspective," *Journal of Economic History*, 34, pp. 131–148.

Hunter, Louis (February 1929), "The Influence of the Market upon Technique in the Iron Industry in Western Pennsylvanian up to 1860," *Journal of Economic and Business History*, 1, pp. 241–281.

Hyde, Charles K. (Spring 1973), "The Adoption of the Hot Blast by the British Iron Industry: A Reinterpretation," *Explorations in Economic History*, 10, pp. 281–294.

———. (Summer 1973), "The Adoption of Coke-Smelting by the British Iron Industry, 1709–1790," *Explorations in Economic History*, 10, pp. 397–419.

———. (May 1974), "Technological Change in the British Wrought Iron Industry, 1750–1815: A Reinterpretation," *Economic History Review*, second series, 27, pp. 190–206.

Ishikawa, Tsuneo (December 1973), "Conceptualization of Learning by Doing: A Note on Paul David's 'Learning by Doing and . . . the Antebellum United States Cotton Textile Industry,'" *Journal of Economic History*, 33, pp. 851–861.

Jeremy, David (January 1973), "Innovation in American Textile Technology during the Early 19th Century," *Technology and Culture*, 14, pp. 40–76.

———. (Spring 1973), "British Textile Technology and Transmission to the United States: The Philadelphia Region Experience, 1770–1820," *Business History Review*, 47, pp. 24–52.

Klingaman, David, Vedder, Richard and Gallaway, Lowell (Spring 1974), "The Ames-Rosenberg Hypothesis Revisited," *Explorations in Economic History*, 11, pp. 315–316.

Klonglan, Gerald E. and Coward, Jr., E. Walter (March 1970), "The Concept of Symbolic Adoption: A Suggested Interpretation," *Rural Sociology*, 35, pp. 77–83.

Knauerhase, Ramon (September 1968), "The Compound Steam Engine and Productivity Changes in the German Merchant Marine Fleet, 1871–1887," *Journal of Economic History*, 28, pp. 390–403.

Kranzberg, M. and Davenport, W. H. (1972), *Technology and Culture: an Anthology*, New York: Schocken.

McCloskey, Donald (1971), "International Differences in Productivity? Coal and Steel in America and Britain Before World War I," (edited by McCloskey, Donald), pp. 285–304, *Essays on a Mature Economy*, London: Methuen.

Mak, James and Walton, Gary (September 1972), "Steamboats and the Great Productivity Surge in River Transportation," *Journal of Economic History*, 22, pp. 619–640.

———. (June 1973), "The Persistence of Old Technologies: The Case of Flatboats," *Journal of Economic History*, 33, pp. 444–451.

Mantoux, Paul (1948), *The Industrial Revolution in the Eighteenth Century*, London.

Murphy, John J. (June 1966), "Entrepreneurship in the Establishment of the American Clock Industry," *Journal of Economic History*, 26, pp. 169–186.

North, Douglass (September/October 1968), "Sources of Productivity Change in Ocean Shipping, 1600–1850," *Journal of Political Economy*, 76, pp. 953–970.

Olmstead, Alan (June 1975), "The Mechanization of Reaping and Mowing in American Agriculture, 1833–1870," *Journal of Economic History*, 35, pp. 327–353.

Parker, William N. and Klein, Judith L. V. (1966), "Productivity Growth in Grain Production in the United States, 1840–1860 and 1900–1910," *Output, Employment and Productivity in the United States After 1800, Studies in Income and Wealth*, Vol. 30, pp. 523–579, New York: Columbia University Press.

Paterson, Donald (August 1971), "'Spin-Off' and the Armaments Industry," *Economic History Review*, second series, 24, pp. 463–464.

Purdue Faculty Papers in Economic History (1967), Homewood. Ill.: Richard D. Irwin.

Rasmussen, Wayne (October 1968), "Advances in American Agriculture: The Mechanical Tomato Harvester as a Case Study," *Technology and Culture*, 9, pp. 531–543.

Robinson, Eric H. (March 1974), "The Early Diffusion of Steam Power," *Journal of Economic History*, 34, pp. 91–104.

Rogers, Everett M. and Havens, A. Eugene (September 1962), "Adoption of Hybrid Corn: A Comment," *Rural Sociology*, 27, pp. 330–332.

Rosenberg, Nathan (December 1963), "Technological Change in the Machine Tool Industry, 1840–1910," *Journal of Economic History*, 23, pp. 414–443.

———. (June 1967), "Anglo-American Wage Differences in the 1820's," *Journal of Economic History*, 27, pp. 221–229.

———. (1969), *The American System of Manufacturers*, Chicago: Aldine Publishing Company.

———. (October 1969), "The Direction of Technological Change: Inducement Mechanisms and Focusing Devices," *Economic Development and Cultural Change*, 18, pp. 1–24.

———. (October 1970), "Economic Development and the Transfer of Technology: Some Historical Perspectives," *Technology and Culture*, 11, pp. 550–575.

———. (October 1971), "Technology and the Environment: An Economic Exploration," *Technology and Culture*, 12, pp. 543–561.

———. (Fall 1972), "Factors Affecting the Diffusion of Technology," *Explorations in Economic History*, 10, pp. 3–34.

Rothbarth, E. (September 1946), "Causes of the Superior Efficiency of U.S.A. Industry as Compared with British Industry," *Economic Journal*, 56, pp. 383–390.

Ruttan, Vernon W. and Hayami, Yujiro (April 1973), "Technology Transfer and Agricul-

tural Development," *Technology and Culture,* 14, pp. 119–151.

Sandberg, Lars (December 1968), "The Draper Loom in New England Textiles: A Comment," *Journal of Economic History,* 28, pp. 624–627.

———. (February 1969), "American Rings and English Mules: The Role of Economic Rationality,"*Quarterly Journal of Economics,* 83, pp. 25–43.

Saul, S. B. (April 1967), "The Market and the Development of the Mechanical Engineering Industries in Britain, 1860–1914," *Economic History Review,* second series, 20, pp. 111–130.

Sawyer, John E. (1954), "The Social Basis of the American System of Manufacturing," *Journal of Economic History,* 24, pp. 361–379.

Saxonhouse, Gary (March 1974), "The Tale of Japanese Technological Diffusion in the Meiji Period," *Journal of Economic History,* 34, pp. 149–165.

Smith, Merritt Roe (October 1973), "John Hall, Simeon North and the Milling Machine: The Nature of Innovation Among Antebellum Arms Makers," *Technology and Culture,* 14, pp. 573–591.

Solo, Robert (July 1968), "The Meaning and Measure of Economic Progress," *Technology and Culture,* 9, pp. 389–414.

Stigler, George (June 1951), "The Division of Labor is Limited by the Extent of the Market," *Journal of Political Economy* pp. 185–193.

Temin, Peter (May 1964), "A New Look at Hunter's Hypothesis About the Antebellum Iron Industry," *American Economic Review,* 54, pp. 344–351.

———. (June 1966), "Steam and Waterpower in the Early Nineteenth Century," *Journal of Economic History,* 26, pp. 187–205.

———. (September 1966), "Labor Scarcity and the Problem of American Industrial Efficiency in the 1850's," *Journal of Economic History,* 26.

———. (Winter 1971), "Labor Scarcity in America," *The Journal of Interdisciplinary History,* 1.

Trebilcock, Clive (December 1969), "'Spin-Off' in British Economic History: Armaments and Industry, 1760–1914," *Economic History Review,* second series, 22, pp. 474–490.

———. "'Spin-Off' and the Armaments Industry: Rejoinder," *Economic History Review,* second series, 24, pp. 463–464.

Uselding, Paul (June 1970), *Studies in the Technological Development of the American Economy During the First Half of the Nineteenth Century,* PhD Thesis, Northwestern University.

———. (June 1970), "Henry Burden and the Question of Anglo-American Technological Transfer in the Nineteenth Century," *Journal of Economic History,* 30, pp. 312–337.

———. (Spring 1972), "Technical Progress at the Springfield Armory, 1820–1850," *Explorations in Economic History,* 9, pp. 291–316.

———. (September 1972), "Factor Substitution and Labor Productivity Growth in American Manufacturing, 1839–1899," *Journal of Economic History,* 32, pp. 670–681.

Uselding, Paul (1973), "An Early Chapter in the Evolution of American Industrial Management," *Business Enterprise and Economic Change,* (edited by Cain, Louis and Uselding, Paul), pp. 51–84, Kent, Ohio: Kent State University Press.

———. (Spring 1974), "The Ames-Rosenberg Hypothesis Revisited: A Rejoinder," *Explorations in Economic History,* 11, pp. 315–316.

———. (October 1974), "Elisha K. Root, Forging, and the 'American System,'" *Technology and Culture,* 15, pp. 543–568.

Uselding, Paul and Juba, Bruce (Fall 1973), "Biased Technical Progress in American Manufacturing," *Explorations in Economic History,* 11, pp. 55–72.

Vernon, Raymond (May 1966), "International Investment and International Trade in the Product Cycle," *Quarterly Journal of Economics,* 80, pp. 190–207.

Walton, Gary (April 1964), "Sources of Productivity Change in American Colonial Shipping, 1675–1775," *Economic History Review,* second series, 20, pp. 67–78.

———. (August 1968), "A Measure of Productivity Change in American Colonial Shipping," *Economic History Review,* second series, 21, pp. 268–282.

———. (June 1970), "Productivity Change in Ocean Shipping After 1870: A Comment," *Journal of Economic History,* 30, pp. 435–442.

———. (Winter 1970/71), "Obstacles to Technical Diffusion in Ocean Shipping, 1675–1775," *Explorations in Economic History,* 8, pp. 123–140.

Watson, Andrew M. (March 1974), "The Arab Agricultural Revolution and its Diffusion, 700–1100," *Journal of Economic History,* 34, pp. 8–35.

Wilkins, Mira (March 1974), "The Role of Private Business in the International Diffusion of Technology," *Journal of Economic History,* 34, pp. 166–188.

Williamson, Jeffrey (November/December 1971), "Optimal Replacement of Capital Goods: The Early New England and British Textile Firm," *Journal of Political Economy,* 79, pp. 1320–1334.

———. (September 1972), "Embodiment, Disembodiment, Learning by Doing, and Returns to Scale in Nineteenth-Century Cotton Textiles," *Journal of Economic History,* 32, pp. 691–705.

———. (May/June 1974), "Optimal Replacement of Capital Goods in Early New England and British Textile Firms: A Reply," *Journal of Political Economy,* 82, pp. 638–640.

Wilkinson, Norman B. (Winter 1963), "Brandywine Borrowings from European Technology," *Technology and Culture,* 4, pp. 1–13.

Woodbury, Robert (1960), "The Legend of Eli Whitney and Interchangeable Parts," *Technology and Culture,* 1.

Zabler, Jeffrey (Fall 1972), "Further Evidence on American Wage Differentials, 1800–1830, *Explorations in Economic History,* 10, pp. 109–117.

———. (Fall 1973), "Wages in the Iron Industry: Reply," *Explorations in Economic History,* 11, pp. 89–99.

RECENT RESEARCH IN JAPANESE ECONOMIC HISTORY, 1600–1945

Kozo Yamamura, UNIVERSITY OF WASHINGTON

This essay is written with two groups of readers in mind. The first consists of nonspecialists who are interested in a summary assessment of our current stock of knowledge on the economic history of Japan, in the most recent research results and in a bibliography useful in familiarizing themselves with Japan's economic history. The second is composed of potential researchers, including graduate students, economic historians interested in comparative work and specialists in Japanese history who may be interested in redirecting or expanding their research efforts into the economic aspects of Japanese history. With the hope of enticing some in the second group to join the ranks of the as yet small number of active researchers, this essay includes brief comments on current trends in research, and suggestions for future research. The periods covered in this essay are limited to the Tokugawa (1600–1867) and the 1868–1945 periods.[1] The appended references, one for each of these period, are not exhaustive. While an effort was made to include all publications that are readily available in U.S. libraries for the Tokugawa period, the works listed for the 1868–1945 period exclude many articles and some books which, in my judgement, are superseded in content by later works (often by the same author) and those that are primarily of interest to economic theorists, and only tangentially to economic historians.[2]

I. TOKUGAWA PERIOD: 1600–1867

Three general observations can be made about the English literature on Tokugawa economic history and the current state of research in this field. First, as

attested by references 1, the English literature on the subject has increased during the past two decades, so that it is possible today for nonspecialists to familiarize themselves with the basic contours of Tokugawa economic history and to gain some insights into several aspects of the economy. However, the total amount of English literature available on this period remains meagre by most standards.

The second observation that may be made is that the field has undergone rapid changes during the past decade, both in research methodology and in the questions asked. Put simply, an increasing number of Japanese and western researchers have recently come to question some of the basic views advanced by many earlier Japanese economic historians. A growing number of Japanese economic historians, though still in the minority, now openly question many of the long-accepted, basically Marxist interpretations concerning various aspects of the Tokugawa economy; and a small number of western scholars who have not accepted the Japanese orthodoxy are being joined by other westerners willing to reevaluate and criticize the orthodoxy systematically and explicitly.

The last observation that can be made is that, because of the recent developments just described, many new questions have been added to a long list of topics awaiting researchers. The signpost reading "Researchers needed" has now been changed to read "Researchers urgently needed. High returns promised for the qualified."[3]

Before elaborating on each of these three observations, we must first present the following summary of the basic outlines of the traditional Tokugawa economic interpretation that emerge as one reads through the Japanese literature. A basic understanding of the dominant Japanese view constitutes an essential background for surveying the current English literature and in understanding the nature of the recent developments.

Most Japanese economic historians continue to use a Marxist framework of analysis. Thus the dominant or orthodox interpretation of the Tokugawa economy which has evolved in Japan is Marxist. Summarized drastically, the major points of consensus existing in the literature in Japanese on the Tokugawa economy are:[4]

(i) Though the economy grew during the seventeenth century, it stagnated during the last century and a half of the Tokugawa period. The growth of the economy was due to the increased amount of paddies created both by the ruling samurai class and the peasants, to increased agricultural productivity, and to the increases in commerce that followed the end of the century-long civil wars, which preceded the establishment of the Tokugawa *bakufu* (samurai government).

The economy failed to grow in most parts of Japan during the eighteenth and nineteenth centuries because of major famines, the increased difficulties in creating new paddies, and because peasants (who made up no less than 80 percent of the population) were "exploited" by the ruling class and by the "rich peasants" (*gono*) who began to emerge during the eighteenth century. The appearance of the *gono* can be traced to the "disintegration of the small peasant class," whose land

was lost to the rich peasants under the increasing burden of taxes and exploitation suffered at the hands of the steadily rising merchant class.

(ii) The samurai class suffered increasing financial hardships because of the development of commerce, which had the effect of forcing the cash-hungry samurai to resort to the high-interest loans from the merchant class.

(iii) By the mid-eighteenth century, the rich peasants who were in the position to exploit peasants most effectively in their capacity as landowners, moneylenders and rural entrepreneurs, grew even richer at the expense of urban merchants and peasants.

(iv) The bleakness of the Tokugawa economic conditions for most of the population, coupled with the occurrence of three major famines, was reflected in a lack of population increase during the last hundred and fifty years of the period. Infanticide among poor peasants was common.

Most Japanese scholars would add that the oppressed majority struggled unsuccessfully and that the struggle was to continue even after the Meiji Restoration, which ushered in a period of "absolutist capitalism" with its new capitalist-oppressors.

This is the orthodox, Marxist interpretation. Non-Marxist western students of the Tokugawa economy (and other aspects of the period as well) have been attempting to reinterpret and reexamine the analyses and data found in Japanese publications. It is important for readers of the English sources on this period to keep this fact in mind.

Nonspecialists and would-be researchers can most profitably begin their study of Tokugawa economic history with a few college textbooks in Japanese history. The best among them are Hall (1970); Fairbank, Reischauer and Craig (1973); and Sansom (1961). In all of these books, those sections that deal with economic aspects of the period are explicitly identified or are easily located. Hall and Fairbank *et al.*, although not economists, are generally successful in reinterpreting the views of Japanese scholars, and analytical slips are few. Sansom's work, which is more informative on many aspects of economic institutions and their change over time, contains a number of analyses and observations that are directly adapted from the Japanese literature. Read with the above *caveats* in mind, these textbooks are useful in providing an outline of Tokugawa economic change and necessary basic terminology. One should be aware that there are several other college textbooks that incorporate Marxist interpretations without the compensating virtues of Sansom's book.

The next step of the student or researcher is to read the literature that deals more directly, perhaps exclusively, with the economic aspects of the Tokugawa period. Among the broadly defined topics, various aspects of agriculture have received most of the attention of western researchers. The most important contributor on the subject is T.C. Smith. His book (Smith, 1959), written in the mid-1950's, remains a good introduction to Tokugawa agriculture. This is a pioneering effort which

demonstrated not only that authors using Japanese literature need not be restricted by it but that westerners using primary sources can make significant contributions toward the understanding of the Tokugawa economy. For "new" economic historians, Smith's work tends to offer more socio-historical explanations of various changes than strictly economic analyses, but the book accomplishes its goal of highlighting the basic characteristics of Tokugawa agriculture and village life. His later articles on by-employments, changes in the effective rates of the peasants' tax burden, and changes in agricultural technology (Smith, November 1958, 1969, 1970) are carefully researched studies providing important findings that are useful in questioning the majority view of the Japanese scholars and expanding our understanding of the Tokugawa economy.

A reading list on agriculture should also include Crawcour's assessment of the Tokugawa economy (Crawcour, 1965); Hanley and Yamamura's essay dealing with the growth of agriculture, which contains rice output data by domain and for the nation as a whole (Hanley and Yamamura, 1972); and Choi's work, which highlights technological changes in Tokugawa agriculture (Choi, August 1971). Chambliss's book, a case study, can provide useful information on the changes experienced in one Tokugawa village during the nineteenth century (Chambliss, 1965). In addition to these discussions about the Tokugawa Period, listed in references 1, the reader should see also, in references 2, two able discussions on Tokugawa agriculture—contained in chapter 4 of Rosovsky's book (Rosovsky, 1961, references 2) and Nakamura's work (Nakamura, 1966, references 2). Rosovsky's book contains useful discussions on many aspects of the Tokugawa economy and Nakamura's work is important in its effort to show the level of agricultural productivity that had been attained by the late Tokugawa period.

In contrasting the traditional Japanese explanation with the economic analytical approach to the reasons for the changes in landholding patterns and in contractual arrangement, Yamamura's article (Yamamura, forthcoming) will be of interest to some readers. That the English literature on agriculture—the most important aspect of the Tokugawa economy—is virtually exhausted by the above list is sad testimony to the yet-limited state of research which has been reported in English.

Another topic which has received much attention during the past several years is demographic change. Two factors account for this: one is the pioneering effort made by Hayami (1966–1967, 1968, 1973), who used the family reconstruction method to analyze religious investigation records (*shumon-aratame-cho*) complied by villages. The other is the usefulness of the demographic data for reexamining not only the long-accepted view of Tokugawa demographic change, but also Tokugawa economic change as well. Hanley's contributions (1971, 1973, March 1974), based on her analysis of the religious investigation records, explicitly question the established Japanese view of Tokugawa demographic change. A comparison of the works of Hayami and Hanley with those of Honjo (1927) and Sansom, cited earlier, clearly demonstrates the significance of these recent studies.

The works of Hayami and Hanley, as well as Fruin (1973) also provide valuable quantitative evidence on mobility, occupational distribution and numerous other demographic characteristics of the Tokugawa population.

Many aspects of the growth of commerce—the merchant class, moneychangers, guilds, land and sea transportation—have also received the sustained attention of specialists. Crawcour's articles (1961, May 1961a and b, August 1963, May 1964, and 1966), carefully written and well-grounded in original sources, should not be missed by those interested in these aspects of the Tokugawa economy. As an introductory survey on Tokugawa commerce, Sheldon's book (Sheldon, 1958) is still informative and Hauser's recent work (Hauser, 1974) constitutes a good institutional history of cotton trade in the Kinai region. The aritcles by Sakai (May 1964) and Flersham (May 1964) are useful for those interested in case studies of trade over water. Crawcour and Yamamura (July 1970) and Duffy and Yamamura (June 1971) are quantitative studies of developments of Tokugawa monetary markets, using daily price data of various media of exchange and rice. Yamamura's book on the samurai (Yamamura, 1974) examines the changes in the living standard of the samurai class and contains estimated deflators (consumer price index) and time series data on the price of rice for the second half of the Tokugawa period.

On other topics, Rozman's comparative study of Tokugawa and Chinese cities (Rozman, Autumn 1974) contains helpful insights and information for economic historians, as does Hall's classic essay on castle towns (Hall, 1968). Beasley's article (Beasley, May 1960) provides quantitative evidence on the rice tax revenues and is useful for obtaining a glimpse of the Tokugawa government's financial resources at the end of the period. "Rule by Status" by Hall (Autumn 1974) and the contributions by Henderson on Tokugawa laws (Henderson, 1964, 1968) provide crucial insights into the working of Tokugawa governance. Henderson's article on contracts in Tokugawa villages (Henderson, Autumn 1974) is a valuable recent addition for economic historians. Hall's substantive work on the domain of Okayama (Hall, 1966) can yield much valuable insight and information for economic historians.

The most recent change in the study of Tokugawa economy (suggested earlier) consists of the explicit questioning of the orthodox interpretations of the Tokugawa economy, both in Japan and in the United States. As pointed out in Hanley and Yamamura (February 1971), the reexamination by a minority of Japanese scholars of the dominant view has been increasing steadily during the past decade. However, those scholars who began to question the long-accepted view often did so only implicitly or only touched upon specific aspects of the orthodoxy, thus avoiding frontal conflicts with the views held by the majority of scholars. This situation has changed during the past few years.

In 1973, several scholars orgainzed a group to study Quantitative Economic History, and in 1975 the first work of this group was published: *Sūryo keizaishi*

nyumon (An Introduction to Quantitative Economic History). This book on the Tokugawa period not only constitutes a call for quantitative economic history but also is the first systematic and explicit "challenge" (in the words of the authors themselves) to the Marxist orthodoxy. The introductory chapter, authored by Shunsaku Nishikawa, an econometrician, acknowledges that their work follows the path of the American new economic historians. The remainder of the book consists of Hayami's quantitative analysis of Tokugawa population; Nishikawa's work on income, consumption and expenditure patterns of peasant households in the domain of Chōshu; and Hiroshi Shimbo's analysis of price data. Nishikawa calculated the production function of Chōshu peasants, and Shimbo's study constitutes the first major Japanese effort to analyze price data explicitly within the framework of modern (non-Marxist) economic analysis. The fact that this book appeared and that more publications are planned by this group of scholars clearl marks a new era in Japan in the study of Tokugawa economic history.

Such a development in Japan is most welcome to American specialists. Now we can expect Japanese scholars to add to the contributions made by Smith, Crawcour, Hanley and others, and to provide important pieces of the mosaic needed to reinterpret Tokugawa economic history. The preliminary efforts made by Hanley and Yamamura (forthcoming) in suggesting a more basic and integrative reevaluation of Tokugawa economic history can now be more easily built upon. In short, it is not an exaggeration to say that the study of Tokugawa economic history is about to embark on a new, much more explicitly analytically oriented course of thorough reexamination.

Due to the very limited number of works in English and also due to the recent development just described, any list of suggested research topics can only be a highly subjective selection among many awaiting the attention of future researchers. Given the state of the English literature, a possible list of priorities would include:

1. Examinations of the reasons for the changes in the landholding system and patterns between the late Sengoku period and the early Tokugawa period. Research in this area and related topics (relative value of factors, policy rationale, etc.) would be valuable in establishing the initial conditions of the Tokugawa economy. Japanese works, emphasizing political aspects of landholding and contractual systems, are of little use to most western economic historians.

2. A major effort to reexamine in as quantitative a manner as possible and within the framework of modern economic theory the changes, and the causes of the changes (technology, management of land use, relative prices of factor inputs, etc.), of agricultural productivity and output. First, following the paths of Smith, Nishikawa and others, more case studies are needed to accumulate empirical evidence. Our goal should be to obtain a much better understanding, in the near future, of these changes at the national level.

3. Studies on the growth of commerce, based more explicitly on an economic analytical framework, rather than oriented toward making additions to the already

existing, good descriptive and institutional studies. Under this general heading, studies on the changing terms of trade between sectors and between regions and on the effects of the *sankin kotai* system on the growth of commerce and the economy as a whole world be valuable.

4. Further examination of demographic changes is highly desirable. While recent research has provided a significant increase in our knowledge of the subject, it also focused attention on the need to increase our knowledge of the demographic characteristics of the urban population, rural-urban mobility, and the relationship between economic and demographic change.

5. Research is needed on the transition to the Meiji period, especially the flow of merchant and *gono* captial and entrepreneurial talents into the early Meiji industries. The nature of the rapid economic changes and of the changes in institutions during the 1830–1867 period are often discussed, but remain poorly understood.

This is a very short list of the high priority areas of research. If one were to list specific topics, suitable for dissertations or articles, for instance, the list would be a long one indeed.

For those who wish to identify the Japanese works useful in researching Tokugawa economic history, Hauser's book (Hauser, 1974) includes a carefully prepared up-to-date bibliography, and Hanley and Yamamura's (Hanley and Yamamura, forthcoming) also includes many recent works in research areas suggested above. The discussion of the data sources contained in Hanley and Yamamura (1971) may be useful to some researchers.[5]

II. THE 1868–1945 PERIOD

The quality and quantity of English literature now existing on this period are such that most nonspecialists and would-be researchers should encounter little difficulty in satisfying their interests in Japanese economic history or in finding inputs necessary for comparative examinations or for lecturing. Unlike the decade immediately following the end of World War II, when economists interested in Japan were forced to rely on the meager stock of literature then available in English, today one can justifiably claim that the English literature on this period of the Japanese economy is, in quantity and perhaps even in quality, superior to that on the comparable period of economic history of European nations, excepting England. As an examination of references 2 makes evident, the fact that many Japanese economists, sharing the same interests and analytical framework of western scholars, contributed to the current stock of English literature accounts in large measure for the quality and quantity of the literature.[6]

Given the quantity of the literature, it is impossible in this brief essay to comment on the content of, and contribution made by, each of the items listed in references 2. Thus, more for the purpose of surveying and identifying the major

research accomplishments to date rather than of attempting a discussion of contributions made by each author, let us first describe briefly the basic analytical
motivation (the reasons for the questions examined and method of analysis
adopted) of most of the English literature. This is important in understanding the
nature of a large number of the works included in the bibliography as well as in
understanding the reasons for several easily identifiable gaps existing in the
literature, despite the quantity of the studies available on this period. We shall then
survey the major contributions, adding brief comments on a few controversies
which were generated by some postwar works, and then present a list of topics for
future research. The suggested topics can be stated much more specifically for this
period than for the Tokugawa period because the gaps in our knowledge are better
identified, due to the quantity of research already existing.

A large proportion of the works listed in references 2 is devoted to explaining the
factors accounting for the rapid industrialization of Japan. This, of course, is
because many economists and some economic historians chose to study Japan as
an example of a successful latecomer to industrialization. With its Asian
background and seemingly unique institutional characteristics, industrializing
Japan was an interesting and useful subject of research for the many dozens of
scholars who became specialists and for several welcome "interlopers." Also,
contributing significantly to economists' interest in this period of Japanese
economic growth, was the fact that there was a large amount of usable quantitative
evidence and that its quality was improved steadily over time, thanks to the tireless
efforts of Japanese economists. Also because of the data and the significance of the
Japanese experience, Japan in this period was often chosen as a testing ground for
new and old theories, especially by economists interested in a broad spectrum of
questions relating to economic development.

This meant, however, that most questions which are not a part of the "explanation" for the rapid growth and which are not directly amenable to quantitative
analysis tended to be neglected. As references 2 discloses, topics such as labor
conditions and the labor movement, the development of economic institutions,
farmer unrest, and the impact of the variety of economic policies tended to be
neglected.

In surveying the current stock of literature, it will be convenient to divide it into
two broad categories. One consists of those works that are of interest primarily, but
not necessarily, to trained economists and that make explicit use of economic
theory. Most of these works rely principally on quantitative evidence in testing
their hypotheses or in advancing their interpretations. The other is composed of the
works of economists and historians who do not make explicit use of economic
theory (though often economic theory figures implicitly as the underpinning of
their analysis) and for whose works quantitative evidence is often enlisted only to
strengthen their analyses, rather than to provide a core for their research. Of
course, this division is for convenience of description, as will be clear in the
following discussion, is arbitrary in some instances.

The most important in the first category of works is the recent book by Ohkawa and Rosovsky (1973).[7] If only one book on Japanese economic growth is to be read or assigned to students, this book must be selected. Using the sources of growth approach (i.e., calculating production functions from aggregate data) and based on a persuasive model of trend acceleration, this book contains rich quantitative evidence and carefully expressed insights on questions that cannot be dealt with directly by quantitative evidence (thus, selected parts are of importance to noneconomists as well). We should note that this book, typifying the quality of the best of the works on Japan, could not have been written were it not for the efforts of many earlier contributors (who are listed in references 2) and especially for the quantitiative data gathered and refined by the Hitotsubashi economists who compiled the *Long Term Economic Statistics*.[8] The coverage of this book extends into the postwar years.

In this same category of works, two conference volumes (which also include a few excellent articles published earlier), one edited by Ohkawa, Johnston and Kaneda (1974) and the other by Klein and Ohkawa (1968), closely follow the Ohkawa-Rosovsky book in importance. In the former, the majority of the essays (Hemmi, 1970; Kaneda, 1970; Kato, 1970; Kawano, 1970; Noda, 1970; Ranis, 1970; Tussing, 1970; and Umemura, 1970) are extremely useful in helping the readers to understand the crucial role played by the agricultural sector in Japan's economic growth. In the latter, the six essays on the prewar period constitute basic contributions on the topics dealt with by the respective authors—Fujino on the construction cycle (Fujino, 1968), Shionoya on patterns of industrial development (Shionoya, 1968), Watanabe on technological change and dual structure (Watanabe, 1968), Hayami and Yamada on technological progress in agriculture (Hayami and Yamada, 1968), Baba and Tatemoto on foreign trade (Baba and Tatemoto, 1968), and Kuznets on the level and structure of consumption (Kuznets, 1968).

On agriculture, Nakamura's contribution (Nakamura, 1966), which generated one of the most active debates among the specialists, should not be missed. Nakamura's finding—that the rate of growth of agricultural output during the first three decades following the beginning of modern economic growth was only about one percent (rather than 2.4 percent as had been believed earlier)—was a crucial contribution that forced others to reexamine the data and to reassess the source of resources that facilitated the first phase of Japan's industrialization. Rosovsky's article (Rosovsky, February 1968) is most useful in understanding the nature of the significance of Nakamura's contribution. Other works important for understanding the growth of agriculture are Hayami's book (Hayami, 1975) and his articles (Hayami, Fall 1972; September/October, 1970).

Important and/or useful articles and books in this category, on a variety of topics, include Shinohara on cyclical changes and related questions (Shinohara, 1962), Odaka (February 1968, June 1970) and Taira (May 1972, Winter 1963, 1970, Spring 1970) on wages, Ranis (September 1957, October 1958) on factor

proportions and on the capital-output ratio, Rapp (Fall 1967, 1976) on changing trade patterns, Watanabe (April 1965) on dual structure, Sato (April 1971), on technological change and Rosovsky-Ohkawa (April 1961) and Gleason (1965) on the changing patterns of consumption and its relationship to economic growth. Minami's book (Minami, 1973) on the so-called "turning point"—principally his efforts at evaluating the validity of the findings made by Ranis and Fei in applying the well-known Ranis-Fei model to Japan—is also of interest to specialists on the controversy relating to the neoclassical versus classical formulation of the analyses of dualism (agricultural and industrial sectors) in economic growth. Confronting Minami's work and contributing much more are the books by Kelley, Williamson, and Cheetham (1972, 1974). Their ambitious efforts—constructing a general equilibrium model and applying it to Meiji Japan—yield many insights which are of prime importance to specialists and nonspecialists alike.[9]

Strictly econometric studies by Klein (July 1961), Klein and Shinkai (January 1963), and Chenery, Shishido, and Watanabe (January 1962) are significant in providing the readers with the type of findings which only such works can yield. The last especially, which makes ingenious use of an input-output table and examines industrial growth as a deviation from a hypothetical balanced growth, is rich in insights useful in understanding the characteristics of Japanese economic growth. Also, their findings merit the attention of those who might undertake a policy-oriented study of Japan's international trade during the 1914–1935 period.

Far from superseded in content by the Rosovsky and Ohkara book is Rosovsky's earlier study (Rosovsky, 1961) on capital accumulation. Analyzing Japanese economic growth within a broad Gerschenkronian framework, the book contains much which is useful and insightful both to economists and historians.

Short of entering into extended technical discussions, it is difficult to summarize the specific contributions made by each author and the mutual reactions shared among them, which serve to advance our understanding of Japan's economic growth during this period. However, it is perhaps accurate to say that, because of the numerous works in this category, we are now in possession of the quantitative evidence and analytical examinations which most economic historians wish to have on this period of Japanese growth. Progress to be made from now on in this category of the literature will be concentrated principally on technical aspects and on refining the earlier findings, rather than on broad interpretive aspects of Japanese growth. Virtual completion of the *Long Term Economic Statistics* and the appearance of the Rosovsky-Ohkawa book, it appears, mark an end to the postwar phase of an intensive effort to understand the essential characteristics of Japanese economic growth that quantitative and economic theoretical analysis could provide.

In the second category of the literature, several dozen works deserve the attention of interested readers. For convenience of description and also for readers who may be interested in specific aspects of the economic history of Japan of this

period, let us group the literature in this category into the following seven subcategories: descriptive-analytical literature on (i) the economy generally and on specific industries or institutions; (ii) the workings of the labor market and labor management; (iii) institutional development and policies relating to the banking and financial sectors of the economy; and policies relating to the banking and financial sectors of the economy; and (iv) business history and entrepreneurship. Then, we shall discuss the articles which cannot be conveniently classified into any of the above four categories but which are of significance and deserving readers' attention. We shall group these articles by the subperiod: (v) the Meiji period (1868–1911) and (vi) the Taisho-Showa periods (1912–1945). The last subcategory (vii) includes the articles which do not belong to any of the above subgroups but are clearly worthy of note.

(i) The literature on the economy as a whole and on specific industries or institutions is not as extensive as one might expect. Most notable in this category is Lockwood's book (Lockwood, 1954). Though some of the the the observations and analyses contained in this book require revision and updating in view of the research results which have appeared during the past two decades, this pioneering work is still rich in useful descriptions and insightful observations and no one seriously interested in Japan can afford to neglect it. Another useful work which must be read for its good descriptive analysis of the interwar years is Allen's short book (Allen, 1946).

Aoki's book (Aoki, 1956) on the cotton industry is informative for those interested in this industry. Emi's short book (Emi, 1963) on the government's fiscal activity is rich in useful data and observations, and is especially useful because the author's discussions are well-grounded in economic theory. Blumenthal (1976) and Yamamura (1976) examine the growth of the shipbuilding industry and the general trading company respectively. Blumenthal's work ably highlights technological change and the role of the government in the growth of the shipbuilding industry.

Maddison's work (Maddison, 1971) is a comparative one by a nonspecialist, and is a good book from which nonspecialists and students can obtain information concerning the quantitative magnitude and basic outlines of Japanese industry vis-a-vis those of the USSR. Both Moulton's and Orchard's books (Moulton, 1931; Orchard, 1930) remain extremely useful for obtaining descriptive accounts of selected industries, financial institutions and international trade for the interwar years.

(ii) On the labor market and management, the work by Abegglen (1958) should be read, although it has been seriously challenged by Taira and others. Taira's works (Taira, Winter 1963, Spring 1970, and 1970) are perhaps central in this category of literature. Evans discusses the so-called convergence hypothesis as it applies to the Japanese labor market (Evans, Spring 1970). An historian, Marshall, has contributed a thoughtful analysis of Japanese labor-management relationships

(Marshall, 1967). Several contributions by sociologists are also of importance: Hazama's essay (Hazama, 1976) is a very useful discussion of the changing life style of industrial workers; and Cole and Tominaga's work (Cole and Tominaga, 1976) and Odaka's recent book (Odaka, 1975) fill an important gap in economists' knowledge. Many other useful works by sociologists are not included in references 2, but interested readers can obtain citations for such sources in the works cited in this subsection.

(iii) On banking and finance, Patrick's works (Patrick, 1967, 1971) are excellent and contain able analyses. For some economists, Hoekendorf's dissertation (Hoekendorf, 1961) and Ott's article (Ott, April 1961) will be invaluable. Sakurai's book (Sakurai, 1964), though difficult to obtain in the U.S., is also worthy of close scrutiny; and Yamamura's essay (Yamamura, 1972) is informative and should be read with Patrick's essay (Patrick 1967). Oshima's work (Oshima, 1965) is an important contribution, most valuable in understanding Meiji finance. Adams's work (Adams, 1964) is descriptive but contains useful facts and observations not readily found in English.

(iv) English works on business history and especially on entrepreneurship are not large in number. Recent books by Yoshino (1968) and Hirschmeier and Yui (1975) are highly informative and are good books with which to begin one's reading on the subject. Hirschmeier's book (1964) and articles (1965, Spring 1970) and Horie's essay (1965) present the majority view of Japanese entrepreneurship while Yamamura's articles (June 1967, April 1968) provide a revisionist view. Yui's (Spring 1970) and Morikawa's (Spring 1970) essays add to our understanding of the zaibatsu structure and leadership. Smith's articles (June 1956, October 1960) too should not be missed as they discuss an important source of Japanese entrepreneurial talents—landlords and their sons. Rosovsky and Yamamura's essay (Spring 1970) suggests the importance of the further study of Japanese entrepreneurship and contains an extended bibliography on the subject.

(v) On the Meiji period, economic historians should not miss essays by Crawcour (1965), Dore (May 1959, October 1960), Horie (1939), Inukai and Tussing (September 1967), and Landes (1965). As the titles of each contribution make clear, each deals with important questions of the Meiji period. Smith's book (1955) is of special importance as it still is a competent examination by an historian of Meiji industrialization. Several articles discussing the rise of capitalism in Japan are worthy of special note and they include Horie (1936), Miyamoto, Sakudo and Yasuba (December 1965) and Norman (1949), the last of which follows the Marxist line. Important contributions added recently are Yasuba's essay (Autumn 1975), which reinterprets, within the neoclassical economic theoretical framework, the Japanese Marxist debate on labor mobility and wage differentials between the agricultural and industrial sectors; and Saxonhouse's two very able articles (March 1974, 1976) on the reasons for industry-wide efforts to adopt new technology and otherwise to achieve rapid growth in the all-important cotton-spinning industry.

(vi) Articles on the interwar years are few in number, as is testified to by the fact that Allen's brief book must still be read by specialists. Perhaps the most useful for economic historians is Patrick's essay (1971), which constitutesn more than an essay on fiscal aspects of the period. Waswo (1974) on agrarian unrest and Totten (1974) on labor problems are useful recent contributions by historians. Yamamura's essays (1974a, 1974b) on various major developments in the interwar period and on the Great Depression provide useful descriptive accounts of the rapidly changing economy during the interwar years.

(vii) In this subgroup of the contributions not easily classifiable, we should make a special note of Taeuber's book (1958) on Japanese population. The articles by Obuchi (1976) and Yasukawa (1963) are also important for anyone interested in the economic history of Japan during this time. (Readers interested in research on demography should see these works for further citations.) Bronfenbrenner's and Patrick's "lessons" of Japanese economic growth are still readable (Bronfenbrenner, Spring 1961; Patrick, October 1961). The neglected "dark" side of the Japanese growth story is finally dealt with in the able essay by Chubachi and Taira (1976) on poverty, and also useful is the carefully researched paper by Ono and Watanabe (1976) on prewar income inequality.

Because of the quantity of research which has already been conducted on the 1868–1945 period, we can identify the areas of future research more specifically than we were able to for the Tokugawa pèriod. The priority areas of research on this period—the gaps ĩn our knowledge represented in references 2—are:

1. Studies of the process of technological adoption and diffusion.

Despite the findings made in such studies as Ohkawa and Rosovsky (1973), Sato (April 1971), and in many other works that indicate that technological change played a crucial role in the economic growth of Japan, very little research has been done to date on the process of technolocial change itself. Clearly needed in increasing our knowledge of this important factor in Japanese economic growth are micro-examinations (at the firm and industry level or by specific innovation) of how and why a specific technology was adopted so rapidly. Our understanding of Japanese economic growth will be significantly enhanced if much more of the type of research contributed by Saxonhouse (March 1974, 1976) on the Meiji cotton textile industry, Blumenthal (1976) on the shipbuilding industry and Minami (1976) on the introduction of electric power is undertaken. Such research, if carried out using the many pertinent existing Japanese studies and data, will allow us to better understand the reasons for the magnitude of the large "residuals" found in the studies made using the sources of growth approach.

2. Selected aspects of the interwar years.

A large quantity of postwar research notwithstanding, our knowledge of this subperiod is still quite limited in comparison to the Meiji period. Because the quantitative studies usually include this period, we are often lulled into thinking

that this subperiod has received as much attention as has the Meiji period. However, as is evident in references 2, only a very small number of articles deal with aspects of this subperiod, such as fiscal-monetary policies (including crucial questions relating to the return to the gold standard and its effects), reasons for the fluctuations in international trade and policies adopted to reduce international trade deficits, policies affecting agriculture and labor, agrarian and labor unrest and many other questions. Such works as those cited under subcategory (vi) above indicate that the needed research on these aspects of the subperiod has just begun. We should also add here that our knowledge of Japanese imperialism is limited to such works as Nakamura (1974) and Hayami and Ruttan (November 1970), both primarily on the changes in agricultural productivity resulting from the introduction of Japanese technology and capital to the colonies. Obviously, there is much more we must know about the multifaceted effects, both in Japan and in the colonies, of Japanese colonialism.

3. Effects of institutional change on economic growth.

Because many economists have examined Japanese economic growth adopting the quantitative sources of growth approach and because others, too, have focused on the success story in analyzing the economic history of the post-Revolution period, studies on institutional changes and their effects on economic growth remain neglected. Strangely enough, as yet not a single book is available that provides competent coverage of the development of some of the important economic institutions since the Meiji Restoration. To date, anyone who wants more than a passing mention of the development of stock exchanges, call money markets, trade associations, commercial laws, patent laws, and the like must rely on Japanese sources.

Since the development of such institutions undoubtedly affected the pattern and the rate of economic growth by reducing the costs of resource use and of transactions, the paucity of information on the development of these institutions must be remedied. When our knowledge of these institutions is increased, we shall be in a position to analyze better not only the effects of the development of these and other institutions on economic growth but also the wide-ranging effects resulting from the development of these institutions. To illustrate the point made here, there exists as yet no English work describing, and analyzing the effects of, the land tax reform (*chiso kaisei*) of the early Meiji period despite the fundamental impact it had on the landholding pattern, on the rights and rent burden of tenant cultivators, and on income distribution both at the time and for the following two generations.

4. The economics of the zaibatsu.

Closely related to 3, above, our knowledge of the effects of organizational change on economic growth, especially the economic significance of the zaibatsu, needs to be increased. What is required is not further descriptive examinations of various organizational aspects of the Japanese economy, but examinations that are

specifically formulated within the economic analytical framework. For example, we need to ask the following questions of the zaibatsu: To what extent did the structural flexibility observed within the prewar, conglomerate zaibatsu reduce the costs associated with the inter- and intra-sectoral and interfirm transfer of financial, technological, managerial and informational resources? Relating to the desirability of studies of technological change and diffusion discussed above, what role did the large amount of prewar zaibatsu financial resources play in enabling them to import and adopt technologies; that is, did the amount of financial resources help overcome the riskiness and long periods of assimilation involved in technological adoption? Last, how significant were the zaibatsu scale and their ability to diversify their activities in enabling them to launch complementary industries simultaneously? These and related questions, if pursued, will undoubtedly aid us substantially in enhancing our understanding of the nature of the large "residuals" found in Japanese industrialization.

5. Demographic changes and their interrelationships with economic growth.

Except for Taeuber (1958, January 1964), Obuchi (forthcoming), Yasukawa (1963), and several others, demographic changes of the 1868–1945 period have received to date only very limited attention from scholars writing in English. As valuable as Taeuber's work is, it deals mostly with aggregate demographic data and little with the interrelationship between economic and demographic change. Obuchi's work, which also uses aggregate data, is limited to offering some useful hints on the interrelationships. What is clearly called for, especially as our knowledge of the interrelationships between economic and demographic changes in both the Tokugawa and postwar periods increases, are studies on the interactions between various demographic and economic changes, especially at less than aggregate levels. Also, no comprehensive effort has yet been made to evaluate various estimates made by Japanese scholars of demographic changes (including birth and death rates) during the period between the Meiji Restoration and the first modern census of 1920.

6. The transitional period between the late Tokugawa period and the early decades of the Meiji period.

Because specialists of the post-Restoration period and the Tokugawa period concentrate their research efforts generally in the areas of their speciality, works bridging these two periods are still few and thus our understanding of this important transitional period is inadequate. While the works of Smith (1955), Huber (May/June 1971), Rosovsky (1966), Crawcour (1965) and others offer some insights, many questions yet remain to be investigated. For example, we know little concerning the magnitude and the mechanism of the capital outflow from the agricultural sectors to industry; the causes and magnitudes of the relative price changes of factors and products during the decades surrounding the Meiji

Restoration (despite the obviously unrealistic magnitudes of changes in prices and the resulting income gains which Huber suggested occurred as the result of the opening of trade in the 1850's, no one has yet challenged his findings); and, changes in the wage level between the late Tokugawa period and the early Meiji years.

7. The World War II Years.

Our collective knowledge of the war years is virtually nonexistent. The only readily accessible English study on the period is Cohen's work (1949), which has little to say on the workings and internal policy problems which Japan faced during these years. It is regrettable indeed that no study esixts as yet which describes and analyzes the economic experience of this period. Today, when much data and pertinent information on the war years has already been declassified and also much of the data and descriptive evidence available in Japan has already been compiled by several Japanese scholars, our collective ignorance of these five years can no longer be justified.

FOOTNOTES

1. Only a few articles have been written in English on economic aspects of pre-Tokugawa Japan.

2. Though only a few articles published in the *Hitotsubashi Journal of Economics* are included in section 2 of the references, this journal publishes numerous, usually high-quality articles on the post-Restoration period. Thus anyone who wishes to specialize in Japanese economic history must examine this journal before embarking on any research project.

3. See also Yamamura (March 1971), "Agenda for Asian Economic History," *Journal of Economic History*, 31, pp. 199–207.

4. Japanese economic historians' views on the Tokugawa economy are much more fully described in an article by Yamamura (September 1975), listed in references 1.

5. Hanley and Yamaura (1971), listed in references 1, includes references to bibliographies and catalogs of Japanese works.

6. Interested readers are referred to Henry Rosovsky's *Quantitative Japanese Economic History – Annotated Bibliography* (Rosovsky, 1961, Berkeley: The Center of Japanese Studies), which is a survey of U.S. holdings of Japanese works and data sources.

7. See Koji Taira's review article on this book entitled "Growth, Trends, and Savings in Japanese Agriculture and Industry" (Taira, January 1976, *Economic Development and Cultural Change*, 24, pp. 423–436).

8. Ohkawa, K., Shinohara, M. and Umemura, M., eds. (1965–1976, Tokyo: Toyo Keizai Shimposha), *Long-Term Economic Statistics of Japan since 1868*, 13 volumes.

9. See Kozo Yamamura's review of these authors' *Dualistic Economic Development* (Kelley, Williamson and Cheetham, 1972, listed in references 2), in *Economic Development and Cultural Change* 23, (April 1975), pp. 539–545.

REFERENCES

1. The Tokugawa Period (1600–1867)

Beasley, W.G. (May 1960), "Feudal Revenue in Japan at the Time of the Meiji Restoration," *The Journal of Asian Studies*, 19.

Chambliss, William J. (1965), *Chiaraijima Village: Land Tenure, Taxation, and Local Trade, 1818–1884*, Tucson: University of Arizona Press.

Choi, Kee II (August 1971), "Technological Diffusion in Agriculture under the Bakuhan System," *Journal of Asian Studies*, 30.

Crawcour, E. Sydney (May 1961), "The Development of a Credit System in Seventeenth Century Japan," *Journal of Asian Studies*, 20.

——.(August 1963), "Changes in Japanese Commerce in the Tokugawa Period," *Journal of Asian Studies*, 22.

——.(1965), "The Tokugawa Heritage," *The State and Economic Enterprise in Japan* (edited by Lockwood, William W.), Princeton: Princeton University Press.

——.(May 1961), "Documentary Sources of Tokugawa Economic and Social History," *Journal of Asian Studies*, 20.

——.(1966), "Kawamura Zuiken: A Seventeenth-Century Entreprenuer," *Transactions of the Asiatic Society of Japan*, third series, 9.

——. (May 1964), "Notes on Shipping and Trade in Japan and the Ryukus," *Journal of Asian Studies*, 33.

——. (1961), "Some Observations on Merchants, A Translation of Mitsui Takafusa's *Chonin Koken Roku*, with an introduction and notes," *Transactions of the Asiatic Society of Japan, third series*, 7.

——. (Autumn 1974), "The Tokugawa Period and Japan's Preparation for Modern Economic Growth," *Journal of Japanese Studies*, 1.

Crawcour, E. Sydney and Yamamura, K. (July 1970), "The Tokugawa Monetary System: 1787–1868," *Economic Development and Cultural Change*,18.

Duffy W. and Yamamura K. (June 1971), "Integration of Tokugawa Monetary Markets, 1787–1867: A Spectral Analysis," *Explorations in Economic History, 8.*

Fairbank J., Reischauer, E.O. and Craig, A. (1973), *A History of East Asian Civilization*, Boston: Houghton Mifflin Co.

Flershem, Robert G. (May 1964), "Some Aspects of Japan Sea Trade in the Tokugawa Period," *Journal of Asian Studies*, 23.

Fruin, W.M. (1973), "Farm Family Migration: The Case of Echizen in the Nineteenth Century," *Keio Economic Studies*, 10.

Hall, John W. (Autumn 1974), "Rule by Status in Tokugawa Japan," *Journal of Japanese Studies*, 1.

——. (1970), *Japan From Prehistory to Modern Times*, New York: Dell Publishing Co.

——. (1968), "The Castle Town and Japan's Modern Urbanization," *Studies in the Institutional History of Early Modern Japan* (edited by Hall, John W. and Jansen, Marius B.), Princeton: Princeton University Press.

——. (1966), *Government and Local Power in Japan, 500–1700: A Study Based on Bizen Province*, Princeton: Princeton University Press.

Hanley, Susan B. (1973), "Migration and Economic Change in Okayama during the Tokugawa Period," *Keio Economic Studies*, 10.

——. (1971), "Population Trends and Economic Development in Tokugawa Japan," unpublished Ph. D. dissertion, Yale University.

————. (March 1974), "Fertility, Mortality and Life Expectancy in Pre-modern Japan," *Population Studies*, 28.

Hanley, Susan B. and Yamamura, K. (1971), "Quantitative Data for Use in Historical Research on Japan," *The Dimensions of the Past: Materials, Problems and Opportunities for Quantitative Work in History* (edited by Lorwin, W.R. and Price, J.M.), New Haven: Yale University Press.

————. (1972), "Population Trends and Economic Growth in Preindustrial Japan," *Historical Population Studies* (edited by Glass, D.V. and Revelle, R.), London: Edward Arnold Publishers.

————. (February 1971), "A Quiet Transformation in Tokugawa Economic History," *Journal of Asian Studies*, 30.

————. (Forthcoming), *Economic and Demographic Change in Preindustrial Japan*, Princeton: Princeton University Press.

Hauser, William B. (1974), *Economic Institutional Change in Tokugawa Japan: Osaka and Kinai Cotton Trade*, New York and London: Cambridge University Press.

Hayami, Akira (1973), "Labor Migration in a Preindustrial Society: A Study Tracing the Life Histories of the Inhabitants of a Village," *Keio Economic Studies*, 10.

————. (1968), "The Demographic Analysis of a Village in Tokugawa Japan: Kando-shinden of Owari Province, 1778–1871," *Keio Economic Studies*, 5.

————. (1966–1967), "The Population at the Beginning of the Tokugawa Period," *Keio Economic Studies*, 4.

Henderson, Dan Fenno (1964), *Conciliation and Japanese Law: Tokugawa and Modern*, 2 vols, Tokyo: Tokyo University Press.

————. (1968), "The Evolution of the Tokugawa Law," *Studies in the Institutional History of Early Modern Japan* (edited by Hall, J.W. and Jansen, M.), Princeton: Princeton University Press.

————. (Autumn 1974), "Contracts in Tokugawa Villages," *Journal of Japanese Studies*, 1.

Honjo, Eijiro (1927), "Population Problems in the Tokugawa Era,"*Kyoto University Economic Review*, 2.

————. (1935), *The Social and Economic History of Japan*, Kyoto: Institute for Research in Economic History of Japan.

Neville, Edward L. (1958), "The Development of Transportation in Japan: A Case Study of Okayama Han, 1600–1868," unpublished Ph.D. thesis, University of Michigan.

Rozman, Gilbert (Autumn 1974), "Edo's Importance in the Changing Tokugawa Society," *Journal of Japanese Studies*, 1.

————. (1975), *Urban Networks in Ch'ing China and Tokugawa Japan*, Princeton: Princeton University Press.

Sakai, Robert (May 1964), "The Satsuma-Ryukyu Trade and the Tokugawa Seclusion Policy," *Journal of Asian Studies*, 23.

Sano, Yoko (January 1963), "The Changes in Real Wages of Construction Workers in Tokyo, 1830–1894," *Management and Labor Studies*, English series, No. 4, the Institute of Management and Labor Studies, Keio University.

Sansom, George B. (1961), *A History of Japan: 1615–1867*, Stanford: Stanford University Press.

Sheldon, Charles D. (1958), *The Rise of the Merchant Class in Tokugawa Japan, 1600– 1868: An Introductory Survey*, New York: J.J. Augustin.

————. (July 1971), "Premodern Merchants and Modernization in Japan," *Modern Asian Studies*, 5.

Smith, Thomas C. (1970), "Okura Nagatsune and the Technologists," *Personality in Japanese History* (edited by Craig, A. and Shively, D.H.), Berkeley: University of California Press.

———. (1959), *The Agrarian Origins of Modern Japan*, Stanford: Stanford University Press.

———. (1969), "Farm Family By-employments in Preindustrial Japan," *The Journal of Economic History*, 29.

———. (1952), "The Japanese Village in the Seventeenth Century," *The Journal of Economic History*, 12. Reprinted in *Studies in the Institutional History of Early Modern Japan* (edited by Hall, John W. and Jansen, Marius B., 1968), Princeton: Princeton University Press.

———. (November 1958), "The Land Tax in the Tokugawa Period," *Journal of Asian Studies*, Vol. XVIII, No. 1. Reprinted in *Studies in the Institutional History of Early Modern Japan* (edited by Hall, John W. and Jansen, Marius B., 1968), Princeton: Princeton University Press.

———. (August 1973), "Pre-modern Economic Growth: Japan and the West," *Past & Present*, 60.

Tsukahira, Toshio G. (1966), *Feudal Control in Tokugawa Japan. The Sankin Kotai System*, Cambridge: East Asian Research Center, Harvard University.

Yamamura, Kozo (1974), *A Study of Samurai Income and Entrepreneurship*, Cambridge: Harvard University Press.

———. (forthcoming), "A Comparative Analysis of Landholding Systems: Preindustrial England and Tokugawa Japan," *Comparative Uses of Japanese Experience* (edited by Craig. A.).

——— (September 1975), "Towards a Reexamination of the Economic History of Tokugawa Japan," *Journal of Economic History*, 33.

2. The 1868–1945 Period

Abegglen, J. C. (1958), *The Japanese Factory: Aspects of its Social Organization*, Glencoe Free Press.

Abegglen, J. C. and Mannari, H. (July 1966), "Leaders of Modern Japan: Social Origins and Mobility," *Economic Development and Cultural Change*, 14.

Adams, T.F.M. (1964), *A Financial History of Modern Japan*, Tokyo: Kōdansha.

Allen, G.C. (1946), *A Short Economic History of Modern Japan*, London: George Allen and Unwin, Ltd.

———. (1940), "Japanese Industry: Its Organization and Development to 1937," *The Industrialization of Japan and Manchukuo 1930–1940* (edited by Schumpeter, E.B.), New York: Macmillian Co.

Aoki, Keizo (1956), *The Cotton Industry of Japan*, Tokyo: Japan Society for the Promotion of Science.

Baba, M. and Tatemoto, M. (1968), "Foreign Trade and Economic Growth in Japan: 1858–1937," *Economic Growth: The Japanese Experience since the Meiji Era* (1976), (edited by Klein & Ohkawa), New Haven: Yale University Press.

Blumenthal, Tuvia (1976), "The Japanese Shipbuilding Industry," *Japanese Industrialization and its Social Consequences* (edited by Patrick, H.T.), Berkeley: University of California Press.

Bronfenbrenner, Martin (Spring 1961), "Some Lessons of Japan's Economic Development, 1853–1938," *Pacific Affairs*, 34.

Chenery, H.B., Shishido, S. and Watanabe, T. (January 1962), "The Pattern of Japanese Growth, 1914–1953," *Econometrica*, 30.

Chubachi, M. and Taira, K. (1976), "Poverty in Modern Japan: Perceptions and Realities," *Japanese Industrialization and its Social Consequences* (edited by Patrick, H.T.), Berkeley: University of California Press.

Cohen, Jerome B. (1949), *Japan's Economy in War and Reconstruction*, Minneapolis: University of Minnesota Press.

Cole, R.E. and Tominaga, K. (1976), "Japan's Changing Occupational Structure and Its Significance," *Japanese Industrialization and its Social Consequences* (edited by Patrick, H.T.), Berkeley: University of California Press.

Crawcour, E.S. (1965), "The Tokugawa Heritage, *The State and Economic Enterprise in Japan* (edited by Lockwood, W.W.), Princeton: Princeton University Press.

Dore, Ronald P. (May 1959), "The Meiji Landlord: Good or Bad?" *Journal of Asian Studies*, 17.

————. (October 1960), "Agricultural Improvement in Japan: 1870–1900," *Economic Development and Cultural Change*, 9.

Emi, Koichi (1963), *Government Fiscal Activity and Economic Growth in Japan 1868–1960*, Tokyo: Kinokuniya Bookstore Co., Ltd.

————. (June 1965), "An Approach to the Measurement of National Saving in Japan, 1878–1940," Hitotsubash: *Journal of Economics*, 6.

Evans, Robert Jr. (Spring 1970), "Evolution of the Japanese System of Employer-Employee Relations, 1868–1945," *Business History Review*, 44.

Fujino, Shozaburo (1968), "Construction Cycles and Their Monetary-Financial Characteristics," *Economic Growth The Japanese Experience Since the Meiji Era* (edited by Klein, L. and Ohkawa, K.), New Haven: Yale University Press.

Gleason, Alan H. (1965), "Economic Growth and Consumption in Japan", *The State and Economic Enterprise in Japan* (edited by Lockwood, W. W.), Princeton: Princeton University Press.

Harootunian, H.D. (August 1960), "The Economic Rehabilitation of the Samurai in the Early Meiji Period", *Journal of Asian Studies*, 19.

Hayami, Yujiro (1975), *A Century of Agricultural Growth in Japan* (edited by Lockwood, W.W.), Minneapolis and University of Tokyo Presses.

————. (Fall 1972), "Rice Policy in Japan's Economic Development," *American Journal of Agricultural Economics*, 54.

Hayami, Yujiro and Ruttan, V. (September/October 1970), "Factor Prices and Technological Change in Agricultural Development: The U.S. and Japan, 1880–1960," *Journal of Political Economy*, 78.

————. (November 1970), "Korean Rice, Taiwan Rice, and Japanese Agricultural Stagnation: An Economic Consequence of Colonialism," *Quarterly Journal of Economics*, 84.

Hayami, Yujiro and Yamada, S. (1968). "Technological Progress in Agriculture," *Economic Growth The Japanese Experience since the Meiji Era* (edited by Klein, L. and Ohkawa, K.), New Haven: Yale University Press.

Hazama, Hiroshi (1976), "Historical Changes in the Life Style of Industrial Workers," *Japanese Industrialization and its Social Consequences*, (edited by Patrick, H.T.), Berkeley: University of California Press.

Hemmi, Kenzo (1970), "Primary Product Exports and Economic Development", *Agriculture and Economic Growth: Japan's Experience* (edited by Ohkawa, K., Johnston, B.F. and Kaneda, H.), Princeton University Press, University of Tokyo Press.

Hirschmeier, Johannes (1965), "Shibusawa Eiichi: Industrial Pioneer," *The State and Economic Enterprise in Japan* (edited by Lockwood, W.W.), Princeton: Princeton University Press.

———. (1964), *The Origins of Entrepreneurship in Meiji Japan*, Cambridge: Harvard University Press.

———. (1975), "The Japanese Spirit of Enterprise, 1868–1970," *Business History Review*, 44.

Hirshmeier, Johannes and Yui, T. (1975), *The Development of Japanese Business*, Cambridge, Mass.: Harvard University Press.

Hoekendorf, W.C. (1961), "The Secular Trend of Income Velocity in Japan, 1879–1940," unpublished Ph.D. thesis, University of Washington.

Horie, Yasuzo (1965), "Modern Entrepreneurship in Meiji Japan," *The State and Economic Enterprise in Japan* (edited by Lockwood, W.W.), Princeton: Princeton University Press.

———. (1939), "The Government and Industry in the Early Years of Meiji Era," *Kyoto University Economic Review*, 14.

———. (1936), "An Outline of the Rise of Capitalism in Japan," *Kyoto University Economic Review*, 11.

Huber, Richard (May/June 1971), "Effect on Prices of Japan's Entry Into World Commerce after 1858," *Journal of Political Economy*, 79.

Inukai, I. and Tussing, A.R. (September 1967), "Kogyo Iken: Japan's Ten Year Plan, 1884," *Economic Development and Cultural Change*, 16.

Johnston, Bruce F. (1966), "Agriculture and Economic Development: The Relevance of the Japanese Experience," *Food Research Institute Studies*, 6.

———. (December 1961), "Agricultural Productivity and Economic Development in Japan," *Journal of Political Economy*, 59.

Kaneda, Hiromitsu (May 1965), "Substitution of Labor and Non-Labor Inputs and Technological Change in Japanese Agriculture," *Review of Economics and Statistics*, 47.

———. (1970), "Long-Term Changes in Food Consumption Patterns in Japan," *Agriculture and Economic Growth: Japan's Experience*, (edited by Okhawa, K., Johnston, B.F. and Kaneda, H.), Princeton University Press and University of Tokyo Press.

Kato, Yuzuru (1970), "Development of Long-Term Agricultural Credit," *Agriculture and Economic Growth: Japan's Experience* (edited by Ohkawa, K., Johnston, B.F. and Kaneda, H.), Princeton University Press and University of Tokyo Press.

Kawano, Shigeto (1970), "Effects of the Land Reform on Consumption and Investment of Farmers," *Agriculture and Economic Growth: Japan's Experience* (edited by Ohkawa, K., Johnston, B.F. and Kaneda, H.), Princeton University Press and University of Tokyo Press.

Kelley, A.C., Williamson, J.G. and Cheetham, R.J. (1972), *Dualistic Economic Development: Theory and History*, University of Chicago Press.

———. (1974), *Lessons from Japanese Development: An Analytical Economic History*, Chicago: University of Chicago Press.

———. (December 1971), "Writing History Backwards: Meiji Japan Revisited," *The Journal of Economic History*, 31.

Klein, Lawrence (July 1961), "A Model of Japanese Economic Growth, 1878–1937," *Econometrica*, 29.

Klein, Lawrence and Ohkawa K., eds. (1968), *Economic Growth: The Japanese Experience since the Meiji Era*, Homewood, Illinois: Richard D. Irwin Inc.

Klein, Lawrence and Shinkai, Y. (January 1963), "An Econometric Model of Japan, 1930–1959," *International Economic Review* 1.

Kuznets, Simon (1968), "Trends in Level and Structure of Consumption," *Economic Growth The Japanese Experience since the Meiji Era* (edited by Klein, L. and Ohkawa, K.), New Haven: Yale University Press.

Landes, David S. (1965), "Japan and Europe: Contrasts in Industrialization," *The State and Economic Enterprise in Japan: Essays in the Political Economy of Growth* (edited by Lockwood, W.W.) Princeton: Princeton University Press.

Lockwood, W.W. (1954), *Economic Development of Japan*, Princeton: Princeton University Press.

————. (ed.) (1965), *The State and Economic Enterprise in Japan*, Princeton: Princeton University Press.

Maddison, Angus (1971), *Economic Growth in Japan and in the USSR*, New York: Allen and Unwin.

Marshall, B.K. (1967), *Capitalism and Nationalism in Prewar Japan*, Stanford: Stanford University Press.

Minami, Ryoshin (1976), "The Introduction of Electric Power and Its Impact on the Manufacturing Industries: With Special Reference to Smaller Scale Plants," *Japanese Industrialization and its Social Consequences* (edited by Patrick, H.T.), Berkeley: University of California Press.

————. (1973), *The Turning Point in Economic Development*, Tokyo: Kinokuniya Bookstore Co., Ltd.

Miyamoto, M., Sakudo, Y. and Yasuba, Y. (December 1965), "Economic Development in Pre-Industrial Japan, 1859–1894," *Journal of Economic History*, 25.

Morikawa, Hidemasa (Spring 1970), "The Organizational Structure of the Mitsubishi and Mitsui Zaibatsu, 1868–1922: A Comparative Study," *Business History Review*, 44.

Morley, James W. (1971), *Dilemma of Growth in Prewar Japan*, Princeton: Princeton University Press.

Moulton, Harold G. (1931), *Japan, An Economic and Financial Appraisal*, Washington, D.C.: The Brookings Institution.

Nakagawa, K. and Rosovsky, H. (Spring/Summer 1963), "The Case of the Dying Kimono: The Influence of Changing Fashions on the Development of the Japanese Woolen Industry," *Business History Review*, 37.

Nakamura, J.I. (1966), *Agricultural Production and Economic Development of Japan*, Princeton: Princeton University Press.

————. (1974), "Incentives, Productivity Gaps, and Agricultural Growth Rates in Prewar Japan, Taiwan and Korea," *Japan in Crisis* (edited by Silberman, B. and Harootunian, H.), Princeton: Princeton University Press.

Noda, Tsutomu (1970), "Savings of Farm Households," *Agriculture and Economic Growth: Japan's Experience* (edited by Ohkawa, K., Johnston, B.F. and Kaneda, H.), Princeton University Press and University of Tokyo Press.

Norman, E.H. (1949), *Japan's Emergence as a Modern State*, New York: The Institute of Pacific Relations.

Odaka, Konosuke (February 1968), "A History of Money Wages in the Northern Kyushu Industrial Area, 1892–1939," *Hitotsubashi Journal of Economics*, 8.

————. (June 1969), "Indices of the Excess Demand for Labor in Prewar Japan, 1929–39: A Preliminary Study," *Hitotsubashi Journal of Economics*, 10.

Odaka, Kunio (1975), *Toward Industrial Democracy–Management and Workers in Modern Japan*, Cambridge, Mass.: Harvard University Press.

Ogura, T. (ed.) (1966), *Agricultural Development in Modern Japan*, Tokyo: Fuji Publishing Co.

Ohbuchi, Hiroshi (1976), "Demographic Transition in the Process of Japanese Industrialization," *Japanese Industrialization and its Social Consequences* (edited by Patrick, H.T.), Berkeley: University of California Press.

Ohkawa, K., Johnston, B.F. and Kaneda, H. (eds.) (1970), *Agriculture and Economic Growth: Japan's Experience*, Princeton and Tokyo: Princeton and Tokyo University Presses.

Ohkawa, K. and Rosovsky, H. (1973), *Japanese Economic Growth–Trend Acceleration in the Twentieth Century*, Stanford: Stanford University Press.

Ono, A. and Watanabe, T. (1976), "Changes in Income Inequality in the Japanese Economy," *Japanese Industrialization and its Social Consequences* (edited by Patrick, H.T.). Berkeley: University of California Press.

Orchard, John E. (1930), *Japan's Economic Position*, New York: McGraw-Hill.

Oshima, Harry T. (1965), "Meiji Fiscal Policy and Economic Progress," *The State and Economic Enterprise in Japan* (edited by Lockwood, W.W.), Princeton: Princeton University Press.

Ott, David J. (April 1961), "The Financial Development of Japan, 1878–1958," *Journal of Political Economy*, 69.

Patrick, Hugh T. (1967), "Japan, 1868–1914," *Banking in The Early Stages of Industrialization* (edited by Cameron, Rondo), New York: Oxford University Press.

———. (October 1961), "Lessons for Underdeveloped Countries from the Japanese Experience of Economic Growth," *Indian Economic Journal*, 14.

———. (June 1965), "External Equilibrium and Internal Convertability: Financial Policy in Meiji Japan," *Journal of Economic History* , 25.

———. (1971), "The Economic Muddle of the 1920's," *Dilemma of Growth in Prewar Japan* (edited by Morley, J.W.), Princeton: Princeton University Press.

———. (1971), "The Development Policy of the Japanese Colonial Government in Taiwan, 1895–1945: Comment" *Government and Economic Development* (edited by Ranis, Gustav), New Haven: Yale University Press.

———. (1972), "Finance, Capital Markets and Economic Growth in Japan," *Financial Development and Economic Growth*, (edited by Sametz, Arnold W.), New York: New York University Press.

———. (ed.) (1976), *Japanese Industrialization and its Social Consequences*, Berkeley: University of California Press.

Pelzel, J.C. (December 1954), "The Small Industrialists in Japan," *Explorations in Entrepreneurial History*, 7.

Ranis, Gustav (1970), "The Financing of Japanese Economic Development," *Agriculture and Economic Growth: Japan's Experience* (edited by Ohkawa, K., Johnston, B.F. and Kaneda, H.), Princeton and Tokyo: Princeton University Press and University of Tokyo Press.

———. (1955), "The Community-Centered Entrepreneur in Japanese Development," *Explorations in Entrepreneurial History*, 13.

———. (September 1957), "Factor Proportions in Japanese Economic Development," *American Economic Review*, 47.

———. (October 1958), "The Capital-Output Ratio in Japanese Economic Development, *Review of Economic Studies*, 26.

Rapp, William V. (Fall 1967), "A Theory of Changing Trade Patterns under Economic Growth: Tested for Japan," *Yale Economic Essays*, 7.

———. (1976), "Firm Size and Japan's Export Structure: A Microview of Japan's Changing Export Competitiveness since Meiji," *Japanese Industrialization and its*

Social Consequences (edited by Patrick, H.T.), Berkeley: University of California Press.

Rosovsky, H. (1966), "Japan's Transition to Economic Growth, 1868–1885," *Industrialization in Two Systems* (edited by Rosovsky, H.), New York: Wiley.

———. (1961), *Captial Formation in Japan*, Glencoe: Free Press.

———. (February 1968), "Rumbles in the Rice Fields: Prof. Nakamura vs. Official Statistics," *Journal of Asian Studies*, 27.

Rosovsky, H. and Ohakawa, K. (October 1961), "The Role of Agriculture in Modern Japanese Economic Development," *Economic Development and Cultural Change*, 9.

———. (April 1961), "The Indigenous Components in the Modern Japanese Economy," *Economic Development and Cultural Change*, 9.

Sakurai, Kinichiro (1964), *Financial Aspects of Economic Development of Japan*, Tokyo: Science Council of Japan.

Sato, Kazuo (April 1971), "Growth and Technological Change in Japan's Non-Primary Economy: 1930–1967," *Economic Studies Quarterly*, 17.

Saxonhouse, Gary R. (1976), "Country Girls and Comunication among Competitors in the Japanese Cotton-Spinning Industry," *Japanese Industrialization and its Social Consequences* (edited by Patrick, H.T.), Berkeley: University of California Press.

———. (March 1974), "A Tale of Japanese Technological Diffusion in the Meiji Period," *Journal of Economic History*, 34,

Shinohara, Miyohei (1962), *Growth and Cycles in the Japanese Economy*, Tokyo: Kinokuniya Book Store Co., Ltd.

———. (1964) Economic Development and Foreign Trade in Pre-War Japan," *The Economic Development of China and Japan* (edited by Cowan, D.C.), London: Allen & Unwin.

Shionoya, Yuichi (1968), "Patterns of Industrial Development," *Economic Growth The Japanese Experience since the Meiji Era* (edited by Klein, L. and Ohkawa, K.), New Haven: Yale University Press.

Smith, Thomas C. (1955), *Political Change and Industrial Development in Japan*, Stanford: Stanford University Press.

———. (June 1956), "Landlords and Rural Captialists in the Modernization of Japan," *Journal of Economic History*, 16.

———. (October 1960), "Landlords' Sons in Business Elite," *Economic Development and Cultural Change*, 9.

Taeuber, Irene B. (January 1964), "Urbanization and Population Change in the Development of Modern Japan," *Economic Development and Cultural Change*, 12.

———. (1958), *The Population of Japan*, Princeton: Princeton University Press.

Taira, Koji (1970), *Economic Development and the Labor Market in Japan*, New York: Columbia University Press.

——— (Spring 1970), "Factory Legislation and Management Modernization During Japan's Industrialization, 1868–1916," *Business History Review*, 44.

——— (Winter 1963), "Market Forces and Public Power in Wage Determination: Early Japanese Experiences," *Social Research*, 30.

———. (May 1962), "The Inter-Sectoral Wage Differential in Japan, 1881–1959," *Journal of Farm Economics*, 44.

Totten, George O. (1974), "Japanese Industrial Relations at the Crossroads: The Great Noda Strike of 1927–1928," *Japan in Crisis* (edited by Silberman, B. and Harootunian, H.), Princeton: Princeton University Press.

Tussing, Arlon R. (1970), "The Labor Force in Meiji Economic Growth: A Quantitative Study of Yamanashi Prefecture," *Agriculture and Economic Growth: Japan's Ex-*

perience (edited by Ohkawa, K., Johnston, B.F. and Kaneda, H.), Princeton: Princeton University Press, and University of Tokyo Press.

Umemura, Mataji (1970), "Agriculture and Labor Supply in the Meihi Era," *Agriculture and Economic Growth: Japan's Experience* (edited by Klein, Ohkawa and Kaneda), Princeton: Princeton University Press.

Waswo, Ann (1974), "The Origins of Tenant Unrest," *Japan in Crisis* (edited by Silberman, B. and Harvotunian, H.), Princeton: Princeton University Press.

Watanabe, Tsunehiko (1968), "Industrialization, Technological Progress, and Dual Structure," *Economic Growth The Japanese Experience since the Meiji Era* (edited by Klein, L. and Ohkawa, K.), New Haven: Yale University Press.

————. (April 1965), "Economic Aspects of Dualism in the Industrial Development of Japan," *Economic Development and Cultural Change,* 13.

Yamada, S (1967), "Changes in Output and in Conventional Inputs in Japanese Agriculture since 1880," *Food Research Institute Studies,* 7.

Yamamura, Kozo (1974), "The Japanese Economy, 1911–1930: Concentration, Conflicts and Crises," *Japan in Crisis* (edited by Silberman, B. and Harootunian, H.), Princeton: Princeton University Press.

————. (1974), "Then Came the Great Depression: Japan's Interwar Years," *The Great Depression Revisited* (edited by van de Wee, Herman), The Hague, Martinus Nijhoff.

————. (June 1967), "The Role of Samurai in the Development of Modern Banking in Japan," *Journal of Economic History,* 27.

————. (April 1968), "A Re-Examination of Entrepreneurship in Meiji Japan," *Economic History Review,* 21.

————. (1972), "Japan: A Revised View," *Banking and Economic Development* (edited by Cameron, R.), Oxford: Oxford University Press.

————. (Spring 1970), "A Note on the *Japan Business History Review* and Recent Books," *Business History Review,* 44.

————. (1976), "General Trading Companies in Japan - Their Origins and Growth," *Japan's Industrialization and its Social Consequences* (edited by Patrick, H.T.), Berkeley: University of California Press.

Yamamura, K. and Rosovsky, H. (Spring 1970), "Entrepreneurial Studies in Japan: An Introduction," *Business History Review,* 44.

Yasuba, Yasukichi (Autumn 1975), "Anatomy of the Debate on Japanese Capitalism," *Journal of Japanese Studies,* 2.

————. (1976), "The Evolution of Dualistic Wage Structure," *Japanese Industrialization and its Social Consequences* (edited by Patrick, H.T.), Berkeley: University of California Press.

Yasukawa, Masaaki (1963), "Estimates of Annual Births and of the General Fertility Rates in Japan, 1890–1920," *Keio Economic Studies,* 1.

Yoshino, M.Y. (1968), *Japan's Managerial System,* Cambridge: MIT Press.

Yui, Tsunehiko (Spring 1970), "The Personality and Career of Hikojiro Nakamigawa 1887–1901," *Business History Review,* 44.

SOME RECENT DEVELOPMENTS IN THE STUDY OF ECONOMIC AND BUSINESS HISTORY IN WESTERN GERMANY

Wolfram Fischer, FREE UNIVERSITY OF BERLIN

Economic history as a profession went through a rapid growth process in the 1960's and early 1970's in Western Germany. While there was only one chair exclusively devoted to economic and social history in the early 1950's (held by Ludwig Beutin in Cologne) and three or four combining economic history with other social sciences (Friedrich Lütge in Munich also taught economics, Carl Jantke in Hamburg and Hans Proesler in Nuremberg combined it with sociology and Wilhelm Abel with agricultural economics), now there exist 30 full professorships and about a dozen associate professorships in the field together with at least 60 junior positions. This rise was caused partly by the general expansion of academic institutions in the Federal Republic of Germany since the early 1960's; old universities grew beyond recognition, some like Munich, Hamburg, Münster, Berlin and Cologne comprising now more than 30,000 students each; about a dozen were newly created—among them the Ruhr-University in Bochum with three chairs in economic, social and technological history. Technical universities were extended to full-fledged universities and teacher colleges were raised to the status of comprehensive universities (*Gesamthochschulen*).

If economic history took its share in this growth this is due to two corresponding internal developments in the "mother sciences," economics and history. Economists turning more and more to theoretical and mathematical work felt a gap; where some of them formerly taught (or believed they taught) economic history (which often was rather the history of economic doctrines), they now were

willing to accomodate specialists in this field. Thus Professors Lütge and Abel in their later active years were able to give up their wider teaching duties in order to concentrate on their main fields, economic and agricultural history. When Friedrich Lütge died, a second professorship in economic and social history was established at the University of Munich. On the other hand, historians felt the need to emphasize social and economic factors in their teaching and research, which improved the career chances of specialists in these fields. Some universities even created new historical professorships with the emphasis on social and economic history (e.g., Münster and Frankfort). The renaissance of regional history, which always was a field for historians interested in agriculture, demography, rural and urban settlements, led in the same direction. The University of Hamburg for a long time had a specialist in the history of the *Hanse*; now Heidelberg created another chair in this field. Bonn and Freiburg, where medieval and modern historians like Franz Steinbach, Herman Aubin and Clemens Bauer had long cultivated the borderlines of economic, social, constitutional, and cultural history of the Rhineland, continued and expanded in these areas. The Swiss medievalist Hektor Ammann introduced economic history first at the University of Mannheim, then at Saarbrücken. Amongst those historians who held general appointments but concentrated largely on social or economic or business history, Percy Ernst Schramm at Göttingen, Otto Brunner at Hamburg, Götz Freiherr von Póllnitz at Nuremberg, Werner Conze first at Münster, then at Heidelberg, and Wilhelm Treue at Hanover and Göttingen, may be mentioned. They trained young historians in diverse fields including historical demography, history of social groups and structure, history of enterprises and of technology. A few technical universities created chairs for the history of technology; others appointed historicans who were willing to devote at least part of their time to it.

Realizing the necessity, but certainly not anticipating the size of this growth, the German counterpart of the Economic History Association, the *Gesellschaft für Sozial- und Wirtschaftsgeschichte*, was founded in the fifties; its first chairman was Friedrich Lütge.   Upon his death Hermann Kellenbenz, first the successor of Ludwig Beutin at Cologne and later of Götz Freiherr von Póllnitz in Nuremberg, was elected. A decade later, 1968, the moribund committee for economic history (*Ausschuss für Wirtschaftsgeschichte*) in the German economic association (*Verein für Socialpolitik*) was revitalized by the younger generation of economic historians, which had grown up after the war and established itself in the 1960's. Though this group emphasizes economic analysis in economic history, it is no full counterpart to the American Young Turks of the same time, the cliometricians. Open to theoretical argument and statistical evidence, it nevertheless did not break the bridges to the more conventional economic and social historians, and even accepts workers in the field without formal economic training. Nevertheless, there is a difference in emphasis in the work of these organizations which may be gathered from the papers of their meetings which are regularly published.[1] While

the *Gesellschaft* tries to accommodate a wide range of interests including, for instance, geographic or socio-cultural variables, the *Ausschuss* concentrates on problems of economic structure and development. But here too questions like the influence of legal changes are not excluded, as is seen in the contributions of P. Martin on early industrial enterprises in the legal form of limited companies[2] or of Karl-Heinrich Kaufhold on the consequences of the restriction of freedom of economic enterprises (*Gewerbefreiheit*) in Prussia 1849.[3] In line with a strong German tradition is the emphasis on the interplay of politics and the economy which Fritz Blaich demonstrates in the case of the law on the sale of potash of 1910.[4] Occasionally, but not regularly, American business and economic historians will find contributions which ask questions and apply methods comparable to the most advanced (or *en vogue* one) in this country. Examples are Helmut Hesse's econometric considerations on the differential of regional incomes in the growth process of 19th-century Germany,[5] or Jürgen Kocka's essay on the growth strategies of big enterprises in pre-World War I Germany; its title, modeled along Chandler's line, needs no translation: "Expansion-Integration-Diversifikation."[6] Papers of this type occasionally can be found also in the collection of the *Gesellschaft* since they are by no means excluded from its proceedings. But they are even rarer there. Examples are the present writer's reflections on the role of handicraft and small business in Germany's economic growth between 1850 and 1914 or Knut Borchardt's ingenious essay measuring regional income differences, in the face of a lack of direct evidence, by an index of the density of medical doctors and students in secondary schools per head of population.[7]

A survey of the papers of the two groups of economic historians reveals, particularly if compared with the annual meetings of the Economic History Association, that German economic historians have very diversified interests and approaches and seem to find it difficult to concentrate on a few common topics. This has been criticized with only marginal success. However, there are examples of more coherent group production; for instance, the discussions an "organized capitalism" at the German historical association's meeting of 1972,[8] or some of the regular gatherings of the *Arbeitskreis für moderne Sozialgeschichte* which, under the chairmanship of Werner Conze, produced, inter alia, volumes on the German *Vormärz*, on the economic and political crises of the Weimar Republic, and on the beginnings of the modern world.[9] A single meeting of an *ad hoc* group at Bochum, on economic, social and political problems of the inter-war-period, sponsored by the *Deutsche Forschungsmeinschaft*, is another example. Through a remarkable effort by the editors and the publisher the voluminous proceedings of this conference were available in print only one year later.[10] For several years a group of historians met at Büdingen Castle to discuss economic, social and political elites. The results are published in several volumes.[11] In the last decade foundations sponsored research in social history which spilled over into economic history as well. Thus the Thyssen-foundation in a multidisciplinary project on the

19th century financed meetings of a group of sociologists, social historians and historians of education who dealt with problems like innovations, social conflict and indicators of social change. Some, though not all of the papers and related monographs have been published by the foundation. Another group in the same Thyseen-program on the 19th century dealt with the interrelations of science, technology and the economy. Some monographs and two remarkable volumes of papers and discussion, delivered mainly by historians of science and technology over the period of one decade, are the result.[12]

The *Deutsche Forschungsgmeinschaft*, the publicly-supported main sponsor of research in Germany, financed two programs in modern economic history: first, "early industrialization," and then, as a chronological sequence, "history of German industry before 1914." The first program resulted in a series of monographs mainly produced by a group of researchers connected with the *Historische Kommission zu Berlin*, first under the guidance of Rudolf Braun, who launched an interdisciplinary approach, then under the leadership of Otto Büsch, who managed to keep the group together as well as to incite nearly every member to a monograph of his (or her) own.[13] The second program, which is still in progress, will produce an even wider range of publications since groups or single researchers in many German universities are involved, reaching from Freiburg, Stuttgart and Heidelberg in the Southwest; to Marburg, Maynce, Aachen, Bonn and Cologne in the Rhine-Main area and the West; to Münster, Bochum, Göttingen and Hamburg in the Northwest and North; and again including Berlin. Topically, at least three major areas are emphasized: problems of industrial finance and capital supply (directed by Tilly at Münster and Winkel at Aachen), technology of modern industries like chemistry and the installation of electrical power (Pohl at Bonn, Timm at Bochum and Ott at Freiburg), and the recruitment and structure of the labor force (Bog at Marburg, Conze at Heidelberg). Within this group also a pilot project was launched, aiming at the creation of a "Historical Statistics of Germany," which—unlike the basically synthetic work of Walther G. Hoffmann and his collaborators[14]—will try to provide comprehensive compilations and explanations of quantitative evidence about the German economy and society, as collected by private, semipublic and public sources. A small group of researchers in Berlin and Göttingen under the responsibility of Otto Büsch, Wolfram Fischer and Karl-Heinrich Kaufhold is working presently on industrial production and employment figures. The latter has produced himself a major piece on early industrial and crafts statistics (*Gewerbestatistik*) in Prussia in his *Habilitationsschrift*. Valuable statistical surveys have been produced on the size and geographical location of manufactures and early industrial enterprises in the Rhineland.[15]

As this survey has shown, cooperative and collective work has certainly increased in Western Germany during the last decade. Does this mean that there is also a tendency to focus on a few, generally accepted basic research goals and

methods? The answer cannot be a clear ''yes'' or ''no.'' It seems that some major themes have developed upon which a number of people tend to concentrate, but the diversity is still great, and no group has established itself in the same way as the cliometricians of the 1960's or the entrepreneurial historians of the 1950's in this country. Before looking at some of these central themes more closely, let us first elaborate on the diversity. Richard Tilly, in his critical review article on recent German economic history has maintained that since the 1870's ''German economic historians, increasingly producing economic history without economics, have been playing Hamlet without the Prince.''[16] He attributes this to the emphasis on legal and institutional studies, but also to the—still persisting— fact that economic history in all German-speaking countries is institutionally intertwined with social history, which up to very recent times seemed less capable of being operationalized. There is certainly more than a grain of truth in this critique, though more recently a shift in emphasis or—with the growing number of practitioners in the field—a greater division of labor can be discerned. Knut Borchardt has offered another explanation of the German emphasis on institutional change. In an intriguing discussion of the North-Thomas property rights approach, he maintains that the German economists of the 19th century lived in a situation in which institutional change was a major, if not *the* major problem for the onset of economic growth; that they witnessed a dramatic breakdown of old structures and institutions and the emergence of new ones; and that as advisers to the government they were confronted with the urgent problem of how to solve economic problems by legal and institutional means (for instance, by drafting a patent law or a law regulating the stock exchange). No wonder, he concludes, that the intellectuals dealt first with questions that really were more urgent than an explanation of one or another price structure.[17] One could strengthen this argument with reference to Adam Smith who, writing in a similar situation of institutional change, did not refrain from dealing with legal and political questions, so that the beginning of modern classical economics was rightly termed ''political economy.'' But the question then remains why German economists after the turn of the century did not take up the same kind of analytical argument which by then was fully established in Marshallian economics. I am not sure whether it would be sufficient to explain this failure by the continuation of major political changes since World War I, as one might be tempted to think, since this whole line of argument does not explain why the Viennese school of economics from Böhm-Bawerk and Menger to Schumpeter, Hayek, Machlup and Haberler deviated so markedly from the Berlin school around Schmoller. The Austrian situation was, after all, not that different from the German one. However this may be, the fact remains that employment of economic theory and use of statistical or econometric methods was until recently rare in the writings of German economic historians and still is rather the exception than the rule.

One indicator Tilly used to demonstrate this situation was the type of articles

published in the *Viertelsjahrsschrift für Sozial-und Wirtschaftsgeschichte* (VSWG), the leading West German periodical in the field. Writing in 1969, he pointed out that roughly 60% of the articles published during the last 10 years dealt with the preindustrial period, as compared with around 45% in the *Economic History Review*, the leading English journal. Also, more than 50% of the articles dealt with social history rather than economic history as compared with only 20% in the *Economic History Review*.[18] I have counted and classified the articles in the VSWG for the following six years (1970–1975). The outcome seems to indicate a major change. Of the 60 articles published in these years—not counting smaller miscellanea—only 30% dealt with the preindustrial period, 63% with the Industrial Revolution and later times, and 7% were of more general, mainly methodological, character. Even if some articles could be classified differently—I put all articles dealing with the transitional period of 1750 to 1850 in the Industrial Revolution and later—the relation would still be markedly different: no more than about 40% can be attributed to pre-industrial-revolution periods. Again the distribution between social and economic topics has changed. According to my account, only 32% can be said to deal mainly with problems of social history, although I counted all articles on historical demography in the social rather than the economic bracket. Fifty-three% dealt with predominantly economic questions, 10% with politico-economic issues (an old topic of German economic history), and 5% were of a more methodological character. Even more astonishing however is the geographical distribution of the themes. Only 40% of the articles deal with Germany, exactly the same percentage with other countries, and 20% either with international economic relations or with wider regions, like Europe or the Atlantic Economy, or with no special geographical area at all. One reason for this distribution may be found in the fact that only 70% of the authors live in Germany, 30% outside—the largest group being Austrian authors, who constitute 7% of the contributors to the journal.[19] The percentage of foreign language articles (English or French) is 12, still smaller than the percentage of foreign authors, which is due not only to the Austrians but also to the fact that some of the articles by American and English authors are in German. The share of foreign contributors and of foreign language articles has been growing recently. Thus all authors of No. 3, 1975, and two-thirds of the authors of the whole year 1975 came from outside Germany.[20]

If this evidence is taken as an indicator of recent tendencies in German economic history, it can be stated that the profession has become more interested in modern history and economic problems, but most of all, that it is being "internationalized" both in respect to fields of interest and to the exchange with non-German scholars. One should not overestimate this evidence, however. I would suggest that it provides a hint that tendencies in these directions exist and gain momentum, but it is still too early to take it as an indicator of a definite trend. Moreover, the empirical basis for making a more reliable judgement must be

broadened considerably, since the VSWG is not the only journal in which German econmic historians publish their articles. Some prefer economic journals, like the *Jahrbücher für Nationalökonomie und Statistik*, *the Zeitschrift für die gesamte Staatswissenschaft*, or the *Zeitschrift für Wirtschafts und Sozialwissenschaften* (formerly known as *Schmollers Jahrbuch*). Others publish mainly in general historical periodicals, in one of the many publications of regional history, or in foreign journals. Business history publications concentrate on the *Tradition, Zeitschrift für Firmengeschichte* and, until recently, on the now defunct *Scripta Mercaturae*. This periodical was started in 1967 by an enthusiastic amateur, a small businessman who had never received a full-time university education, but was an active researcher in fields such as the history of mining, of industrial enterprises and of international trade. After returning from emigration to Brazil in the 1950's, he used the earnings from a small ship in Munich to edit, print and publish this journal all by himself. At first he was also the principal author, but he proved able to recruit more and more professional economic historians as contributors.[21]

A comparison of the two journals of business history shows a fairly distinct division of labor. While *Tradition* concentrates mainly on the 19th and 20th centuries and on Germany, *Scripta Mercaturae* emphasizes the pre-industrial period and international trade. Though particularly *Tradition*, which was founded in 1956 by Wilhelm Treue and has been edited by him since, has been criticized because of lack of analytical perspective and too much emphasis on individual entrepreneurs or enterprises,[22] it certainly filled a need for assembling materials and studies on business enterprises and enterpreneurs. Together both journals covered an important field of German economic history and provided an opportunity of publication also for business archivists and occasional writers on the history of business affairs.

Articles on business history, as on economic history in general, are being accepted more and more also by many of the regional historical periodicals. Their number is so great and their quality so uneven that nobody would be able to keep track of their activities, had not the association of regional historical societies long ago decided to found a yearbook of general reference. This, the *Blätter für deutsche Landesgeschichte*, provides not only original articles and regional surveys but also topical review articles which try to cover the whole field of regional economic and business history and are a most valuable source of bibliographical information.[23] Among the regional journals themselves, the *Rheinische Vierteljahrsblätter* are probably the most important for economic and business historians since they have a long tradition of devoting part of their space to problems of the Rhenish economy. For most of these journals, Tilly's statement might still hold true, that older periods and social history have some priority over modern economic history, particularly in its more analytical approach. But even in regional journals the number of articles devoted to the development of modern

businesses, transport, urbanized areas and the like are becoming not only more frequent but also more important. Moreover, there is a growing concern of regional historians with the local repercussions of recent economic and general policies, such as rearmament in the Third Reich, the dismantlement after World War II, or the influx of refugees, and the establishment of new enterprises. Here the old preference of German economic historians for the relations between government and the economy has found a fresh field for exploration. It has also become a favorite theme for those members of the New Left—sociologists and political scientists more often than economic historians—who are eager to demonstrate (rather than to explore) why Western Germany failed to become a socialist country after 1945. This will be an even more popular field in the immediate future as the sources of the military governments become more widely available and research funds are channeled into it.[24] The *Vierteljahrshefte für Zeitgeschichte* (VFZG) edited by the *Institut für Zeitgeschichte*, can be regarded as the best reference for this field, since they not only publish articles related to it but also provide a current bibliography.[25] Two short but reliable surveys up to 1970 are provided by Harald Winkel.[26] They supplement the earlier survey of Knut Borchardt, which is part of the most comprehensive book on the German economy since 1970.[27] Another short survey, also covering the 1920s, has been written by a recent German emigré to the United States, Karl Hardach of Rutgers University.[28] A very interesting comparison of economic development and structural change in both Germanies since the late 1950's is available in two official government publications (the materials for Willy Brandt's "State of the Nation" Message in 1970 and 1972), which in their economic sections were prepared by a team of economists, mainly from the *Deutsches Institut für Wirtschaftsforschung* in Berlin.[29] The present writer has tried to integrate some of their results in his contribution on mining, industry and crafts, 1914–1972, in the *Handbuch der deutschen Sozial- und Wirtschaftsgeschichte*.[30]

This handbook, the first volume of which was published in 1971,[31] may be seen as a cross section of the present state of German economic history. Conceived in the early 1960's with a publication date of 1967 in mind, it took nearly a decade longer to be finished. Some of the authors died—H. Aubin, F. Lütge and H. Ammann; others gave up and had to be replaced by younger ones who had different conceptions about how to tackle their subject. Thus the part about economic policy in the 19th and 20th century taken over by Eckart Schremmer from Friedrich Lütge became much more theoretically oriented and abstract. Other sections, because of the lack of any specialist in the field, had to be filled by the editor himself to avoid intolerable gaps (e.g., the part on public finance in the 19th and 20th century). For the second volume, the appearance of Walther Hoffmann's estimates on economic growth in German since 1850 (Hoffmann, 1965), certainly was a turning point. The sections on growth and business cycles (by Borchardt), as those on industry (by myself), rely heavily on his findings. Karl-Heinrich Kaufhold, in his contribu-

tion on German industry and crafts 1800–1850, was able to rely on his own research on Prussia (Abel, 1970); so did Wolfgang Köllmann in his contributions on the history of population and Wilhelm Abel in his, on agriculture. Others remained more in the traditional descriptive and selective style while Werner Conze tried to draw conventional wisdom and recent scholarship together in his sections on 19th century social structure and movements. The two volumes are organized topically as well as chronologically. Topics like population, agriculture, trade and industry, economic policy and public finance are treated separately over periods of different lengths, reaching from the half century during the "transitional" period, 1800–1850, to several centuries in earlier time. This is certainly not a "new" economic history, organized around a common set of theoretical assumptions and techniques of research, but some traces of novel approaches may be discernible in it even for the most critical user. Though it is far from being perfect or definitive, it probably will not be replaceable by a similar enterprise for at least one or two decades to come.

It is always easier for a single author to produce a coherent book than for a group. Nevertheless, no really "new" textbook on German economic history has been published during the recent years. What comes closest to it is Friedrich Wilhelm Henning's three-volume paperback, which grew out of his lectures and aims at students who prepare for exams.[32] Compared with the older works of Friedrich Lütge, Heinrich Bechtel and the East-German Hans Mottek,[33] it is a step forward. Economics is certainly not left out of it. It also draws on many new results of research, to a great extent on Henning's own. It is stuffed with tables and graphs and it is well-organized. Unfortunately it also has some considerable drawbacks: it is written in a telegraphic kind of style, often only throwing out key-words; therefore, it does not unfold an argument but just gives results without indicating how the author arrived at them. Henning does not even give the sources for his tables and graphs. Some, particularly for the earlier times, are clearly estimates and informed judgements—very reasonable judgements most of the time. But the unexperienced student is made to believe that evidence exists where it really does not. It is all right to put such sketches out in a lecture where tthey can be explained orally. In a book which people would like to use not only for memorizing but for further and more detailed work, they are wrongly placed. The uninformed student may think the proofs are to be found in the books and articles given in the bibliographies at the end of each volume; but often they are not. Thus the books, while providing a short and mostly reliable survey, do not explain the course and structure of German economic history. Pending a new two-volume successor to Lütge's standard work by new authors,[34] general readers have either to live with Henning and the older works or to turn to shorter surveys, e.g., those in Carlo Cipolla's Fontana Economic History of Europe written by Knut Borchardt (18/19th century) and Karl Hardach (20th century), which do much better in explaining what happened in recent German economic history.[35] Two other short surveys try

to cover the whole German social and economic history from the Middle Ages to the present and cannot, therefore, claim to give more than an elementary introduction.[36]

Any general treatment of a country's economic history has, of course, to rely on extensive monographic literature. Richard Tilly stated in 1969 that "our knowledge of German economic history is spotty" because "such an extensive literature" as was available to Clapham for Britain as early as the 1920's, did not yet exist at the end of the 1960's and that, therefore, in his judgement "time may even now not yet be ripe for such an effort."[37] Let us see now where and in which respect some progress has been made in the last six years or so. Fortunately, two bibliographical guides are now available.[38] In addition, some helpful statistical compilations exist for the times after 1870—except the voluminous work of Hoffmann and collaborators (Hoffman, Grumback and Hesse, 1965)—which is difficult to use. One is an abstract of the official statistics of Germany, published by the *Statistisches Bundesamt* to commemorate the centennial of the central statistical office in Germany.[39] It comes as close as one can get to a "Historical Statistics of Germany," if one confines oneself to the official data as they were collected and published at different times. It does not try, as Hoffmann did, to improve them or supplement estimated figures for earlier times when certain data—e.g., on physical production—were not yet actually collected. Thus the figures on industrial production before 1950 rest on selective inquiries made first mainly for customs purposes and, since 1936, for rearmament; national income data begin in 1925. Nevertheless, with its careful explanation of what was collected, why, by whom and by which methods, this short and moderately priced volume ($6.-) provides an excellent groundwork for the last hundred years. No wonder that a collection which was begun somewhat later, in order to provide students of history with quantitative material, draws liberally from this official publication.[40] It extends the scope of the collection into educational and social mobility figures taken from other official statistics and recent research. No wonder too, that the first volume, covering the time before 1870, for which the present writer has taken up responsibility, will have to wait until the above mentioned monographic research into problems of the historical statistics of Germany has produced some satisfactory results. A very useful collection of data on structural change since the turn of the century has been provided by one of the foremost scholars in 20th-century German economic history, Dietmar Petzina.[41] As far as the availability of quantitative data for a modern economic history of Germany is concerned, the situation has definitely improved since the mid-1960's, at least the access to data is now much easier. Nearly all the data—except Hoffman's synthetic ones—had been available before, but they were buried in hundreds of volumes of the official statistics and semi-official work, and there, of course, much more detailed data are still assembled for any searching scholar.[42]

Some progress can be stated also in the field of methodology and research techniques. First of all, a debate about methodology has begun and is being carried

on.[43] More important, some younger scholars, well trained in economics and statistics and aware of the gains and pitfalls of quantification in history, have entered the field. Most, though not all of them, received their economic training through Walter G. Hoffmann, and the majority were launched on their historical research by Richard Tilly. Not surprisingly, their special topics reflect the concern to identify the main sectors of economic growth in 19th-century Germany and to measure their contribution. In a useful though somewhat oddly arranged dissertation, Günter Kirchhain has dealt with the growth of the German cotton industry.[44] At the same time Carl-Ludwig Holtrerich has devoted a very careful and balanced study to the Ruhr coal industry.[45] He works with a clear theoretical concept of economic growth and the role of a leading sector, and masters the statistical techniques necessary to analyze the mechanism of development. His argument is cohesive and convincing. The progress he made becomes particularly clear if one compares his approach with the nontheoretical study of nearly the same subject by another young economist which appeared only two years earlier.[46] Not surprisingly either, three studies center around the contribution of the railroads to German economic growth. Horst Wagenblass, a student of Erich Maschke's and Eckart Schremmer's at Heidelberg, tried to evaluate the effect of demand from railroads on the German iron and engineering industries at the early period of industrialization.[47] Rainer Fremdling took up the Fogel-Fishlow topic for Germany and measured the role of the railroads in German economic growth until the 1870's,[48] and Reinhard Spree in Berlin, in what is perhaps the most ambitious quantitative study by a young economic historian in Germany in recent years,[49] devoted one crucial chapter to the same question. The main thrust of his study is, however, not the linear trend of growth but its cyclical patterns between 1840 and 1880. Constructing a reference cycle out of several distinct cycles—such as swings in the production of basic goods, in monetary flows and investments, etc.—he tries to determine the nature and course of German economic development in a crucial phase. His findings are open to criticism mainly because he neglected two possibly major factors in this development, agriculture and foreign trade; but within its limits, his dissertation constitutes a definite contribution to the economic history of 19th century Germany.

International trade in the earlier parts of the century has been the topic of two dissertations written under the supervision of Wolfgang Zorn, then in Bonn.[50] The study by Kutz is remarkable insofar as it tries to overcome the lack of German sources for German foreign trade by exploiting the statistics and consular reports of the trade partners of the German states: England, France, the Netherlands and Belgium, Austria, Russia (including Poland), Scandinavia, the United States and Latin America contribute auxiliary sources to shed light on German economic history. In this context also the somewhat older studies of Hermann Kellenbenz and Herbert Hassinger on German and Austrain foreign trade at the end of the 18th century should be mentioned, studies which form part of the conference papers of the first meeting of the *Gesellschaft für Sozial- und Wirtschaftsgeschichte*.[51] There

are, moreover, some monographs dealing with special areas of foreign trade in 19th-century Germany, most of them written by students of Hermann Kellenbenz.[52] Other deal with international trade relations of German trading centers or with specific products of foreign trade in earlier centuries. A symposium under the chairmanship of Ingomar Bog explored the trade relations with Eastern Central Europe in early modern time.[53] Also the old tradition of publishing source material for foreign trade has been continued.[54]

International trade is one economic activity which lends itself to quantification better than most others, since very early records are available, although most of them remain rather spotty. Another field where such progress seems possible is the economic history of cities. For two of the most important trading places of medieval Germany quantitative studies have been recently tried. Wilhelm Schönfelder's book on the economic development of late medieval Cologne has, however, met much criticism, since he seems not to have mastered the intricacies of reading late medieval sources in their context.[55] More careful is a shorter study of the economic development of late medieval Hamburg;[56] more traditional, but with interesting results, is a monograph about Strassburg in early modern times.[57] Some monographs, mainly dissertations, deal with 19th-century cities. For a long time the Rhenish-Westfalian cities and towns around the Ruhr have been a preferred research object. Middle classes in southwest Germany were the topic of a symposium of urban historians.[58] In recent years urbanization as a socio-economic process has become more prominent as a topic of research. A new periodical has been founded in 1974 and some case studies have been published.[59]

Some of these studies also deal with population development. Historical demography has been rather neglected in post-war Germany, due to the ideological bent demographic and family research had received in Nazi-Germany. For many years Wolfgang Kollmann was nearly the only historian active in the field. His essays are now conveniently collected.[60] He also edited a reader which deals with methodological as well as substantive questions.[61] An edition of basic German population statistics of the 19th century by him and his collaborators is still in preparation. One of his students devoted himself to German emigration,[62] another one to the change in generative structures in peasant and bourgeois families since 1950.[63] A student of Richard Tilly's worked on the interactionof demographic and economic factors in a Westfalian district in the 19th century, T. Angel on Italian immigration into Rhenish cities in the 17th and 18th centuries.[64] Historical demography in the French (and English) manner of family reconstitution has only recently been taken up seriously, foremost by a Swiss scholar who taught first at Giessen and now in Berlin. His main work is on Scandinavia, but while at Giessen he introduced a group of students to the methods of demographical research and

Historical demography is, of course, also closely related to agricultural history. In Germany this tradition has been never quite lost, as the work of Günther Franz testifies, though agricultural history was mainly regarded from two different

angles, the legal and social relations of peasants and their Lords (*Agrarverfassungsgeschichte*), the realm of Friedrich Lütge and other, and the history of agricultural prices and wages, of agrarian production and structure (*Agrarwirtschasftsgeschichte*). The latter branch is mainly connected with the name of Wilhelm Abel in Göttingen and his pupils. Only a few of the recent studies can be mentioned here. Current research can be followed up through a periodical.[67] Most though not all of the monographs are published in a series which was founded by Friedrich Lütge and Günther Franz and is now edited by the latter together with Wilhelm Abel.[68] Outstanding examples of recent research in agricultural history are the books and articles by Friedrich-Wilhelm Henning.[69] Also two *Habilitationsschriften* ought to be mentioned which continue the tradition of *Agrarverfassungsgeschichte*, though in somewhat different directions. Hugo Ott explores the agricultural foundations of some later medieval rulers (*Grundherrschaften*), mainly monasteries, in the upper Rhine Valley and the southern black forest,[70] Willi A. Boelcke the interrelations of economic structure and changes in the political power base of noble rulers (*Adelsherrschaften*) in Eastern Germany throughout the later middle-ages and early modern times.[71] Some dissertations follow the same lines or trace legal and economic conditions of peasants in smaller German territories.[72] The five-volume standard text on German agriculture history, which began to appear in 1962, was finished in 1970 with the volume on the social history of the German peasantry by Günther Franz, while the earlier volumes by Abel and Lütge had already gone through a second edition.[73] In addition, there is now also a shorter textbook by Ernst Klein on agriculture in the age of industrialization and a comprehensive volume by Wilhelm Abel on pre-industrial mass poverty and famines.[74]

One author, Eckart Schremmer, who has successfully tried to inject new economics into traditional agrarian history and to combine both,[75] has in recent years turned mainly to other sectors and problems, sometimes amassing huge materials into comprehensive studies,[76] sometimes singling out specific problems and trying out new methods.[77] In his last study he resumes a difficult problem which was taken up more extensively by an economist.[78] Using her data and Hoffmann's to calculate the contribution of the "residual" to German economic growth in the second half of the 19th century, he arrives at 42% for the economy as a whole, but at 53% for agriculture and only 38% for industry and crafts; while questioning the validity of the method of measuring total factor productivity to find out the magnitude of the residual, he does not, however, try to interpret the somewhat puzzling results or to propose alternative techniques of measurement.

Most of the studies that use Hoffmann's data are done, as mentioned earlier, by his students or collaborators and do not concern themselves with the question of how the results thus achieved fit into the conventional wisdom of German economic history and how the techniques or data employed might account for their results.[79] The authors see themselves as applied economists rather than as new

economic historians, an understanding which tends to widen the gulf between them and the economic historians proper, even more than that between the old and the new economic historians in this country. Only a few economic historians like Knut Borchardt, Eckart Schremmer, Richard Tilly, myself, and some of our students have tried to bridge this gap. Nevertheless, the tendency of some recently trained economists to occupy themselves with problems of modern German economic development and the attempts of some economic historians to enter this discussion should not go unnoticed, since they promise some fruit for the future.

Another gulf that seems to develop is that between political historians turning to problems of economic influence in politics, and economic historians proper, dealing with the same interrelation but aiming mainly at an explanation of the performance of the economy. As stated above, the relations between government and the economy occupy a prominent place in the tradition of German economic history. In recent years, stimulated mainly by the controversy between Fritz Fischer and his opponents about the causes of World War I and German war aims therein, partly also by discussion with East German old and West German neo Marxists on the causes of the rise of Hitler and of fascism in general (or even wider: on the roots and nature of imperialism), a fairly remarkable stream of literature has developed which aims at the revision of German (or Western) history in general, particularly in the later 19th and earlier 20th century. Problems of the structure and course of industrial societies have been taken up and the old discussion about the nature of capitalism has been revived. Only some of the more important or more pertinent problems connected with this discussion (which seems to have dominated the German historical profession during the last years) can be dealt with here. At its best, this discussion has produced some outstanding books on Bismarck's (and American) imperialism, the social structure of Germany during World War I, and the role of the German lower-middle classes in the rise of Hitler's Germany.[80] Some interesting comparative work has been done on the so-called "organized capitalism," the Great Depression, and agricultural movements in Germany, America and France[81]—work that is similar in intention to Charles Maier's comparative analysis of interwar Germany, Italy and France.[82] The volume on the the interplay of economic interests and politics in the Weimar Republic (Mommsen, Petzina and Weisbrod, 1974) also belongs in this category, which can be described as politico-social history, with strong emphasis on theoretical concepts and on an evaluation or analysis of underlying economic forces.

Such a search for economic factors or causes of political organizations and developments is very popular among the younger generation of German historians; the results of these searches are, however, not always convincing, since only a few of the participants have an adequate conception of or training in economics. At their worst they display preconceived value-judgements about the character of business enterprises or naive astonishment about the interplay between economic and political interests. Sometimes there is only a small step taken to a wholesale

verdict on captialism, particularly big business, without a well-founded economic analysis.[83] Selected readings on economics, and not-too-well-understood statistics—particularly if taken from the synthetic work of Hoffmann—are sometimes thrown out to prove the working of economic factors in every major political decision. Nevertheless, at least two areas of recent German history have become much better known through these endeavours: financial and agricultural politics in Imperial and Weimar Germany,[84] and the foundation, organization, social base and politics of nearly all major interest groups.[85]

Other fields of economic policy that have been explored are protectionist customs policy (e.g., in its effect on the international monetary system before World War I[86],) the economic preparation for this war[87] and the politics and economics of reparations after World War I.[88] The belated publication of an official history of the genesis of the Young-plan, which was ordered by the Brüning government to defend its policy against the accusation of Dr. Schacht, should also be mentioned in this context.[89]

There is a revival of interest in German colonial policy before World War I with a marked emphasis on economic factors.[90] This coincides with a renewed interested in German colonial history by English and American historians and a drive toward comparative analysis of imperialism.[91] There are also two valuable German readers summarizing the international debate on colonialism and imperialism and an intelligent interpretation of Marx's and Engles' views on imperialism.[92]

As stated before, most of these studies aim at an interpretation of the political history of Germany; economic and social forces serve mainly to explain the particular course of German political events and structures, and many are motivated by the question: why was it possible that Hitler came to power?[93] Thus a century after Marx and half a century after Beard an economic explanation of recent German history has come *en vogue*. There are many facets to this explanation, and I do not intend to deal with their relative merit in this review. They are often influenced by basic political beliefs of the authors and sometimes by their epistomology, though it may be noted that there is no clear-cut parallel between a "progressive" political view and a "progressive" scholarly approach. Some of the most outspoken critics of traditional interpretation of German history employ the most traditional tools of research, and it is usually the more moderate or circumspect researchers who take great pain in clearing up their concepts and selecting adequate techniques. One of the centers of this discussion is still the question of *who* brought Hitler to power, and it is here where the orthodox Marxist point of view, that it was big industry, has been revived and revoked most eloquently.[94]

Equally, the discussion about the relations of business and government, of economic and political-military interests during the Third Reich, has continued; and more detailed knowledge about the conduct of economic policy, its problems and contingencies has been the result. Much of the discussion centers still around

Hitler's last minister of armament, Albert Speer, who has himself entered the discussion with his memoirs "Inside the Third Reich."[95] One of his major assistants has also published his memoirs.[96] A diligent but not very inspiring doctoral dissertation has been written about the ministry of Speer.[97] But more weight is now being attributed to the skill of his forerunner, Todt, and quite a number of different problems of economic planning and distribution for and in the war economy have been tackled, often concentrating on resource procurement and allocation,[98] but also on the role of certain personalities or groups like the engineers.[99] Rearmament as a goal and as a means of policy has remained a favorite topic.[100] There are also new studies about labor, particularly a massive collection of documents on Nazi labor and wage policy by a British historian who has worked for many years in Berlin,[101] and on employment policy before and after 1933.[102] A neo-Marxist sociologist has tried his hand—not very successfully—at a reinterpretation of the economic and social history of peacetime Nazi-Germany, relying partly on the book of the French Marxist, Charles Bettelheim, which has been translated into German.[103]

Only a few economists and economic historians focus in their work more on the economic than on the political order of Nazi-Germany.[104] A Berlin dissertation in economics has treated the concentration of enterprises as consequence and as means of national socialist economic policy.[105] Similar problems formed part of a study by Peter Czada and myself, in which we tried to tackle the structural changes in 20th-century German industry.[106] They are also present in the work of Dietmar Petzina who, after his book on the *Vierjahresplan* and related studies, has written a very valuable survey of German economic history between 1918 and 1945.[107]

Equally rare are studies of the economic order for earlier periods of German history. The most prolific author in this respect is Fritz Blaich, who has published on the economic legislation and policy of the German Empire in the 16th and 17th centuries, as well as on problems of cartel and trust policies in the late 19th and early 20th centuries.[108] Another example is Friedrich Zunkel's book on the discussion and power-struggle for a "new economic order" during World War I.[109] Altogether we find that by far the majority of those who study the relationship between the state and the economy are mainly interested in the structure and nature of the political world; the economy for them is an important *explanans* of the political system but not the *explanandum* it self. It is possible, therefore, to vary Tilly's verdict: While German economic historians cautiously try to draw the prince into the center of the play, many historians insist that the play itself is not about the economy but about politics. What they want to find out is not how the economic system functions and changes over time but how power is distributed and exercised via economic interests.

Small wonder, then, that business history as a historical analysis of the business world, its structure and development, does not make much headway. The number of those historians who think it worthwhile to study it, not for the sake of political

or socio-political history but *per se*, is still small. It is true, small and large studies of single businessmen and firms are not lacking, but most are not done by professional scholars and their value is very uneven. Hans Jäger has reported recently about some of the more important works.[110] I can concentrate, therefore, on a few developments and would like to stress mainly areas of relative strength: one is, in continuation of an old tradition, the history of the great merchant houses, particularly in Upper Germany in early modern time. The late Götz Freiherr von Pölnitz's massive biography of Anton Fugger, basically a chronologically arranged narrative, has come to volume 3, part I, covering in 769 pages less then a decade.[111] Wolfgang Freiherr Stromer von Reichenbach in a similar voluminous study has extended research in these southern German merchant and banking houses back to the later middle-ages.[112] Reinhardt Hildebrandt, who in an earlier study covered the later Fugger years of decline,[113] has explored an interesting group of employees in early modern merchant houses, the leading business clerks, who sometimes managed to become partners or owners of enterprises. Most, however, remained in the position of *Angestellte*, white-collar workers of a pre-industrial merchant society.[114]

For a more recent period, Jürgen Kocka has undertaken a major study of this group, beginning with the House of Siemens.[115] From there he moved into more general and methodological questions,[116] and recently he has published the first comprehensive study of German entrepreneurship in a long time.[117] It will be available in a modified version also to the English-reading public in volume VII of the *Cambridge Economic History of Europe*, due for publication in 1976 or 1977. Besides Kocka the number of authors who devote themselves to more general problems of business history remains small. Richard Tilly's contribtion to the Copenhagen Congress of the International Economic History Association deserves, however, mention.[118] Like Kocka he has been inspired by Chandler's "Strategy and Structure" and related studies. Hartmut Kaelble has explored the social origins of Berlin entrepreneurs, their social status and political influence, mainly in the second third of the 19th century;[119] Gerhard Adelmann, leading entrepreneurs in Rhineland and Westfalia in the second half of the 19th century,[120] and the late Percy Ernst Schramm added to his many books on Hamburg families another one on two members of the ruling merchants class.[121] Hermann Kellenbenz and Klara van Eyll dealt with the organizations of businessmen, mainly the chamber of commerce, in Cologne from the French rule to the beginning of World War I.

All these studies tend to be dominated by two topics: a) organization and b) social recruitment, training and status of businessmen and managers. They are often conceived as social histories of particular groups or classes rather than as contributions to the management of firms.[122] One part of the vital function of business-leadership and decision making has received, however, some attention: financing. Ernst Klein and P. Coym wrote about problems of industrial finance in

the early 19th century,[123] Ernest Hieke, about financing the German trade in crude oil and the beginning of the German-American Petroleum Company,[124] and Richard Tilly provided some material and considerations about the capital market in 19th-century Germany.[125] At present he is attempting to analyze the financial decisions of the fifty largest German corporations in late 19th and early 20th century. Earlier he wrote about the role of banks in early industrialization;[126] and this problem, a classic German economic history, has been revived by several authors.[127] Though it still awaits more detailed studies of certain regions and types of institutions (e.g., the saving-bank and benevolent societies),[128] a new general treatment of money and banks in the 19th and 20th century has just appeared.[129] Sponsored by the *Deutsche Bank* and other German banks, an Institute for Research in the History of Banking has been founded in Frankfurt, which started to publish a journal for the history of banking. In its first two issues a review article surveyed banking history, mainly in Germany.[130]

If we compare this rather limited output in studies on business history with that of more general economic history, we have to state that the exploration of the business world certainly has not been a favorite subject of German economic historians. Whatever the reasons for this avoidance may be, it demonstrates that the recent growth of the profession in Germany has not led to a marked upswing in this crucial area of economic development.

FOOTNOTES

1. Lütge, March 1963, 1964, March 1965, 1968; Kellenbenz, April 1969, 1971, April 1971, 1974, 1975; Fischer, 1971; Winkel, 1973, 1975.
2. Martin, in Fischer (1971), pp. 195–214.
3. Kaufhold, in Winkel (1975) pp. 165–188.
4. Blaich, in Winkel (1975), pp. 189–201.
5. Hesse, in Fischer (1971), pp. 261–279.
6. Kocka, in Winkel (1975), pp. 203–226.
7. Borchardt, in Lütge (1968), pp. 115–130; and Fischer, in Lütge (1968), pp. 131–142.
8. Winkler (1974), Vol. 9.
9. Conze (1962, 1970), Vol. 1; Conze (1976); Conze and Raupach (1967), Vol. 8.
10. Mommsen, Petzina and Weisbrod (1974).
11. Franz (1972), Vol. 5; Helbig (1973), Vol. 6; Helbig (1974), Vol. 7; Franz (1975), Vol. 8.
12. Freudenberger and Mensch (1975), Vol. 13; Noll (1976), Vol. 10; Pfetsch (1975), Vol. 14; Rüegg and Neuloh (1971), Vol. 1; Teuteberg and Wiegelmann (1972), Vol. 3; Burchardt (1974), Vol. 1; Treue and Mauel (1976), Vols. 2 and 3; Kroker (1975), Vol. 4; Heggen (1975), Vol. 5; and Weber (1976), Vol. 6.
13. Büsch (1971a) Vol. 6; Büsch (1971b), Vol. 9; Bergmann (1973), Vol. 11; Thienel (1973), Vol. 3; Lundgreen (1973), Vol. 5; Lundgreen (1975), Vol. 16; Rarisch (1976), Vol. 17; Fischer (1972), Vol. 1.
14. Hoffmann (1965).

15. Abel (1970), Vol. 16; Kaufhold (1976); Kaufhold, in Abel (1968), Vol. 13; Hahn and Zorn (1971); and Kermann (1972), Vol. 82.

16. Tilly (1969), Vol. XXIX, No. 2. p. 298.

17. Borchardt, in Kocka (1976).

18. Tilly (1969), Vol. XXIX, No. 2, p. 301.

19. I have classified according to residence, not to nationality—Richard Tilly himself thus being counted as German.

20. According to information obtained by Prof. Wolfgang Zorn, one of the editors, this is due to a conscious effort of the editors who want to widen the scope and horizon of the journal. About three-quarters of the incoming articles are now being rejected.

21. Kellenbenz (1975), pp. 391–412; *Scripta Mercaturae* (1967 ff).

22. Jaeger (1974), pp. 28–48; Jaeger (1972), pp. 107–124; Kocka (1975), p. 11.

23. For many years Wolfgang Zorn wrote most of the surveys on economic history. This task has now been taken over by Karl-Friedrich Kaufhold at Göttingen.

24. Hastings (1976), pp. 75–101. There exists a program to film the files of the U.S. Military Government for Germany for the *Bundesarchiv* in Koblenz and for some research institutes like the *Institut für Zeitgeschichte* in Munich or the *Zentralinstitut für sozialwissenschaftliche Forschung* of the Free University of Berlin. The *Deutsche Forschungsgemeinschaft* made the immediate postwar German history, including its economic aspects, one of its focuses of research promotion for the next five years.

25. Abelshauser (1975); Mey (1971), pp. 160–186.

26. Winkel (1971, 1974).

27. Borchardt (1966), pp. 253–333, 335–360.

28. Hardach (1976).

29. *Materialien zum Bericht zur Lage der Nation* (1970–1972).

30. Fischer (1976).

31. Aubin and Zorn (1971, 1976).

32. Henning (1973, 1974).

33. Lütge (1952, 1960, 1966); Bechtel (1951, 1952, 1956, 1967); and Mottek (1957, 1964, 1974).

34. The present writer has agreed to write the second volume covering the 19th and 20th centuries. It will appear also in an English language edition at Columbia University Press. But he has still a long way to go.

35. Borchardt (1972, 1973); Hardach (forthcoming).

36. Droege (1972); Engelsing (1973, 1976), Hassinger (1964) pp. 61–98, Köppen (1973).

37. Tilly (1969); Hardach (1972).

38. Wehler (1976), Vols. 1 and 2.

39. *Bevölkerung und Wirtschaft 1872–1972* (1972).

40. Hohorst, Kocka and Ritter (1975), Vol 1. A second volume, covering 1914 to the present, is in preparation, by Dietmar Petzina.

41. Petzina (1969), pp. 308–338.

42. It may be noted that some very useful older statistical compilations have been reprinted: Bratring (1968), Krug (1970), Gülich (1972).

43. Fischer (1972); Kocka (1972a, 1972b, 1972c, 1975a, 1975b); Sarrazin (1974), Wehler (1970, 1973). The literature regarding social history is much broader.

44. Kirchhain (1971).

45. Holtfrerich (1973).

46. Poth (1971).

47. Wagenblass (1973).

48. Fremdling (1975); Hertz-Eichenrode (1969).

49. Spree (1976).

50. von Borries (1970); Kutz (1974).

51. Kellenbenz (1964); Hassinger (1964); Lütge (1963, 1964).

52. Bläsing (1973); Brockstedt (1975); Dane (1971); Köppen (1973); Pitsch (1974); Schawacht (1973).

53. Eyll (1971); Gramulla (1972); Westermann (1971); Bog (1971).

54. *Deutsche Handelsakten des Mittelalters und der Neuzeit* (1923 ff); Scholz-Babisch (1971); Schremmer (1971), Vol. 15; Kellenbenz (1974).

55. Schònfelder (1970), Vol. 1.

56. Baum and Sprandel (1972), 59, pp. 473–488.

57. Hertner (1973), Vol. 8.

58. Fränken (1969), Vol. 19; Herbig (1976), Vol. 3; Maschke and Sydow (1972), Series B, Vol. 69.

59. *Zeitschrift für Stadtgeschichte, Stadtsoziologie und Denkmalpflege* (1974 ff), Vol. 1. It supplements the older *Archiv für Kommunalwissenschaften* (1962 ff), Vol. 1. An example of a case study (Berlin) is Thienel (1973). A more comprehensive study of the urbanization process in Prussia is being prepared by Horst Matzerath, Berlin.

60. Köllmann (1974), Vol. 12.

61. Köllmann and Marschalck (1972), Vol. 54.

62. Marschalck (1973), Vol. 14.

63. von Nell (1973).

64. Hohorst (1974); Augel (1971), Vol. 78.

65. Imhof (1975a), Vol. 31, Parts 1 and 2; Imhof (1975b), pp. 190–227; Imhof and Larsen (1976), Vol. 12.

66. Crew (1975); Knodel (1974); Hubbard (1973); Sabean (1972), Vol. 26. (Sabean is now working at a historical demography of a Württemberg village—Neckarhausen.) Shorter (1972).

67. *Zeitschrift für Agrargeschichte und Agrarsoziologie* (1953 ff).

68. *Quellen und Forschungen zur Agrargeschichte* (1955 ff).

69. Henning (1969a), Vol. XXX; Henning (1969b), Vol. 21; Henning (1970), Vol. 18.

70. Ott (1970), Vol. XXIII.

71. Boelcke (1969), Vol. VIII.

72. Stenle (1971), Thumm (1971), Strobel (1972). See also Sabean (1972).

73. Franz (1962 ff), 5 volumes; Jankuhn (1969), Vol. 1; Abel (1962, 1967), Vol 2; Lütge (1963, 1967), Vol. 3; Franz (1970), Vol. 4; Haushofer (1963, 1972), Vol. 5.

74. Klein (1973), Vol. 1; Abel (1974).

75. For a more recent study of Bavarian agriculture following several studies on southwest Germany's agricultural history, see Schremmer (1972), pp. 42–65.

76. Schremmer (1970). This is a study of 780 pages, which, however, leaves out agriculture.

77. Schremmer (1972), pp. 1–40; (1973), pp. 433–458.

78. André (1971), Vol. 16.

79. Gahlen (1968), Vol. 19; Hesse (1971), Vol. 63, pp. 261–279; von Knorring (1970), Vol. 29; Müller and Geisenberger (1972), Vol. 10. Similar studies by economists outside the "Hoffmann school" are Jeck (1970), Vol. 9; Eistert (1970), Vol. 51.

80. Wehler (1969, ³1972), (1974), Vol. 10; Kocka (1973), Vol. 8; Winkler (1972).

81. Winkler (1973), Vol. 6; (1974), Vol. 9; Puhle (1975), Vol. 16.

82. Maier (1975).

83. This holds true for some of the more radical students of Fritz Fischer. See Krohn (1974), Vol. 13.

84. Witt (1970); Menges (1971), Vol. 7; Maurer (1973), Vol. 1; Hansmeyer (1973); Krosigk (1974). For an earlier period and a more specific topic, see Lenz (1970). Vol. 11. See Herzt-Eichenrode (1969), Vol. 23; Panzer (1970), Vol. 1; (1975), 23, pp. 71–85; Schildt (1975), 14, pp. 128–142; Schremmer (1975), Vol. 23. pp. 216–220.

85. Barmeyer (1971), Vol. XXIV; Kaelble (1967), Vol. 27; Kolb (1973), pp. 343–385; Mielke (1976), Vol. 17; Puhle (1975), Vol. 16; Puhle (1975); (1972), Vol. 54; (1971), pp. 145–162. Saul (1974); Stegmann (1970); Ullmann (1976), Vol. 21.

86. Fechter (1974), Vol. 11.

87. Burchardt (1968), Vol. 6; Ott (1974), pp 333–357.

88. Link (1970); Wandel (1971), Vol. 11; Rupieper (1974).

89. Vogt (1970), Vol. 15.

90. Bade (1975), Vol. 13; Schiefel (1974), Vol. 11; Bald (1970), Vol. 54; Baumgart (1971), 58, pp. 468–481; Bley (1968), Vol. 5; Hausen (1970), Vol. 6; Louis (1971), Vol. 6; Tetzlaff (1970), Vol. 17; Treue (1976), Vol. 26; Washausen (1968), Vol. 23.

91. Gifford and Louis (1967); Austen (1968); Iliffe (1969); Baumgart (1975), Vol. 7.

92. Albertini (1970), Vol. 39; Wehler (1970), Vol. 37; Schröder (1968), pp. 31–103.

93. Very outspoken in the successful textbook by Wehler (1973, 1975). For an elaborate critique of this view see Thomas Nipperdey, "Wehlers Kaiserreich," *Geschichte und Gesellschaft*, 1 (1975), pp. 539–560; and Hans-Günter Zmarzlik, "Das Kaiserreich in Neuer Sicht?" *Historische Zeitschrift*, 222 (1976), pp. 105–126.

94. The most orthodox proponents of this theory of monopoly capitalism are some East-German historians like Gossweiler (1971). The most outspoken opponent is an American. For summaries of these discussions (with all the literature quoted) see Turner, Jr. (1972, 1975a, 1975 b).

95. Speer (1969).

96. Kehrl (1973).

97. Janssen (1968).

98. Jäger (1969); Riedel (1973); Fritz (1974).

99. Ludwig (1974).

100. Forstmeier and Volkmann (1975).

101. Mason (1975).

102. Marcon (1974); Wolffsohn (1975).

103. Hennig (1973); Bettelheim (1974).

104. To these belong those mentioned in footnote 98. See also Hanau and Plate (1975).

105. Swatek (1972).

106. Fischer and Czada (1970), pp. 116–165.

107. Petzina (1973), Vol. 2, pp. 663–784.

108. Blaich (1970, 1973, 1975).

109. Zunkel (1974). Vol. 3.

110. Jaeger (1974).

111. Pölnitz (1971).

112. Stromer (1970).

113. Hildebrandt (1966).

114. Hildebrandt (1971).

115. Kocka (1969).

116. Kocka (1969; 1972; in Winkel, 1975; 1971).

117. Kocka (1975). See also Stahl (1973).

118. Tilly (1974), pp. 145–169.

119. Kaelble (1972).

120. Adelmann (1971), 35, pp. 335–352.

121. Schramm (1969).
122. Kellenbenz and Eyll (1972). A social history of the West German bourgeoisie in the later 19th century has been begun by H.J. Henning. His first volume does not, however, cover—like Zunkel's earlier work on the Rhenish entrepreneurs—businessmen, but intellectuals and civil servants, the *Bildungsbürgertum.* (Henning, 1972).
123. Klein (1971); Coym (1971).
124. Hieke (1971), 16, pp. 16–48.
125. Tilly (1973), 60, pp. 145–165.
126. Tilly (1967), pp. 151–182.
127. Jaeger (1974).
128. Wysocki (1969); Hasselmann (1971).
129. Born (1975).
130. Pohl (1975).

REFERENCES

Abel, Wilhelm (1962, 1967), *Geschichte der deutschen Landwirtschaft vom frühen Mittelalter bis zum 19. Jahrhundert,* Deutsche Agrargeschichte (edited by Franz, G.), Vol. 2, Stuttgart: Eugen Ulmer.

———. (1974), *Massenarmut und Hungerkrisen im vorindustriellen Europa. Versuch einer Synopsis,* Hamburg and Berlin: Paul Parey.

———. (ed.) (1970), *Handwerksgeschichte in neuer Sicht,* Göttinger Handwerkswirtschaftliche Studien, Vol. 16, Göttingen: Schwartz & Co.

Abelshauser, Werner (1975), *Wirtschaft in Westdeutschland 1945–1948. Rekonstruktion und Wachstumsbedingungen in der amerikanischen und britischen Zone,* Schriftenreihe der Vierteljahrshefte für Zeitgeschichte, Vol. 30, Stuttgart: Deutsche Verlags-Anstalt.

Adelmann, Gerhard (1971), "Führende Unternehmer im Rheinland und in Westfalen 1850–1914," *Rheinische Vierteljahrsblätter, 35, pp. 335–352.*

Albertini, Rudolf von (ed.) (1970), *Moderne Kolonialgeschichte,* Neue Wissenschaftliche Bibliothek, Vol. 39, Köln and Berlin: Kiepenheuer & Witsch.

André, Doris (1971), *Indikatoren des technischen Fortschritts. Eine Analyse der Wirtschaftsentwicklung in Deutschland von 1850 bis 1913,* Weltwirtschaftliche Studien (edited by Jürgensen, Harald and Predöhl, Andreas), Vol. 16, Göttingen: Vandenhoeck & Ruprecht.

Archiv für Kommunalwissenschaften (1962ff), (edited by Herzfeld, Hans, Hillebrecht, Rudolf and others, and the Verein zur Pflege kommunalwissenschaftlicher Aufgaben e.V. Berlin, Vol. 1 Stuttgart: W. Kohlhammer; Köln: Deutscher Gemeindeverlag.

Aubin, Hermann and Zorn, Wolfgang, (eds.) (1971), *Handbuch der deutschen Wirtschafts- und Sozialgeschichte,* Vol. I: Von der Frühzeit bis zum Ende des 18. Jahrhunderts, Stuttgart: Union.

———. (1976), *Handbuch der deutschen Wirtschafts- und Sozialgeschichte, Vol. II: Das 19. und 20. Jahrhundert,* Stuttgart: Klett, in Vorbereitung.

Augel, Johannes (1971), *Italienische Einwanderung und Wirtschaftstätigkeit in rheinischen Städten des 17. und 18. Jahrhunderts,* Rheinisches Archiv, Vol. 78, Bonn: Röhrscheid.

Austen, Ralph Albert (1968), *Northwest Tanzania under German and British Rule. Colonial Policy and Tribal Politics, 1889–1939,* New Haven and London: Yale.

Bade, Klaus J. (1975), *Friedrich Fabri und der Imperialismus in der Bismarckzeit.*

Revolution - Depression - Expansion, Beiträge zur Kolonial- und Überseegeschichte, Vol. 13, Freiburg: Atlantis.

Bald, Detlef (1970), *Deutsch-Ostafrika 1900–1914. Eine Studie über Verwaltung, Interessengruppen und wirtschaftliche Erschliebung*, (edited by IFO-Institut für Wirtschaftsforschung München, Afrika-Studienstelle, Afrika-Studien), Vol. 54, München: Weltforum-Verlag.

Barmeyer, Heide (1971), *Andreas Hermes und die Organisationen der deutschen Landwirtschaft. Quellen und Forschungen zur Agrargeschichte*, Vol. XXIV. Stuttgart: Gustav Fischer.

Baum, Hans Peter and Sprandel, Rolf (1972), "Zur Wirtschaftsentwicklung im spätmittelalterlichen Hamburg," *Vierteljahrschrift für Sozial-und Wirtschaftsgeschichte*, 59, pp. 473–488.

Baumgart, Winfried (1975), *Der Imperialismus. Idee und Wirklichkeit der englischen und französischen Kolonialexpansion 1880–1914*, Wissenschaftliche Paperbacks, Sozial- und Wirtschaftsgeschichte (edited by Pohl, Hans), Vol. 7, Wiesbaden: Franz Steiner.

———. (1971), "Die deutsche Kolonialherrschaft in Afrika. Neue Wege der Forschung," *Vierteljahrschrift für Sozial- und Wirtschaftsgeschichte*, 58, pp. 468–481.

Bechtel, Heinrich (1951, 1952, 1956), *Wirtschaftsgeschichte Deutschlands*, 3 vols, München: Georg D.W. Callwey.

———. (1967), *Wirtschafts- und Sozialgeschichte Deutschlands*. Wirtschaftsstile und Lebensformen von der Vorzeit bis zur Gegenwart, München: Georg D.W. Callwey.

Bergmann, Jürgen (1973), *Das Berliner Handwerk in den Frühphasen der Industrialisierung*, Einzelveröffentlichungen der Historischen Kommission zu Berlin, Vol. 11, Berlin: Colloquium Verlag.

Bettelheim, Charles (1974), *Die deutsche Wirtschaft unter dem National-sozialismus*, Müchen: Trikont.

Bevölkerung und Wirtschaft 1872–1972 (1972), herausgegeben anläßlich des 100jährigen Bestehens der zentralen amtlichen Statistik vom Statistischen Bundesamt, Stuttgart and Mainz: Kohlhammer.

Bläsing, Joachim F.E. (1973), *Das goldene Delta und sein eisernes Hinterland 1815–1851. Von niederländisch-preußischen zu deutschniederländischen Wirtschaftsbeziehungen*, Leiden: H.E. Stenfert Kroese.

Blätter für deutsche Landesgeschichte (1864 ff.), edited by Gesamtverein der deutschen Geschichts- und Altertumsvereine, Hannover: Selbstverlag. (Later, im Auftrage des Gesamtvereins der deutschen Geschichts- und Altertumsvereine, edited by Renkhoff, Otto, Wiesbaden: Selbstverlag.)

Blaich, Fritz (1973), *Kartell- und Monopolpolitik im kaiserlichen Deutschland. Das Problem der Marktmacht im Deutschen Reichstag zwischen 1879 und 1914*, Beiträge zur Geschichte des Parlamentarismus und der politischen Parteien, Vol. 50, Düsseldorf: Droste.

———. (1975), *Der Trustkampf (1901–1915). Ein Beitrag zum Verhalten der Ministerialbürokratie gegenüber Verbandsinteressen im Wilhelminischen Deutschland*, Schriften zur Wirtschafts- und Sozialgeschichte, edited by Fischer, Wolfram, Vol. 24, Berlin: Duncker & Humblot.

———. (1970), *Die Wirtschaftspolitik des Reichstags im Heiligen Römischen Reich. Ein Beitrag zur Problemgeschichte wirtschaftlichen Gestaltens*, Schriften zum Vergleich von Wirtschaftsordnungen, edited by Hensel, K. Paul and Pleyer, Klemens, Vol. 16, Stuttgart: Gustav Fischer.

Bley, Helmut (1968), *Kolonialherrschaft und Sozialstruktur in Deutsch-Südwestafrika 1894–1914*, Hamburger Beiträge zur Zeitgeschichte, Vol. 5, Hamburg: Leibniz.

Boelcke, Willi A. (1969), *Verfassungswandel und Wirtschaftsstruktur. Die mittelalter-liche und neuzeitliche Territorialgeschicht ostmitteldeutscher Adelsherrschaften als Beispiel*, Beihefte zum Jahrbuch der schlesischen Friedrich-Wilhelms-Universität zu Breslau, Vol. VIII, Würzburg: Holzner.

Bog, Ingomar (ed.)(1971), *Der Aussenhandel Ostmitteleuropas 1450–1650*, Köln and Wien: Böhlau.

Borchardt, Knut (1966), *Die Bundsrepublik Deutschland* (pp. 253–333) and *Im anderen Teil Deutschland* (pp. 335–360), in Deutsche Wirtschaft seit 1870 (edited by Stolper, Gustav, Hauser, Karl and Borchardt, Knut), Tübingen: J.C.B. Mohr.[2]

Borchardt, Knut (1966), *Die Bundesrepublik Deutschland* (pp. 253–333) and *Im anderen Teil Deutschland* (pp. 335–360), in Deutsche Wirtschaftseit 1870 (edited by Stolper, Gustav, Hauser, Karl and Borchardt, Knut), Tübingen: J.C.B. Mohr.

————. (1972), *Die Industrielle Revolution in Deutschland*, Serie Piper, Vol. 40, München: R. Piper & Co.

————. (1976), Der Property Rights Ansatz in der Wirtschaftsgeschichte - Zeichen für eine systematische Neuorientierung des Faches? in *Theorien in der Sozial- und Wirtschaftsgeschichte*, (ed. by Kocka Jürgen), Beihett, Z.W., Geschichte und Gesellschaft, Göttingen: Vandenhoeck & Ruprecht.

Born, Karl Erich, (1975), *Geld und Banken im 19. und 20. Jahrhundert*, Stuttgart: Alfred Kröner.

Borries, Bodo von (1970), *Deutschland Außenhandle 1836 bis 1856. Eine statistische Untersuchung zur Frühindustrialisierung*, Forschungen zur Sozial- und Wirtschaftsgeschichte (edited by Borchardt, K, Schremmer, E. and Zorn, W., Vol. 13, Stuttgart: Gustav Fischer.

Bratring, F.W.A. (1968), *Statistisch-Topographische Beschreibung der gesamten Mark Brandenburg*, Veröffentlichungen der Historischen Kommission zu Berlin, Vol. 22, Berlin: de Gruyter.

Braun, Hans-Joachim (1974), *Technoligische Beziehungen zwischen Deutschland und England von der Mitte des 17. bis zum Ausgang des 18. Jahrhunderts*, Geschichte und Gessellschafts, Bochumer Historische Studien (edited by Alföldy, Géza, Seibt, Ferdinand und Timm, Albrecht, Düsseldorf: Pädagogischer Verlag Schwann.

Brockstedt, Jürgen (1975), *Die Schiffahrts-und Handelsbeziehungen Schleswig-Holsteins nach Lateinameraka 1815–1848*, Forschungen zur internationalen Social-und Wirtschaftsgeschichte (ed. by Kellenbenz, Hermann), Vol. 10, Köln and Wien: Böhlau.

Burchardt, Lothar (1968), *Friedenswirtschaft und Kriegsvorsorge. Deutschlands wirtschaftliche Rüstungsbestrebungen vor 1914*, Wehrwissenschaftliche Forschungen, Abt. Militärgeschichtliche Studien, (edited by Militärgeschichtliches Forschungsamt), Vol. 6, Boppard/Rh.: Harald Boldt.

————. (1974), *Wissenschaftspolitik im Wilhelminischen Deutschland. Vorgeschichte, Gründung und Aufbau der Kaiser-Wilhelm-Gesellschaft zur Förderung der Wissenschaften*, Studien zu Naturwissenschaft, Technik und Wirtschaft im 19. Jahrhundert (edited by Treue, Wilhelm,) Vol. 1, Göttingen: Vandenhoeck & Ruprecht.

Büsch, Otto (1971), *Industrialisierung und Gewerbe im Raum Berlin/Brandenburg 1800–1850. Eine empirische Untersuchung zur gewerblichen Wirtschaft einer hauptstadtgebundenen Wirtschaftsregion in frühindustrieller Zeit. Mit einer Statistik und einer thematischen Karte zum Jahr 1849*, Einzelveröffentlichungen der Historischen Kommission zu Berlin, Vol. 9, Berlin: Colloquium Verlag.

————. (ed.)(1971), *Untersuchungen zur Geschichte der frühen Industrialisierung vornehmlich im Wirtschaftsraum Berlin/Brandenburg*, Publikationen zur Geschichte der

Industrialisierung, Einzelveröffentlichung der Historischen Kommission zu Berlin, Vol. 6, Berlin: Colloquium Verlag.

Cipolla, Carlo Maria (ed.) (1973), *The Fontana Economic History of Europe,* Vol. 4 (*The Emergence of Industrial Societies*), parts I, II, London: Collins.

Conze, Werner, (ed.) (1976), *Industrielle Welt. Sonderband: Soziale Bewegung und politische Verfassung,* Beiträge zur Geschichte der modernen Welt (edited by Engelhardt, Uwe, Sellin, Volker and Stuke, Horst), Stuttgart: Ernst Klett.

———. (1962, 1970), *Staat und Gesellschaft im deutschen Vormärz 1815–1848,* Industrielle Welt, Schriftenreihe des Arbeitskreises für moderne Sozialgeschichte, Vol. 1, Stuttgart: Ernst Klett.

Conze, Werner and Raupach, Hans (eds.) (1967), *Die Staats- und Wirtschafts-krise des deutschen Reichs 1929/33,* Industrielle Welt, Schriftenreihe des Arbeitskreises für moderne Sozialgeschichte, Vol. 8, Stuttgart: Ernst Klett.

Coym, P. (1971), *Unternehmensfinanzierung im frühen 19. Jahrhundert. Dargestellt am Beispiel der Rheinprovinz und Westfalens,* Diss. Hamburg.

Crew, David Francis (1975), *Industry and Community. The Social History of a German Town, 1860–1914,* Cornell University Ph.D.

Dane, Hendrik (1971), *Die wirtschaftlichen Beziehungen Deutschlands zu Mexiko und Mittelamerika im 19. Jahrhundert,* Forschungen zur internationalen Sozial- und Wirtschaftsgeschichte (edited by Kellenbenz, Hermann), Vol. 1, Köln and Wien: Böhlau.

Droege, Georg (1972), *Deutsche Wirtschafts- und Sozialgeschichte,* Deutsche Geschichte. Ereignisse und Probleme (edited by Hubatsch, Walther), Frankfurt/M./Berlin/Wein: Ullstein.

Eistert, Ekkehard (1970), *Die Beeinflussung des Wirtschaftswachstums in Deutschland von 1883 bis 1913 durch das Bankensystem. Eine theoretisch-empirische Untersuchung.* Untersuchungen über das Spar-, Giro- und Kreditwesen (edited by Voigt, Fritz, Vol. 51, Berlin: Duncker & Humblot.

Engelsing, Rolf (1973), *Sozial- und Wirtschaftsgeschichte Deutschlands,* Göttingen: Vandenhoech & Ruprecht. (Also in bibliographisch erweiterte Auflage 1976 in Vorbereitung.)

Eyll, Clara van (1971), *Die Kupfermeister im Stolberger Tal. Zur wirtschaftlichen Aktivität einer religiösen Minderheit,* Kölner Vorträge zur Sozial- und Wirtschaftsgeschichte (edited by Kellenbenz, H.), Vol. 17, Köln: Selbstverlag Forschungsinstitut für Sozial- und Wirtschaftsgeschichte an der Universität zu Köln.

Fechter, Ursula (1974), *Schutzzoll und Goldstandard im Deutschen Reich (1849–1914) Der Einfluß der Schutzzollpolitik auf den internationalen Goldwährungsmechanismus,* Neue Wirtschaftsgeschichte, (edited by Bog, Ingomar), Vol. 11, Köln/Wien: Böhlau.

Fischer, Wolfram (in Vorbereitung), *Bergbau, Industrie und Handwerk 1914–1972,* in Aubin, Hermann and Zorn, Wolfgang, Handbuch der deutschen Sozial- und Wirtschaftsgeschicht, Vol. II.

———. (1972), *Sozialgeschichte und Wirtschaftsgeschichte. Abgenzungen und Zusammenhänge,* in Soziologie und Sozialgeschichte. Aspekte und Probleme. Kölner Zeitschrift für Soziologie und Sozialpsychologie, Sonderheft 16, pp. 132–152, Opladen: Westdeutscher Verlag.

———. (1972), (edited by Ritter, Gerhard A.), *Wirtschaft und Gesellschaft im Zeitalter der Industrialisierung. Aufsätze - Studien - Vorträge,* Kritische Studien zur Geschichtswissenschaft, Vol. 1, Göttingen: Vandenhoeck & Ruprecht.

Fischer, Wolfram (ed.) (1971), *Beiträge zu Wirtschaftswachstum und Wirtschaftsstruktur*

im 16. und 19. Jahrhundert, Schriften des Vereins für Socialpolitik. Gesellschaft für Wirtschafts- und Sozialwissenschaften, Neue Folge, Vol. 63, Berlin: Duncker & Humblot.

Fischer, Wolfram und Czada, Peter (1970), "Wandlungen in der deutschen Industriestruktur im 20. Jahrhundert. Ein statistisch-deskriptiver Ansatz," in *Entstehung und Wandel der modernen Gesellschaft. Festschrift für Hans Rosenberg zum 65. Geburtstag* (edited by Ritter, Gerhard A.), pp. 116–165, Berlin: de Gruyter.

Forstmeier, Friedrich and Volkmann, Hans-Erich (eds.) (1975), *Wirtschaft und Rüstung am Vorabend des Zeiten Weltkrieges,* Düsseldorf: Droste.

Fränken, Willy (1969), *Die Entwicklung des Gewerbes in den Städten Möchengladbach und Rheydt im 19. Jahrhundert,* Schriften zur Rheinisch-Westfälischen Wirtschaftsgeschichte, Vol. 19, Köln: Rheinisch-Westfälisches Wirtschaftsarchiv.

Franz, Günther (ed.) (1963, 1970–1972), *Deutsche Agrargeschichte,* 5 vols. Stuttgart: Eugen Ulmer.

———. (1972), *Beamtentum und Pfarrerstand 1400–1800,* Deutsche Führungsschichten in der Neuzeit, Vol. 5, Limburg and Lahn: C.A. Starke.

———. (1975), *Bauernschaft und Bauernstand 1500–1970. Büdinger Vorträge 1971–72,* Deutsche Führungsschichten in der Neuzeit, Vol. 8, Limburg and Lahn: C.A. Starke.

———. *Deutsche Führungsschichten in der Neuzeit. Vorträge der jährlichen "Büdinger Tagungen."* Limburg and Lahn: C. A. Starke

———. (1970), *Geschichte des deutschen Bauernstandes vom frühen Mittelalter bis zum 19. Jahrhundert,* Deutsche Agrargeschichte (edited by Franz, G., Vol. 4, Stuttgart: Eugen Ulmer.

Fremdling, Rainer (1975), *Eisenbahnen und deutsches Wirtschafts-wachstum 1840–1879. Ein Beitrag zur Entwicklungstheorie und zur Theorie der Infrastruktur,* Unterschungen zur Wirtschafts-, Sozial- und Technikgeschichte (edited by the Gesellschaft für Westfälische Wirtschaftsgeschichte e. V), Vol. 2, Dortmund: Ardey.

Freudenberger, Herman and Mensch, Gerhard (1975), *Von der Provinzstadt zur Industrieregion (Brünn Studie). Ein Beitrag zur Politökonomie der Sozialinnovation, dargestellt am Innovationsschub der industriellen Revolution im Raume Brünn,* Studien zum Wandel von Gesellschaft und Bildung im Neunzehnten Jahrhundert (edited by Neuloh, O. and Rüegg, W.), Vol. 13, Göttingen: Vandenhoeck & Ruprecht.

Fritz, Martin (1974), *German Steel and Swedish Iron Ore 1939–1945,* Göteborg: The Institute of Economic History of Gothenburg University.

Gahlen, Bernhard (1968), *Die Überprüfung produktionstheoretischer Hypothesen für Deutschland 1850–1913,* Schriften zur angewandten Wirtschaftsforschung (edited by Hoffman, Walther G.), Vol. 19, Tübingen: J.C.B. Mohr.

Gifford, Prosser and Louis, William Roger (eds.) (1967), *Britain and Germany in Africa, Imperial Rivalry and Colonial Rule,* New Haven and London: Yale.

Gossweiler, Kurt (1971), *Großbanken - Industriemonopole - Staat. Ökonomie und Politik des staatsmonopolistischen Kapitalismus in Deutschland 1914–1932,* Berlin-East: VEB Deutscher Verlag der Wissenschaften.

Gramulla, Gertrud Susanna (1972), *Handelsbeziehungen Kölner Kaufleute zwischen 1500 and 1650,* Forschungen zur internationalen Sozial- und Wirtschaftsgeschichte (edited by Kellenbenz, Hermann), Vol. 4, Köln and Wien: Böhlau.

Gülich, Gustav von (1972), *Geschichtliche Darstellung des Handels, der Gewerbe und des Ackerbaus der bedeutendsten handeltreibenden Staaten unserer Zeit.* Bd. 1/2, 3/4, 5, Tabellarische Übersichten der Bde. 1-5. Unveränderter Nachdruck d. 1830 b. Friedrich Frommann in Jena erschienenen Ausgabe, Graz: Akad. Druck- und Verlagsanstalt.

Hahn, H. and Zorn, Wolfgang, unter Jansen, Mitarbeit von H. und Krings, W. (1971), *Wirtschaftskarte der Rheinlande um 1820*. Rheinisches Archiv, Vol. 87, und Arbeiten zur rheinisches Landeskunde, Vol. 37, Bonn: Röhrscheid.

Hanau, Arthur and Plate, Roderich (1975), *Die deutsche landwirtschaftliche Preis- und Marktpolitik im Zweiten Weltkrieg*, Quellen und Forschungen zur Agrargeschichte, Vol. 28, Stuttgart: Gustav Fischer.

Deutsche Handelsakten des Mittelalters und der Neuzeit (edited by Historische Kommission bei der Bayerischen Akademie der Wissenschaften) (1923 ff), Wiesbaden: Franz Steiner. Vol. 12: Scholz-Babisch, Marie, Quellen zur Geschichte des Klevischen Rheinzollwesens vom 11. bis 18. Jh., 1971, part I; Vol. 13: Scholz-Babisch, Marie, Quellen zur Geschichte des Klevischen Rheinzollwesens vom 11. bis 18. Jh., 1971, part II; Vol. 14: Schremmer, Eckart (ed.), Handelsstrategie und betriebswirtschaftliche Kalkulation im ausgehenden 18. Jh. Der süddeutsche Salzmarkt, 1971; Vol. 15: Kellenbenz, Hermann (ed.), Handelsbräuche des 16. Jh. Das Medersche Handelsbuch und die Welserschen Nachträge, 1974.

Hansmeyer, Karl-Heinrich (ed.), (1973), *Kommunale Finanzpolitik in der Weimarer Republik*, Stuttgart: Kohlhammer.

Hardach, Karl (1976), *Wirtschaftsgeschichte Deutschlands im 20. Jahrhundert*, Göttingen: Vandenhoech & Ruprecht.

Hasselmann, Erich (1971), *Geschichte der deutschen Konsumgenossenschaften*, Frankfurt: Fritz Knapp.

Hassinger, Herbert (1964), *Der Außenhandel der Habsburger Monarchie in der zweiten Hälfte des 18. Jahrhunderts*, in Lütge, Friedrich (ed.), Die wirtschaftliche Situation in Deutschland und Österreich um die Wende vom 18. zum 19. Jahrhundert, pp. 61–98, Stuttgart: Gustav Fischer.

Hastings, James J. (1976), "Die Akten des Office of Military Government for Germany (US)," *Vierteljahrshefte für Zeitgeschichte*, Vol. 24, part I, pp. 75–101.

Hausen, Karin (1970), *Deutsche Kolonialherrschaft in Afrika. Wirtschaftsinteressen und Kolonialverwaltung in Kamerun vor 1914*, Beiträge zur Kolonial- und Überseesgeschichte (edited by Albertini, R. von and Gollwitzer, H.), Vol. 6, Zürich and Freiburg: Atlantis.

Haushofer, Heinz (1963, 1972), *Die deutsche Landwirtschaft im technischen Zeitalter*, Deutsche Agrargeschichte (edited by Franz, G.), Vol. 5, Stuttgart: Eugen Ulmer, 2., verb. Auflage.

Heggen, Alfred (1975), *Erfindungsschutz und Industrialisierung in Preussen 1793–1877*. Studien zu Naturwissenschaft, Technik und Wirtschaft im 19. Jahrhundert (edited by Treue, Wilhelm), Vol. 5, Göttingen: Vandenhoeck & Ruprecht.

Helbig, Herbert (ed.) (1974), *Führungskräfte der Wirtschaft in Mittelalter und Neuzeit 1790–1918. Büdinger Vorträge*, Deutsche Führungsschichten in der Neuzeit (edited by Franz, G.), Vol. 7, Limburg and Lahn: C. A. Starke.

———. (1973), *Führungskräfte der Wirtschaft in Mittelalter und Neuzeit 1350–1850. Büdinger Vorträge 1968–1969*, part I, Deutsche Führungsschichten in der Neuzeit, Vol. 6 (edited by Franz, G.), Limburg and Lahn: C. A. Starke.

Hennig, Eike (1973), *Thesen zur deutschen Sozialgeschichte und Wirtschaftsgeschichte 1933–1938*, Edition Suhrkamp, Vol. 662, Frankfurt and Main: Suhrkamp.

Henning, Friedrich-Wilhelm (1969), *Bauernwirtschaft und Bauerneinkommen in Ostpreußen im 18. Jahrhundert;* Beihefte zum Jahrbuch der Albertus-Universität Konigsberg/Pr., Vol. XXX, Würzberg: Holzner.

———. (1970), *Bauernwirtschaft und Bauerneinkommen im Fürstentum Paderborn im 18. Jahrhundert*, Schriften zur Wirtschafts- und Sozialgeschichte (edited by Fischer, Wolfram), Vol. 18, Berlin: Duncker & Humblot.

————. (1970), *Bauernwirtschaft und Bauerneinkommen im Fürstentum Paderborn im 18. Jahrhundert*, Schriften zur Wirtschafts- und Sozialgeschichte (edited by Fischer, Wolfram), Vol. 18, Berlin: Duncker & Humbolt.

————. (1969), *Dienste und Abgaben der Bauern im 18. Jahrhundert*, Quellen und Forschungen zur Agrargeschichte, Vol. XXI, Stuttgart: Gustav Fischer.

————. (1974, 1973, 1974), *Das vorindustrielle Deutschland 800–1800*, Wirtschafts- u. Sozialgeschichte, Vol. 1, Paderborn: Ferdinand Schöningh; *Die Industrialisierung in Deutschland 1800–1914*, Wirtschafts- u. Sozialgeschichte, Vol. 2, Paderborn: Ferdinand Schöningh; *Das industrialisierte Deutschland 1914–1972*, Wirtschafts- u. Sozialgeschichte, Vol. 3, Paderborn: Ferdinand Schöningh.

Henning, Hans-Joachim (1972), *Das westdeutsche Bürgertum in der Epoche der Hochindustrialisierung 1860–1914. Soziales Verhalten und soziale Strukturen*. Part I: *Das Bildungsbürgertum in den preussischen Westprovinzen*. Historische Forschungen im Auftrage der Historischen Kommission der Akademie der Wissenschaften und Literatur, Mainz, Vol. VI, Wiesbaden: Steiner.

Herbig, Wolfgang (1976), *Wirtschaft und Bevölkerung der Stadt Lüdenscheid im 19. Jahrhundert*, Untersuchungen zur Wirtschafts-, Sozial- ung Technikgeschichte (edited by the Gesellschaft für Westfälische Wirtschaftsgeschichte), Vol. 3, Dortmund: Ardey.

Hertner, Peter (1973), *Stadtwirtschaft zwischen Reich und Frankreich. Wirtschaft und Gesellschaft Straßburgs 1650–1714*, Neue Wirtschaftsgeschichte (edited by Bog, Ingomar), Vol. 8, Köln and Wien: Böhlau.

Hertz-Eichenrode, Dieter (1969), *Politik und Landwirtschaft in Ostpreußen 1919–1930. Untersuchungen eines Strukturproblems in der Weimarer Republik*, Schriften des Instituts für Politische Wissenschaft (edited by Stammer, O.), Vol. 23, Köln and Opladen: Westdeutscher Verlag.

Hesse, Helmut (1971), "Die Entwicklung der regionalen Einkommensdifferenzen im Wachstumsprozß der deutschen Wirtschaft vor *1913*," in Fischer, Wolfram (ed), *Beiträge zu Wirtschaftswachstum und Wirtschaftsstruktur im 16. und 19. Jahrhundert*, Schriften des Vereins für Socialpolitik, N.F.., Vol. 63, pp. 261–279, Berlin: Duncker & Humblot.

Hieke, Ernst (1971), "Gründung, Kapital und Kapitalgeber der Deutsch- Amerikanischen Petroleum-Gesellschaft (DAPG) 1890–1904. Ein Beitrag zur Geschichte des internationalen und zur Finanzie-rung des deutschen Petroleumhandels," *Tradition. Zeitschrift für Firmengeschichte und Unternehmerbiographie*, 16, pp. 16–48.

Hildebrandt, Reinhard (1971), *Diener und Herren*. Eine historisch-statistische Untersuchung zur Entstehung der kaufmännischen Angestelltenschaft am Beispiel des Personals der großen oberdeutschen Handelshäuser 1450–1650. Unpublished Habilitationsschrift, FU Berlin.

————. (1966), *Die "Georg Fuggerischen Erben." Kaufmännische Tätigkeit und sozialer Status 1555–1600*, Schriften zur Wirtschafts- und Sozialgeschichte (edited by Fischer, W.), Vol. 6, Berlin: Duncker & Humblot.

Hoffmann, Walther G. (1965), unter Grumbach, Mitarbeit von Franz und Hess, Helmut *Das Wachstum der deutschen Wirtschaft seit der Mitte des 19. Jahrhunderts*, Enzyklopädie der Rechts- und Staats-wissenschafts, Abt. Staatswissenschaft, Berlin and Heidelberg and New York: Springer.

Hohorst, Gerd, Kocka, Jürgen and Ritter, Gerhard A. (eds.) (1975), *Sozial- geschichtliches Arbeitsbuch. Materialien zur Statistik des Kaiserreichs 1870–1914*, Statistische Arbeitsbücher zur neueren deutschen Geschichte (edited by Kocka, Jürgen and Ritter, Gerhard A.), Müchen: C. H. Beck.

———. (1974), *Entwicklung und Entwicklungstendenzen des demographischen und ökonomischen Systems im Kreise Hagen 1814–1913*, Diss. Münster.

Holtfrerich, Carl-Ludwig (1973), *Quantitative Wirtschaftsgeschichte des Ruhrkohlenbergbaus im 19. Jahrhundert. Eine Führungssektoranalyse*, Untersuchungen zur Wirtschafts-, Sozial- und Technikgeschichte (edited by the Gesellschaft für Westfälische Wirtschaftsgeschichte), Vol. 1, Dortmund: Ardey.

Hubbard, William Henry (1973), *A Social History of Graz, Austria 1861–1914*, Columbia University: Ph. Diss., History modern.

Iliffe, John (1969), *Tanganyika under German Rule 1905–1912*, Cambridge.

Imhof, Arthur E. (1975), "Demographische Stadtstrukturen der frühen Neuzeit. Gießen in seiner Umgebung im 17. und 18. Jahrhundert als Fallstudie," *Zeitschrift für Stadtgeschichte, Stadtsoziologie und Denkmalpflege*, 2, pp. 190–227.

Imhof, Arthur E. (ed.) (1975), *Historische Demographie als Sozialgeschichte. Gießen und Umgebung vom 17. zum 19. Jahrhundert*, Quellen und Forschungen zur hessischen Geschichte, Vol. 31, parts 1 and 2, Darmstadt and Marburg: Selbstverlag der Hessischen Historischen Kommission Darmstadt und der Historischen Kommission für Hessen.

Imhof, Arthur E. and Larsen, Øivind (1976), *Sozialgeschichte und Medizin. Probleme der quantifizierenden Quellenbearbeitung in der Sozial- und Medizingeschichte*, Medizin in Geschichte und Kultur (edited by Rothschuh, K.E.), Vol. 12, Oslo: Universitetsforlaget. Stuttgart: Gustav Fischer.

Jaeger, Hans (1974), "Business History in Germany: A Survey of Recent Developments," *Business History Review*, XLVIII, pp. 28–48.

———. (1974), "Business History in Germany," *Business History Review XLVIII*, p. 34, footnote 15: Festschriften.

———. (1972), "Gegenwart und Zukunft der historischen Unternehmerforschung," *Tradition*, 17, pp. 107–124.

Jäger, Jörg-Johannes (1969), *Die wirtschaftliche Abhängigkeit des Dritten Reiches vom Ausland, dargestellt am Beispiel der Stahlindustrie*, Berlin: Berlin Verlag.

Jankuhn, Herbert (1969), *Vor- und Frühgeschichte vom Neolithikum bis zur Völkerwanderungszeit*, Deutsche Agrargeschichte (edited by Franz, Günther), Vol. 1, Stuttgart: Eugen Ulmer.

Janssen, Gregor (1968), *Das Ministerium Speer. Deutschlands Rüstung im Krieg*, Berlin: Ullstein.

Jeck, Albert (1970), *Wachstum und Verteilung des Volkseinkommens. Untersuchungen und Materialien zur Entwicklung der Einkommensverteilung in Deutschland 1870–1913*, Tübinger Wirtschaftswissenschaftliche Abhandlungen, Vol. 9, Tübingen: J.C.B. Mohr.

Kaelble, Hartmut (1967), *Industrielle Interessenpolitik in der Wilhelminischen Gesellschaft. Centralverband Deutscher Industrieller 1895–1914*, Veröffentlichungen der Historischen Kommission zu Berlin, Vol. 27, Berlin: de Gruyter.

———. (1972), *Berliner Unternehmer während der frühen Industrialisierung. Herkunft, sozialer Status und Politischer Einfluß*, Veröffentlichungen der Historishen Kommission zu Berlin, Vol. 40, Berlin: de Gruyter.

Kaufhold, Karl Heinrich (1976), *Das Gewerbe in Preußen um 1800*, Göttinger Handwerkswirtschaftliche Studien, Göttingen: Schwartz & Co.

———. (1968), *Das Handwerk der Stadt Hildeschim im 18. Jahrhundert. Eine wirtschaftsgeschichtliche Studie*, Göttinger Handwerkswirtschaftliche Studien (edited by Abel, W.), Vol. 13, Göttinger: Schwartz & Co.

Kehrl, Hans (1973), *Krisenmanager im Dritten Reich. 6 Jahre Frieden - 6 Jahre Krieg, Erinnerungen*, Düsseldorf: Drost.

Kellenbenz, Hermann (1964), "Der deutsche Außenhandel gegen Ausgang des 18. Jahrhundert," in Lütge, Friedrich (ed.), Die wirtschaftliche Situation in Deutschland und Österreich um die Wende vom 18. zum 19. Jahrhundert, pp.4–6, Stuttgart: Gustav Fischer.

——. (1975), "Theodor Gustave Werner und die Zeitschrift Scripta Mercaturae," *Vierteljahrschrift für Sozial- und Wirtschaftsgeschichte*, 62, pp. 391–412.

Kellenbenz, Hermann (ed.) (1975), *Agrarisches Nebengewerbe und Formen der Reagrarisierung im Spätmittelalter und 19./20. Jahrhundert*, Forschungen zur Sozial- und Wirtschaftsgeschichte (edited by Borchardt, K., Schremmer, E. and Zorn, W.), Vol. 21, Stuttgart: Gustav Fischer.

——. (1971), *Öffentliche Finanzen und privates Kapital im späten Mittelalter und in der ersten Hälfte des 19. Jahrhunderts*, Forschungen zur Sozial -und Wirtschaftsgeschichte (edited by Borchardt, K., Schremmer, E., and Zorn, W.), Vol. 16, Stuttgart: Gustav Fischer.

——. (1974), *Handelsbräuche des 16. Jahrhunderts. Das Medersche Handelsbuch und die Welserschen Nachträge*, Deutsche Handelsakten des Mittelalters und der Neuzeit (edited by Historische Kommission bei der Bayerischen Akademie der Wissenschaften), Vol. XV, Wiesbaden: Franz Steiner.

——. (1974), *Wirtschaftspolitik und Arbeitsmarkt, Bericht über die 4. Arbeitstagung der Gesellschaft für Sozial- und Wirtschaftsgeschichte in Wien am 14. und 15. April 1971*, Sozial- und wirstchaftshistorische Studien, Müchen: Oldenbourg.

Kellenbenz, Hermann and Eyll, Klara van (1972), *Die Geschichte der unternehmerischen Selbstverwaltung in Köln 1797–1914*, Hrsg. aus Anlaß des 175jährigen Bestehens der Industrie- und Handelskammer zu Köln am 8. November 1972, Köln: Rheinisch-Westfälisches Wirtschaftsarchiv zu Köln.

Kermann, Joachim (1972), *Die Manufakturen im Rheinland 1750–1833*, Rheinisches Archiv, Vol. 82, Bonn: Röhrscheid.

Kirchhain, Günter (1971), *Das Wachstum der deutschen Baumwollindustrie im 19. Jahrhundert*, Diss. Münster.

Klein, Ernst (1971), "Zur Frage der Industriefinanzierung im frühen 19. Jahrhundert," in Kellenbenz, Hermann (ed.), *Öffentliche Finanzen und privates Kapital im späten Mittelalter und in der ersten Hälfte des 19. Jahrhunderts; Forschungen zur Sozial- und Wirtschaftsgeschichte* (edited by Borchardt, K., Schremmer, E. and Zorn, W.), Vol. 16, pp. 118–128, Stuttgart: Gustav Fischer.

——. (1973), *Geschichte der deutschen Landwirtschaft im Industriezeitalter*, Wissenschaftliche Paperbacks Sozial- und Wirtschaftsgeschichte (edited by Pohl, Hans), Vol. 1, Wiesbaden: Franz Steiner.

Knodel, John E. (1974), *The Decline of Fertility in Germany 1871–1939*, Princeton: Princeton UP.

Knorring, Ekkehard von (1970), *Die Berechnung makroökonomischer Konsumfunktionen für Deutschland 1851–1913*, Schriften zur angewandten Wirtschaftsforschung (edited by Hoffmann, W.G.), Vol. 29, Tübingen: J.C.B. Mohr.

Kocka, Jürgen (1975), "Expansion - Integration - Diversifikation. Wachstumsstrategien industrieller Großunternehmen in Deutschland vor 1914," in Winkel, Harald (ed.), Vom Kleingewerbe zur Großindustrie. Quantitativ-regionale und politisch-rechtliche Aspekte zur Erforschung der Wirtschafts- und Gesellschaftsstruktur im 19. Jahrhundert. *Schriften der Vereins für Socialpolitik*, N.F., Vol. 83, pp. 203–226, Berlin: Duncker & Humblot.

———. (1971), "Family and Bureaucracy in German Industrial Management; 1850–1914: Siemens in Comparative Perspective," *Business History Review*, XLV, pp. 133–156.

———. (1969), "Industrielles Management: Konzeptionen und Modelle in Deutschland vor 1914," *Vierteljahrschrift für Sozial- und Wirtschaftsgeschichte*, 56, pp. 332–373.

———. (1973), *Klassengesellschaft im Krieg. Deutsche Sozial- geschichte 1914–1918*, Kritische Studien zur Geschichtswissenschaft, Vol. 8, Göttingen: Vandenhoeck & Ruprecht.

———. (1972), "Siemens und der aufhaltsame Aufstieg der AEG," *Tradition. Zeitschrift für Firmengeschichte und Unternehmerbiographie*, 17, pp. 125–142.

———. (1975), "Sozialgeschichte - Strukturgeschichte - Gesellschaftsgeschichte," *Archiv für Sozialgeschichte*, XV, pp. 1–42.

———. (1972), "Sozial - und Wirtschaftsgeschichte," in Kernig, Claus Dieter (ed.), *Sowjetsystem und demokratische Gesellschaft*, Eine vergleichende Enzyklopädie, Vol. 6, pp. 5–7, Freiburg/Basel/Wien: Herder.

———. (1975), "Recent historiography of Germany and Austria. Theoretical Approaches to Social and Economic History of Modern Germany: Some Recent Trends, Concepts and Problems in Western and Eastern Germany," *Journal of Modern History*, 47, pp. 101–119.

———. (1972), "Theorieprobleme der Sozial- und Wirtschaftsgeschichte. Begriffe, Tendenzen und Funktionen in West und Ost." in Wehler, Hans-Ulrich (ed.), *Geschichte und Soziologie*, Neue Wissenschaftliche Bibliotek, Vol. 53, pp. 305–330, Köln: Keipenheuer & Witsch.

———. (1969), *Unternehmensverwaltung und Angestelltenschaft am Beispiel Siemens 1847–1914. Zum Verhältnis von Kapitalismus und Bürokratie in der deutschen Industrialisierung*, Industrielle Welt, Schriftenreihe des Arbeitskreises für moderne Sozialgeschichte (edited by Conze, W.), Vol. 11, Stuttgart: Ernst Klett.

———. (1975), *Unternehmer in der deutschen Industrialisierung*, Göttingen: Vandenhoeck & Ruprecht.

Kolb, Eberhard (1973), "Ökonomische Interessen und politischer Entscheidungsprozeß. Zur Aktivität deutscher Wirtschaftskreise und zur Rolle wirtschaftlicher Erwägungen in der Frage von Annexion und Grenzziehung 1870/71," *Vierteljahrschrift für Sozial- und Wirtschaftsgeschichte*, 60, pp. 343–385.

Köllmann, Wolfgang (1974), *Bevölkerung in der industriellen Revolution. Studien zur Bevölkerungsgeschichte Deutschlands*, Kritische Studien zur Geschichtswissenschaft (edited by Berding, H. Kocka, J., Schröder, H.-Chr. and Wehler, H.-U.), Vol. 12, Göttingen: Vanderhoeck & Ruprecht.

Köllmann, Wolfgang and Marschalck, Peter (eds.) (1972), *Bevölkerungsgeschichte*, Neue Wissenschafliche Bibliotek, Vol. 54, Köln: Kiepenheuer & Witsch.

Köppen, Heinrich Ernst (1973), *Die Handelsbeziehungen Hamburgs zu den Vereinigten Staaten von Nordamerika bis zur Mitte des 19. Jahrhundert*, Diss. Köln.

Krohn, Claus-Dieter (1974), *Stabilisierung und ökonomische Interessen. Die Finanzpolitik des Deutschen Reiches 1923–1927*, Studien zur modernen Geschichte (edited by Fischer, F., Grothusen, K.D. and Moltmann, G.), Vol. 13, Düsseldorf: Bertelsmann Universitätsverlag.

Kroker, Evelyn (1975), *Die Weltausstellungen im 19. Jahrhundert. Industrieller Leistungsnachweis, Konkurrenzverhalten und Kommunikationsfunktion unter Berücksichtigung der Montanindustrie des Ruhrgebiets zwischen 1851 und 1880*, Studien zu Naturwissenschaft, Technik und Wirtschaft im 19. Jahrhundert. (edited by Treue, Wilhelm), Vol. 4, Göttingen: Vandenhoeck & Ruprecht.

Kroker, Werner (1971), *Wege zur Verbreitung technologischer Kenntnisse zwischen Eng-*

land und Deutschland in der zweiten Hälfte des 18. Jahrhunderts, Schriften zur Wirtschafts-und Sozialgeschichte (edited by Fischer, Wolfram), Vol. 19, Berlin: Duncker & Humblot.

Krug, Leopold (1970), *Betrachtungen* über den Nationalreichtum des preußischen Staates und über den Wohlstand seiner Bewohner. In zwei Teilen, Neudruck der Ausgabe Berlin 1805, Aalen: Scientia Verlag.

Kutz, Martin (1974), Deutschlands Außenhandel von der Französischen Revolution bis zur Gründung des Zollvereins. Eine statistische Strukturuntersuchung zur vorindustriellen Zeit, *Vierteljahrschrift für Sozial- und Wirschaftsgeschichte,* (edited by Brunner, O., Kellenbenz, H., Pohl, H., Maschke, E., Zorn, W.), Beihefte No. 61, Wiesbaden: Franz Steiner.

Lenz, Rudolf (1970), *Kosten und Finanzierung des Deutsch- Französischen Krieges 1870–1871. Dargestellt am Beispiel Württembergs, Badens und Bayerns,* Wehrwissenschaftliche Forschungen, Abt. Militärgeschichtliche Studien, Vol. 11, Boppard a. Rh.: Harald Boldt.

Link, Werner (1970), *Die amerikanische Stabilisierungspolitik in Deutschland 1921–32,* Düsseldorf: Droste.

Louis, William Roger (1971), *Das Ende des deutschen Kolonialreiches. Britischer Imperialismus und die deutschen Kolonien 1914–19,* Studien zur modernen Geschichte, Vol. 6, Düsseldorf: Bertelsmann Univ.-Verlag.

Ludwig, Karl-Heinz (1974), *Technik und Ingenieure im Dritten Reich,* Düsseldorf: Droste.

Lundgreen, Peter (1973), *Bildung und Wirtschaftswachstum im Industrialisierungsprozeß des 19. Jahrhunderts. Methodische Ansätze, empirische Studien und internationale Vergleiche,* Historische und Pädagogische Studien (edited by Büsch, Otto and Heinrich, Gerd), Vol. 5, Berlin: Colloquium-Verlag.

————. (1975), *Techniker in Preußen während der Frühen Industrialisierung. Ausbildung und Berufsfeld einer entstehenden sozialen Gruppe,* Einzelveröffentlichungen der Historischen Kommission zu Berlin, Vol. 16, Berlin: Colloquium-Verlag.

Lütge, Friedrich (1963,1967), *Geschichte der deutschen Agrarverfassung vom Frühen Mittelalter bis zum 19. Jahrhundert,* Deutsche Agrargeschichte (edited by Franz, G.), Vol. 3, Stuttgart: Eugen Ulmer.

————. (1952), *Deutsche Sozial- und Wirtschaftsgeschichte,* Ein Überblick. Enzyklopädie der Rechts- und Staatswissenschaft, Abt. Staatswissenschaft; 2. wesentlich vermehrte und verbesserte Auflage, 1960; 3. wesentlich vermehrte und verbesserte Auflage, 1966, Berlin/Göttingen/Heidelberg: Springer.

Lütge, Friedrich (ed.) (1968), *Wirtschaftliche und soziale Probleme der gewerblichen Entwicklung im 15.-16. und 19. Jahrhundert,* Forschungen zur Sozial- und Wirtschaftsgeschichte (edited by Lütge, F.), Vol. 10, Stuttgart: Gustav Fischer.

————. (1964), *Die wirtschaftliche Situation in Deutschland und Österreich um die Wende vom 18. zum 19. Jahrhundert,* Bericht über die Erste Arbeitstagung der Gesellschaft für Sozial- und Wirtschaftsgeschichte in Mainz, 4.-6. März 1963, Forschungen zur Sozial- und Wirtschaftsgeschichte (edited by Lütge, F.), Vol. 6, Stuttgart: Gustav Fischer.

Maier, Charles S. (1975), *Recasting Bourgeois Europe: Stabilization in France, Germany and Italy in the Decade after World War I,* Princeton.

Marcon, Helmut (1974), *Arbeitsbeschaffungspolitik der Regierungen Papen und Schleicher. Grundsteinlegung für die Beschäftigungspolitik im Dritten Reich,* Moderne Geschichte und Politik (edited by Schulz, Gerhard, Born, K. Erich and Scholder, Klaus), Bern: Herbert Lang; Frankfurt/Main: Peter Lang.

Marschalck, Peter (1973), *Deutsche Überseewanderung im 19. Jahrhundert. Ein Beitrag*

zur soziologischen Theorie der Bevölkerung, Industrielle Welt. Schriftenreihe des Arbeitskreises für moderne Sozialgeschichte (edited by Conze, Werner), Vol. 14, Stuttgart: Ernst Klett.

Maschke, Erich and Sydow, J. (eds.), (1972), *Städtische Mittelschichten,* Protokoll der 8. Arbeitstagung des Arbeitskreises für südwestdeutsche Stadtgeschichtsforschung. Veröffentlichungen der Kommission für geschichtliche Landeskunde Baden-Württembergs, series B, Vol. 69, Stuttgart: Kohlhammer.

Mason, Timothy W. (1975), *Arbeiterklasse und Volksgemeinschaft. Dokumente und Materialien zur deutschen Arbeiterpolitik 1936–1939,* Schriften des Zentralinstituts für sozialwissenschaftliche Forschung der Freien Universität Berlin, Vol. 22, Opladen: Westdeutscher Verlag.

Materialien zum Bericht zur Lage der Nation (1974 ff), edited by Ministerium f. innerdeutsche Beziehungen, Berlin: Elsnerdruck; Bonn: Selbstverlag. (Earlier, 1970–1972), under the title *Bericht der Bundesregierung und Materialien zur Lage der Nation,* edited by Bundesministerium f. innerdeutsche Beziehungen, Bonn: Selbstverlag.

Maurer, Ilse (1973), *Reichsfinanzen und Große Koalition. Zur Geschichte des Reichskabinetts Müller* (1928–1930), Moderne Geschichte und Politik, Vol. 1, Bern/ Frankfurt a.M.: Herbert Lang.

Menges, Franz (1971), *Reichsreform und Finanzpolitik. Die Aushöhlung der Eigenstaatlichkeit Bayerns afu finanzpolitischem Wege in der Zeit der Weimarer Republik,* Beiträge zu einer historischen Strukturanalyse Bayerns im Industriezeitalter (edited by Bosl, K.), Vol. 7, Berlin: Duncker & Humblot.

Mey, Harald (1971), "Marktwirtschaft und Demokratie. Betrachtungen zur Grundlegung der Bundesrepublik," in VfZG, 19, pp. 160–186.

Mielke, Siegfried (1976), *Der Hansa-Bund für Gewerbe, Handel und Industrie 1909–1914. Der gescheiterte Versuch einer antifeudalen Sammlungspolitik,* Kritische Studien zur Geschichtswissenschaft, Vol. 17, Göttingen: Vandenhoeck & Ruprecht.

Mommsen, Hans, Petzina, Dietmar and Weisbrod, Bernd (eds.) (1974), *Industrielles System und politische Entwicklung in der Weimarer Republik. Verhandlungen des Internationlen Symposiums in Bochum vom 12.-17. Juni 1973,* Düsseldorf: Droste.

Panzer, Arno (1975), "Industrie und Landwirtschaft in Deutschland im Spiegel der Außenwirtschafts- und Zollpolitik von 1870 bis heute," in *Zeitschrift für Agrargeschichte und Agrarsoziologie,* 231, pp. 71–85.

———. (1970), *Das Ringen um die deutsche Agrarpolitik von der Währungsstabilisierung bis zur Agrardebatte im Reichstag im Dezember 1928,* Beiträge zur Sozial- und Wirtschaftsgeschichte (edited by Koppe, W.), Vol. 1, (Kiel: Kommissionsverlag Walter G. Mühlau.

Petzina, Dieter (1969), "Materialien zum sozialen und wirtschaftlichen Wandel in Deutschland seit dem Ende des 19. Jahrhunderts," in *Vierteljahrschefte für Zeitgeschichte,* (edited by Rothfels, H. and Eschenburg, Th.), 17, pp. 308–338.

———. (1973), *Grundriß der deutschen Wirstchaftsgeschichte 1918–1945,* in Institut für Zeitgeschichte (edited by Deutsche Geschichte seit dem Ersten Weltkrieg), Vol. 2, pp. 663–784, Stuttgart: Deutsche Verlagsanstalt.

Pfetsch, Frank R. (1974), *Zur Entwicklung der Wissenschaftspolitik in Deutschland 1750–1914,* Berlin: Duncker & Humblot.

Pfetsch, Frank R. (ed.) (1975), *Innovationsforschung als multidisziplinäre Aufgabe. Beiträge zur Theorie und Wiklichkeit von Innovationen im 19. Jahrhundert,* Studien zum Wandel von Gesellschaft und Bildung im 19. Jahrhundert, Vol. 14, Göttingen: Vandenhoeck & Ruprecht.

Pitsch, Franz Josef (1974), *Die wirtschaftlichen Beziehungen Bremens zu den Vereinigten Staaten von Amerika bis zur Mitte des 19. Jahrhunderts*, Veröffentlichungen aus dem Staatsarchiv der Freien Hansestadt Bermen, Vol. 42, Bremen: Selbstverlag.

Pohl, Manfred (ed.) (1975), *Banhistorisches Archiv Zeitschrift zur Bankengeschichte*, Vol. 1, Frankfurt/M:Fritz Knapp.

Pölnitz, Götz Freiherr von (1971), *Anton Fugger*, Vol. 3, 1548–1560, Part I, 1548–1554; Schwäbische Forschungsgemeinschaft bei der Kommission für bayerische Landesgeschichte, series 4, Vol. 13; Studien zur Fuggergeschichte, Vol. 22, Tübingen: J.C.B. Mohr.

Poth, L. (1971), *Die Stellung des Steinkohlenbergbaus im Industrialisierungsprozeß unter besonderer Berücksichtigung des Ruhrgebietes*, Schriftenreihe zur Industrie- und Entwicklungspolitik (edited by Voigt, F.), Vol. 7, Berlin: Duncker & Humblot.

Puhle, Hans-Jürgen (1967, 1975), *Agrarische Interessenpolitik und preußischer Konservativismus im wilhelminischen Reich (1893–1914). Ein Beitrag zur Analyse des Nationalismus in Deutschland am Beispiel des Bundes der Landwirte und der Deutsch-Konservativen Partei*, Schriftenreihe des Forschungsinstituts der Friedrich-Ebert-Stiftung, Vol. B, Historisch-Politische Schriften, Hannover: Verlag f. Literatur und Zeitgeschehen, Bonn: 2nd ed.

————. (1972), *Von der Agrarkrise zum Präfaschismus. Thesen zum Stellenwert der agrarischen Interessenverbände in der deutschen Politik am Ende des 19. Jahrhunderts*, Institut f. Europäische Geschichte, Mainz, Vorträge, Vol. 54, Wiesbaden: Franz Steiner.

————. (1971), *Der Bund der Landwirte im Wilhelminischen Reich–Struktur, Ideologie und politische Wirksamkeit eines Interessenverbandes in der konstitutionellen Monarchie (1893–1914)*, in Rüegg, Walter and Neuloh, Otto (eds.), Zur soziologischen Theorie und Analyse des 19. Jahrhunderts, pp. 145–162, Göttingen: Vandenhoeck & Ruprecht.

————. (1974, 1975), *Politische Agrarbewegungen in kapitalistischen Industriegesellschaften. Deutschland, USA und Frankreich im 20. Jahrhundert*, Kritische Studien zur Geschichtswissenschaft, Vol. 16, Hab. Schr. Univ. Münster, FB Geschichte, Göttingen: Vandenhoeck & Ruprecht.

Quellen und Forschungen zur Agrargeschichte (edited by Abel, W., Franz, G. and Lütge F.) (since 1955), Stuttgart: Gustav Fischer.

Rarisch, Ilsedore (1976), *Das Unternehmerbild in der deutschen Erzählliteratur der ersten Hälfte des 19. Jahrhunderts*, Veröffentlichungen der Historischen Kommission zu Berlin, Berlin: Colloquium Verlag.

Riedel, Matthias (1973), *Eisen und Kohle für das Dritte Reich. Paul Pleigers Stellung in der NS–Wirtschaft*, Göttingen/Frankfurt/Zürich: Musterschmidt.

Rüegg Walter and Neuloh, Otto (eds.) (1971), *Zur soziologischen Theorie und Analyse des 19. Jahrhunderts*, Studien zum Wandel von Gesellschaft und Bildung im Neunzehnten Jahrhundert, Vol. 1, Göttingen: Vandenhoeck & Ruprecht.

Rupieper, Hermann-Josef (1974), *Politics and Economics. The Cuno Government and Reparations 1922/1923*, Ph. Diss. Stanford.

Sabean, David (1972), *Landbesitz und Gesellschaft am Vorabend des Bauernkrieges. Eine Studie der sozialen Verhältnisse im südlichen Oberschwaben in den Jahren vor 1525*, Quellen und Forschungen zur Agrargeschichte (edited by Abel, W. and Franz, G.), Vol. 26, Stuttgart: Gustav Fischer.

Sarrazin, Thilo (1974), *Ökonomie und Logik der historischen Erklärung. Zur Wissenschaftslogik der New Economic History*, Schriftenreihe des Forschungsinstituts der Friedrich-Ebert-Stiftung, Vol. 109, Bonn-Bad Godesberg: Verlag Neue Gesellschaft.

Saul, Klaus (1974), *Staat, Industrie, Arbeiterbewegung im Kaiserreich. Zur Innen- und Außenpolitik des Wilhelminischen Deutschland 1903–1914*, Düsseldorf: Bertelsmann Universitätsverlag.

Schawacht, Jürgen Heinz (1973), *Schiffahrt und Güterverkehr zeischen den Häfen des deutschen Niederrheins (insbes. Köln) und Rotterdam vom Ende des 18. bis zur Mitte des 19. Jahrhunderts (1794–1850/51)*, Schriften zur Rheinisch-Westfälischen Wirtschaftsgeschichte, Vol. 26, Köln: Rheinisch-Westfälisches Wirtschaftsarchiv.

Schiefel, Werner (1974), *Bernhard Dernburg 1865–1937. Kolonialpolitiker und Bankier im wilhel minischen Deutschland*, Beiträge zur Kolonial- und Überseegeschichte, (edited by Albertini, R. V., und Gollwitzer, H.), Vol. 11, (Zurich/Freiburg: Atlantis.

Schildt, Gerhard (1975), *Die Auswirkungen der deutschen Agrarzölle unter Bismarck und Caprivi auf den russischen Getreide-export*, in Jahrbuch für die Geschichte Mittel- und Ost-deutschlands, 14, pp. 128—142.

Scholz-Babisch, Marie (1971), *Quellen zur Geschichte des Klevischen Rheinzollwesens vom 11. bis 18. Jahrhundert, Erste und Zweite Hälfte*, Deutsche Handelskaten des Mittelalters und der Neuzeit (edited by Historische Kommission bei der Bayerischen Akademie der Wissenschaften), Vols. XII and XIII: Deutsche Zolltarife des Mittelalters und der Neuzeit, parts III and IV, Wiesbaden: Franz Steiner.

Schönfelder, Wilhelm (1970), *Die wirtschaftliche Entwicklung Kölns von 1370–1513. Dargestellt mit linearen Trendfunktionen samt Analyse inhrer Bestimmungsfaktoren*, Neue Wirtschaftsgeschichte, (edited by Bog, Ingomar), Vol. 1, Köln/Wien:Böhlau.

Schramm, Percy Ernst (1969), *Gewinn und Verlust. Die Geschichte der Hamburger Senatorenfamilien Jencquel und Luis (16. bis 19. Jahrhundert)*. Zwei Beispiele für den wirtschaftlichen und sozialen Wandel in Norddeutschland; Veröffentlichung des Vereins für Hamburgische Geschichte, Vol. XXIV, Hamburg: Christians.

Schremmer, Eckart (1972), "Agrarverfassung und Wirtschaftsstruktur. Die südostdeutsche Hofmark- eine Wirtschaftsherrschaft?" in *Zeitschrift für Agrargeschichte und Agrarsoziologie*, 20, pp. 42–65.

———. (1975), "Über den Faktoreinsatz in der deutschen (Land-) Wirtschaft in der 2. Hälfte des 19. Jahrhunderts. Industrialisierung, wirtschaftliche Rückständigkeit und strukturstabilisierender Fortschritt," in *Zeitschrift für Agrargeschichte und Agrarsoziologie*, Vol. 23, pp. 216–220.

———. (1972), "Standortausweitung der Warenproduktion im langfristigen Wirtschaftswachstum. Zur Stadt-Land- Arbeitsteilung im Gewerbe des 18. Jahrhunderts," *Vierteljahrschrift für Sozial- und Wirtschaftsgeschichte*, 59, pp. 1–40.

———. (1973), "Wie groß war der 'technische Fortschritt' während der Industriellen Revolution in Deutschland 1850—1913?", *Vierteljahrschrift für Sozial- und Wirtschaftsgeschichte*, 60, pp. 433–458.

———. (1970), *Die Wirtschaft Bayerns. Vom hohen Mittelalter bis zum Beginn der Industrialisierung. Bergbau, Gewerbe, Handel*, München: C. H. Beck.

Schriften zur Rheinisch-Westfälischen Wirtschaftsgeschichte (1959 ff), N.F. der Veröffentlichungen des Archivs für Rh.-Westfälische Wirtschaftsgeschichte, Verlag Rheinisch-Westfälisches Wirtschaftssarchiv zu Köln.

Scripta Mercaturae, Halbjahresveröffentlichung von Urkunden und Abhandlungen zur Geschichte des Handels und der Weltwirtschaft, München: Eigenverlag, 1967 ff.

Schröder, Hans-Christoph (1968), *Karl Marx, Friedrich Engels und das Problem des Imperialismus*, in Sozialismus und Imperialismus. Die Auseinandersetzung der deutschen Sozialdemokratie mit dem Imperialismusproblem und der "Weltpolitik" vor 1914, part I; Schriftenreihe des Forschungsinstituts der Friedrich-Ebert-Stiftung, Vol. B, Historischpolitische Schriften, Hannover: Verlag f. Literatur und Zeitgeschehen, pp. 31–103.

Schwerin von Krosigk, Lutz Graf (1974), *Staatsbankrott. Die Geschichte der Finanzpolitik des Deutschen Reiches von 1920 bis 1945*, geschrieben vom letzten Reichsfinanzminister, Göttingen/Zürich/Frankfurt: Musterschmidt.

Shorter, Edward (1972), *"La vie intime." Beiträge zu seiner Geschichte am Beispiel des kulturellen Wandels in den bayerischen Untershchichten im 19. Jahrhundert*, in Ludz, P.Chr., Soziologie und Sozialgeschichte, Opladen: Westdt. Verl.

Speer, Albert (1969), *Erinnerungen*, Berlin: Propyläen.

Spree, Reinhard (1976), *Die Wachstumszyklen der deutschen Wirtschaft von 1840 bis 1880*, Schriften zur Wirtschafts- und Sozialgeschichte (edited by Fischer, W.), Berlin: Duncker & Humblot.

Stahl, Wilhelm (1973), *Der Elitekreislauf in der Unternehmerschaft. Eine empirische Untersuchung für den deutschsprachigen Raum*, Frankfurt/M., Zürich: Harri Deutsch.

Stegmann, Dirk (1970), *Die Erben Bismarcks. Parteien und Verbände in der Spätphase des Wilhelminischen Deutschlands. Sammlungspolitik 1897–1918*, Berlin/Köln: Kiepenheuer & Witsch.

Steitz, Walter (1976), *Feudalwesen und Staatssteursystem. Vol. 1: Due Realbesteuerung der Landwirtschaft in den süddeutschen Staaten im 19. Jahrhundert*, Studien zu Naturwissenschaft, Technik und Wirtschaft im 19. Jahrhundert (edited by Treue, Wilhelm), Vol. 7, Göttingen: Vandenhoeck & Ruprecht.

Stenle, Peter (1971), *Die Vermögensverhältnisse der Landbevölkerung in Hohenlohe im 17. und 18. Jahrhundert*, wirtschaftswiss. und sozialwiss, Diss., Hohenheim.

Strobel, Albrecht (1972), *Agrarverfassung im Übergang. Studien zur Agrargeschichte des Badischen Breisgaus vom Beginn des 16. bis zum Ausgang des 18. Jahrhunderts*, Forschungen zur Oberrheinischen Landesgeschichte, Freiburg/München: Karl Alber.

Stromer, Wolfgang von (1970), *Oberdeutsche Hochfinanz 1350–1450*, 3 vols., Vierteljahrschrift für Sozial- und Wirtschaftsgeschichte, Beihefte 55—57, Wiesbaden: Franz Steiner.

Swatek, Dieter (1972), *Unternehmenskonzentration als Ergebnis und Mittel nationalsozialistischer Wirtschaftspolitik*, Volkswirtschaftliche Schriften (edited by Broermann, J.), Vol. 181, Berlin: Duncker & Humblot.

Tetzlaff, Rainer (1970), *Koloniale Entwicklung und Ausbeutung. Wirtschafts- und Sozialgeschichte Deutsch-Ostafrikas 1885–1914*, Schriften zur Wirtschafts- und Sozialgeschichte (edited by Fischer, W.), Vol. 17, Berlin: Duncker & Humblot.

Teuteberg, Hans-Jürgen and Wiegelmann, Günter (1972), *Der Wandel der Nahrungsgewohnheiten unter dem Einfluß der Industrialisierung*, Studien zum Wandel von Gesellschaft und Bildung im 19. Jahrhundert, Vol. 3, Göttingen: Vandenhoeck & Ruprecht.

Thienel, Ingrid (1973), *Städtewachstum im Industrialisierungsprozeß des 19. Jahrhunderts. Das Berliner Beispiel*, Veröffentlichungen der Historischen Kommission zu Berlin, Vol. 39; Publikationen zur Geschichte der Industrialisierung, Vol. 3, Berlin: Walter de Gruyter.

Thumm, Gustav Adolf (1971), *Die bäuerlichen und dörflichen Rechtsverhältnisse des Fürstentums Hohenlohe im 17. und 18. Jahrhundert*, agrarwissenschaftliche Diss., Hohenheim.

Tilly, Richard (1973), "Zur Entwicklung des Kapitalmarktes und Industrialisierung im 19. Jahrhundert unter besonderer Berücksichtigung Deutschlands," in *Vierteljahrschrift für Sozial- und Wirtschaftsgeschichte*, 60, pp. 145–165.

———. (1967), *Germany, 1815–1870*, in Cameron, Rondo (ed.), *Banking in the Early Stages of Industrialization*, pp. 151–182, New York: Oxford UP.

————. (1974), *The Growth of Large-Scale Enterprise in Germany*, in Daems, Herman and Wee, Herman van der (eds.), *The Rise of Managerial Capitalism*, pp. 145–169, Den Haag: Leuven UP.

————. (1969), *Soll und Haben:* Recent German Economic History and the Problem of Economic Development, in *The Journal of Economic History*, XXIX, No. 2, pp. 298–319.

Tradition (1956 ff), Zeitschrift für Firmengeschichte und Unternehmerbiographie, Baden-Baden: August Lutzeyer.

Treue, Wilhelm und Mauel, Kurt (eds.) (1976), *Naturwissenschaft, Technik und Wirtschaft im 19. Jahrhundert.* Acht Gespräche der Georg-Agricola-Gesellschaft zur Forderung der Geschichte der Naturwissenschaften und der Technik, Studien zu Naturwissenschaft, Technik und Wirtschaft im 19. Jahrhundert, Vols. 2 and 3, Göttingen; Vandenhoeck & Ruprecht.

Treue, Wolfgang (1976), *Die Jaluit-Gesellschaft auf den Marshall-Inseln 1887–1914.* Ein Beitrag zur Kolonial- und Verwaltungsgeschichte in der Epoche des deutschen Kaiserreichs, Schriften zur Wirtschafts- und Sozialgeschichte, Vol. 26, Berlin: Duncker & Humblot.

Turner, Jr., Henry Ashby (1972), *Faschismus und Kapitalismus in Deutschland,* Studien zum Verhältnis zwischen Nationalsozialismus und Wirtschaft, Göttingen: Vandenhoeck & Ruprecht.

————. (1975a), "Großunternehmertum und Nationalsozialismus 1930–33. Kritishches und Ergänzendes zu zwei neuen Forschungsbeiträgen," in *Historische Zeitschrift,* 221, pp. 18–68.

————. (ed.) (1975b), *Reappraisals of fascism.* Edited with an introduction, New York: New Viewpoints, A division of Franklin Watts.

Ullmann, Hans-Peter (1976), *Der Bund der Industriellen.* Organisation, Einfluß und Politik klein- und mittelbetrieblicher Industrie im Deutschen Kaiserreich 1895–1914; Kritische Studien zur Geschichtswissenschaft, Vol. 21, Göttingen: Vandenhoeck & Ruprecht.

Vierteljahrschrift (1903 ff), für Sozial- und Wirtschaftsgeschichte, Wiesbaden: Franz Steiner.

Vierteljahrshefte (1953 ff), für Zeitgeschichte herausgg. im Auftrag des Instituts für Zeitgeschichte München von Hans Rothfels and Theodore Eschenburg, Stuttgart: Deutsche Verlagsanstalt.

Rheinische Vierteljahrsblätter (1935 ff), (edited by Meisen, Karl and Weisgerber, Franz Steinbach L.; later by Besch, W., Ennen, E., Lewald, U. and Zender, M.), Mitteilungen d. Instituts f. geschichtl. Landeskunde der Rheinlande an der Universität Bonn, Bonn: Röhrscheid.

Vogt, Martin (ed.) (1970), *Die Entstehung des Youngplans, dargestellt vom Reichsarchiv 1931–1933,* Schriften des Bundesarchivs, Vol. 15, Boppard/Rh.: Harald Boldt.

Wagenblass, Horst (1973), *Der Eisenbahnbau und das Wachstum der deutschen Eisen- und Maschinenbauindustrie 1835 bis 1860.* Ein Beitrag zur Geschichte der Industrialisierung Deutschlands, Forschungen zur Sozial- und Wirtschaftsgeschichte (edited by Borchardt, K., Schremmer, E. and Zorn, W.), Vol. 18, Stuttgart: Gustav Fischer.

Wandel, Eckhard (1971), *Die Bedeutung der Vereinigten Staaten von Amerika für das deutsche Reparationsproblem 1924–1929,* Tübinger Wirtschaftswissenschaftliche Abhandlungen, Vol. 11, Tübingen: J.C.B. Mohr.

Washausen, Helmut (1968), *Hamburg und die Kolonialpolitik des Deutschen Reiches 1880–1890,* Veröffentlichungen des Vereins für Hamburgische Geschichte, Vol. 23, Hamburg: Hans Christians.

Weber, Wolfhard (1976), *Innovationen im frühindustriellen deutschen Bergbau und Hüttenweisen* (Friedrich Anton von Heynitz), Studien zu Naturwissenschaft, Technik und Wirtschaft im 19. Jahrhundert (edited by Treue, Wilhem), Vol. 6, Göttingen: Vandenhoeck & Ruprecht.

Wehler, Hans-Ulrich (1974), *Der Aufstieg des amerikanischen Imperialismus. Studien zur Entwicklung des Imperium Americanum 1865–1900*, Kritische Studien zur Geschichtswissenschaft, Vol. 10, Göttingen: Vandenhoeck & Ruprecht.

————. (1976), *Bibliographie zur modernen deutschen Sozialgeschichte, 18.–20. Jahrhundert*, Arbeitsbücher zur modernen Geschichte, Vol. 1, Göttingen: Vandenhoeck & Ruprecht.

————. (1976), *Bibliographie zur modernen deutschen Wirtschaftsgeschichte*, Arbeitsbücher zur modernen Geschichte, Vol. 2, Göttingen: Vandenhoeck & Ruprecht.

————. (1969, 1972), *Bismarck und der Imperialismus*, Köln/Berlin: Kiepenheuer & Witsch.

————. (1973, 1975), *Das deutsche Kaiserreich, 1871–1914*, Deutsche Geschichte (edited by Leuschner, J.), Vol. 9, Göttingen; Vandenhoeck & Ruprecht.

————. (1970), "Theorieprobleme der modernen deutschen Wirtschaftsgeschichte (1800–1945)," in Ritter, Gerhard A. (ed.), *Entstehung und Wandel der modernen Gesellschaft. Festischrift für Hans Rosenberg zum 65. Geburtstag*, pp. 66–107, Berlin: de Gruyter.

Wehler, Hans-Ulrich, (ed.) (1973), *Geschichte und Ökonomie*, Köln: Kiepenheuer & Witsch.

————. (1970) *Imperialismus*, Neue Wissenschaftliche Bibliothek, Vol. 37, Köen/Berlin: Kiepenheuer and Witsch.

Westermann, Ekkehard (1971), *Das Eislebener Garkupfer und seine Bedeutung für den europäischen Kupfermarkt 1460–1560*, Köln/Wien: Böhlau.

Winkel, Harald (1971), *Die deutsche Wirtschaft seit Kriegsende. Entwicklung und Probleme*, Mainz: Hase & Koehler.

————. (1974), *Die Wirtschaft im geteilten Deutschland 1945–1970*, Wissenschaftliche Paperbacks (edited by Pohl, Hans), Vol. 4: Sozial- und Wirtschaftsgeschichte, Wiesbaden: Steiner.

Winkel, Harald (ed.) (1975), *Vom Kleingewerbe zur Großindustrie. Quantitativ-regionale und politisch-rechtliche Aspekte zur Erforschung der Wirtschafts- und Gesellschaftsstruktur im 19. Jahrhundert*, Schriften des Vereins für Social- politik, Gesellschaft für Sozial- und Wirtschaftswissenschaften, Neue Folge, Vol. 83, Berlin: Duncker & Humblot.

————. (1973), *Finanz- und wirtschaftspolitische Fragen der Zwischenkriegszeit*, Schriften des Vereins für Socialpolitik. Gesellschaft für Sozial- und Wirschaftswissenschaften, Neue Folge, Vol. 73, Berlin: Duncker & Humblot.

Winkler, Heinrich August (1972), *Mittelstand, Demokratie und Nationalsozialismus. Die politische Entwicklung von Handwerk und Kleinhandel in der Weimarer Republik*, Köln: Kiepenheuer & Witsch.

Winkler, Heinrich August (ed.) (1974), *Organisierter Kapitalismus. Voraussetzungen und Anfänge*, Kritische Studien zur Geschichtswissenschaft, Vol. 9, Göttingen: Vandenhoeck & Ruprecht.

————. (1973), *Die Große Krise in Amerika. Vergleichende Studien zur politischen Sozialgeschichte 1929–1939*, Kritische Studien zur Geschichtswissenschaft, Vol. 6, Göttingen: Vandenhoeck & Ruprecht.

Witt, Peter Christian (1970), *Die Finanzpolitik des Deutschen Reiches von 1903 bis 1913*. Eine Studie zur Innenpolitik des Wilhelminischen Deutschland, Historische Studien (edited by Berges, W. *et al*), Lübeck/Hamburg: Matthiesen.

Wolffsohn, Michael (1975), *Industrie und Handwerk im Konflikt mit staatlicher Wirtschaftspolitik? Studien zur Politik der Arbeitsbeschaffung in Deutschland 1930– 1934*, unpublished Diss. Berlin.

Wysocki, Josef (1969), *Zahlungsverkehr und Mittelstandsidee. Zum Wirken von Johann Christian Eberle nach dem Ersten Wiltkrieg*, Untersuchungen über das Spar-, Giro- und Kreditwesen, Vol. 41, Berlin: Duncker & Humblot.

Zeitschrift für Agrargeschichte und Agrarsoziologie (since 1953), (edited by Franz, Günther), Frankfurt/M: DLG-Verlag.

Zeitschrift für die gesamte Staatswissenschaft (1844 ff), (edited by Böhm, Franz *et al.*), Tübingen: J.C.B. Mohr.

Zeitschrift für Stadtgeschichte, Stadtsoziologie und Denkmalpflege (1974 ff), (edited by Borst, Otto), Vol. 1, Stuttgart: Kohlhammer.

Zeitschrift für Wirtschafts- und Sozialwissenschaften (1972 ff). Earlier, Schmollers Jahrbuch für Gesetzgebung, Verwaltung und Volkswirtschaft im Deutschen Reich (edited by Kruse, Alfred); since 1974, edited by the Gesellschaft für Wirtschafts- und Sozialwissenschaften, Berlin: Duncker & Humblot.

Zunkel, Friedrich (1974), *Industrie und Staatssozialismus. Der Kampf um die Wirtschaftsordnung in Deutschland 1914–1918*, Tübinger Schriften zur Sozial- und Zeitgeschichte (edited by Schulz, G.), Vol. 3, Düsseldorf: Droste.

COMPARATIVE ECONOMIC HISTORY

Rondo Cameron, EMORY UNIVERSITY

Comparative economic history, long the object of lip service, has in recent years begun to mature into a recognizable subdiscipline. Its problems, primarily methodological, have by no means all been resolved, but genuine progress has been achieved. This chapter is not intended as a comprehensive bibliographic survey—the literature is much too large and dispersed for that—but traces the main outlines of the development of the subject, gives pertinent examples drawn from recent publications and focuses on selected problems of methodology.[1] The Appendix lists articles that are more or less explicitly comparative at the international level published since 1965 in the principal English-language journals of economic history; it does not list articles that are comparative at the subnational level, although a number of those exist as well.

I. ANTECEDENTS AND EARLY DEVELOPMENT

Both parent disciplines have prepared the way for the use of the comparative method in economic history. Since the 1920's courses in comparative economic systems have become standard fare in most economics departments, with a consequent proliferation of textbooks on the subject. Recently a special conference was devoted to the methodological problems of the comparison of economic systems, resulting in the publication of a book on the subject.[2] Moreover, since

about 1950 scholarly concern with the problems of underdeveloped countries has stimulated a greater interest in alternative methods of economic organization. Influences from general history are much older, however, and have been, on the whole, more decisive in formulating the methodological problems and procedures for comparative economic history.

Interest in the comparison of social institutions is as old as written history itself, as Fritz Redlich pointed out in his lucid survey of the subject almost two decades ago.[3] Herodotus, Thucydides and Plutarch, as well as Aristotle, made comparative observations on social phenomena. Plutarch's *Lives*, in fact, was intended as comparative biography. Casual, impressionistic, frequently implicit comparisons occasionally appeared in the writings of subsequent historians. Nevertheless, not much was done to systematize or formalize the comparative method until the eighteenth or even the nineteenth century. Even then the most effective catalysts came from outside the field of history: from anthropology (or what was to become anthropology), jurisprudence, comparative religion, geology, even anatomy and botany.

Probably the single most influential statement of the virtues of the comparative method in history was Marc Bloch's address to the International Congress of Historical Sciences in Oslo in 1928.[4] Although he addressed historians in general, Bloch drew most of his illustrative material from the fields of economic and social history, of which he was a master. Bloch's driving interest was in the causes of social phenomena, causes not merely in the sense of historical origins, but also in terms of theoretical or scientific explanation—the "why" of things.

According to Bloch, the comparative method in history could be applied in two distinct ways. It could, in the first place, be applied to "societies far removed from one another in time or space."[5] The goals of such comparisons would be to discover uniformities in human nature or social institutions that are independent of time and place, or to overcome gaps in documentation "by hypotheses based on analogies," a kind of grand "procedure of interpolation of lines of development."[6]

The second type of comparison, the one that Bloch himself favored, is "that in which the units of comparison are societies that are geographical neighbors and historical contemporaries, constantly influenced by one another."[7] This type of comparison aims: (1) to test hypotheses with respect to the causes of historical events and the functions of social institutions; (2) to discover the uniqueness of different societies (this is not a paradox; one cannot know what is unique about a society until one knows what it has in common with other societies); and (3) to assist in formulating problems for historical research.[8]

Bloch's plea for, and demonstration of the utility of, the comparative method was widely applauded. Nevertheless, until after World War II almost no works envinced Bloch's influence except those written by himself, notably *Les caractères originaux de l'histoire rurale française*[9] and *La société féodale*.[10] Among

the significant exceptions to the above generalization were a series of remarkable articles and a small book by J. U. Nef: "A Comparison of Industrial Growth in France and England from 1540 to 1640,"[11] "Prices and Industrial Capitalism in France and England, 1540–1640"[12] and *Industry and Government in France and England, 1540–1640*.[13] (Another apparent exception—actually published before Bloch's address—is J. H. Clapham's well-known and durable *Economic Development of France and Germany, 1815–1914*,[14] although it is actually an example of "parallel history" rather than comparative history. Insofar as it employs comparisons, they are more often with Britain than between France and Germany.)

Since its formation in 1940, the Economic History Association has from time to time directed the attention of its members to comparative economic history. At the sixth annual meeting in 1946 one session was devoted to the subject, with papers on "Other Wests than Ours" by Herbert Heaton[15] and "Inner Asian Frontiers" by Owen Lattimore.[16] At the seventeenth annual meeting in 1957, more famous for having launched the controversy on the economics of slavery and what eventually became known as cliometrics, an entire day was devoted to discussion of comparative economic history, with principal papers by Sylvia Thrupp and W. T. Easterbrook.[17] Finally, at the thirty-fourth annual meeting in 1974, under the presidency of Miss Thrupp, the entire program was devoted to "Comparative Economic History: Promises and Problems."[18]

Meanwhile, in 1958, Miss Thrupp founded a new journal, *Comparative Studies in Society and History*, in the expectation that it would become not only a forum for the publication of comparative articles but also a workshop where theoretical and methodological tools would be refined and honed. Response to the latter expectation has been disappointing, on the whole. The practitioners of the comparative method do not appear to be especially concerned about the theoretical bases of their enterprise. This might indicate that all is well, theoretically speaking; but even a casual acquaintance with the literature suggests otherwise.

An equally or even more powerful impulse toward comparative economic history, at least among economists, came from the work of Simon Kuznets. After establishing himself as the *doyen* of national income accountants and expert on the economic growth of the United States, Kuznets turned after World War II to a series of wide-ranging research efforts in the field of international quantitative comparisons of economic growth. These efforts resulted in the publication of two magisterial volumes, *Modern Economic Growth: Rate, Structure, and Spread*[19] and *The Economic Growth of Nations: Total Output and Production Structure*.[20] Along the way, Kuznets inspired dozens of students and colleagues to similar work. As chairman of the Committee on Economic Growth of the Social Science Research Council, he was directly responsible for the production of a number of volumes featuring international comparisons;[21] as principal instigator of the International Association for Research in Income and Wealth, he was indirectly

responsible for several volumes of historical national accounts for individual countries which form the basis for uniform international comparisons.[22] Other significant works in the Kuznets tradition, although not directly inspired by him, are *Why Growth Rates Differ* by Edward F. Denison[23] and *Economic Growth in the West* by Angus Maddison.[24]

II. RECENT DEVELOPMENTS

In recent years the proliferation of books and articles that might, by some stretch of the imagination, be labeled as comparative economic history has been such that no single scholar can hope to comprehend them all. Some of them are self-consciously comparative in a methodological sense; the majority are not, or are only haphazardly so. The following brief survey is restricted to examples primarily from the former category and, for convenience, to those that involve international comparisons. There is no valid reason why the comparative method should not be applied to phe nomena of less than national scope; indeed, as I shall argue in the methodological sections, there are many good reasons why it should be. But some limits are necessary in so brief a survey, and the international comparisons illustrate all the main problems.

Almost any textbook or general work that covers more than one country contains the elements for international comparisons. Usually, however, the comparisons are not made explicit; it is up to the reader to draw such inferences as he can from the material presented. This is especially true of such collaborative works as the *Cambridge Economic History of Europe* and the *Fontana Economic History of Europe*. Although some of the contributors seek to make overtly comparative judgments within their fields of specialization, most do not. The problem is exemplified in Volumes 3 and 4 of the *Fontana Economic History*. Volume 3, *The Industrial Revolution*, consists of topical chapters on population, the labor force, patterns of demand, the role of the state, and so on, and chapters devoted to sectors of the economy (agriculture, banking, the service sector—but, curiously, not manufacturing as such). Some of the authors make brief comparisons in passing; yet, in the one chapter that might be regarded as the heart of the volume, "Technological Progress and the Industrial Revolution, 1750–1914," by Samuel Lilley, the author focuses almost exclusively on Great Britain, and that mainly in the late eighteenth and early nineteenth centuries. Volume 4, *The Emergence of Industrial Societies*, covers virtually the same chronological era as Volume 3, but is given over almost entirely to country-by-country treatment, each in a separate chapter (except for "The Low Countries, 1700–1914," by Jan Dhondt and Marinette Bruwier, and "The Nordic Countries, 1850–1914," by Lennart Jör-berg). The result is that, except for Jörberg's excellent comparative study of Denmark, Norway, Sweden and Finland, what we have is a series of "parallel histories" rather than true comparative history.

Comparison should be facilitated when a book is the product of a single author, or of a very few who, working in close collaboration, consciously attend to the comparative aspects of their subject. Bagwell and Mingay, for example, introduce their elementary text as follows: "While textbooks that deal with Britain and America separately abound, there is, so far as we are aware, no book that compares the two countries' development over even so limited a period as we have selected. . . . The attempt that we make in this volume is therefore something of an elementary pioneer effort in comparative economic history."[25]

Few other authors of textbooks with which I am familiar are so explicit about their method, but some achieve good results nevertheless. While Ralph Davis makes no statement about the comparative method in *The Rise of the Atlantic Economies*,[26] he is clearly aware of its existence and utility. Similarly, Milward and Saul openly strive to compare and contrast in their text devoted to continental Europe,[27] although they do not altogether avoid the appearance of parallel histories. The deliberate omission of Britain from their book, however, partially undermines their purpose. Their argument that "by putting the economic development of the Continent itself in the forefront of the picture the perspective will be less distorted"[28] has some validity; at the same time, however, it ignores the further distortions immanent in this limited perspective.

David S. Landes, in *The Unbound Prometheus: Technological Change and Industrial Development in Western Europe from 1750 to the Present*,[29] appears to have fallen into the trap that Milward and Saul sought to escape. Although he is very much concerned with economic comparisons, especially among the three great powers of Western Europe, his simultaneous concern with political and military strength, and his frequent use of the analogy of a footrace, distort the economic validity of his argument. The statement in the concluding chapter, that "there was one leader, Britain, and all the rest were pursuers,"[30] even though qualified in the next sentence, scarcely does justice to the wellsprings, to the multiplicity of interest, ambitions and energies involved in the struggles for economic improvement in Europe in the nineteenth century. Reification—the treatment of nations as organic entities with wills and ambitions of their own—is one of the dangers of international macroeconomic comparisons to be diligently avoided. Even in Landes's own terms, however, from the perspective of the 1970's, with Spain gaining rapidly on Great Britain in per capita income, the above citation has a definitely archaic ring.

Douglass C. North and Robert Paul Thomas, in *The Rise of the Western World*,[31] also succumb to the problem of reification; but their essay in comparative economic history is beset by a still more common problem, oversimplification. They are more interested in applying a model, one that emphasizes the importance of the efficient protection of property rights as a condition of economic development, than in exploring the variety of possible factors that encourage and retard economic development. As a result, the evidence they present to support their argument is both too sketchy and one-sided to be convincing.

Although we have by no means exhausted the field of multinational macroeconomic comparisons, even the preceding brief review of the most noteworthy examples of their kind suggests the need for much more spadework before we can draw meaningful generalizations about the causes of differential overall economic performance, as opposed to useful descriptions of such performances. This, in turn suggests the need to reduce the level of aggregation involved. One way of going about this is to reduce the number of national economies being compared, as in the comparisons of France and Britain by Crouzet, Kindleberger, Marczewski and O'Brien,[32] or that of India and China by Swamy.[33] It is also possible, of course, to go to still lower levels of aggregation, to that of specific sectors, industries and even specific firms in two or more national economies. Such a procedure is both commonsensical and straightforward. It clearly delineates what is being compared, and at the same time provides criteria for judging the relative effectiveness or efficiency of differing forms of economic organization, investment or marketing strategies, official government policies, and so on.

Labor historians have been especially prolific in this type of comparative study, for which they were able to borrow a number of the techniques of comparative politics to study trade union structure, working class politics, and so on. Some of the earlier works in this genre resembled "parallel histories" more than genuinely comparative histories, but recent contributions bring a more sophisticated approach to the study of cross-national working class institutions.[34] Moreover, proponents of the so-called new social history are going beyond formal working class organizations, which have rarely enrolled even a majority of workers, in an effort to write "history from below." So far, most of this work has been confined to a national framework,[35] but there have been a few bold efforts to transcend political boundaries. Peter N. Stearns dealt the always shaky concept of "national character" an additional blow with his stimulating essay on "National Character and European Labor History,"[36] and he and Harvey Mitchell engaged in a unique published debate on a like subject, *The European Labor Movement, the Working Classes, and the Origins of Social Democracy, 1890–1914.*[37] Another similar work, as interesting for its methodology (to be commented on below) as for its substantive findings, is *The Rebellious Century, 1830–1930* by Charles, Louise and Richard Tilly.[38]

Other sectors of the economy have received less intensive comparative treatment than organized labor and the working classes, but notable examples do exist that might well serve as models for further studies. For agriculture, there is Folke Dovring's *Land and Labor in Europe in the Twentieth Century: A Comparative Survey of Recent Agrarian History,*[39] as well as the same author's contribution to the *Cambridge Economic History of Europe,* "The Transformation of European Agriculture."[40] Even more wide-ranging is B. H. Slicher van Bath's *The Agrarian History of Western Europe, A.D. 500–1850;*[41] this book is less a manifestly comparative study than an attempt to treat Western Europe comprehensively as a

single geographical and economic unit, although inevitably it contains many insights and observations of value for comparative purposes.

Banking and the financial sector generally have been the subject of a number of comparative treatments. Along with my own entries in this field,[42] these include Maurice Levy-Leboyer, *Les banques européenes et l'industrialisation internationale dans la première moitié du XIXe siècle*,[43] Raymond W. Goldsmith, *Financial Structure and Development: An International Comparison*[44] and various books and articles by the late Raymond de Roover dealing with the medieval and early modern periods.[45] In addition, there is a sizable periodical literature.[46] To some extent this work has been inspired by Alexander Gerschenkron who, although he himself did not write specifically on banking or financial history, scattered references and allusions to it throughout his numerous stimulating essays.[47]

One would expect that foreign trade would be a promising area for comparative quantitative treatments in view of the interests of governments in collecting statistics (and revenue) on it. Unfortunately, the statistics, especially for the nineteenth and earlier centuries, are inaccurate, frequently incommensurable, and, in general, highly untrustworthy.[4X] Paul Bairoch has made a valiant beginning in an effort to bring some order out of the chaos,[49] but the problems may be insuperable. On the nonquantitative side, C. P. Kindleberger recently provided a stimulating comparative analysis of the movement for free trade.[50] He has also made forays into quantitative comparisons of aspects of international trade with *The Terms of Trade: A European Case Study*[51] and earlier articles leading thereto. Kindleberger, although he disclaims credentials as an economic historian, has in fact been one of the most prolific contributors to the field of comparative economic history. In addition to the articles just cited and the macroeconomic comparison of France and Britain previously cited (footnote 32), he has also authored a comparative study of postwar European economic growth.[52] H.J. Habakkuk provoked a lively controversy on the roles of factor proportions and institutional features in technological change with the publication of *American and British Technology in the Nineteenth Century* in 1962. Parts of the ensuing debate have been conveniently collected by S. B. Saul in *Technological Charge: The United States and Britain in the Nineteenth Century*.[53]

Industry studies are natural vehicles for the comparative method. Two older but still very respectable examples of this genre are D. L. Burn, *The Economic History of Steelmaking, 1867–1939: A Study in Competition*, and L. F. Haber, *The Chemical Industry in the Nineteenth Century: A Study of the Economic Aspect of Applied Chemistry in Europe and North America*.[54] Elements for a comparative history of railway-building, although not comparative history as such, are contained in my *France and the Economic Development of Europe, 1800–1914*, chapter VIII-X.[55] A promising field for research at a still lower level of aggregation than an entire industry is the comparison of individual firms. Alfred D.

Chandler, Jr.'s studies of the rise of big business in America[56] are noteworthy examples of intranational comparison; internationally, little has been done except for J. R. Harris' excellent pioneering effort. Using both archival sources and microeconomic analysis, Harris has made a study of two large-scale firms in the eighteenth-century plate glass industry, one in France and the other in Britain.[57]

Price histories lend themselves admirably to comparative study. The International Scientific Commission on the History of Prices was created in 1928 with the hope that a sufficient number of such histories would enable policy makers to control the business cycle; but the downturn of 1929–30 and the depression that followed threw the work into disarray, and such studies as were completed were done by individual scholars on different countries, without a true comparative format. More recently, a team of researchers under the direction of Professor L. H. Dupriez has completed a wide-ranging study of the international convergence of prices as a result of technological progress.[58] Similarly, in *A Century of Pay*.[59] E. H. Phelps Brown and M. H. Browne have traced and compared the evolution of real wages in several industrial countries.

Economic policy should provide a fruitful field for the application of the comparative method. Unfortunately, not much has been done to cultivate it. Most discussions of comparative economic policy have been casual and haphazard, with very little attempt at systematic application of the comparative method. An exception was E. F. Heckscher's pathbreaking but controversial study of mercantilism;[60] but, from the viewpoint of comparative economic history, this monumental effort was vitiated by the author's search for the uniformities of policies of the early national states, to the neglect of important differences, and by his insistence on seeing mercantilism as "a system," or rather an interrelated series of systems.[61] Another older work in which economic policies figure prominently is William A. Lewis's *Economic Survey, 1919–1939*;[62] yet Lewis, while he compared international trends and national policies, did not do so within a systematic comparative framework. Possibly the most successful application of the comparative method to the subject of economic policy—a deliberately restricted policy area—is Gaston V. Rimlinger's study of the evolution of welfare policies in the major industrial nations.[63] Rimlinger's success is traceable in good part to his carefully prepared methodological framework.

III. QUESTIONS OF METHOD: UNITS OF COMPARISON

What is the appropriate unit to study in comparative economic history? The answer that comes most readily to mind, and the one that has been emphasized in the preceding survey, is the modern nation-state and its equivalent (or substitute) in more remote times. By far the greater number of studies labeled as comparative use nationality or political boundaries as a criterion for defining their units. Such need not be the case, however. Bloch himself stigmatized the notion that comparisons

must be international as oversimplified and inflexible.[64] He preferred the more inclusive term, society, but recognizing that comparisons can be made within as well as between societies, he finally opted for units possessing "a difference of environment" as "more flexible and more precise."[65]

In an effort to secure still greater flexibility and precision, one of Bloch's expositors suggested that the most appropriate unit is the concept of a social system, noting that the term "can designate social aggregates ranging all the way from a single family to the whole of human civilization."[66] The suggestion has merit, although one might wonder with what "the whole of human civilization" could be compared (possibly a counterfactual civilization?), but even it may be too restrictive. For example, one might wish to compare the economic policies of two statesmen, such as Disraeli and Gladstone, or Cavour and Bismarck, or the economic achievements of notable entrepreneurs.[67] Nevertheless, for most purposes the concept of a social system (and economic systems are also social systems) seems both adequate and appropriate.

If social systems be accepted as the standard units for comparison, then it becomes still more clear that comparisons need not be international in scope to be meaningful. Insofar as geography enters into the definition of the unit, regions both larger and smaller than nation-states may be used.[6X] One of the most revolutionary developments in the field of historical demography in recent years has been the method of family reconstitution by means of data contained in parish records; once the data have been collected and coded, it is a simple matter to compare the demographic experience of one parish with that of another.[69] Sylvia Thrupp, unquestionably the most committed comparativist to grace our profession, has urged us to "buckle down to micro-comparative study grounded in local ecosystems,"[70]—good advice reminiscent of Marc Bloch's emphasis on "difference of environment" as the basis for comparative study.

IV. QUESTIONS OF METHOD: PROCEDURES

Granted that social systems are the most suitable units for comparison, how does one proceed? According to Sewell, "If an historian attributes the appearance of phenomenon A in one society to the existence of condition B, he can check his hypothesis by trying to find other societies where A occurs without B or vice versa. If he finds no cases which contradict the hypothesis, his confidence in its validity will increase, the level of his confidence depending upon the number and variety of comparisons made. If he finds contradictory cases, he will either reject the hypothesis outright or reformulate and refine it so as to take into account the contradictory evidence and then subject it again to comparative testing. . . . Whether employed by historians or by social scientists, the comparative method is an adaptation of experimental logic to investigations in which actual experimentation is impossible. The comparative method, like the experimental method, is a

means of systematically gathering evidence to test the validity of our explanations."[71]

This procedure, apparently straightforward, and commendable in principle, may nevertheless lead to ambiguities. How does one define a "phenomenon" in social systems? What is a "condition"? These are terms with considerable latitude. Particular phenomena and conditions must be carefully specified, for in history and the social sciences, unlike the physical sciences, entities such as "feudalism," "the manorial system," "the balance of trade," "the gold standard" and even "national income" exist only as concepts in the minds of investigators, not as concrete physical objects. This suggests that the phenomena to be compared, and the conditions that presumably give rise to them, not only should be carefully specified but narrowly defined as well, to prevent the intrusion of possibly nonobserved or nonobservable elements of a situation. The inability to control for all possible variables is the principal reason why macroeconomic comparisons, such as explanations of observed differences in economic growth rates of nations, are rarely convincing.[72]

In *Banking in the Early Stages of Industrialization* my collaborators and I selected as the phenomenon to be explained (the dependent variable) "the relative effectiveness of the banking system in promoting industrialization" and, as the principal independent variable (making allowances for random occurrences exogenous to the banking system), the structure of the system (more explicitly defined) as determined by custom, legislation, and so on. We were criticized, not without reason, for (among other things) not defining the dependent variable more explicitly and exactly so as to rule out the possibility of subjective judgments with respect to "relative effectiveness." The Tillys, in *The Rebellious Century*, are open to the criticism that by lumping food riots, labor strikes, and political demonstrations under one rubric as instances of "collective violence," they have failed to specify adequately their dependent variable. These instances, among many others that might be cited, argue for selecting as the unit of comparison as small a social system as possible given the nature of the phenomenon to be explained.

In designing a research project in comparative economic history, it should go almost without saying that the units to be compared should be generally similar, in order that the differences may be clearly outlined. This guideline accords with Bloch's preference for "units of comparison . . . that are geographical neighbors and historical contemporaries. . . ."[73] It should not rule out altogether, however, Bloch's other type of comparison, that of "societies far removed from one another in time and space." For example, it could be interesting to compare the causes and consequences of soil erosion or water pollution in several widely spaced societies—ancient Rome, medieval Europe, ancient or modern China, modern industrial and modern underdeveloped countries—in spite of the admittedly great difficulties in controlling for all relevant variables.[74]

Another question that arises is, what kind of evidence is admissible in comparative economic history? In general, it admits the same kind of evidence that is used in more conventional research. The relevance and admissibility of specific items of evidence can be established only in relation to a given project. There are no comprehensive rules. But what about the appropriate types of documentation? Can secondary sources be relied on exclusively, or must every comparative study be based at least in part on primary sources? Again, there are no set rules. Most of the broad-brush comparative studies mentioned above rely mainly or exclusively on secondary sources, which may help to explain their inadequacies. But Kindleberger argues that "there is considerable room in economic history for economists, not historians, to analyze historical material in two, or preferably three and four countries in Europe, using secondary materials already in existence which have insufficiently taken account of experience in other countries."[75] On the other hand, Thrupp exhorts and Harris demonstrates the value of primary sources.[76] In the final analysis the decision must be governed by the nature of the problem and the suitability of the available evidence; new primary sources are always welcome in economic history, but in some cases the available secondary sources may be sufficient.

Finally, there remains the question of who should write comparative economic history. Obviously, in cases of cross-national comparisons where languages other than English are involved, the researcher must command at least a reading knowledge of the relevant languages;[77] comparative studies in which a significant portion of the evidence is drawn from already existing translations is highly suspect to begin with. Kindleberger concedes that "there may be a place" for historians "involving examination of primary materials and documents, and working up original materials such as income, crop, [and] output estimates," but his preference is "not so much [for] economic historians as economists interested in analyzing historical materials on a comparative basis."[7X] Bloch, in contrast, addressed his appeal to all historians. Kindleberger is equally adamant on the desirability of "the strict comparability which comes from having two sets of facts examined by a single brain."[79] There is no doubt that the numerous conference volumes and other collective works in which various authors are invited to address a comparative theme from the point of view of their particular specialty leave much to be desired;[X0] and yet it is also possible that a tightly knit team of specialists working in close collaboration from a common outline may produce work that is superior to that of any single author, even if it were possible for one author to command the relevant languages, area and period specialties, and so on. Ultimately, any work of comparative economic history, whether by a single author or a specialized team, by historians or economists, will be judged on its intrinsic merits, as befits any scholarly undertaking. Let there be more of them.

APPENDIX

Articles of comparative interest published since 1965 in *Explorations in Economic History (EEH), Economic History Review (EHR),* and the *Journal of Economic History (JEH).*

Adams, Jr., Donald R. (September 1970), "Some Evidence on English and American Wage Rates, 1790–1830," *JEH,* XXX, 3.

Alden, Dauril (March 1965), "The Growth and Decline of Indigo Production in Colonial Brazil: A Study in Comparative Economic History," *JEH,* XXV, 1.

Asher, Ephraim (June 1972), "Industrial Efficiency and Biased Technical Change in American and British Manufacturing: The Case of Textiles in the Nineteenth Century," *JEH,* XXXII, 2.

Barsby, Stephen L. (September 1969), "Economic Backwardness and the Characteristics of Development," *JEH,* XXIX, 3.

Black, R. D. Collison (May 1968), "Economic Policy in Ireland and India in the Time of J. S. Mill," *EHR,* XXVI, 2.

Davis, Lance (May 1966), "The Capital Markets and Industrial Concentration: The United States and United Kingdom, a Comparative Study," *EHR,* XIX, 2.

Don, Yehuda (February 1968), "Comparability of International Trade Statistics: Great Britain and Austria-Hungary Before World War I, *EHR,* XXI, 1.

Goldsmith, Raymond W. (March 1975), "The Quantitative International Comparison of Financial Structure and Development," *JEH,* XXXV, 1.

Good, David F. (December 1973), "Backwardness and the Role of Banking in Nineteenth-Century European Industrialization," *JEH,* XXXIII, 4.

Gross, Nachum (December 1971), "Economic Growth and the Consumption of Coal in Austria and Hungary," *JEH,* XXXI, 4.

Kahan, Arcadius (March 1973), "Notes on Serfdom in Western and Eastern Europe," *JEH,* XXXIII, 1.

Kindleberger, C. P. (March 1975), "The Rise of Free Trade in Western Europe, 1820–1875," *JEH,* XXXV, 1.

Lampe, John R. (March 1975), "Varieties of Unsuccessful Industrialization: The Balkan States Before 1914," *JEH,* XXXV, 1.

Lane, Frederic C. (March 1975), "The Role of Governments in Economic Growth in Early Modern Times," *JEH,* XXXV, 1.

Malowist, M. (February 1966), "The Problem of Inequality of Economic Development in Europe in the Later Middle Ages," *EHR,* XIX, 1.

Mokyr, Joel (June 1974), "The Industrial Revolution in the Low Countries in the First Half of the Nineteenth Century: A Comparative Case Study," *JEH,* XXXIV, 2.

Neuberger, H. M. and Stokes, H. H. (March 1975), "German Banking and Japanese Banking: A Comparative Analysis," *JEH,* XXXV, 1.

Pollard, Sidney (November 1973), "Industrialization and the European Economy," *EHR,* XXVI, 4.

Rapp, Richard T. (September 1975), "The Unmaking of the Mediterranean Trade Hegemony: International Trade Rivalry and the Commercial Revolution," *JEH,* XXXV, 3.

Reed, Clyde (March 1973), "Transactions Costs and Differential Growth in Seventeenth Century Western Europe," *JEH,* XXXIII, 1.

Resnick, Stephen A. (March 1970), "The Decline of Rural Industry Under Export Expansion: A Comparison Among Burma, Philippines, and Thailand, 1870–1938," *JEH,* XXX, 1.

Rimlinger, Gaston V. (December 1966), "Welfare Policy and Economic Development: A Comparative Historical Perspective," *JEH,* XXVI, 4.

Schwartz, Anna Jacobson (March 1975), "Monetary Trends in the United States and the United Kingdom, 1878–1970: Selected Findings," *JEH*, XXXV, 1.

Schweitzer, Arthur (Summer 1970), "Comparative Enterprise and Economic Systems," *EEH*, VII, 4.

Temin, Peter (May 1974), "The Anglo-American Business Cycle, 1820–1860," *EHR*, XXVII, 2.

Thrupp. Sylvia L. (March 1975), "Comparative Study in the Barnyard," *JEH*, XXXV, 1.

FOOTNOTES

1. The final draft of this chapter was completed in Africa, without access to the usual bibliographic aids. It has, however, benefited from the editorial and secretarial assistance of Cynthia Anne Walsh. I alone am responsible for its content.

2. Eckstein (1971). This publication evolved from both the papers and discussions presented during a two-and-a-half-day conference held at the University of Michigan in November, 1968.

3. Redlich (1958). Reprinted in Redlich (1971), *Steeped in Two Cultures,* pp. 312–338, New York: Harper Torchbook.

4. Bloch (1928).

5. Bloch (1953), p. 496.

6. *Ibid.*, p. 497.

7. *Ibid.*, p. 498.

8. See Sewell, Jr. (1967), for an even more systematic exposition of Bloch's method than Bloch himself provided.

9. Bloch (1931).

10. Bloch (1939–1940)

11. Nef (1936).

12. Nef (1937).

13. Nef (1957). First published in the *Memoirs of the American Philosophical Society,* XV (1940).

14. Clapham (1921). Reprinted numerous times, the fourth edition (little changed) in 1936.

15. Heaton (1946).

16. Lattimore (May 1947).

17. Thrupp (December 1957); Easterbrook (December 1957). See also Heaton (December 1957). Among those taking part in the discussions, in addition to Heaton, were Rondo Cameron, Shepard B. Clough, Bert F. Hoselitz, Sanford A. Mosk, Warren C. Scoville, George Soule and Barry E. Supple.

18. Most of the papers, some of which will be commented on below, were published in the *Journal of Economic History*, XXXV (March 1975). Unfortunately, a complete record of the methodological discussion that took place in the opening session was not made; Michael Edelstein and Richard T. Rapp (Spring 1975) make reference to it, however.

19. Kuznets (1966).

20. Kuznets (1971).

21. See, among others, Kuznets, Moore and Spengler (1966); Aitken (1959).

22. Notably Deane and Cole (1967), and the multivolume *Histoire quantitative de l'économie française,* still in progress. See also the several volumes in the series *Income and Wealth,* some of which were edited by Kuznets himself.

23. Denison (1967).

24. Maddison (1964).

25. Bagwell and Mingay (1970), p. v.

26. Davis (1973).
27. Milward and Saul (1973), Vol. I. Vol. II is forthcoming.
28. *Ibid.*, p. 7.
29. Landes (1969).
30. *Ibid.*, p. 538.
31. North and Thomas (1973).
32. Crouzet (1967); Kindleberger (1964); Marczewski (1965); and O'Brien (forthcoming).
33. Swamy (1973).
34. For example, Kassalow (1969), and Sturmthal (1964).
35. As pointed out above, this does not rule out use of the comparative method. Kathryn Amdur has a doctoral dissertation underway at Stanford University comparing the political affiliations of workers in Toulouse and St. Etienne in the 1920s.
36. Stearns (1974).
37. Stearns and Mitchell (1971). Each of the authors makes critical comments on the other's essay. Robert Wohl provides a general introduction.
38. Tilly (1975).
39. Dovring (1965a).
40. Dovring (1965b). In principle, all of the chapters in this ongoing scholarly enterprise, except those devoted to individual countries, should be comparative in nature; but some are more successful than others.
41. Slicher van Bath (1963).
42. Rondo Cameron *et al.* (1967), (Japanese translation, Tokyo: Nihon Hyonronsha, 1973; Spanish translation, Madrid: Editorial Tecnos, 1974; Italian translation, Bologna: Società editrice il Mulino, 1975), Cameron ed. (1972). See also Cameron (1963, 1965).
43. Levy-Leboyer (1964).
44. Goldsmith (1969).
45. Notably "New Interpretations in the History of Banking," *Cahiers d'histoire mundiale/Journal of World History,* II (1954), 38–76; reprinted in Kirshner, Julius, ed. (1974), *Business, Banking, and Economic Thought in Late Medieval and Early Modern Europe: Selected Studies of Raymond de Roover,* Chicago and London: University of Chicago Press.
46. See the items by Lance E. Davis, Raymond W. Goldsmith, David F. Good, Hugh M. Neuberger and Houston H. Stokes, and Anna Jacobson Schwartz cited in the Appendix.
47. Gerschenkron (1962, 1968, 1970). For an evaluation of Gerschenkron's influence on comparative financial history, see Cameron (1972), pp. 9–15.
48. See Morgenstern (1955, 1963).
49. Bairoch (Spring 1973); Bairoch (1976).
50. Kindleberger (March 1975).
51. Kindleberger (1956).
52. Kindleberger (1967). For Kindleberger's views on methodology, see the last two paragraphs of this article.
53. Habakkuk (1962); Saul (1970).
54. Burn (1940, 1961); Haber (1958).
55. Cameron (1961). Abridged edition, Chicago: Rand, McNally & Co., 1966.
56. Notably, Chandler (1962).
57. J. R. Harris, "Saint-Gobain and Ravenhead," in B. Ratcliffe, ed., *Great Britain and Her World: Essays in Honour of W. O. Henderson,* Manchester: Manchester University Press, 1975, pp. 27–70.
58. Dupriez, *et al.* (1966).
59. Brown and Browne (1968).

60. Heckscher (1955). First published in Swedish in 1931. The English translation, prepared from the German edition and revised by the author, published in 1935.

61. For a comprehensive evaluation, see Coleman (1969).

62. Lewis (1949).

63. Rimlinger (1971).

64. Bloch (1928, 1953), p. 496.

65. *Ibid.*

66. Sewell (1967), p. 213.

67. Hughes (1966).

68. See, for example, Rockoff (March 1975); Bateman and Weiss (March 1975).

69. See Franklin F. Mendels, "Recent Research in European Historical Demography," *American Historical Review*, LXXV (April 1970), 1065–1073, for a concise survey of the literature.

70. Thrupp (March 1975). At the other extreme, see the provocative article by Mauro (August 1971).

71. Sewell (1967).

72. Even this assumes that the growth rates have been correctly observed and recorded. A common source of confusion regarding the relative effectiveness of the French, British and German economies in the last century or so resulted from the simple failure to reduce the respective growth rates to a per capita basis. See my "L'économie française: passé, présent, avenir," (Cameron, October-December 1970).

73. Bloch (1953), p. 498.

74. See Rondo Cameron, "Economic History, Pure and Applied," *Journal of Economic History*, XXXVI (March 1976), 3–27, for a very rough comparison of this type.

75. Personal communication to the author. See Edelstein and Rapp (Spring 1975).

76. See Thrupp (March 1975), and Harris (1975, footnote 57).

77. An extreme case is illustrated by Lampe's article (Lampe, March 1975), cited in the Appendix.

78. Edelstein and Rapp (Spring 1975).

79. *Ibid.*

80. There are too many candidates for this distinction to single out any one for invidious mention.

REFERENCES

Aitken, Hugh G. J., ed. (1959), *The State and Economic Growth*, New York: Social Science Research Council.

Bagwell, Philip S. and Mingay, G. E. (1970), *Britain and America, 1850–1939: A Study of Economic Change*, New York and Washington: Praeger Publishers.

Bairoch, Paul (Spring 1973), "European Foreign Trade in the XIX Century: The Development of the Value and Volume of Exports, (Preliminary Results)," *Journal of European Economic History*, 2, 5–36.

———. (1976), *Commerce exterieur et development economique de l' Europe an XIX siècle;* Paris and The Hayue: Mouton.

Bateman, Fred and Weiss, Thomas (March 1975), "Comparative Regional Development in Antebellum Manufacturing," *Journal of Economic History*, XXXV, 182–208.

Bloch, Marc (1939–40), *La société féodale*, 2 vols., Paris. Translated by Manyon, L. A. (1961), *Feudal Society*, London.

————. (1931), *Les caractères originaux de l'histoire rurale française*. Translated by Sondheimer, Janet (1970), *French Rural History: An Essay on its Basic Characteristics*, Berkeley and Los Angeles: University of California Press.

————. (1928), "Pour une histoire comparée des sociétés européenes." Translated by Riemersma, J. C., (1953) "Toward a Comparative History of European Societies," *Enterprise and Secular Change* (edited by Lane, Frederic C. and Riemersma, Jelle C.), pp. 494–521, Homewood, Ill.: Richard D. Irwin, Inc.

Brown, E. H. and Browne, M. H. (1968), *A Century of Pay*, London: Macmillan; New York: St. Martin's Press.

Burn, Duncan L. (1940), *The Economic History of Steelmaking, 1867–1939: A Study in Competition*, Cambridge: Cambridge University Press. (2nd ed., 1961).

————. (1961), *The Steel Industry, 1939–1959: A Study in Competition and Planning*, Cambridge: Cambridge University Press.

Cameron, Rondo (1963), "Banking in the Early Stages of Industrialization: A Preliminary Survey," *Scandinavian Economic History Review*, XI, 117–134.

————. (September/October 1970), "L'économie française: passé, présent, avenir," *Annales (E. S. C.)*, 25.

————. (1961), *France and the Economic Development of Europe*, Princeton: Princeton University Press.

————. (1965), "Theoretical Bases of a Comparative Study of the Role of Financial Institutions in the Early Stages of Industrialization," *Deuxième Conference Internationale d'Histoire Economique, Aix-en-Provence, 1962*, Paris and The Hague: Mouton & Co.

————. (ed). (1972), *Banking and Economic Development: Some Lessons of History*, New York, London, Toronto: Oxford University Press.

Cameron, Rondo, *et al*. (1967), *Banking in the Early Stages of Industrialization: A Study in Comparative Economic History*, New York, London, Toronto: Oxford University Press.

Chandler, Jr., Alfred D. (1962), *Strategy and Structure: Chapters in the History of the Industrial Enterprise*, Cambridge, Mass. and London: The M. I. T. Press.

Clapham, J. H. (1921), *Economic Development of France and Germany, 1815–1914*, Cambridge: Cambridge University Press. (4th ed., 1936).

Coleman, D. C., ed. (1969), *Revisions in Mercantilism*, London: Methuen & Co.

Crouzet, François (1966), "Angleterre et France au XVIIIᵉ siècle: essai d'analyse comparée de deux croissances économiques." Translated (1967), as "England and France in the Eighteenth Century: A Comparative Analysis of Two Economic Growths," *The Causes of the Industrial Revolution in England*. (edited by Hartwell, R. M), pp. 139–174, London: Methuen & Co.

Davis, Ralph (1973), *The Rise of the Atlantic Economies*, Ithaca, N. Y.: Cornell University Press.

Deane, Phyllis and Cole, W. A. (1967), *British Economic Growth, 1688–1959*, 2nd ed., Cambridge: Cambridge University Press.

Denison, Edward F. (1967), *Why Growth Rates Differ*, Washington, D. C.: The Brookings Institution.

De Roover, Raymond (1954), "New Interpretations in the History of Banking." Rpt. (1974), *Business, Banking, and Economic Thought in Late Medieval and Early Modern Europe: Selected Studies of Raymond de Roover, (edited by Kirshner, Julius)* Chicago and London: University of Chicago Press.

Dovring, Folke (1965), *Land and Labor in Europe in the Twentieth Century: A Comparative Survey of Recent Agrarian History*, 3rd ed., The Hague: Martinus Nijhoff.

———. (1965), "The Transformation of European Agriculture," *Cambridge Economic History of Europe*, Vol. VI, Pt. II, pp. 604–672, Cambridge: Cambridge University Press.

Dupriez, L. H., *et al.* (1966), *Diffusion du progrès et convergence des prix: Etudes internationales*, 2 vols., Louvain and Paris: Nauwelaerts.

Easterbrook, W. T. (December 1957), "Long-Period Comparative Study: Some Historical Cases," *Journal of Economic History*, XVII, 571–595.

Eckstein, Alexander, ed. (1971), *The Comparison of Economic Systems*, Berkeley, Los Angeles, London: University of California Press.

Edelstein, Michael and Rapp, Richard (Spring 1975), "Comparative Economic History: Promises and Problems. A Report of the Meeting of the Economic History Association," *Journal of European Economic History*, 4, 209–214.

Gerschenkron, Alexander (1968), *Continuity in History and Other Essays*, Cambridge, Mass.: The Belknap Press of Harvard University Press.

———. (1962), *Economic Backwardness in Historical Perspective: A Book of Essays*, Cambridge, Mass.: The Belknap Press of Harvard University Press.

———. (1970), *Europe in the Russian Mirror: Four Lectures in Economic History*, Cambridge: The University Press.

Goldsmith, Raymond W. (1969), *Financial Structure and Development: An International Comparison*, New Haven and London: Yale University Press.

Habakkuk, H. J. (1962), *American and British Technology in the Nineteenth Century*, Cambridge: Cambridge University Press.

Haber, L. F., *The Chemical Industry During the Nineteenth Century: A Study of the Economic Aspect of Applied Chemistry in Europe*.

Heaton, Herbert (1946), "Other Wests Than Ours," *Journal of Economic History*, Supplement VI, 50–62.

———. (December 1957), "Summary of Discussion," *Journal of Economic History*, XVII, 596–602.

Heckscher, Eli (1931), *Mercantilism*. Translated by Mendel Shapiro. Edited by E. F. Söderlund. Rev. ed (1955), London: Allen and Unwin; New York: Macmillan.

Hughes, Jonathan R. T. (1966), *The Vital Few: American Economic Progress and Its Protagonists*, New York: Houghton Mifflin.

Kassalow, Everett M. (1969), *Trade Unions and Industrial Relations: An International Comparison*, New York: Random House.

Kindleberger, C. P. (1964), *Economic Growth in France and Britain, 1851–1950*, Cambridge, Mass.: Harvard University Press.

———. (1967), *Europe's Postwar Growth: The Role of Labor Supply*, Cambridge: Mass.: Harvard University Press.

———. (March 1975), "The Rise of Free Trade in Western Europe, 1820–1875," *Journal of Economic History*, XXXV, 20–55.

———. (1956), *The Terms of Trade: A European Case Study*, New York: Technology Press of M. I. T. and Wiley.

Kuznets, Simon (1971), *The Economic Growth of Nations: Total Output and Production Structure*, Cambridge, Mass.: The Belknap Press of Harvard University Press.

———. (1966), *Modern Economic Growth: Rate, Structure, and Spread*, Studies in Comparative Economics, No. 7, New Haven and London: Yale University Press.

Kuznets, Simon, Moore, Wilbert E. and Spengler, Joseph J., eds. (1955), *Economic Growth: Brazil, India, Japan*, Durham, N. C.: Duke University Press.

Landes, David S. (1969), *The Unbound Prometheus: Technological Change and Industrial Development in Western Europe from 1750 to the Present*, Cambridge: At the University Press.

Lattimore, Owen (May 1947), "Inner Asian Frontiers," *Journal of Economic History,* VII, 24–52.

Levy-Leboyer, Maurice (1964), *Les banques européenes et l'industrialisation internationale dans la première moitié de XIXe siècle,* Paris: Presses Universitares de France.

Lewis, William A. (1949), *Economic Survey, 1919–1939,* London: G. Allen & Unwin.

Maddison, Angus (1964), *Economic Growth in the West,* New York: The Twentieth Century Fund, Inc.

Marczewski, Jean (1965), *Introduction à l'histoire quantative,* Part II, Geneva: Librairie Droz.

Mauro, Frederic (August 1961), "Towards an 'Intercontinental Model': European Overseas Expansion Between 1500 and 1800," *Economic History Review,* 2nd ser., XIV, 1–17.

Milward, Alan S. and Saul, S. B. (1973), *The Economic Development of Continental Europe, 1780–1870,* London: George Allen & Unwin; Totowa, N. J.: Rowman & Littlefield.

Mitchell, Harvey (1971), "Labor and the Origins of Social Democracy in Britain, France, and Germany, 1890–1914," *The European Labor Movement, the Working Classes, and the Origins of Social Democracy,* (edited by Stearns Peter N. and Mitchell, Harvey) Itaska; Ill.: F. E. Peacock.

Morgenstern, Oskar (1963), *On the Accuracy of Economic Observations,* Princeton: Princeton University Press.

———. (1955), *The Validity of International Gold Movement Statistics,* Princeton: Princeton University Press.

Nef. J. U. (1936), "A Comparison of Industrial Growth in France and England from 1540 to 1640," *Journal of Political Economy,* XLIV, 289–317, 505–533, 643–666.

———. (1957), *Industry and Government in France and England,* London: Oxford University Press; Ithaca, N. Y.: Cornell University Press. (First published in 1940.)

———. (1937), "Prices and Industrial Capitalism in France and England, 1540–1640," *Economic History Review,* VII, 155–185.

North, Douglass C. and Thomas, Robert Paul (1973), *The Rise of the Western World,* New York and Cambridge: The Cambridge University Press.

O'Brien, Patrick K. (forthcoming), *Levels of Welfare and Productivity in Britain and France.*

Redlich, Fritz (1958), "Toward Comparative Historiography: Background and Problems," *Kyklos,* XI, 3, 362–389.

Rimlinger, Gaston V. (1971), *Welfare Policy and Industrialization in Europe, America, and Russia,* New York: Wiley.

Rockoff, Hugh T. (March 1975), "Varieties of Banking and Regional Economic Development in the United States, 1840–1860," *Journal of Economic History,* XXXV, 160–181.

Saul, S. B. (ed.) (1970), *Technological Change: The United States and Britain in the 19th Century,* London: Methuen and Company.

Sewell, Jr., William H. (1967), "Marc Bloch and the Logic of Comparative History," *History and Theory,* VI, 2, 208–218.

Slicher van Bath, B. H., (1963), *The Agrarian History of Western Europe* (translated by Olive Ordish), London: Edward Arnold

Stearns, Peter N. (1971), "The European Labor Movement and the Working Classes, 1890–1914," *The European Labor Movement, the Working Classes, and the Origins of Social Democracy,* (edited by Stearns, Peter N. and Mitchell, Harvey). Ithaca, N. Y.: F. E. Peacock.

————. (1974), "National Character and European Labor History," *Workers in the Industrial Revolution: Recent Studies of Labor in the United States and Europe.* (edited by Stearns, Peter N. and Walkowitz, Daniel J.), New Brunswick, N. J.: Transaction Books.

Sturmthal, Adolf (1964), *Workers Councils: A Study of Workplace Organization on Both Sides of the Iron Curtain,* Cambridge, Mass.: Harvard University Press.

Swamy, Subramanian (1973), *Economic Growth in China and India, 1925–1970,* Chicago: University of Chicago Press.

Thrupp, Sylvia L. (March 1975), "Comparative Study in the Barnyard," *Journal of Economic History,* XXXV.

————. (December 1957), "The Role of Comparison in the Development of Economic Theory," *Journal of Economic History,* XVII, 554–570.

Tilly, Charles, Louise, and Richard (1975), *The Rebellious Century, 1830–1930,* Cambridge, Mass.: Harvard University Press.

RESEARCH IN ECONOMIC HISTORY

An Annual Compilation of Research

Series Editor: Paul Uselding, Department of Economics, University of Illinois.

Volume 1.   Published 1976.   384 pages   Institutions: $25.00
ISBN NUMBER: 0-89232-001-X   Individuals: $18.50

CONTENTS:

MANUFACTURING IN THE ANTEBELLUM SOUTH, Fred Bateman, Indiana University and Thomas Weiss, University of Kansas. TRANSFERENCE AND DEVELOPMENT OF INSTITUTIONAL CONSTRAINTS UPON ECONOMIC ACTIVITY, Jonathan R.T. Hughes, Northwestern University. THE BUSINESS ADVISORY COUNCIL, 1933–1961: A Study in Corporate-Government Relations, Kim McQuaid, Northwestern University. THREE CENTURIES OF AMERICAN INEQUALITY, Peter Lindert and Jeffrey Williamson, University of Wisconsin. ENGLISH OPEN FIELDS AS BEHAVIOR TOWARDS RISK, Donald McCloskey, University of Chicago. STAGFLATION IN HISTORICAL PERSPECTIVES: The Napoleonic Wars Revisited, Joel Mokyr, Northwestern University and N. Eugene Savin, University of British Columbia and Cambridge University. CROSS-SPECTRAL ANALYSIS OF LONG SWINGS IN ATLANTIC MIGRATION, Larry Neal, University of Illinois. SOCIO-ECONOMIC PATTERNS OF MIGRATION FROM THE NETHERLANDS IN THE NINETEENTH CENTURY, Robert Swierenga, Kent State University and Harry Stout, University of Connecticut. IN DISPRAISE OF THE MUCKRAKERS: United States Occupational Mortality, 1890–1910, Paul Uselding, University of Illinois.

Volume 2.   November 1977   Approx. 375 pages   Institutions: $25.00
ISBN NUMBER: 0-89232-036-2   Individuals: $18.50

CONTENTS:

LAND AND MONEY IN THE SPARTAN ECONOMY, 404-371 B.C., John Buckler, University of Illinois. THE ECONOMIC HISTORY OF URBAN LOCATION AND SANITATION IN CHICAGO, Louis P. Cain, Loyola University of Chicago. DEPLETION AND DIPLOMACY: The Dynamics of the Northern Fur Sealing Industry, Donald Paterson and James Wilen, University of British Columbia. HIGH FERTILITY IN MID-NINETEENTH CENTURY FRANCE: A Multivariate Analysis of Fertiliy Patterns in the Arrondissement of Lille, Paul Spagnoli, Boston College. THE GROWTH OF THE GREAT LAKES AS A MAJOR TRANSPORTATION RESOURCE, 1870–1911, Samuel H. Williamson, University of Iowa. IMPERIALISM AND ECONOMIC DEVELOPMENT: Comparisons of England, India and the United States, Harold Woodman, Purdue University.

 JAI PRESS

P.O. Box 1285, 321 Greenwich Avenue
Greenwich, Connecticut 06830, (203) 661-7602

MARQUETTE UNIVERSITY LIBRARIES

3 5039 01203048 9

SUBJECT TO
DATE DUE LIBRARY RECALL